PRAISE FOR CALLINGS

"Gregg Levoy offers a discerning eye for peering into one's life to translate the recurring symptoms of refusing the inner voices, to gather the courage to answer what calls. He does this with good writing, humor, and a strong clarion voice."—Clarissa Pinkola Estes, Ph.D., author of *Women Who Run with the Wolves*

"*Callings* can help you discover your true vocation and help you hear the still small voice that calls you by name."—Sam Keen, Ph.D., author of *Fire in the Belly* and *Hymns to an Unknown God*

"Gregg Levoy has written about the nature of guidance with a ringing clarity. *Callings* is a spiritual seduction that gives form to a universal mystery. I'd recommend it to anyone who is seeking to hold the divine hand through a transition in their lives."—Caroline Myss, Ph.D., author of *Anatomy of the Spirit*

Stunning! Wonderful! Levoy writes like a poet. His material is both spiritual and practical. I don't know another book that deals with callings in quite the same way."

—Larry Dossey, M.D., author of *Healing Words* and *Prayer in Medicine*

"*Callings* is the best book I know for re-working the way we work."

—Jeff Berner, contributing editor, *Work at Home* magazine

"*Callings* is elegantly researched, beautifully written, and intelligently uplifting. It works brilliantly."—*Spirit at Work* newsletter

"Ravishing! This book is going to charge off the shelves. It's the kind of book people call each other about to share favorite passages. A book to savor."

—Booklist

"A marvelous work."—*Albuquerque Journal*

"Levoy's book is a feast of prose, filled with wise observations."

—*Intuition* magazine

"Solid and wise."—*Utne Reader*

"In the crowded field of books about listening to the heart, Levoy's guidance and encouragement are rewarding."—*Publisher's Weekly*

"A great book that helps support all of us on our life's journey."

—*Personal Transformation*

"Gregg Levoy intelligently and articulately explores the process of encountering one's callings and offers hope to anyone embarking on this mysterious journey."—*Body Mind Spirit* magazine

Callings is stunning and profound, one of those rare and precious books that enfold you in its pages and engage your soul. Gregg Levoy is adept both at his craft of writing and his authentic presentation of the material. He's written a powerful book."—*Viewpoints Forum*, Compuserve

"*Callings* is a touchstone for anyone seeking something more out of their work or making a transition."—*Kansas City Star*

Callings has been a selection of the Book of the Month Club. Quality Paperback Books, and One Spirit Book Club.

CALLINGS

FINDING AND FOLLOWING AN AUTHENTIC LIFE

GREGG LEVOY

THREE RIVERS PRESS • NEW YORK

Portions of this book originally appeared in different form in the following publications: *San Francisco Chronicle, New Age Journal, Writer's Digest Magazine, The Sun, Christian Science Monitor, Hemispheres, America West Magazine,* and *Utne Reader.*

Published by Three Rivers Press, New York, New York.
Member of the Crown Publishing Group.

Random House, Inc. New York, Toronto, London, Sydney, Auckland
www.randomhouse.com

THREE RIVERS PRESS is a registered trademark and the Three Rivers Press colophon is a trademark of Random House, Inc.

Originally published in hardcover by Harmony Books in 1997.

First paperback edition printed in 1998.

Printed in the United States of America

Design by Lynne Amft

Library of Congress Cataloging-in-Publication Data
Levoy, Gregg, 1955–
Callings: Finding and following an authentic life / by Gregg Levoy.—1st ed.
Includes bibliographical references.
1. Self-actualization (Psychology) 2. Vocation—Psychological aspects.
3. Spirituality. I. Title.
BF637.S4L487   1997
158—dc21   97-6116

ISBN 0-609-80370-0

14 16 18 20 19 17 15 13

To Robin,

for being a teacher to me in the search for an authentic life

C O N T E N T S

ACKNOWLEDGMENTS

It is with the grace of Providence that I was led into the company of the following people, whose generosity, enthusiasm, and good shepherding sustained me in writing this book: Kitty Farmer, Ned Leavitt, Leslie Meredith, Larry Dossey, and all of the people who generously shared their stories of calling with me.

To them all, my deepest gratitude.

INTRODUCTION

The wind, one brilliant day, called.

—ANTONIO MACHADO

Some years ago, along a country road outside of Fresno, California, on a windy spring day, a part of the invisible world was made, for a brief moment, visible to me.

I saw, in the light lancing through a row of trees, great streams of yellow pollen sweeping by on the wind, every speck filled with information—blueprints for making perfect blue flowers, the dark musculature of trees, meadow grasses.

I saw in that moment that the whole sky is filled with furtive transmissions—pollen and seeds, radio waves and subatomic particles, the songs of birds, satellite broadcasts of the six o'clock news and the Home Shopping Network. And I saw that what is necessary to make substance or meaning out of any of it is a receiver, somebody to receive.

Years later, struggling to make sense of a stunning aggregate of symptoms and synchronicities in my own life that appeared to cluster around the question of whether or not I should leave a job, I realized that my own life was similarly flooded with signals of which I was only dimly aware but that seemed to indicate the necessary steps I should take to make my life literally "come true." Until then, unfortunately, the receiver had usually been turned off, so these incoming calls fell lemming-like into silence.

❧

In many traditions, calls—in the form of sounds—precede prayer, rites of initiation, spiritual healings, and major life events. The purpose of calls is to summon adherents away from their daily grinds to a new level of awareness, into a sacred frame of mind, into communion with that which is bigger than themselves. The calls may come from bull-roarers, trumpets, rattles, wooden clackers, songs, bells, or the chanting of muezzins atop minarets.

In the primary creation myth of Western cosmology, the very first call came through the voice that said "Let there be light," and there was light, the words then becoming flesh. Every call since then has also been a call to form, a call to each of us to materialize ourselves.

Calls, of course, beg the question "Who, or what, is calling?" But in attempting to answer this question even an exhaustive list of every name for Soul or Destiny or God would be beside the point. It simply doesn't matter whether we call it God, the Patterning Intelligence, the Design Mind, the Unconscious, the Soul, the Force of Completion, the Center Court, or simply "life's longing for itself," as Kahlil Gibran envisioned. It is clear, however, that "living means being addressed," as the theologian Martin Buber once said, and whatever or whoever is addressing us is a power like wind or fusion or faith: We can't see the force, but we can see what it does.

Primarily this force announces the need for change, and the response for which it calls is an awakening of some kind. A call is only a monologue. A return call, a response, creates a dialogue. Our own unfolding requires that we be in constant dialogue with whatever is calling us. The call and one's response to it are also a central metaphor for the spiritual life, and in Latin there is even a correspondence between the words for *listening* and *following*.

❧

This book, then, is about putting on a lens through which we can see our lives as a process of calls and responses. To me, this is a much more appealing and meaningful vision than, as I heard a character on television remark recently, seeing life as "Just a bunch of stuff that happens." This book is about religion in the original sense of the word—re-*ligare*, to re-connect—to re-member what has been dis-membered: our own selves, the deep life within us that is a strong "religious" impulse despite whatever outward waywardness our lives may exhibit. This is the sense of "religion" that psychologist William James meant when he described religion as "the attempt to be in harmony with an unseen order of things," to remember what we already know.

"When my daughter was seven years old," says artist Howard Ikemoto, "she asked me one day what I did at work. I told her I worked at the college, that my job was to teach people how to draw. She stared back at me, incredulous, and said, 'You mean they forget?' "

Yes, we forget, and this book is about remembering our vocations, again in the true sense of the word—our callings—whether they are vocations in the arenas of work, relationship, lifestyle, or service. They may be calls to *do* something (become self-employed, go back to school, leave or start a relationship, move to the country, change careers, have a child) or calls to *be* something (more creative, less judgmental, more loving, less fearful). They may be calls toward something or away from something; calls to change something, review our commitment to it, or come back to it in an entirely new way; calls toward whatever we've dared and double-dared ourselves to do for as long as we can remember.

CENTRIFUGAL FORCE

Unfortunately, we often simply tune out the longings we feel, rather than confront and act on them. Perhaps we do not really forget our calls but we fear what they might demand of us in pursuing them. Anticipating the connip-tions of change blocks us from acknowledging that we do know, and always have known, what our calls are. Perhaps we also fear the *hope* that such calls evoke in us, and the power that we know is dammed up behind our resistance.

A multitude of forces in this world certainly conspires to divide us against ourselves, our power and authenticity, our voices, even our ability simply to listen to ourselves and believe what we hear: parents who either told us or modeled for us that dreams aren't bankable; schooling that braided into our brain stems the message that we must live up to certain standards, but seldom do; the wheedlings of advertising and consumerism; a patriarchal culture that taught us—by the brute force of reason—to abandon our instincts and intu-itions; the juggernaut of conformity, without which culture couldn't exist but that exacts from us in return a stiff price in individuality; and even the instinct for survival.

"Nature places a simple constraint on those who leave the flock to go their own way," say David Bayles and Ted Orland in *Art and Fear*. "They get eaten! In society, it's a bit more complicated, but the admonition stands: avoiding the unknown has considerable survival value. Society and nature . . . tend to produce guarded creatures." The upshot is that we often end up trading our authenticity for what we perceive as survival, terrified to swap security for our heart's deep desires, which is the imperative of all callings and one of the dominant fears in responding to them.

Saying yes to the calls tends to place you on a path that half of yourself thinks doesn't make a bit of sense, but the other half knows your life won't make sense without. This latter part, continually pushing out from within us with a centrifugal force, keeps driving us toward authenticity, against the tyranny of fear and inertia and occasionally reason, against terrific odds, and against the knocking in our hearts that signals the hour.

We find ourselves compelled to follow the sometimes blind spiritual instinct that tells us our lives have purpose and meaning. We find that we must act on this imperative despite the temptations—to back down and run for cover—that will divide even the most grimly resolute against themselves. We must persist with the sort of hope about which playwright and former Czechoslovakian president Vaclav Havel spoke when he said, "Hope is not the conviction that something will turn out well, but the certainty that something makes sense, regardless of how it turns out."

This requires a cussed determination to prevail, especially in the face of a bewildering paradox that lies at the heart of each of our calls and each of our lives: Both are incredibly important and incredibly insignificant. Our lives are like giant earthquakes: in geologic terms, they are muscle twitches; yet in human terms, they are titanic. Knowing such a thing, we can't help but approach the prospect of following our deepest callings with both exhilaration and terror.

T H E   V E I L   I N   T H E   T E M P L E

Because the notion of a call is historically tied up with religion, we tend to think of it as divinely inspired, which induces a good measure of terror. Calls are, in our minds, big, and we feel we have to respond in a big way, which, of course, can be paralyzing. It is therefore important to remember, first, that a call isn't something that comes from on high as an order, a sort of divine subpoena, irrespective of our own free will and desire. We have a choice. We have a vote! "Thunder doesn't rent the sky," Rod Serling once said, "and a bony finger come down from the clouds and point at you, and a great voice boom, 'You! You're the anointed!' "

Second, few people actually receive big calls, in visions of flaming chariots and burning bushes. Most of the calls we receive and ignore are the proverbial still, small voices that the biblical prophets heard, the daily calls to pay attention to our intuitions, to be authentic, to live by our own codes of honor.

Our lives are measured out in coffee spoons, wrote T. S. Eliot; they are measured out not in the grand sweeps but in the small gestures. The great breakthroughs in our lives generally happen only as a result of the accumulation of innumerable small steps and minor achievements. We're called to reach out to someone, to pick up an odd book on the library shelf, to sign up for a class even though we're convinced we don't have the time or money, to go to our desks each day, to turn left instead of right. These are the fire drills for our bigger calls.

"I don't ask for the full ringing of the bell," wrote the poet Wallace Stevens. "I don't ask for a clap of thunder that would rend the veil in the temple. A scrawny cry will do, from far off there among the willows and the cattails, from far off there among the galaxies."

Perhaps our callings, the wisdom of our true natures, can only be hinted at, anyway—filtered through symbols, dreams, symptoms, happenstances, and synchronicities. They are not shown to us directly but only mediated, for the same reason that the goddess Athena had to come to the aid of Ulysses disguised as a mortal, and for the same reason we can't look directly at the sun. The ancients believed that if gods or goddesses were to appear to us in their true forms, the sight would sear the flesh off our bones, as happened to Semele, mother of Dionysus, who was incinerated with lightning and thunderbolts after being granted her request to see her lover, Zeus, in his full immortal splendor.

We thus need to learn to recognize our calls in many disguises. The channels through which they come are also like pierced ears—we have to keep earrings in them or they close up. We have to stay in dialogue, stay vigilant, and be willing to be seized by our encounters, by what comes our way.

And we have to act! Responding to a call means doing something about it.

If passion is the call, as psychologist Rollo May has said, then form is the response and the way we ground our calls in the world. Passion—or as Plato said, Eros (Love)—moves instinctively toward the creation of form. It wants to take shape, fashion of itself a vehicle, and, as the mystic poet Rumi once wrote, "There are hundreds of ways to kneel and kiss the ground."

‹⁙›

In this book we'll apply the oracular arts of sign reading to the search for authenticity, deciphering the calls that issue from our lives and point us toward action. They come in a tremendous variety of forms, all of which should be considered as divining rods to help us locate the underground streams, so we'll know where to dig. They include:

- A dream that keeps coming back, or what it is that pursues you in dreams;
- A symptom that recurs and is exquisitely metaphoric, such as a pain in the neck from shouldering too much responsibility;
- A conversation you overhear in a restaurant that seems as though it was spoken directly to you;
- Places in your life where there's friction. As in nature, friction occurs where changes are taking place, or trying to. Where, for example, do your words not match your deeds; where do you fight with others; where do your longings rub against your security;
- Song lyrics you can't get out of your head;
- Instructions that arise unbidden from the silence of meditation;
- An ultimatum your partner gives you: either go to couples counseling or the relationship is over;
- What you would preach about if given an hour of prime time;
- What decisions you need to make in your life right now; what issues are hanging in midair waiting for resolution.

In reading all these signs, we are searching for the power inherent in simply naming things, for that which we cannot name is lost to us, and that which we can name is coaxed into life. The danger, of course, is that we tend to overexplain and overinterpret, which, as the playwright Eugène Ionesco once said, "separates us from astonishment."

Calls are essentially questions. They aren't questions you necessarily need to answer outright; they are questions to which you need to respond, expose yourself, and kneel before. You don't want an answer you can put in a box and set on a shelf. You want a question that will become a chariot to carry you across the breadth of your life, a question that will offer you a lifetime of pondering, that will lead you toward what you need to know for your integrity, draw to you what you need for your journey, and help you understand what it means to burst at the seams. These questions will also lead you to others whose lives are propelled by the same questions, and from them you will receive "oh, never an answer," as writer P. L. Travers says, "but a spark of instructive fire."

A PATH BETWEEN TWO QUESTIONS

The critical challenge of discernment—knowing whether our calls are true or false, knowing how and when to respond to them, knowing whether a call really belongs to us or not—requires that we also tread a path *between* two essential questions: "What is right for me?" and "Where am I willing to be led?" Discernment also requires that we ask these two questions continually and devotedly, in hopes that by doing so Providence will, in due course, be alerted to our desires and answers will find us.

In stone sculpting, an artist taps a stone lightly with a hammer to see if it's "true." If it emits a dull tone, it has faults running through it that will crack it apart when you work on it. A clear ring, one that hangs in the air for a moment, means it's true, has integrity, and, most importantly, will hold up under repeated blows. This is the same information we seek about our callings, and we need to be continually "tapping in" to discern their truth.

Thus we cannot know whether a cigar is indeed just a cigar without studying it. We cannot declare a happenstance "just a coincidence" without looking at whether it corresponds to a theme or an issue in our lives. Without submitting to the ceaseless thrum of our own intuitions over a period of time, we cannot know whether the voices we hear are those of inner guides or just the babble in Babylon.

If you're bored with your work, for instance, does that mean you need to leave it or change it? Does falling in love with Someone Else signal that your marriage needs dissolution or attention? If you didn't get the job, does that mean you weren't supposed to pursue the career, or that the rejection is a test of your resolve? If you can't get pregnant, is it that you're not meant to, you're meant to redefine the meaning of parenting for yourself, or that you simply have a medical condition that means nothing? Is a calling true if it's propelled, in part, by a desire to prove something? If you're afraid, does it suggest the need for courage and a leap of faith, or do you need to back up and reevaluate? How do you know when you're procrastinating or when the answer you seek simply hasn't revealed itself to you yet?

The channels through which callings come—whether dreams and symptoms or intuitions and accidents—are like oracles of any kind. They aren't meant to be treated as psychic vending machines, merely dispensing information. They are to be approached for dialogue, entered into in the spirit of correspondence and what the poet William Butler Yeats called "radical innocence." Their answers are typically metaphoric, paradoxical, poetic, and dreamlike, and they require reflection and conversation.

S H A K E N   U P

Recently, an acquaintance of mine who has searched for many years for a sense of direction and mission revealed that he was waiting for "an unshakable vision." I immediately thought of the work of the Belgian physicist Ilya Prigogine, who was awarded the Nobel Prize for his theory of what he calls "dissipative structures," part of which contends that friction is a fundamental property of nature and nothing grows without it—not mountains, not pearls, not people. It is precisely the quality of fragility, he says, the capacity for being "shaken up," that is paradoxically the key to growth. Any structure—whether at the molecular, chemical, physical, social, or psychological level—that is insulated from disturbance is also protected from change. It becomes stagnant. Any vision—or any thing—that is true to life, to the imperatives of creation and evolution, will not be unshakable.

We must therefore be willing to get shaken up, to submit ourselves to the dark blossomings of chaos, in order to reap the blessings of growth. Much of this is axiomatic: stress often prompts breakthroughs; crises point toward opportunities; chaos is an integral phase of the creative process; and protest abets the cause of democracy. The whole science of immunization is based on this wisdom: We introduce a little bit of chaos in order to prevent a lot of chaos. Just enough, but not too much. We shake up the system for the sake of helping it evolve and become stronger.

If you aren't willing to get shaken up, if you hang on to the belief that you can have an unshakable vision, when your call falters in any way—say you follow it and something painful happens, or you hear it once but then it goes

away, or you drive into a tunnel and lose the reception—then you will probably conclude that the call wasn't true to begin with because . . . it shook!
Almost by definition, calls shake us up because in the same breath that a call is
uttered, so is suffering. As Jonah discovered, a call rocks the boat, because it
often points to passions, and the word *passion* derives from the Latin *passio* for
suffering.

Being unwilling to bear the hurly-burly of faithfulness to our call, we
court *disaster*—Latin for "against one's stars"—and we end up agitated anyway.
Although we have the choice not to follow a call, if we do not do so, the Sufi
poet Kabir said, our lives will be infected with a kind of "weird failure." We'll
feel alienated from ourselves, listless and frustrated, and fitful with boredom,
the common cold of the soul. Life will feel so penetratingly dull and pointless
that we may become angry, and turn the anger inward against ourselves (one
definition of depression) or feel seized by the impulse to run madly out of the
house, down to the river, and search among the bullrushes for a miracle. The
calls we will not name or follow coalesce into entities that will attempt to tunnel their way into consciousness using any rough tool at hand to remind us of
their imperatives, and they will do so through the impeccable logic of pain. As
an old Roman saying goes: The fates lead those who will. Those who won't
they drag.

Callings keep surfacing until we deal with them. They return, in Freud's
words, as "repetition compulsions": the same marital fight over and over; the
symptom that recurs; the fantasy that won't go away; the urge drawing us to
the same type of partner; being fired again. In the Bible, God often called to
the prophets by repeating their names twice. "Abraham, Abraham." "Jacob,
Jacob." "Moses, Moses." Once, it seems, wasn't enough. Indeed, repetition is
fundamental to learning. Ask teachers, ask advertisers, ask parents. "Still, small
voices" may not have enough voltage to rattle the status quo, but they do have
staying power. I have, for instance, dreamed for more than thirty years of a
certain house where I once lived in New York. Ever since my parents' divorce
and my mother's remarriage, my mind is still working it out, my soul is still
unresolved.

Those who refuse their calls, though, who are afraid to become what they
perhaps already are—unhappy—will not, of course, experience the unrest (or
the joy) that usually accompanies the embrace of a calling. Having attempted
nothing, they haven't failed, and they can console themselves that if none of
their dreams come true, then at least neither will their nightmares.

Generally, people won't pursue their callings until the fear of doing so is finally exceeded by the pain of *not* doing so, but it's appalling how high a threshold people have for this quality of pain. Too many of us, it seems, have cultivated the ability to live with the unacceptable, and I hope that this book will make a convincing case for the benefits of allowing ourselves to get shaken up, to trade some of our stagnating certainties and securities for the generative effect of a little friction.

VIRGINS AND VOLCANOES

Perhaps the main reason that we ignore calls is that we instinctively know the price they'll exact. In order to become authentic, we're going to have to give up something dear: a job, a house, a relationship, a belief, a lifestyle to which we've become accustomed, the prestige of being a big fish in *any* size pond, security, money, precious time, anger at somebody, or just the pleasures of cynicism.

In recent years, a lot of people have taken as a personal motto and policy statement Joseph Campbell's admonition to "follow your bliss," believing, perhaps, that by doing so their lives will be blissful. Unfortunately, "follow your bliss" is more about following than about bliss. The flat-out truth is that if you follow your bliss you'll have your bliss, but nothing else is promised. Having your "bliss" is not a trifle, for grievously few people possess it. But all calls lead to some sacrifice because even just one choice closes the door on another, and some calls lead to much sacrifice, which may feel anything but blissful. If you're unwilling to make sacrifices, though, you can end up losing a great deal more than whatever you might have sacrificed.

The natives of some Asian countries have a tradition of trapping monkeys, by placing a piece of fruit in a gourd, with a small hole bored in its side, that is tied to the ground. Monkeys reach in for the fruit, but by grabbing it, and thereby making a fist, they can't get their hands out of the gourds. The natives then bag them and eat them. If the monkeys would only let go of the fruit, they could escape, but for some reason this doesn't enter their monkey minds, and it costs them their lives. We are only a notch up the evolutionary ladder and often act as if we, too, are hardwired with the same suicidal attachments.

We have to be willing to surrender. It's no coincidence that at all times in all cultures throughout history, the wisest among us have said that surrender is about liberation, not defeat! Historically, surrender has involved giving up the transitory for the sake of the transcendent. It has been a way of dis-possessing ourselves in the hopes of bringing good graces down upon us. The question sacrifice asks is: "What are you willing to give up to ensure your own unfolding, and the unfolding of what is holy in your life?"

Unfortunately, sacrifice is typically seen as deprivation—belt tightening, inconvenience, the tossing of virgins into volcanoes, the nailing of men onto crosses. Its reputation is one of punishment, but also, according to most of the world's religions, one of redemption and rebirth. Hopi Indians, for instance, buried their dead in the fetal position. In dying, we come back around to life. Sacrifice is an essential fact of life however, not an isolated act of appeasement. Rock eventually crumbles and becomes dirt that feeds plants. Grain is crushed to make flour. Snow melts to become water that nourishes the earth and makes for good river rafting in the spring. Each time we sacrifice—each time we let go of something, die to an old way of being, relinquish our grip on the fruit— we are practicing for bigger and bigger surrenders, and eventually for what M. Scott Peck calls "the final vocation": growing old gracefully and—a tough call—dying. We all owe God a death, Shakespeare once said, so we owe it to ourselves to practice for the occasion whenever possible.

One way we do so is by tending to the small surrenders that come our way almost daily: letting go of a bad mood, making a choice or a compromise, forgiving someone, parting with fear and saying the truth in a moment, spending time with our children instead of working late again.

Every sacrifice, though, every step toward action, every response to a call necessitates a leap of faith and is done without knowing the outcome. It is, as the philosopher Søren Kierkegaard described, the epitome of anxiety meeting courage. It is Jonah leaping overboard, which seems like madness, yet often in following our own calls, we're told by others that we're crazy. At some level, we, too, have to make an ultimate sacrifice to our callings. We need to devote everything, our whole selves. A part-time effort, a sorta-kinda commitment, an untested promise, won't suffice. You must know that you mean business, that you're going to jump into it up to your eye sockets and not turn back at the last minute. In making the leap from vision to form, you will be tested and suffer setbacks, occasionally severe. At our first steps toward authenticity—or love or compassion or any high calling—every devil in hell will come out to meet us. Only when you try your vision in the world can you test whether it's true.

How will you fare, for instance, when the higher calling meets the bottom line? What will you do when what seemed so meaningful in the solitude of introspection or retreat or an altered state suddenly begins to unravel in the cold light of practicality, of having to pay the rent and go to work and shuttle the children to day care and music lessons? What will happen when the backlash hits, when you're bombarded by the implorings of old roles and responsibilities, by the blank stares of loved ones, by fear and doubt and impatience—yours or others'—and by the sheer force of entropy in your life?

What happens when you discover, too, that you *yourself* are the prime saboteur, that whenever you have a breakthrough, it's followed by a breakdown, that you unconsciously blow a fuse every time you think too big, move too fast, get too excited, run too much juice through the system, as if you're sending up balloons in a room whose ceiling is studded with nails.

It is equally disconcerting to realize that you *can* have what you want. In most cases, this is true, if the call is. It is also a test to realize that if you really wanted, you could quit your job tomorrow. You might be in a pickle, but you could do it. You could get on a plane and fly to the Orient this week. You could pack a few things and take a retreat first thing in the morning. You could leave this marriage tonight. You could start saving the whales or the children or the planet right now! Of course, when you realize this you run into the paralysis of freedom.

Granted, there are real limitations in the world—poverty, racial discrimination, sexual stereotypes, disability, lack of access to education, financial responsibilities. Yet people do prevail against what conventional wisdom would suggest are impassables. They find ways of making end runs around such odds. This book is filled with stories of people who have successfully negotiated the tight passages to authenticity and personal power. They will describe, in detail, the process of how they responded to their callings, from the moment they first heard them; how they figured out what those calls were; where they found the courage to pursue the call in the face of opposition from within and without; and what in their characters helped (and hindered) them on their journeys.

ARIADNE'S THREAD

In attempting to weather the tests and win our spurs, it is essential to know how to gain and regain strength—to what people, places, teachings, practices, beliefs, and sanctuaries can we turn? Who and what are our allies?

In the story of Theseus and the Minotaur, after Theseus has slain the beast in the center of the underground labyrinth, he guides himself back to the surface by a length of thread given him by Ariadne, the king's daughter, retracing his steps through the dark maze of tunnels.

What is that thread for you? What can guide you through the labyrinth back to safety, back from your encounters with the dark? Perhaps it is the lamp of someone's love, the support and feedback of people who genuinely believe you can do it, your connection to something bigger than yourself (family, community, nature, music, God), your own courage and humor, even your own desperation. Whatever the forms, these parts of you, of your life, can help you remember who you are. These are the parts of you that haven't gone to sleep or forgotten.

If our allies help us stay the course, though, our "enemies"—whatever forces thwart us—provide us with the true tests of our spirit. They offer us the best opportunities to learn strength, resolve, patience, and compassion—skills that are easy in the abstract and damnably hard in the doing. Sometimes, however, what first appears to be an enemy turns out not to be, and it is the better part of valor to exercise a heroic quality of discretion in following our calls. Be willing to approach obstacles as if they might be allies, and make your leaps of faith accordingly.

When Jonah went overboard, he leapt not into the swallowing sea but into an unexpected benediction—the belly of the whale. The whale served as Ariadne's thread for Jonah, leading him to safety, delivering him to his own fate for resolution. The whale is an inspired bit of symbolism. The only other time we are inside another's belly is before birth, so the image reflects the anticipated birth that follows sacrifice. In that belly, drunk on evolution, we are not so much acting as being acted upon by Something Bigger than ourselves. It is our preparation before we are spilled forth into life, into the world, ready at last to carry out our missions.

The psychologist Ira Progoff once said that each of our lives is like a well, and we're meant to go down deeply enough into our own wells so that we finally reach the stream that's the source of all the wells. There, says theologian Frederick Buechner, in the place where "our deep gladness and the world's deep hunger meet," we hear a further call. This call leads us out into the world to test our bright swords in real combat—to teach love, save lives, change minds, educate, minister.

But the question must arise in our minds whether our deep gladness can satisfy the world's deep hunger. This, also, is a test of our faith. The difference that any of us will ultimately make in the world is equivalent to our throwing a stone into the sea. Science tells us that because the stone is lying on the bottom, the level of the water *must* have risen, but there is no way to measure it. We must take it entirely on faith.

part one

THE CALL

TO

ATTENTION

one

T H E
E A R   O F   T H E
A N I M A L

Some years ago, at a hands-on science museum in San Francisco known as the Exploratorium, I saw an exhibit called a particle chamber. It was a glass box about the size of an oven in which subatomic particles were made visible, appearing as if they were ordinary dust motes caught in a beam of light, or the "snow" in paperweight winter scenes. These particles, however, are not dust that settles *on* things but are dust that floats right *through* them. As I leaned my head over the glass chamber, the particles I saw beneath my face were those that had just passed through my own skull, like parachutists through a cloud. They were the remains of stars that exploded before earth was even a gleam in God's eye; radioactive fossils falling through space like the skeletons of marine animals on their way to building a coral reef; the parts that flew out when stars collided like demolition derbies in space.

The particle chamber is a container for making the invisible visible. So are the compass, microscope, telescope, radio and television; so are scientists, psychologists, and artists; so is conscious attention. The right instrument is essential, but turning it on is even more important. By turning on our devoted attention, by becoming students of our lives, archivists of life's details, we may distinguish the calls that are raining on us constantly, though they are obscured by our inattention. We need to listen "as if to hear from behind the wall the songs of birds who populate the secret garden," as the sculptor Auguste Rodin once said. If we don't listen, the callings go unnoticed, and we are the worse for it. Our lives become absurd—*ab-surdus* meaning to be absolutely deaf.

Aspire to be like a good animal—on the alert—or like someone in love. As the theologian Paul Tillich once said, the first duty of love is to listen. Furthermore, if you sense that the world is animated by a loving presence and your own life somehow witnessed, you listen back in the spirit of conversation, appreciation, *courtesy.* If you *don't* sense the world to be animated by a loving presence, if, like the ancient Greeks perhaps, you sense it animated by gods who have become mean-spirited with boredom, and have taken to messing with the mortals' minds to relieve the ennui born of immortality, then you listen in the spirit of self-defense.

Either way, listening is hard work. The discipline of paying close attention to ourselves, to the vital signs that blip across the screen of our lives in forms such as dreams, intuitions, feedback, and longings, will help us know what our calls are. This practice of listening will tell us what's true and what's not, when to proceed and when to postpone, whom to trust and whom not, which direction to take at the crossroads, whose voices are brawling in our heads, what's right for us and where we're willing to be led.

Part of this discipline is being willing to contend with what we hear when we turn on our receivers. By being willing to receive, we, in a sense, *will* the calls to happen, to make themselves known. We draw them to us, but we never know quite what kind of marching orders we're going to get. We may not be entirely happy with them, but, as with following your bliss, following them, not happiness, is the point. We're on a scavenger hunt, tracking, searching for arrowheads. When we find them we turn them over and over in the warm expectant tremble of our hands, polishing them with curiosity, rubbing them as if they might be magic lamps. Which they might be.

"The first track is the end of a string," wrote Tom Brown in his book *The Tracker.* "At the far end a being is moving. A mystery that leaves itself like a trail of bread crumbs, and by the time your mind has eaten its way to the maker of the tracks, the mystery is inside you."

G U I D A N C E   S Y S T E M

Certain tribes of South Pacific Islanders can sail for a thousand miles over open ocean under complete cloud cover—with no sun, moon, or stars to usher them from island to island—and yet know exactly where they are by the kind of waves beneath their rafts.

This is a hard act to follow, but those who are the most attuned to their callings aspire to just this quality of mindfulness. With senses adequate to their potential and to the passions they feel, they try to make their way, listening, as social activist Fran Peavey puts it, "as if there is a thief in the house."

Gordon Hempton is one such person, and as what he calls a "sound tracker" he operates on this level of subtlety, earning his living by recording the vanishing sounds of nature. He wasn't always this way. In fact, for many years he had a hard time even keeping himself *among* the living, due to his inattention in a line of work that has little mercy for such lapses: He was a bike messenger in Seattle. For seven years, it was a way to support his true love, recording nature sounds.

Because he tended to pay more attention out in the field than on the job, Hempton found himself bloodied up in more than a few run-ins with automobiles. These encounters, though, did wonders for his hearing. "I learned that these ears are hanging on to my head for more than just listening to the radio. They're the watchdogs of my life. My guidance system. And I now use them as if my life depended on it."

Biking eventually became for him, of necessity, a kind of mindfulness practice, the exercise of keeping his receivers turned on to the subtleties in and around him, and one bright sunrise, biking up a steep hill, he was struck again, this time by a call: to follow dawn, as he put it, around the world, recording the sounds of nature. It took another year of planning, $15,000 out of his own pocket, and four months of traveling, but it also became an Emmy Award–winning PBS documentary called *The Vanishing Dawn Chorus,* which took him seventy thousand miles around the globe tracking, as he wrote in a grant proposal for the project, "a never-ending wave of birdsong that follows the rhythm of the Earth's rotation as if the sun never stopped rising and the birds never stopped singing."

Hempton now possesses what the Eskimos call *seuketat,* "the ear of the animal." He can listen to a recording of wind in the pines and tell you length of the pine needles. He can hear the sound of water running under-ground. He will tell you that quiet places, including those on the inside of us, are "the think tanks of the soul." And he will tell you that having the ear of the animal has more than once saved not only his soul but his skin.

Once, while tracking frogs and dripping water in Sri Lanka, he had a sud-den anxiety attack, an intuition of danger that he almost waved off as paranoia or some misfiring synapse in the brain. But *seuketat* informed him otherwise, and not wishing to tempt another accident, he took off quickly, leaving behind his recording equipment, which was still running. Later, when he retrieved it and played it back, he heard first the sound of his own footsteps departing . . . and then the sound of a leopard come out of the forest. "I was being a listener," he said of the incident. "I was being a whole-body listener, and my rational mind was trying to fight it."

This is typical of the rational mind. It is the nature of the beast whose habitat is an era and a culture that mistrust and denigrate the impulses of the deeper brain—intuition, feeling, sensing, instinct, dream. These functions of our guidance system are rejected by the rational within us in part because they're primitive, in part because we can't measure and control them, and in part because they smack of the feminine. We disassociate from them because they scare us. Unfortunately for us, much power is embedded in the deep brain, including survival skills and many of the underground flumes through which callings well to the surface.

We would do well to follow the example of "creative types," argues physi-cian and author Larry Dossey, to follow those who seem to maintain a healthy respect for the powers in themselves of the irrational and unconscious—"the primitive, uncultured, inexplicable and wild"—and court these forces as the Muses they are.

A   FAUSTIAN   BARGAIN

During a somewhat aimless period in my early adulthood, I was in the habit of driving, late at night, to a parking lot near my house which had, in the center of it, a small, round island, perhaps ten feet in diameter, planted with flowers. There I would roll down my window, turn my steering wheel all the way to the right, and just drive slowly around and around, feeling the cen-trifugal force push me gently against the door.

The size of the island was perfectly matched to the turning radius of my car, and I could drift in a sleepy orbit for as long as I liked, slouched in my seat and staring up at the stars wheeling overhead, or watching the lights of nearby streetlamps and buildings and traffic float by like glowing streamers or the lights of a merry-go-round captured at slow shutter speed.

Only with the hindsight of a decade or more, however, did I come to understand what I had been doing: I was unconsciously acting out, with metaphoric precision, an inner experience—the feeling I then had that my life was going in circles. My attempts to dizzy myself in the parking lot, to scramble my inner compass, seemed an appropriate reflection of my stout refusal to search for true north, to make heads or tails of my direction in life.

~※~

The mythologist Joseph Campbell used to say that we're having experiences all the time that hint at our hungers. He insisted that we must learn to listen for them, learn to recognize them. The great sacrilege, he said, in terms of the soul's integrity, is that of "inadvertence, of not being alert, not awake."

What we're up against in trying to awaken, though, is the power of repression in ourselves. At our core, we know that pain isn't subtle when anesthesia wears off, so we're tempted to keep slathering on the soothing unction of inattention, especially when the possibility of pain is involved—whether it's the pain of knowing what we must sacrifice; of what change may demand of us; or of dreams deferred and time rushing by. Sometimes we just don't want to hear about it, and it doesn't matter if we have songs to sing, feelings and intuitions like ten-car pileups inside us, or calls to answer and lines gone dead.

We strike a Faustian bargain: In return for the attenuation of our anxiety, we agree to foreswear awareness, as if we were pleading with a mobster—if you let me go, I promise I won't tell a soul—or paying blackmail in the hope that some dangerous secret won't come to light. The natural equation is this: pain up, awareness down.

A friend of mine, Joe Mowry, recently published an anthology of poems by people who were sexually abused as children. He was struck, he said, by the number of images he found of people being up in the branches of trees, as if they were trying to rise above the pain, to look down on it from a height, perhaps even to see the bigger picture—the *purpose* for the pain.

Denial no doubt serves a palliative function. It can prevent overload on explosive issues, ease us into the hot bath of whatever we're not entirely ready to tackle yet. Says theologian Frederich Buechner in *The Hungering Dark,* "We shy away from introspection because, however fearful the surface seems, we fear the depths still more. And we are right. There is much to fear there. If there is terror about darkness because we cannot see, there is also terror about light because we *can* see. Would rather not see." If we do not climb down willingly with our eyes open, he said, we risk falling in with our eyes closed. If we ignore *seuketat,* we end up turning our backs on the leopard, tempting fate, putting our souls in the position of having to come after us, teeth bared. The only conscious observations we'll make will be those forced on us by crises.

You have to be pretty motivated, though, to want to submit yourself to the cloud chamber. You really have to want, or *need,* to start paying closer attention to yourself, to wake up. You have to be willing to suffer what you hear. It's probably fair to say that awakening is attached to suffering like a rope to a bell, and you're not going to pull on it without making some noise.

"Perhaps this is the lack in my work," the writer Michele Murray once wrote, "what prevents me from leaping into the full power which is mine— that I cannot face myself." Perhaps this is what Gordon Hempton most learned from listening to *birds*—the need to take a chance in what you'll attract with your calls. "The love songs birds sing to attract mates," he says, "also draw the attention of predators."

We have to be open to hearing things we may not want to hear, he says, to attract the attention of bad news as well as good, suffering as well as passion. "In following the call I heard telling me I had to be a sound tracker, I had to be willing to inflict economic hardship on my family. In fifteen years, there have been times I deeply regretted becoming a listener, and I put my equipment up for sale. But that was harder than the economic hardship, and I always kept going. Besides, what kind of example would I be setting for my kids? Tuning out the call is the real risk. A full listener has to be willing to hear it all."

"Attention must be paid!" cried Willy Loman at the end of *Death of a Salesman*—and found out too late that he hadn't.

THE   CURE   IN   CURIOSITY

According to those I interviewed for this book, who are people very responsive to their callings, any practice that strengthens our powers of observation and our ability to see subtleties within ourselves, any practice that allows us to step outside and look back through the shop window, will help us overcome the kind of inadvertence of which Joseph Campbell spoke and from which Willy Loman suffered. These practices include anything that helps us pay attention to our lives, gently sanding our fingertips to make them more sensitive to the feel of things, such as: a daily journal, meditation, therapy, artwork, movement work, martial arts, dream interpretation, music, long walks, intimate conversation, retreats, fasting, rituals. These practices also remind us not to spend so much time awaiting big booming voices from on high that we stumble over the whispers that are right at our feet. "If you listen down below," instructs the Torah, "you will deserve to hear from above."

Start small, says psychologist Charles Tart in his book *Waking Up,* lest you overwhelm yourself with your psychic revelations. Observe yourself walking and eating first. Watch yourself working, thinking about your future, talking to your parents. Then move up—or rather inward—to observing your dreams, physical symptoms, spiritual conundrums, loves and hates.

While traveling on the Amazon River, I once participated in a hunt for caimans (a member of the crocodile family) officiated by a local guide. We conducted this bloodless affair at night by shining a flashlight along the darkened banks of the river. Whenever the light hit a caiman, its eyes glowed red. The light also mesmerized it. If its eyes glowed no farther apart than two inches or so, it wasn't too big to capture easily, which the natives did partly to collect the teeth to use for blow-gun darts. We would glide in a raft up to the caiman, flashlight in one hand, the other hand ready to grab it *quickly* behind the jaws and lift it out of the water in one deft motion. It was arguably one of the more exciting and stupid things I've ever done, but it provides a fitting analogy to the initial efforts at self-awareness. The darkness is pervasive, the light modest. Look for eyes that glow no farther than a few inches apart.

Self-awareness also requires that we have *curiosity* about ourselves, Tart says. We need to resurrect the sort of basic inquisitiveness we had as children, that we usually directed *outward,* the curiosity that had us down on our knees staring into puddles looking for upside-down worlds, pulling seeds apart to figure out how a tree could possibly fit in there, asking why why why.

Remember to start small. Just observe at first, don't analyze. Use curiosity, not interrogation. Save that for later. Just as we get better mileage when we separate the creative and critical functions in our attempts to write or paint or invent, so, too, we make self-awareness more palatable by holding off the impulse to be critical so that we focus initially on the desire simply to see. Observation in itself will be considered an intrusion by those undiscovered parts of us hiding along the banks of our consciousness. Keep in mind that the laws of cause and effect are not so strict that merely thinking about a thing automatically brings it into being, and promise yourself that for now you don't have to *do* anything about what you find with your curiosity.

POWER LOUNGING

I used to think of Sisyphus as the patron saint of workaholics, one of whom I somewhat provisionally consider myself to be, though more out of necessity than compulsion. Freelance writing is a heavy stone and demands a steady labor to keep it rolling. Until recently, though, I'd overlooked the true instruction of Sisyphus's life, which is that each time his grindstone rolls to the bottom of the mountain, he is granted a rest while he walks back down to retrieve it. Though he must work for all time, according to the myth, he doesn't work all the time.

Nor, I decided a few years ago, should I. Having just completed a book that took me fifteen months of twelve-hour days, I suddenly hit a wall I had never hit in my life as a working man—burnout. The thought of doing another day's work on anything even remotely related to the machinations of building a career, producing income, or generally "getting ahead" was nearly enough to buckle me at the knees. As it was, in the waning days of the book project, I pulled myself up to my desk each morning as if to a chin-up bar.

After such an intemperance of work, no trip seemed too extravagant or protracted, no binge too vulgar, no amount of goofing-off too unreasonable. So I decided to take a break. In fact, I decided to extend the spirit of Sabbath to outlandish proportions—by taking four months off, living off savings, and for a brief period in the middle of my life seeing what it would feel like simply not to work. I wanted to make time for the kind of creative idleness that an acquaintance of mine calls "power lounging." I needed "space"—distance from all that was pressing in on me. I needed a penetrating quiet inside, and I needed to hold that silence up to my ears, like an empty shell, and listen to the roar of my own life. I had to try to make out what direction to take next.

When I told a colleague what I planned to do now that the book was done, he asked, "What are you, rich?"

"No," I replied. "Desperate."

Through some trial and error, I have discovered that often the best bait to use in luring a call is a little space. We need time when we're not engaged in what the Taoists refer to as "the ten thousand things." When we give off nothing but busy signals, calls simply don't get through. There's no room for them. Make some room. Get off the line once in a while.

A psychotherapist of my acquaintance, Eric Maisel, whose practice is devoted to people in the arts who are struggling with the vicissitudes of that blood sport, has a technique he calls "hushing." Of all the exercises in his new book, *Fearless Creating*, hushing is, in his estimation, the most important, probably because it's the most difficult. Hushing is what we do when we meditate; when we go into a museum and sit before a painting for fifteen minutes; when we succumb to the lazy lure of a spring afternoon spent in our own backyards watching the shadows of clouds bend in the folds of the hills. It's a quieting and an opening, a way to stop the mind from operating on autoscan. "Hush your thoughts just as if you were comforting a baby," he says. "A wild person with a calm mind can create anything."

Perhaps such a person can even tackle the advanced course in hushing. This involves clearing the decks of the clutter of beliefs that have outlived their usefulness, second-guessing all parental injunctions and moral admonitions, making decisions one way or another, and avoiding all activities that no longer—if they ever did—hold any juice for you. This is, of course, a lifetime's worth of work. It involves going through the psyche with a metal detector, flushing out those beliefs and behaviors that are not consonant with your integrity, and refusing to do business with them anymore.

If my little sabbatical from work was any indication, hushing is unfortunately easier said than done. Whenever I assumed an angle of repose and attempted to quiet my mind, or understand how it worked, I immediately noticed how much it behaved like a roomful of toddlers. In the first phase of my vocational celibacy, I had a postpartum depression. A big project and a lifetime of working build up a tremendous momentum that doesn't end just because the work does. As in any collision, the car stops, but the passenger doesn't.

For my entire leave of absence, I experienced a bewildering freedom marked by a maddening restlessness that despite my intentions routinely propelled me, as if I were in a trance, back into my office. I would sit there sometimes for hours, twisting back and forth on my chair and pulling at my lower lip, listening to the blathering traffic of noises in my head, my legs vibrating like tuning forks under the desk.

"This is what it must be like when men retire," my partner, Robin, declared after a morning of watching me pace around the house aimlessly, opening the refrigerator half a dozen times.

I began to realize with crackling clarity during this supposed time off that I come from a long line of doers, starting with a workaholic family that had hardwired me to excel, to stay on top of things, to expect that hard work and material wealth would put me in line to receive the key to the cosmic washroom. On his deathbed, my grandfather asked my mother what day it was.

"Tuesday," she said.

"Pay the gardener," he instructed her.

His obituary was like most others, betraying the compulsive preoccupation with work, and helping me understand why I had such a devil of a time *not* working. Obits are little more than posthumous résumés, lists of accomplishments: books authored, titles held, military ranks attained, degrees earned. They're summary statements of our lives, testaments to what we hold in esteem.

There are no hallelujahs for idleness, for time spent with family or on retreat, for afternoons given over to long, dreamy walks, for time spent in a state of being rather than a state of doing. Listening is a state of being, but droning away in the boiler room of the culture is a juggernaut of a machine that heaves out a message strong enough to pump cement through the pipes: work! Value adheres to what we produce, so we're constantly doing. When we're busy doing, we don't have to be busy feeling. Feeling that maybe we're burned out, pinned to the ground by the gravity of our endeavors, that we need a change, or that working, which normally offers us a sense of control over our lives, has instead made our lives feel like a parody of being in control, like we're frantically trying to shovel coal into a furnace that's burning it up faster and faster.

Having your nose to the grindstone, your shoulder to the wheel, and your back to the wall for long periods of time is simply not the most comfortable position. Sometimes lying in the bathtub is, or sitting in front of a painting. By adopting postures of receptivity in relation to whatever shy thing hankers for our attention, we build for it an entryway. We clear a strip in the jungle for the planes to land. We come to understand the irony that we can experience progress even while standing still, that going inward can be going forward.

Sitting quietly, hushing, for even a few minutes a day gives us a place in which to catch our breath, and a chance for our callings and intuitions to catch up with us. Just as the ear needs "rests" when listening to music, or the eye and mind need the respite of occasional paragraph breaks when reading a book, we all need a place to linger and reflect in the onrushing of our story or song, an eddy into which we can turn our canoe from the current.

B E Y O N D   W O R D S

Years ago, I knew a man who possessed the uncanny ability to meditate in the middle of a crowd. He could submerge into a trance, his mouth dropping open un-self-consciously, in the bustling cafeteria of a ski lodge at lunchtime. A novice meditator myself at the time, I was astonished at his imperturbability. He could find silence in the most improbable circumstances and tolerate it in the most impressive quantities.

Whenever I hear someone declared a "strong, silent type," I think of *him*, not of the kind of person who slips into silence as one would into a bullet-proof vest, in the emotional equivalent of clamping your hands over your ears. True silence takes guts to face, and the double-dare of it lies first in finding it at all, and then in holding yourself to it amid the static of a thousand competing impulses.

In the beginning was the Word, and that Word grew out of silence. So, to the degree we're each waiting for Word of our callings, we ought to tend the soil of silence. We need to teach ourselves to sit quietly and listen, just listen, long enough to leave a decent indentation on the couch. If all our moments are filled with words and thoughts, with noise however joyous, then when it comes time to convey our deepest intuitions, when our lives demand guidance from within, we'll be speechless.

We also need to teach ourselves to *recognize* silence, which is not *relative*. Silence lacks the usual background accompaniment of droning white noises—cars, refrigerators, air conditioners. I recently visited for the first time a retreat center that I had been promised would have a ringing-in-the-ears quiet. I arrived after a five-hour drive, however, to discover that a highway lay a hundred yards from the retreat center's front door. The sound of traffic was a constant noise, both outside and inside. I was told that I was the only guest ever to complain about the lack of quiet.

It isn't easy finding silence anymore. For most people relative quiet is the only kind of quiet they know. In fact, those who specialize in the study of sound marvel when they chance upon a spot on earth—a remote desert, a cloister, an inaccessible flank of mountainside, a swatch of the canopied rain forest still far from the chain saws and flight patterns—where they can record an hour's worth of silence unblemished by the din of humanity.

We live on a noisy planet. In the rest of the universe, however, silence is the rule, for the simple reason that sound needs air in order to travel. If there is no air there's no sound. If you were in deep space and a fiery comet blasted by not five feet away, you would hear absolutely nothing.

The fabulous struggle for quiet on the set is also exacerbated by the fact that, as Thomas Merton once observed, many of us are in love with our own noise, so we constantly defile silence, fearing that it might accuse us of our own emptiness. There *is* an emptiness at the center of our lives—the place Paradise once filled—and an infinity of silence, I suspect, awaits us at the end of it. Maybe we fear silence, Merton said, because we sense that we may hear there the sound of our own suffering, and the suffering of the world, and in a single moment our hearts will turn over and grow old. Or maybe we're afraid that if we remain silent for too long we might burst into tears that will never stop and we'll end up flooding the basement.

Sitting quietly also feels an awful lot like doing nothing, and for those who are used to feeling power through action and oratory and feel naked without language, nothingness is maybe a bit too close to the void, too much like their image of death, that great escarpment of silence. "Death," said Merton, "is the enemy who seems to confront them at every moment in the deep darkness and silence of their own being. So they keep shouting at death."

When we want to communicate quietly with ourselves or with whomever put us here, however, language is more a hindrance than a help. We get tangled too easily, caught in a net of discursiveness. We're after something that lies beneath all that noise, something literally un-thinkable, something that is not so much communication as it is communion—a felt language, a silence filled not with emptiness but with presence. This presence reveals itself to us only *in* silence, says P. L. Travers, author of *Mary Poppins.* "Be still long enough, I thought, and the trees would take no notice of me and continue whatever it was they were doing or saying before I happened upon them."

ॐ

Rachel Bagby, a New Hampshire vocal artist who presides over an independent record label called Out of the Box, has a practice she calls "media celibacy," which she has engaged in for stretches of up to four months, as a way to hush the blistering hubbub of messages brought to her by radio, television, magazines, and newspapers. It means not tuning into any of them for a period of time. Start with an hour, she suggests. Build up. And be patient with yourself. We've all taken a soaking for centuries.

"It does something to your ears. You receive messages in a new way. You're better able to discern your own voices from those of the culture, the voices that are aligned with life from those that are not. And when you come back to it [the media], you hear more clearly the cultural assumptions, the emotional appeals, the tones of voice, the motivations."

Not only the *way* she hears but also *what* she hears have been changed by her media fasting. "Rather than just the classical and church-related gospel music I grew up with, I began to hear, oddly, East Indian songs and rhythms, and only later discovered that my eldest maternal relative, a great-grandmother, is *from* East India."

Bagby considers this practice of "listening beneath the surface" to be preparation for the work she did with the singer/composer Bobbie McFerrin. For a master class she took with him, she had to prepare a fifteen-minute demo tape, and some of the material she put on it—along with a certain "fearlessness and faith" she brought *to* it—grew directly out of her silencing practice, which occasionally included verbal celibacy. As a result of the tape, she was invited to audition for a vocal performance group that McFerrin was then putting together, called Voicestra.

When she walked in, McFerrin drew a line with his foot on the floor and said to her, "Step into this stream of music and sing what you hear." As she describes it, she heard a thousand different things at once, chose one, and began to sing—about following a single note, "following where it led, building on it, respecting it, revering it, loving it."

She got the job.

"You have to be willing to step into a mysterious unknown situation and listen to the creative response within you, whether it be music, a voice of wisdom, an inspirational idea, or a calling to just be spontaneous."

It's equally important, though, she adds, not to deify silence, even if it greatly tunes the ear. "For those who are culturally habituated to silence—women, children, whole classes of people—perhaps we have to *give* voice to what has been silenced."

The power of silence, and of holding to it, has never been more clearly demonstrated to *me* than by a trip I made in my twenties—during my going-in-circles phase—to a Trappist monastery in Kentucky, the Abbey of Gethsemani, where Thomas Merton is buried beneath a plain white cross in the graveyard out back, and where the monks practice the vows of silence. In the front lobby of the guest house there is a guest register that, in addition to having columns for name and address, has one for "Observations." And under that heading are the most eloquent arguments I have ever encountered for the benedictions of silence:

"53rd annual retreat here."

"I, the poet, stand wordless at your gates."

"In silence, a goal is set and a decision made."

"A return to the deep well of peace."

"I came to talk, discuss and argue. I learned to listen."

"For once I let God do all the talking."

"The eye of the hurricane."

"A welcome comma in my life."

"Where is the man who has no need of words? There is the man I would like to talk to."

"A place out of this world to go to, so that I have the strength to go back into it."

"Beyond words."

"A point of stillness in the search for the stillpoint."

"In this silence, the thread of the world is kept from breaking."

"Ahhhhh."

CONSULT YOUR DEATH

Sometimes my partner, Robin, will leave the house on some errand, turn around halfway down the front steps, and come back to where I'm standing at the door. "Forget something?" I'll ask. "Yeah," she says, looking me in the eye and stroking my face with her hand. "I just wanted to look at you in case I never see you again."

I hate good-byes because I always prefer to assume that I will see people again. It obviates the need for all that awkwardness; it avoids the issue, which is that we may never see each other again. Saying good-bye is understanding that existential fact. Our paths may never cross again.

The first time Robin did this, I simply couldn't take it in. "You're only going shopping," I reminded her, as if the sheer mundaneness of it was a guarantee of safety. Her remark was too full of truth and foreboding for me to let it in. With each such farewell I've become better at receiving it, though when it really sinks in, a hot shot of adrenaline tends to thump through my solar plexus, similar to the sensation of falling when an airplane hits an air pocket. Impermanence is one of the things we share with those we love. We can go at any moment.

I have kept a file for years on some of the abrupt and unnatural ways in which we make exits from life, "in the swish of a horse's tail," as Confucius said. Hit by a bolt of lightning that comes right through the telephone. Killed by a meteor. Struck by a truck tire flying over the median strip at seventy miles an hour that crashes through your windshield. Being drowned in molasses when a truck carrying a ton of it tips over.

Thomas Merton once remarked that in considering any important decision in life, it's imperative to "consult your death" because, as the English writer Samuel Johnson once put it, "When a man knows he is to be hanged in a fortnight, it concentrates his mind wonderfully." Death is a strip search. It points the barrel of mortality at your head and demands to see what you have hidden under your garments. It also asks the question "What do you love?" As you listen for callings keep such a question poised in your mind to help tune out some of the static. In fact, "What do you love" is the question that callings pose.

Many years ago, I interviewed a number of people who were *forced* to consult their deaths because their doctors had told them that they were dying. A few of them were shattered by the news, but most were liberated. They spoke about feeling no longer trapped by life, feeling free to speak their minds and follow their hearts, free from imaginary fears, tyrannical conformities and pleasantries, and petty authorities. One woman told me that her cancer diagnosis was "not a death sentence, but a life sentence." She no longer wondered how to spend her precious nick of time. Her passions and loves were finally released.

Because I tend to turn away from the subject of death myself, from acknowledging that, as an acquaintance of mine put it, I have an expiration date, I find that visual aids help to focus my attention. For instance, I keep rolled up and stashed in the closet in my office a large X ray of my own skeleton, from the top of my skull to the bottom of my pelvis. It was taken by the chiropractor who worked on my back after a diving accident tore up some of the ligaments in my lower back. I unravel that X ray from time to time, just to gape at my innards. One's own skeleton is a thing both monstrous and divine and points to only one conclusion: There is a kingdom come and I'm in for it. There will come a day when I die and do not rise, so I would rather die doing what I love than what I don't. Everybody should have a memento mori, like my X ray, somewhere in their house.

For similar effect, I also visit *ruins* whenever I can, for they, too, are skeletons of a sort. When I travel, I prefer going to places where they abound: the crumbling walls of stone fortresses still bearing the scars of cannonballs, the remains of mummies blown out of the sand by the wind, the broken rim of a volcano whose eruption destroyed an entire civilization—anything to remind me that every castle, like the sun, goes down.

I remember my father telling me once of hosting a friend from Europe who laughed at him when with great enthusiasm he led him through some New England woods to the site of an old log cabin from the 1800s. That's no ruin, his friend scoffed. A mere hundred years old. People *live* that long. Ruins, he said, have to remind you that all your greatest efforts, all the greatest efforts of even hundreds of generations of men and women, thousands of years of human history, will yield nothing absolute, nothing that will last, and that the great thing, the real accomplishment, is building your house in full view of the volcano.

two

THE CHALLENGE
OF FINDING
CLARITY

In the marble corridors of an Egyptian temple, a man glimpses a veiled statue and is warned that underneath the veil is Truth, and that mortals must not look upon it. He cannot resist laying his eyes on Truth, though, so he sneaks into the temple one night and unveils it. In the morning, the priests discover him knocked senseless, lying at the foot of the statue.

When Ann Kreilkamp was twenty-six years old, Truth came flapping out of the wild place in her life, cloaked in the sackcloth of illness, and propelled her into an immense struggle to figure out what it meant. Was it a call? If so, from where was it coming, why, and what sort of response was it calling for? Furthermore, how would she know that whatever response she devised was the right one?

The year was 1969. She was in graduate school, married with children, trying to be all things to all people: the perfect mom, perfect wife, perfect graduate student, perfect Catholic girl. She was also coming apart at the seams. "I thought I was going crazy. I kept asking 'Why do I feel so trapped, why am I so unhappy, why am I so unsatisfied, why do I want to kill my children even though I love them?' " She didn't know that a whole generation of women was asking similar questions and unraveling in similar ways.

One day she just seized up, literally and figuratively. She landed in Massachusetts General Hospital in Boston with generalized peritonitis, an inflammation of the lining that cradles the guts. She couldn't digest. She couldn't absorb. Nothing moved, either in or out. During the seven days she was in the hospital, her stomach ballooned to the equivalent of a six-month pregnancy. It was more than the peritonitis, she sensed. Something was brewing. When she got up the nerve to ask the doctor if she was going to die, he shrugged and walked out of the room.

This provoked something good Catholic girls are not supposed to do: She got angry at God. Her logic was: "Not only is there no God to pray to, there's no God to give the finger to. If there's no God, I'm therefore free—and responsible." At which point, she describes, "For the first time in my life, my soul came down inside my body and said to me, 'Live or die. You have a choice.' "

Within twenty-four hours, Ann Kreilkamp experienced something the medical community is reluctant even to document, let alone investigate. She had a spontaneous remission, or what most doctors, in a massive failure of the imagination, call a misdiagnosis. The peritonitis completely disappeared, leaving her doctor once again shrugging.

Before she left the hospital, she glanced in the mirror and was astonished to see that her physical shape had changed. Her body weight had redistributed itself, her contours were now different and have remained so ever since. Her soul, it seemed, had a shape all its own.

For the next year she struggled to discern what specifically her soul was calling her to do, besides choosing between life and death. Her graduate studies in philosophy, she discovered, were largely the search for certainty, for justification of some of the choices she was considering, for truth—an attempt, perhaps, to unveil the statue. "And when I found out that there *is* no Truth, that ultimately there's no way to be certain, it terrified me. It threw me into an intellectual panic. I realized I just had to jump, to leap with my whole self, which is tricky when you're not entirely whole. But you take your best guess."

At that time, Kreilkamp had to leave her marriage, true to D. H. Lawrence's dictum that every human being is treacherous to every other because we have to follow our own souls. Two years later, she also relinquished custody of her two boys to her husband; it was "the most painful, unnatural act of my life." These broad jumps, however, taught her that the most reliable test of a calling's veracity and meaning comes only in the results. There was no way she could have *analyzed* her way to clarity, bent over her dilemma as if over an anvil, trying to beat shape into it, trying to confirm whether the call to part ways with her family was her soul's voice or just the voice of restlessness, some misguided sense of self-preservation, or even the spawn of her own anger at God.

The answer is in the outcome, she insists. "What is the *feedback* your life gives you? Is your energy growing or shriveling? Moving or getting jammed up? Is your life deepening? And don't jump to conclusions about results. Maybe you have to wait for more evidence before deciding what a thing means. Ultimately, we may make some decisions and never know if they're justifiable, if they'll ever make sense in a way we can fully understand. For example, I still don't know if I was justified in leaving my children, though they now understand my decision, and as adults we're very close. Maybe I wasn't justified. But I had to do it. And that's another sign that a call is true, I think. No matter how uncomfortable, it *feels* right."

Even though the proof lies in the results, pleasing results do not mean a true call, or unpleasant results a false call. Cheap logic would like to believe in a simplistic cause-and-effect universe where if *X* happens, then it was meant to be. Wishing doesn't make it so, however, any more than calling it a calling necessarily makes it one. A "true" call can occasionally have disastrous results—as it did in splitting Ann's family apart—especially if you're breaking with traditions and taboos, pushing old boundaries, running up against the system in all its ferocious stubbornness. Sometimes hell breaks loose, a chunk of it floating right into the shipping lanes.

Certain patterns of a life can only be understood in retrospect. What at first seemed like a calamity may turn out to have been merely the path. Among Tibetan Buddhists, "the mishap lineage" teaches how to make a *practice* out of using misfortune as a means for spiritual growth. Given their belief that "life is suffering," Buddhists are able to turn all of life into a spiritual quest.

THE TRUTH IS NOT SIMPLE

In order to distinguish whether the calls we hear are authentic or siren song, true to our trajectory or dangerous distraction—and whether the interpretations and responses we offer them are befitting—we need to follow the example of Ulysses and strap ourselves to the mast so that we can listen first without reacting, without jumping ship. To be distracted means to be pulled apart.

Our powers of discernment—of clarity—are routinely clouded and informed by all manner of impulses, hankerings, emotions, ulterior motives, and intuitions that may, in fact, be fear. Discerning means separating, so before we attempt to separate the true from the false, the ripe from the unripe, the gold from the fool's gold, first we do a bit of hunting and gathering, drawing together those raw materials and listening to the various voices within us, that are sure to have an opinion on anything as important, as *interesting*, as a calling.

For instance, if you are contemplating whether to start up a new venture and you find money on the sidewalk, is that a sign that you're supposed to proceed, that your enterprise is now divinely sanctioned, or just that someone dropped a bunch of change on the street in pulling car keys from her pocket? How would you even begin to guess without submitting this little shred of evidence to the skeptic *and* the wishful thinker in you, the head *and* the heart, the higher self, the lower self *and* the middle self? If you feel you need to go back to school, do you really need the further education, or are you simply casting about for a good excuse to avoid putting yourself on the line? Have you talked to someone who's done what you want to do without that education, and someone else who's done it with the education? In addition, have you consulted the voices of fear and faith, the voices of time and death, and the voice of anyone who would be directly affected by such a decision?

In discerning a call, we use our judgment. We evaluate something that speaks to us at so many different levels that we may feel as if we're deciphering the Dead Sea scrolls. We are all judges, but few of us are *good* judges who listen to all sides of a story and bear their tiresome debate. Good judges understand that the truth is not simple. Good judges eventually reach a decision and act on it, which is perhaps the best way to practice discernment. Exercising good judgment will occasionally have us up nights mainlining the serenity prayer.

In searching for the veracity of a calling, the meaning of a sign, the answer to the question of readiness, we can't overlook a full accounting of facts and feelings just because we resent the inconvenience of the truth. Discernment is

stringy, hard work. It's also fallible. "Trying to define yourself," the philosopher Alan Watts once said, "is like trying to bite your own teeth."

Once, during the question-and-answer period at the end of a lecture given
by M. Scott Peck, author of *The Road Less Traveled,* I stood up and asked how,
in struggling with an important personal decision, I would know I was doing
the right thing. Dr. Peck said the question is the single most common one he
is asked and that "there is no such formula. The unconscious is always one step
ahead of the conscious mind—the one that *knows* things—so it's impossible to
know for sure. But if you're willing to sit with ambiguity, to accept uncertainties and contradictory meanings, then your unconscious will always be a step
ahead of your conscious mind in the right direction. You'll therefore do the
right thing, although you won't know it at the time."

Uncertainty normally drives us daft, but although knowledge is power,
not knowing also has its own power. There is the power in trusting ourselves,
relying on our intuitions, being able to act even in the face of uncertainty,
rather than drone on for sometimes years with yes-no-yes-no-yes-no-yes-no,
the very onomatopoeia of indecision. It can be more heroic to be willing to act
in the absence of certainty than to refuse to act *without* absolute certainty.

C O N N E C T I N G   T H E   D O T S

There is no checklist against which we can test our callings with dead reck-
oning, much as we might desire it; no list of ingredients for a "true" call. We
can only try to make sense of signs by drawing lines between them, connecting
the dots so that a form, a pattern, a rough road map, emerges.

The truest calls seem not only to keep coming back but also to make their
way to us through *many* different channels, so we can use this as a starting
point. Make a tally of the signals you've been receiving around any given
issue—through dreams, fantasies, cravings and ambitions, persistent symptoms, the fears and resistances that have been preoccupying you lately, any
opportunity whose sudden appearance in your life borders on synchronicity,
whatever people have been telling you a lot lately, what books are on your
nightstand, what notes to yourself are tacked under fruit magnets on the
refrigerator door. Then do the mathematics. What, if anything, do these all
add up to?

The children's magazine *Highlights* features puzzles that involve finding a hidden object, such as a toothbrush, pitchfork, or lightbulb, in an otherwise ordinary scene of a farmhouse or a forest. These objects are fairly well hidden until you know what to look for, and then you wonder how you missed them before. Similarly, as you seek to discern your callings, it might help to define what *you* look for in a calling to test whether it's the genuine article—to come up with something of a portrait, a mug shot of your calling. Think back on previous calls that panned out and list them: the job you knew you should quit, and you were right; the relationship you waffled about committing to until you wore holes in your shoes, but you finally said yes and it turned out to be the best thing that ever happened to you; the time you took a moral stand and felt tremendously empowered.

The point is: How did it *feel* to act on a calling? Did you feel more awake? Was there a kind of rightness to your actions? Did you experience a flood of energy? Did you discover you had surprising forbearance for the mundane tasks involved in the undertaking, and that after a month or a year your enthusiasm didn't falter? Did you feel gratitude? Did you experience gales of resistance to committing (which can indicate the *importance* of a call)? Did your friends declare that they haven't seen you so excited in a long time?

While you're at it, list those calls that *didn't* pan out, too, and their attending signals. The most critical discernment skill, M. Scott Peck insists, is being able to distinguish between the sound of integrity and the sound of its absence. In order to recognize a true call, you must be able to recognize a false one, just as in order to spot a truth you must be able to spot a lie. Keep in mind that if a pursuit does not strike oil, it doesn't mean your effort lacked integrity or value. Perhaps you learned something from the experience that you hadn't *expected* to learn. Perhaps you were meant to try something and find it *not* to your liking, so that you could cross it off your list once and for all. It's important to know what you *don't* want, too.

Maybe you're following the mishap lineage, and your "failures" are actually the path itself. How do you know, for instance, that the hit-and-run nature of your love life isn't part of the unfolding of something you can't even fathom at the moment? Maybe you're called to continue leaving relationships because you're going to be a marriage counselor someday and this is part of your training! It is not uncommon to hear people say, "If you told me that five years from now I would be a marriage counselor (a full-time artist, a father, living in Europe, not painting anymore, fill in the blank), I would have told you that you were out of your mind."

TRUE OR FALSE

In gauging the veracity of a call, using the terms "true calling" and "false calling" is a more useful criterion for discernment than the more common "higher" and "lower" callings. These latter terms, so deeply brined in religious overtones, suggest that a true call emanates from a higher place and a false one from a lower place, and this is an illusion and a mistake. Heaven is not up and hell is not down. When we stand on the earth, we are not standing *up* but sticking *out,* into space. There is no top or bottom. There is as much spirit in things downwind as upwind. Light is not morally superior to darkness. Up is no more populated with angels than down. Calls emerge as readily from the ground as from the sky, as much from the exhortations of the common life as from our spiritual ideals. Dreams and symptoms and hidden passions—those fountainheads of our callings—all grow in the dark, and dark nights of the soul are just as instructive as days of wine and roses, if not more so.

It is also bewildering to try to determine whether a call is "of God" or of some other source, like ego or willfulness or self-interest. We could tie ourselves in knots by trying to determine if the ego, for example, is or isn't an aspect of God. If we were to say it is, then by extension aren't pride, and anger, and revenge, and evil? Some would say that either all is of God or none is. Others would say that someone trying to get a grip on all this business is a baby on the back of an elephant.

Attempts to divide ourselves into divine and not divine break us apart. Better for our overall composure to focus on whether a particular call has *integrity* or not, whether it makes us feel more or less *authentic,* more or less *connected* to ourselves and others, more or less *right,* not morally but intuitively. Better to ask whether a call will give us a feeling of *aliveness,* which, as mythologist Joseph Campbell argued, is more important than even meaning for people to experience. "People say that what we're all seeking is a meaning for life," Campbell explained in *The Power of Myth.* "I don't think that's what we're really seeking. I think what we're seeking is an experience of being alive . . . of the rapture of being alive."

When we hold that our "lower" selves are incompatible with true calls, we're also forgetting that wounds can become gifts, that moral outrage can move mountains, that righteous anger propels social action—all of these are primary motivators of people's pursuit of callings, and none of them can be cut away without bloodletting. Our "lower selves" are also forms of tremendous energy: the tunnel-boring power of compassionate anger, the strategic genius of ego, the perfectly understandable desire to show the bastards, the plaintive longing to know that we are, finally, acceptable. "Purifying" ourselves of these energies would be burning out part of the being that is being called. The *totality* of us is called. Thus, all parts of ourselves become part of the call. We simply have to work out among all our selves what action we'll eventually take.

There is, however, a dark side to callings. In acting on a calling, we may not necessarily act in complete accordance with our deepest values, with grace and humility, with compassion, or even with the law. Our actions may not be met with approval from a panel of experts or a jury of our peers. Saints and sinners alike are called, and some calls do run us up against "the system." The path toward an authentic life is rife with the dangers of inflation and grandiosity. More than a few wars have been waged because someone felt called by God to crush an enemy, snatch back holy lands from "infidels," expand their holdings, acquire a little more real estate from the country next door.

The presence of grass stains on a calling does not automatically disqualify it from the running.

L I S T E N I N G   T H E   S O U L

Uncertainty accompanies our most rugged attempts at discernment, which explains why the Quakers have a tradition of providing what they call "clearness committees" to any member struggling for clarity in discerning a call and responding to it. In addition to helping people test their calls, the committees also demonstrate that we don't have to go it alone, and that community is closely allied with the unfolding of an individual calling.

In fact, the bigger a call, the more it is by *definition* a public affair, a community concern, because it's going to affect others. Going on the road is going to affect your marriage. Quitting your job is going to affect your family. Changing your product line is going to affect your employees. Leaving town is going to affect your men's group. Scaling back your practice is going to affect your clients and patients. That makes it, to some degree, public domain, though clearness committees aren't meant to represent the interests of those whom your calling might affect; they are to help you find clarity.

Before a clearness committee meets, you, the "focus person," compose a brief synopsis of the matter about which you seek clarity. This is circulated among the committee members who will attend the actual session. Members are made up of half a dozen people whom you choose from among friends, colleagues, mentors, and even strangers, or whom you request be gathered by the local "Meeting."

Once in committee, members first observe a period of silence. This is not the perfunctory "moment of silence" that is merely a polite curtsy to the divine before getting on with business, or a chance to merely figure out what you're going to say when the time's up. It is a sincere attempt to shift the center of gravity from the personal toward the transpersonal, toward bringing to an individual dilemma something of the divine, or at least communal. The silence is also a gracious confession that discernment is a mysterious process and that absolute clarity is more an ideal than a real attainment. Yet it's still amazing what can be accomplished, as Quaker Douglas Steere puts it, by "listening each other's souls into disclosure and discovery."

After the silence, the rules are so simple they're radical: Ask questions only! No advice, no storytelling, no windy narratives, no problem solving, no challenging (though the focus person may request any of these at the end). Simply pose questions in a spirit of caring rather than even curiosity, evocation rather than imposition. The goal is not so much to comprehend as it is to apprehend.

"People often find it hard to believe that questions can be so powerful and helpful," says Jan Hoffman, clerk of Ministry and Counsel for the New England Yearly Meeting of Friends, and who has been both focus person and a member of clearness committees. "But again and again, that's what people discover. We find that though individuals have their own integrity, it's easy to obscure their perception of that integrity with advice and devil's advocacy.

"Our tendency as a culture is toward being very proactive, solving problems and fixing things. By assuming the answer is in the person seeking clarity and that we help by listening, not by 'fixing,' the clearness process is counter-cultural. What we seek is the truth in the context of the *focus person's* integrity, not a more general external truth. Asking questions seems to engage the focus person in a way that makes hearing his or her own inner guidance more possible, even questions that seem off the wall."

Jan recalls one focus person who was trying to decide whether to take on a new project, though her life was already on avalanche alert. She was asked what seemed like a preposterous question: "How big is your garden?" The focus person suddenly burst into laughter and remarked, "Good question!" Her garden, it turned out, was already bigger than she could handle.

C A L L   W A I T I N G

In his autobiography, Nikos Kazantzakis, author of *Zorba the Greek*, described an incident in which he came upon a cocoon cradled in the bark of an olive tree just as the butterfly was making a hole and attempting to emerge. Impatient for results, he bent over it and warmed it under his breath, by which he succeeded in speeding up the process. The butterfly, however, emerged prematurely, its wings hopelessly crumpled and stuck to its own body, which needed the sun's patient warmth, not the man's impertinent breath, to transform it. Moments later, after a desperate struggle, the butterfly died in the palm of his hand.

"That little body," he wrote toward the end of his life, "is the greatest weight I have on my conscience."

We do much damage by not being patient with our own evolution, which by design and necessity luxuriates in an abundance of time and plot twists. We communicate to our own souls that we don't have faith in them, in their intimacy with the creative force of life. We sneak downstairs in the middle of the night to see if elves are sewing things up. We force the fauna with our hot insistent breath. We rush a verdict so we can get home in time for dinner. We try to *make* things happen, hoping that in doing so we don't inadvertently open the darkroom door while fate is developing our pictures.

Patience is the missing link in the discernment process, in the search for clarity of calling and readiness of heart, and in the waiting for events to unfurl and talents to ripen. These things seldom burst into being all at once. They accrete like the shells of oysters, bubble up and cool like lava, adding layer by layer onto the armature of themselves. Drumming our fingers won't make events move any faster.

We suffer from the cultural misapprehension that waiting means doing nothing. Great fanfare, for example, usually attends the moment of inspiration, the aha, the eureka—Sir Isaac Newton's revelation upon the apple, Archimedes' bathtub epiphany about specific gravity, Samuel Coleridge's epic poem *Kubla Khan*, which is said to have popped into his consciousness whole. Little notice, however, is taken of the usually lengthy period that precedes it— the period of observation, meditation, experiment, uncertainty, frustration, fits and starts; the period of asking the questions over and over, of sleeping on it and pitching in our sleep. We love the answers and suffer the questions. We worship the flower and ignore the soil. We covet the diamond and overlook the pressure it took to make it.

Far from being the transcendent experience we imagine, though, this hero or heroine's journey, this search for what is truest in ourselves, turns out to be largely pick-and-shovel work. "The more characteristic American hero in the earlier day," the writer Mark Sullivan once observed, "and the more beloved type at all times, was not the hustler but the whittler." Psychologist and minister John Sanford says that whenever we wrestle with our spiritual and psychological conundrums, and refuse to let go until we have some sense of meaning, we're having something of the Jacob experience. We're wrestling with a spirit through a dark night of the soul until the sun comes up—symbolically speaking, until illumination.

On the other hand, whenever we refuse to acquiesce to the true complexity of these struggles and the time they take to unfold, the truth we seek becomes like a knot that only gets tighter when we become impatient and start yanking on it.

But time in itself won't suffice, because the discernment process isn't just about being patient but about being *actively* patient, using the time we have to submit the evidence we gather to the compassionate scrutiny of the mind, the adjudication of the heart, the gut reaction of the body. It is about taking up the pickax and digging, chipping away a bit at a time at our stony questions, or feeling our way like a bird that travels for thousands of miles guided only by instinct and the whisper of magnetism.

THE UNFOLDING

Certain Indians, Annie Dillard reports in her book *Pilgrim at Tinker Creek,* used to carve grooves called lightning marks along the shafts of their hunting arrows because the grooves resembled the jagged fissures that lightning slices down the trunks of trees. If an arrow failed to kill the game outright, blood from the wound would channel down the grooves and spatter on the ground, leaving a trail.

Such is the way a certain calling for Robin Samuel Sierra has led her for nearly a decade, drawing her through the forest, leaving a trail of moist clues. Like the hunters who encountered their quarry only briefly and then had to give chase sometimes for days before crossing paths with it again in the flesh, she, too, glimpsed a certain call only fleetingly—in a daydream—and then spent the next ten years trying to fashion a likeness of the vision she saw there: herself onstage in front of a large audience.

Nothing could have been further from the day-to-day reality of her life as a painter. And nothing could have thrilled and terrified her more, since she had long harbored a desire to be on a stage, though she could never articulate what it was she would be *doing* up there. She only knew that some vital part of her was going unused and using it would have something to do with being outspoken, with regaining a certain exuberance she had lost at childhood's end, and with being of service. This sense was, as she put it, "always a background noise in my life," always a voice telling her that painting wasn't enough, that she wanted to be doing "something for people," something that wasn't satisfied by the argument that she was already serving others by contributing beauty to the world. As service, she felt—rightly or wrongly—beauty wasn't hands-on enough.

The questions she needed to answer piled quickly one on top of another. "Should I let go of art as a vocation? What exactly do I have to offer people? How badly do I really want this? Is this a vision I'm meant to fulfill or just a grandiose fantasy, a way my ego is trying to compensate for the isolated, relatively invisible life of the artist?"

To say the vision triggered fear would be like calling World War II a skirmish. The idea of changing from a very private life to a very public life filled her with an anxiety that bordered on terror and sent her down the trail with her emotional shoelaces tied together. The vision also brought a drive to find the answers she needed, and she went about this the way Ann Kreilkamp suggested: by trying things and studying the outcomes.

First she enrolled in a three-week summer workshop at a retreat center in Washington State where she had the opportunity to work with performance artists—actors, singers, dancers. She started practicing stage skills. Soon afterward she took acting lessons but discovered she didn't want to recite *other* people's lines. Then she began offering art classes to small groups of people. Down the road a bit she experimented with the idea of becoming a therapist and enrolled in graduate school.

Then she took a public speaking class in which the instructor mentioned that stage fright only happens to people who have something they desperately want to say, otherwise they don't have enough at stake to warrant being scared. The public speaking rang true for her in a way none of the other pursuits had, and the next five years were largely spent struggling to define what it was she had to say to the world, which was in turn the struggle "to articulate what I knew in my heart. One thing I learned in the speaking classes was that when people speak from their hearts, *everyone* is interesting. I needed to learn how to be really authentic in front of people, which by itself, I think, is of tremendous value to people."

She also had to learn what she refers to as "masculine skills"—a certain broad-shouldered confidence, outer directedness, derring-do—which she felt would act as a catapult for her endeavors, to help get her *out*. You've got to have heart, she knew, but heart's got to work out in the world.

As it turned out, she learned much in this arena precisely through all the *doing* over the course of ten years, which, when compared to the tasks of *being*, could certainly be said to be a "masculine" trait.

Today Robin is what she calls a "creative consultant," speaking about and counseling others in the vicissitudes of making creative change. Still, it took ten years to go from dreading the prospect of leaving her art behind to dreading continuing it as a profession. It took ten years for the pain of staying finally to overcome the fear of leaving; it took ten years "to become desperate enough finally to be my real self, to take the risks, and to walk away from a gift when it wasn't what I really needed to be doing now, which was a big part of the struggle for clarity, and a source of a lot of grief.

"Maybe I could have done it all sooner, I don't know. It was frustrating that it took so long, though sometimes it just does, and plenty of my own role models took a lot longer than ten years. Or maybe I wasn't ready until I was ready. I know that a certain amount of unfolding had to happen. Unfolding of the answers, and unfolding of myself, which might be one and the same."

THE PROBLEM WITH WIGGLES

It took me two years of fight-and-flight before I finally acted on a call to leave city life—where I had always lived—and move to the country. Even then, I wasn't entirely sure why I submitted myself to such a disruption, and I continued for months trying to figure it out, which I suspect was an attempt to control what I couldn't control—namely, feeling *out* of control—to rise above my panic by barricading myself in the stone tower of the mind, to make the wild world a little less wild.

On my first night in the new house, I was awakened abruptly and harshly at 2 A.M. by an awful commotion in the back of my throat. It felt like something big was stuck there, similar to the sensation I get when one of my vita-mins the size of a horse pill doesn't go all the way down, only worse.

I awoke to a voice in my head, a kind of inner narration, which explained, "The appendage that hangs at the back of your throat, the uvula, the 'punch-ing bag,' is a reminder of the uselessness of trying to wrestle the sacred down to earth. It doesn't touch the ground and never will. It's like the finger of God up there on the ceiling of the Sistine Chapel, almost touching the finger of Adam, but not quite. A part of you, too, will remain forever unreconciled."

That unreconciled part, I came to understand, is the control freak who goes after meaning with a pitchfork; who uses reason the way children use fuzzy blankets; who uses discernment as a way of gaining mastery over events in the particular and over life in general. It is related to the part of me that loves to quantify things: how many miles from here to there; how much rain or snow fell last night; at what elevation are we; how big across is that meadow; what direction is home from here? It is also the part of me to whom the philosopher Alan Watts was referring when he said, "Rigid people feel some basic disgust with wiggles. They want to get things straight. But who can straighten out water? Water is the essence of life."

A doctrine called Vitalism, a sort of love child of philosophy and biology, holds that what separates living from nonliving matter isn't merely mechanics and more complicated flowcharts but a life force, a dynamism that animates everything from the most rudimentary cleavage of cells to the big bang, from the secret life of plants to the grand sprawl of evolution. The nature of this vital principle can only be grasped by someone willing to step beyond the lim-its of intellect and reason and apprehend it with the soul, which some consider to *be* that creative force, whether it's called soul, or anima, prana, élan vital, atman jiva, the spark of life, the apple of Prometheus's eye.

According to the Vitalists, there is *purpose* in this life force, a kind of design or will, a process of development within every being that aims at a des-tination unknown to the conscious mind (or one step ahead of it, as M. Scott Peck would say). They speak of an urge toward completion that is irrepressible in us, and for which we yearn almost dumbly, the way a beast seeks water. We go astray, however, when we attempt to *figure out* this purpose, trying to force consciousness to catch up with the unconscious, trying to force God and Adam to finally touch.

To whatever degree we *can* figure out the design, finding the hidden toothbrush and lightbulb is too big a job for the mind to tackle all by itself, and no amount of "talkers talking their talk," as Walt Whitman put it, will be able to pin it down. For one thing, many of the channels through which calls reveal themselves to us—dreams, symptoms, synchronicities, voices and visions, intuitions, even just the way events sometimes unwind—tend to exude an oracular sort of wisdom, a cryptic, symbolic, and poetic lingo that reveals itself most readily to those with a poetic frame of mind—one rooted as much in faith as in forensics—and impelled by what Eudora Welty called "the Geiger counter of the charged imagination." We imagine what our calls might mean, play with their many possible meanings, experiment and try them on for size, look to see if they fit, follow those that do and part with those that don't.

A tradition in both Middle Eastern and Hebraic mysticism holds that any passage of sacred text, any teaching, any story, must be examined from at least three points of view: literal, metaphorical, and universal (mystical or wordless). None excludes the others. Meaning thus becomes a thing of layers. Those with a poetic basis of mind understand this. Where science goes for the unified theory, poetry voluptuates in nuances. Where logic studies the wind, poetry regards how the boughs are bent. A poetic basis of mind is, in a manner of speaking, the opposable thumb of discernment, because with it we are able to grasp things we simply couldn't before.

Shakespeare's *Macbeth* offers an excellent example of the kind of enigmatic guidance in which callings seem to specialize, and which require of us not so much a suspension as an expansion of our usual faculties of discernment. The witches, the "wyrd sisters," who advise Macbeth are not just forces of evil, but, as Macbeth's friend Banquo rightly understands, "instruments of darkness telling us truths." Macbeth himself later comes to realize that they "have more in them than mortal knowledge." Their wisdom is referred to as "strange intelligence," which seems to me a fine description of callings.

To my mind, though, the tradition to emulate in these matters is the Delphic tradition. The Delphic Oracle north of Athens in Greece was a sort of watering hole where the gods and mortals all came to drink. It was originally a shrine to Gaia, the earth goddess, who was replaced by Apollo, the god of, among other things, poetry. But as a way to honor the homesteading deity, only women were used as Apollo's mouthpieces, his oracles—and all of them older than fifty; thus they were, at least theoretically, mature, wise, and calm in both spirit and temperament. Through these priestesses, the will of Apollo was expressed. Women were also used because at that time and in that part of the world shamanesses were considered to be more powerful in magic than shamans, more receptive to the divine.

Those in need of counsel first passed beneath the Oracle's entrance, above which was inscribed Socrates' proclamation "Know Thyself," and cleansed themselves in a nearby stream, which still bubbles out of the ground today at the site. They paid a fee, sacrificed an animal, and then posed their questions to the resident priestess in a loud and clear voice.

Suitable to the god of poetry, the answers were typically given in verse or prose, which, like Rorschachs, took the imagination as a dancing partner. Though the Oracle answered mostly questions of politics and religion and morality—which gods to propitiate in order to birth a son, which sea route ensured safe passage, how to heal disease, colonize other lands, win wars, make and unmake kings—mostly it answered the crying need for contact with the divine. Although the Delphic tradition is long since gone and the stones of the temple have long since toppled, we can still pass through Socrates' archway by presenting ourselves to our own callings in a poetic frame of mind, in a spirit of earnest devotion, with Geigers turned on.

T H I N K I N G   T O O   M U C H

No matter how charged our imaginations, we are always in danger of over-interpreting and forgetting that a call is a missive from the province of mystery. As E. B. White once said about analyzing humor, it is like a frog that dies under dissection. Better to approach with wonder, which is the knowledge that we can never fully explain the thing. "Let the bird sing without deciphering the song," wrote Ralph Waldo Emerson.

There *is* such a thing as thinking too much about a calling, which is like leaving a hot iron too long in one place while you're trying to smooth the wrinkles out of your shirt. Not only can studying it to death—turning it inside out like an old sock rather than, to some degree, simply exposing yourself before it—make it go bony with refusal, but it can also be a pretty good way of *avoiding* the call altogether. We can analyze every facet of it. We can probe every consequence of following it, not following it, procrastinating in following it, jumping on it right away, or trading it in for another. We can ponder whether it's really ours or whether we're appropriating someone else's, whether the time is now or later, whether it's being murmured to us by God or not-God. We can hold off and then beat ourselves up for not taking action, or we can take action and beat ourselves up for not being more patient. We can scare the backbone out of ourselves by contemplating the enormity of the call and the modest talents we bring to bear on it. We can break ourselves against the rock of debate.

We can spend so much time, in other words, dithering with definitions and exactitudes, possibilities and probabilities, that we do little more than chase our own tails and eventually collapse into bed too exhausted to do anything at all.

You *can* think too much, which is something Dante and his guide, Virgil, discovered on their outing to the Inferno. They were not permitted to pass through one particular threshold until they left all reason and intellect behind. These faculties are useful, in other words, but only up to a point. Beyond that, the door will be barred to us if we attempt to cross by way of reason. No amount of intellectual authority, arrogant confidence, name dropping, or ego and ambition pounding on the door demanding to be admitted will allow us passage. Beyond a certain point, faith is the magic lamp and humility the abracadabra.

Faith begins, if it begins at all, where knowledge leaves off.

Even scientists will admit that they do all the homework they can but eventually rely on an intuitive leap. They call it informed intuition, and though it grows naturally out of periods of dogged rational work—which provides the raw material it needs to go on, the bits of clothing laced with scent—reason, again, only goes so far. Intuition is the last baton carrier. It doesn't win the race alone, but it's the one that crosses the finish line. The more practiced it is, the less likely it is to get winded at crucial moments.

One of the reasons we practice intuition is that the psyche traffics in all sorts of knockoffs, and we need to distinguish between true intuition and, say, fear or anger or wishful thinking or the desire to be right. I recently had an "intuition," for example, that a friend's project wouldn't succeed, and only after it succeeded did I recognize that I was angry at him for something and only *hoped* it wouldn't succeed.

Intuition has receptors that seem able to hook all manner of passing emotions, like a bus that rolls through downtown picking up passengers. The passengers aren't the bus, however, they're merely hitching a ride.

Practicing intuition is, ironically, best accomplished the scientific way. Test and observe. Keep a record of your hunches over time and see how often they're accurate. If you feel you're meant to work with someone, to accept an invitation by a stranger, to slow down as you approach a particular intersection, to encourage your child in a certain direction, to intervene in a situation or bite your tongue, to make a move or stay put—try it out and document the results.

You might even *try* acting on impulse as a way to practice your intuition, suggests Philip Goldberg in his book *The Intuitive Edge*. Make quick decisions, within ten seconds, on minor matters: ordering from a menu, picking up the phone or not, deciding what to wear, choosing which books to buy. Or practice making predictions. Who's calling? Who'll win the game? Who'll get the Grammy? How will the movie end? Or cover the captions on photographs and guess what's going on.

With enough practice, when intuition finally tips the scales in favor of following a calling, precisely *because* you have devoted time to practicing it, you will know that "just a feeling" now carries a weight of authority you can trust.

Still, a calling is ultimately mysterious, and the process of discernment is always a bit of a guessing game. In Greek, the word *mystery* means to close the mouth, which, says Lewis Hyde in *The Gift*, may refer to the secrecy to which initiates into ancient mysteries were sworn. It may also refer to the belief that ultimately a mystery could not be spoken of or fully explained. "Shown, witnessed, revealed," says Hyde, "but not explained."

three

B R A V I N G
C O N F L I C T

F. Scott Fitzgerald declared that the test of a first-rate intelligence is being able to hold two contrary ideas in the mind at the same time and still retain the ability to function.

William Wendt is someone Fitzgerald would have liked. An Episcopalian minister in Washington, D.C., he was possessed in 1975 of the unpopular clerical notion that women had as much right to be priests as men did. This sentiment was not shared by his bishops, nor by his religion, which held to the dubious logic that women could not be priests for the simple reason that they never had been; none of the twelve apostles had been a woman.

One day, after great deliberation, and with his conviction that sometimes it's easier to seek forgiveness than permission, he invited a woman who had been illicitly ordained by an insurgent bishop in Philadelphia, up to the altar to celebrate mass. For this breach in the pecking order, he was summarily tried by the church, in the equivalent of a grand jury trial in civil law, for violating the vow of obedience to "the godly admonitions of the bishop," as church canon puts it.

The call to take action, "to make a statement of some kind, if not in word then in deed," prompted a considerable debate in his own mind, Reverend Wendt said, which revolved around the question of whether ultimate authority for his conscience and his actions lay with God or with the bishops. He prayed for clarity and took solo retreats in search of guidance to resolve these two competing inclinations. His priestly vows and a two-thousand-year-old tradition required that he honor the laws of the church through which he had been able to conduct his life's work. The imperatives of his conscience, however—as author H. L. Mencken described it, "the inner voice that warns us someone may be looking"—required that he honor what he felt was God and God's authority.

Reverend Wendt eventually decided that ultimate authority lay with God and not with the bishops and that his path lay in "upholding the rights of people." He was willing to endure conflict—both within himself and between him and his superiors—in order to honor a calling, rather than avoid contrariety just for its sedative effect.

Furthermore, he felt this decision did nothing to undermine his commitment to the Bible, which instructed him to consult the highest authority in matters of conscience. "An individual who breaks a law that conscience tells him is unjust," said Martin Luther King Jr., with whom Reverend Wendt worked in the 1960s during the civil rights movement, "and who willingly accepts the penalty . . . in order to arouse the conscience of the community over its injustice, is in reality expressing the highest respect for the law."

The church, however, didn't agree. Over the next several weeks, with lawyers on both sides quoting from the Bible, William Wendt stood trial for insubordination. He was eventually found guilty and censured, and lost again on appeal. By that time, however, publicity had begun to turn the tide in his favor, and two years after his original trial, at the General Convention of the Episcopal Church, the very same bishops relented in the face of rising opposition, and probably the dictates of public relations, and granted women access to the altar.

Today, largely because of William Wendt, more than a third of the Episcopal clergy is female, and though he no longer works at his old parish, St. Stephens (fittingly, the church's first martyr), the new priest there is a priestess.

Also because of him, the Episcopal Church now has what it calls the Rule of Conscience, which states that conscience is acceptable grounds on which a priest can make a decision.

꜅

I have heard it said that heroism can be redefined for our age as the ability to tolerate paradox, to embrace *seemingly* opposing forces without rejecting one or the other just for the sheer relief of it, and to understand that life is the game played between two paradoxical goalposts: winning is good and so is losing; freedom is good and so is authority; having and giving; action and passivity; sex and celibacy; income and outgo; courage and fear. One doesn't cancel out the other. Both are true. They may sit on opposite sides of the table, but beneath it their legs are entwined.

A similar heroic quality of intelligence is required in the face of a calling, which flings often opposing energies into our lives. One part of us wants to awaken, another to sleep. One part of us wants to follow, another wants to run like hell. One part may be certain of a call by way of inner knowing, while another is completely dumbstruck by the lack of objective proof; we understand the call psychologically, but not logically. One part of us may feel it is chosen, and another that it is ordained. We may feel both the forces of impulsiveness and caution—of idealism joined at the hip with cynicism. We may feel we have to do the irrational to bring some rationale to our lives. ("It's absurd to pursue your art," the painter Willem de Kooning once said, "but it's absurd not to.") When we stretch our arms to reach for *anything,* some muscles contract and some expand.

Sometimes these contrary exertions inside us feel like gladiators tied together for a fight to the finish, and sometimes like the swimming bodies of yin and yang swirling around in the same fishbowl. Either way, the opposing forces occupy a space that is like an ecotone, a transition zone between two ecological communities like forest and grassland or river and desert. They compete, yes; the word *ecotone* means a house divided, a system in tension. But they also exchange, swapping juices, information, and resources. Ecotones have tremendous biological diversity and resilience.

Likewise, a spirit of fruitfulness might best serve your own antagonisms. Don't just suffer. Suffer creatively. Write about your inner conflicts around a calling. Draw them out. Play them up. Dance a two-step, one for each. Compose a dialogue between two tectonic plates, a suite for clashing cymbals, a pas de deux for fire and water. Creative suffering burns clean, the psychologist Marion Woodman says. Neurotic suffering only builds up more soot.

Somewhat unrealistic, we generally don't want to suffer—i.e., to bear—conflict at *all;* not creatively, not neurotically, not if we can avoid it. We thus generate a kind of approach-avoidance pattern: If I don't approach the conflict, I can avoid feeling uncomfortable—though the end result is that I also avoid responding to the *call.*

I found myself in just such a situation recently, making an end run around conflict and entirely missing the call that was hidden in its folds.

I was facilitating a five-day writers' retreat in New Mexico during which two of the participants became fast foes, rubbing each other constantly the wrong way. One morning, one of the two women, I'll call her Carol, described an incident in her younger life when she was almost raped. The other woman, Diane, asked, "Were you disappointed?"

Carol's jaw dropped open wide enough to drive a semi through. She glared at Diane and said, "That's a *stupid* question!"

We moved smartly onto something else.

The next day Carol talked more about the rape attempt and mentioned that she had avoided being raped only because another man had intervened, a man who later told her, "Young lady, if you don't want to get dirty, stay away from the mud." He was referring to the circumstances of her situation, which Carol had earlier thought, as a result perhaps of youthful naïveté, would be "adventurous." Whereupon Diane blurted out, "That's what I meant yesterday when I asked if you were disappointed."

Carol turned on Diane as if she were going to physically bite her, and yelled, "If you say that one more time I'm going to drown you in the goddamn bathtub"—only she didn't say it quite that nicely.

There was another stunned silence, and then everyone turned and looked at *me.*

I have absolutely no recollection of what I might have said at that moment. I blanked out. It was the sort of beneficent unconsciousness that people are often said to experience when falling from a height or being attacked by a wild animal—perhaps nature's way of sparing us unbearable pain. All I know is that a moment later we were on to another subject, though I was aware of feeling sweaty all over.

In retrospect, I knew I blew it. I was so uncomfortable with the conflict, with the open hostilities that had suddenly broken out between these two peo-ple, that I completely missed a great opportunity to have a group of writers write about what is at the heart of any good story: conflict. "Two worlds col-lide" best describes the basis of every story ever written or told, I once read.

The collision that took place in the retreat was a rare chance for them all to write something with emotional immediacy, right from their guts. I should have told them to grab a piece of paper, take ten minutes, and write about their own reactions to the scene that had just unfolded in front of them, to record without censure whatever emotions, memories, associations, and preju-dices flooded to the surface. To practice something, in fact, that we had earlier been discussing: dialogue. Take the dialogue between Carol and Diane, for instance, and continue it, let the two characters have at it, find out what accounted for their opposing points of view and what was of value in both. And perhaps then share some of those stories.

But because I went dormant, I succeeded only in facilitating our further avoidance of the real drama of life. Although we stepped gingerly around the mud, and got to keep our feet clean, we lost an exceptional opportunity to learn something, to let conflict be a teacher.

At the end of Goethe's *Faust,* the protagonist and his partner, Mephistopheles, have tempered each other until they are very nearly indistin-guishable. I now believe that it's similarly vital to allow the tensions we feel regarding a call to coexist long enough to inform us, to teach us something. If you give your soul time to deliberate, perhaps it will render an insight or response that serves your competing urges. Meanwhile, as William Wendt did, pray hard for clarity. And be patient.

In the middle of the Amazon rain forest 1,500 miles up from the Atlantic, is a place called the Wedding of the Waters. There, the black waters of the Rio Negro join with the café-au-lait-colored waters of the Amazon, and the two flow side by side, without mixing, for more than fifteen miles. The waters do eventually wed, but first there is a long courtship.

PROCEED WITH OUR BURNING

Psychologist Robert Johnson speaks of the ground between conflicting forces as a holy place. The struggle to hold paradox is ultimately a "religious" experience, in the sense that *re-ligare* means to re-join, to bind together oppo-sites, to restore them to each other. Heresy, he says, is giving domination to one principle over all others. "When the unstoppable bullet hits the impenetrable wall," he writes in his book *Transformation*, "we find the religious experience. It is precisely here that one will grow. Conflict to paradox to revelation: this is the divine progression."

What, then, is unstoppable in you, and what is your impenetrable wall? According to Johnson, by witnessing their collision in full consciousness, by juggling them both without allowing one or the other to fall between the floorboards, we reconcile ourselves, we make ourselves enormously resilient, we exercise first-rate intelligence. Let's say you feel called to bring more creativity and freedom into your life in the form of starting up a new business. Just the *thought* of this will probably send the gladiators of head and heart strutting into the arena.

HEAD: "Have you taken a look at your savings account lately? The thing's all skin and bones, and that's *with* a regular paycheck. It couldn't possibly support a shaky new venture. Better hold your horses. Better not listen to that drama queen, the heart. And say, aren't you just a few years away from that pension?"

HEART: "I want out. I want some of the creativity I left back in college. I want to live in California, by the sea. I want to be my own boss. I want to do the brave thing. Do something for love. Where would the world be if all its heroes followed the bottom line?"

Where would *you* be if you ignored one or the other of these voices, if just to be rid of the tension you barred the door to what is, after all, a part of yourself? What does *experience* tell you typically ensues if you don't let them both have a say? How did you feel, for instance, when your parents only listened to your brother's side of the story in an argument? How did you feel when the principal heard only the other kid's version of the fight? The gods are no less fussy. They gave us head and heart, and the ears with which to hear them. Who wants to insult the powers that hand out callings?

We need to learn to allow the tensions between head and heart to hammer out a compromise—meaning a promise together. Perhaps you tighten the budget and work for another year to build up the money to leave sooner, or borrow. You move to a city in California where the business opportunities are good. You take the company you work for as your first client. You come up with a Plan B, just in case. You surround yourself with people who are working on dreams of their own. In other words, you encourage head and heart to meet at the bargaining table, not to retreat to their respective ramparts.

In a syndicated newspaper column appropriately called "News of the Weird," I read recently about what can happen when we attempt to bury our bones of contention in the backyard. A young woman in California was arrested for driving down a freeway swinging a baseball bat out her window at a truck she felt was moving too slowly. The arresting officer happened to notice her license plate: PEACE 95.

"We are both of us walking through fire," the writer P. L. Travers once wrote of paradox. "One single flame enfolds us both. So let us together proceed with our burning. There is no other way. Arms wide, we bend toward each other, and a passing angel pauses for a moment, standing imponderably on the air, to witness our embrace." Wherever there are two, Travers goes on to say, there are three. The third is the One That Reconciles, the Unnameable, without which there is no possibility of true relationship.

A STRETCH OF THE IMAGINATION

There is a big difference between being divided *within* ourselves and being divided *against* ourselves. The former expresses the creative suffering of paradox; the latter expresses only paralysis. One happens quite seldom, the other quite often. And the latter is mirrored most painfully to us by the dividedness of the world: families splitting apart; countries splintering into smaller countries; environmental summits pitting North against South, rich against poor; crazy people swinging baseball bats at others while sporting license plates that say PEACE.

Gene Knudsen Hoffman sees it most abundantly in the tendency toward enemy making in the world—the tragic inability of people and groups of people to *manage* the differences between them. For this reason among others, in 1952 she was called to join the Fellowship of Reconciliation, the oldest interfaith pacifist organization in the world, which is comprised of thousands of "citizen diplomats." Through the Fellowship, she has traveled from her Santa Barbara home to Russia, Libya, and the Middle East, primarily in order to listen to the grievances of those whom we as Americans call our enemies.

"My mother used to take me to all kinds of different churches while I was growing up," she says, "and she told me there was truth in all of them, and it was up to me to find it." In her travels, she discovered that there is no one truth. There are only stories. "If each side can listen to the stories of the other, the suffering of the other, the history of the other, reconciliation is made much easier." If we could read the secret history of our enemies, the poet Henry Wadsworth Longfellow once wrote, "we should find, in each person's life, sorrow and suffering enough to disarm all hostilities."

Gene doesn't soft-sell the challenge of refusing to take sides, of setting aside biases in contending with conflicts outside or inside herself. Biases come with the territory, and they come on strong. "I have often found fantastic opposition to my listening work even from fellow peace workers. Very few helped me, and none went with me on certain trips. They have an enemy and they don't want to listen to them, as if by listening they would be condoning.

"I understand this. I felt the same way about Richard Nixon, though his name was a holy word in the house where I grew up. But I once interviewed him for a magazine article and found that he had some wonderful ideas, spoke some important truths, and was a very good statesman in some ways. And many people were outraged that I could condone him. But I didn't condone him. I interviewed him. If I'd stuck with only the part of me that opposed him, I never would have found out the truths that he held."

If you can hold paradox, Gene says, you can hold tremendous energy within you and be a force for mediation in the world. Equanimity is an ability that naturally mitigates against tyranny both within and among people. Furthermore, by not subjugating parts of yourself and parts of others, you *belong* to more of yourself and the world, and the world belongs more to you. You're not "fighting it" all the time.

One of the toughest challenges in holding paradox is in admitting that all the contraries exist inside each of us (and then admitting them *in*). We are both courageous and cowardly. We both want to know ourselves and don't. We both want to follow our calls and want to fall fast asleep under the nearest palm frond.

It takes tremendous courage and hard work, Gene says, not to take sides when we experience conflict but to stretch the soul wide enough to encompass *both* sides, stretch the imagination almost to the bursting point and understand that two utterly contrary stories can coexist even within the same person. In part, this is why it typically takes Gene three months to "process" the stories she gathers on her listening journeys before she can sit down to write her articles and books, or proceed with speaking tours. For instance, after interviewing both Israelis and Palestinians on the staggering number of issues that divide what is essentially, ethnically, the same people, she had to wait for the two halves of the paradox to sink in, to fashion of themselves something of a whole in her mind, and for an informed response to emerge from the demilitarized zone between them, from the holy place between the two colliding worlds.

PARADOXES AND PECKING ORDERS

In Santa Fe, a high-ceilinged lobby connects the main post office to the government offices next door. An archway looks into the lobby from the post office, and in this archway I would often sit as I waited for the line in the post office to wind down.

On the far wall of the lobby is an enormous mural, ten feet high by thirty feet long, depicting a band of Indians, their pueblo far in the distance behind them. In full battle regalia, they are coming over the rise of a hill and are led by what appears to be an elder. All of them look curious and pensive and are staring intently at something unseen.

One day, having a bit more time to wait than usual, I strolled into the middle of the lobby, and as I turned around I saw, for the first time in all the months I had been coming there, what the Indians are staring at. High on the opposite wall is another mural, equally large, of a band of Spanish soldiers on horseback, led by Francisco Coronado, who was searching for the legendary Seven Cities of Cibola, gold, and new converts to Christianity. They are fully armored up to their metal helmets and armed with muskets, lances, and crossbows, as was the custom when seeking converts to Christianity. Standing on the ground before them is a monk, a Franciscan friar in long brown robes, wearing a large cross around his neck and holding an open Bible.

Across that lobby, across that space between two worlds, each band exchanges the most piercing scrutiny. Each beholds for the first time the Other, and between them is the solemn and urgent anticipation of what would happen next, of which history speaks with brutal and protracted eloquence.

Western culture, which includes the Spanish, is hierarchical and patriarchal and finds it difficult to live with paradoxes without "resolving" them in favor of one side or the other. In our political, religious, personal, and intrapersonal relationships, paradoxes become hierarchies in which we revere one side while denigrating the other, elevate one and push the other down. Power is up and vulnerability is down. Courage is up, fear is down. Career up, family down. Masculine up, feminine down. Mind up, body down. Christianity up, nature religions down. Opposites are separated and pecking orders established. If we ever honor dualities, we do so more in the spirit of analysis than contemplation, more for the sake of knowledge than wisdom.

P O L Y D O X

Woody Allen once said that when we've mastered Oneness, we move up to Twoness. Perhaps when we are able to manage paradox, to hold two contrary ideas in the mind without splitting down the middle, we are better prepared to tackle what might be called polydox, the notion that we may be possessed of not merely two competing impulses regarding a given calling, but three or four or five. We can understand not just yes and no but also a few shades of maybe. We can hear the voices of fear, hope, and curiosity; of ancestry, progeny, father, and mother; of the blood swimming in our veins and the words on the tip of our tongue.

At a party, I once overheard a stranger ask my twin brother, Ross, the requisite introductory question, "So what do you do?" After a brief silence, Ross replied, "When?"

I don't believe he meant to be smug, merely honest, and in that one-word answer he recited the challenge of polydox: accepting that we are many things, not one, however hard we strive for unity, for a more perfect union, for one nation indivisible; we try to "get ourselves together," to answer the question "Who am I?" when really the question might be better put, "Who am *we?*" We're a chorus, a circus, an ecosystem, a quiver of arrows. We're a multiple personality, usually acting in concert, but even those with disordered multiple personalities have much to teach us about the extraordinary plasticity with which we are each possessed. There are cases on record of such people whose characteristics—diseases, eye color, handedness, linguistic abilities and talents, among others—have changed as one personality shifted to another.

The only time we were ever really unified was when we were one-celled organisms, before we began dividing, and the incredibly small number of people in history who have entered the state of unity and *stayed* there tend to have religions named after them. As a rule, we come and go, we touch unity and lose touch, remember and then forget again. We join with it and then, in the next moment, are cleaved from it with a broadax.

Even with so many cooks in the kitchen, however, it is still possible to stir up a single effective response to a calling, just as the brain oversees a bodyful of organs that can still think and walk at the same time. But if the brain decided to ignore, say, the signals emanating from all but the "sweet" receptors on the tongue, or interrupt the dialogue between heart and lung, or play eeny-meeny-miny-moe with systole and diastole, it would all come to a grinding halt. The healthiest response to a calling is the one that is informed by all the parts of us.

part two

RECEIVING

CALLS

four

THE WAY

OF

PASSION

Maurice Sendak, author of *Where the Wild Things Are,* once recounted that he sent to a young reader a card with a picture of a Wild Thing on it, and the boy's mother wrote back that her son loved the card so much he ate it. He didn't seem to care that it was an original Maurice Sendak drawing. He just saw it, he loved it, he ate it.

Passion is a state of love, and hunger. It is also a state of enthusiasm, which means to be possessed by a god or a goddess, by a Wild Thing. One could be possessed by the god of poetry or the goddess of animals, the god of commerce or the goddess of home and hearth. If we imagine that calls issue from the gods, then we are as close as we ever get to them—the calls *and* the gods—when we are enthusiastic. We move toward a kind of divine *presence* because, through our passions, we are utterly present. We are utterly charged and focused. We are oblivious, we forget ourselves, our troubles, our day-to-day living-on-Mulberry-Street lives. We hitch ourselves to something bigger.

❧

Mark Dubois once asked a friend of his, a city planner in Moscow who worked as an environmentalist in Mikhail Gorbachev's government, how they could get more people involved in saving the environment.

"First," his friend responded, "I think it is important that one fall in love."

At sixteen, Mark had fallen in love with a river. That river, the Stanislaus in Northern California, became a passion that would lead him to places he never imagined he would go.

Tradition has it that our gifts and our talents are the most likely places to find callings, which is largely true but not always. Sometimes we're called toward arenas in which we seem to have scant abilities and little experience or know-how. Sometimes we're called to things to which we have distinct aversions, or to what we have always thought of as our weaknesses, whether it's leadership, public speaking, or the practice of compassion for some group we were taught to despise.

A passion is not necessarily a talent (or vice versa), however, and there's no telling where it may lead. It struck Mark as bizarre, for instance, that he—always a loner who preferred the backwaters to the mainstreams—would be called to become an environmental activist, a river politician, to come down from the mountains into Sacramento, where the decisions are made, and add his voice to the public debate, to widen his field of affections to include "everything in the universe." But the river called him, he says, to go out and defend its honor. All love will eventually do that, will call on us to go to the front lines on its behalf—to testify, to serve, to be faithful. We're love's heroes, love's harem.

Mark was a river guide on the Stanislaus, writing the occasional letter to his congressman about the New Melones Dam, which was slated to turn the river into a reservoir, when a friend asked if he would head the Sacramento campaign to save it. His initial reaction was something along the lines of, "Who, *me?*" "I thought, 'I can barely coordinate myself, no less a political campaign!' "

Politics definitely wasn't his forte, as a journalist once noted about him. "He is more at home on the river, where he can walk barefoot, wear cutoffs, and greet friends with a bear hug that leaves their feet dangling" (he's six feet eight inches). But at one time, he says, sports had not been his forte either, and now he was a river guide. So Mark agreed to lead the campaign, and what was supposed to be a commitment of a few hours a week turned into a twenty-four-hour-a-day passion. "I was called to give far more of myself than I ever imagined I could give."

The river, however, had given *him* much, he says—his first passion, confidence, connection to his own emotions and "the magic of the universe," a sense of priorities, a job, freedom from fear—and his environmental enthusiasm has been, in fact, a kind of payback, a matter of returning the favor. The river also *continues* to give him much, helping propel him through the struggles and misgivings involved in politics by providing him, he says, with countless analogies. "It's taught me not to panic when there are sharp rocks, that the current dances past them. And it's the same in politics. I've learned how to dance past the old curmudgeons, not to get hung up on the rocks.

"It's also taught me how to look way downstream to figure out where the currents and channels are so I don't have to work as hard at the last minute or get bounced around so much. And when the river rips an oar out of your hand, you don't get mad. The river brings you back to attention. It's very similar in the human arena, though humans are much harder."

Perhaps the river even prepared him for what he felt called to do on its behalf some years down the road, which was to offer to sacrifice his *life*.

In the spring of 1979, the New Melones Dam was completed, and the engineers and politicians gave their word to the environmentalists that they would honor the law and fill it no higher than an old bridge at a place called Parrott's Ferry, four miles up the Stanislaus canyon. Through the early months of 1979, as the water was slowly rising, Friends of the River, which Mark had cofounded, began a series of "witness encampments," where people could take their last look at the meadows, beaches, archaeological sites, and waterways they loved.

Then word got out that the engineers were going to let the water rise well past Parrott's Ferry, and the environmentalists cried foul. The engineers said, in effect, tough! This is when Mark made a decision that the time had come to draw a line in the sand, to make a personal statement about his feelings both for the river and about the efforts to destroy it. For over five years, every legal and political string had been pulled on behalf of the Stanislaus, and for him it came down to this: He wrote a letter to the Corps of Engineers, with copies going to the White House and various state and federal offices. He said, "I plan to have my feet permanently anchored to a rock in the canyon at the elevation of Parrott's Ferry the day the water reaches that elevation. I urge you to do all in your power to prevent the flooding of the canyon above Parrott's Ferry."

The day he delivered the letters, he went to a hardware store and, pretending to be a miner, asked how he might secure something to a rock, since he had, he claimed, some equipment to stash in the hills. He was told that you do it the same way the old-timers did it: with a sledgehammer and a star drill.

On the appointed day, not unaware of the terrible irony of possibly being killed by the very river that had called him, he kayaked to a remote spot on the rising reservoir, weeping much of the way there—not out of fear but grief— and chained himself to a large boulder, having first hidden a key well out of reach. He had only a sleeping bag, poncho, some books, and a cup to scoop water from the reservoir, which was only two feet below his perch (and rising). Mark told only one friend—dubbed Deep Paddle—where he was so that he could bring him news. Mark told him that if the water reached his knees not to come back.

The water never did get to his knees, though. The politicians got to theirs first, and the water began to level off. But Mark only told Deep Paddle the whereabouts of the key when he had written assurance that the water wouldn't begin rising again once he had come out.

Mark became known to many Californians as "that guy who chained himself to a rock." His gesture, however, gave the river and its lovers, human and animal alike, a three-year reprieve before the Stanislaus was finally lost to the imperatives of "progress" and what Mark considers the "sad and wasteful habits" of water users. Mark's campaign also lit a fire under the California environmental movement and was instrumental in bringing increased awareness, and protection, to other threatened rivers.

In retrospect, he says of the incident, "I wish I could have been more creative, that I didn't have to do something so . . . simple. I wanted to work the system more, but I couldn't figure another way. It was a last resort, and a personal statement I needed to make, and never imagined I would, or could, make. I am boggled, though, by how many people were touched by that one gesture, which generated more attention than all my environmental work in the ten years before it and the fifteen years after it.

"One of the largest and most effective environmental groups is Greenpeace, and this is partly due to the fact that one of the images people have of it is of people willing to put their lives on the line for the earth. I think that's why my tying myself to that rock made such an impact."

Today, Mark is director of Worldwise, a grassroots campaign to ensure the environmental, social, and economic sustainability of multilateral bank loans.

The fact that his own financial life has been something less than inspiring—
that, again, he appears ill-suited to the task—hasn't stopped him, though,
from contending with the grand moguls of global finance like the World Bank
and International Monetary Fund. "One thing I've learned," he says, "is that
of all the horrendous problems we face in the world, one strikes me as the root
cause of them all, and it's a myth: 'I don't have any power.'"

CASTANETS IN THE HEART

Passion is power. On the color spectrum from faint interest to rabid obses-
sion, it is toward the red end of the continuum. Passion is accompanied by the
sound of primal yahoos, castanets in the heart, the beating of wings. It is the
natural exudation of love, any kind of love, and spills from us like heat from a
fire. Passion is the smelling salts of the soul. Passion's message is the same one
that love brings: follow.

Passion is what we are most deeply curious about, most hungry for, will
most hate to lose in life. It is the most desperate wish we need to yell down the
well of our lives. It is whatever we pursue merely for its own sake, what we
study when there are no tests to take, what we create though no one may ever
see it. It makes us forget that the sun rose and set, that we have bodily functions and personal relations that could use a little tending. It is what we'd do if
we weren't worried about consequences, about money, about making anybody
happy but ourselves. It is whatever we could be tempted to sell our souls for in
order to have a hundred extra years just to devote to it, whatever fills us with
the feeling poet Anne Sexton was referring to when she said that "when I'm
writing, I know I'm doing the thing I was born to do." It is what matters most,
whether we're doing it or not.

"There is a sudden knock at your door," says author Deena Metzger in her
book *Writing for Your Life*. "A trusted friend enters to warn you that the Dream
Police will arrive in twenty minutes. Everything, everything in your life that
you have not written down will evaporate upon their arrival. You have only
twenty minutes to preserve what is most precious in your life, what has formed
you, what sustains you, what is essential, what you cannot live without.

"Whatever you forget will disappear. Everything, to be saved, must be
named, in its particularity. Not trees, but oak. Not animals, but wolf. Not people, but Alicia. As in reality, what has no name, no specificity, vanishes."

Whatever passions you can specify, know that there are also passions within those passions that constitute their emotional cores, which is what you're *really* after, the *needs* your passions satisfy, what you want them to bring to you. The passion may be painting, parenting, solving mysteries, making people laugh, solitude, social action, or a certain country, but within it are metapassions: the need for freedom, creative fulfillment, security, belonging, influence, love.

Our passions call us to follow not just the painting or the inventing or the public speaking but also the need for expression; to follow not just politics or martial arts but also the need for power or empowerment; to honor not just our hunger for retreat or meditation or a move to the country but also for serenity. A woman I know is ardent about carving statues of Buddha and has come to understand that she is also trying to teach herself about compassion. A man I know has a passion for Ireland—the country of his ancestors—and it has led him to explore his own lifelong feelings of rootlessness and exile, and his need for bearings.

"The thing is to stalk your calling in a certain skilled and supple way," the author Annie Dillard once wrote, "to locate the most tender and live spot and plug into the pulse."

OBEY YOUR THIRST

In the fall of 1986, north of the Inside Passage along Alaska's coastline, a glacier pushed its way across the narrow neck of a fjord, creating an ice dam that formed a thirty-four-mile-long lake, which became a death trap for the hundreds of marine mammals—porpoises, sea lions, seals—that were now imprisoned in the new lake. Millions of gallons a week of meltwater from the glacier poured into the new lake, and naturalists expected the animals to die slowly of starvation in the rising freshwater as the marine fish on which they feed died off.

Four months later, at midnight, the dam burst from the pressure backed up behind it, and in little more than half a day the entire lake, which had risen eighty-two feet above sea level, poured back into the ocean at four million cubic feet per second, more than fourteen times the amount of water that roars over Niagara Falls every second. The only person anywhere around at the time, a hydrologist working for the U.S. Geological Survey, heard in the dark "a cracking, booming roar and the very large sound of rushing water," an immense sideways-spilling waterfall that pushed icebergs the size of four-bedroom houses out to sea at twenty miles per hour, and in the thrash of which the marine animals were swept violently to freedom.

Sometimes a collapse is the only way *to* freedom. Sometimes the pressure builds to such proportions that we have no other route to equilibrium. The freshwaters of natural desire have continued to pour in from the hills, but their power has been blocked up for so long inside us that the soul, seeking its true level, finds a way out. Hopefully, it sets you free and doesn't drown you in the process. That which doesn't kill you, the philosopher Nietzsche once said, will probably make you stronger.

Thomas Moore, author of *Care of the Soul,* wrote that "repression of the life-force" is the most common reason he sees people in therapy. By ignoring our passions, we dam up our energies and cut ourselves off from a vigorous source of calls, and rather than demonstrating our passions in the world, we put them in the position of having to demon-strate themselves to us. Passions become needs, and if those needs are not met, they become symptoms of one sort or another. "Summoned or not, the god will come," reads the inscription carved over the stone door of psychologist Carl Jung's house.

Sometimes, of course, it's painful to admit a passion because we may feel we can't *do* anything about it. We can't afford to go sailing, don't have the free-dom to travel, no time to read books. Our lack of choices is too depressing to think about, so we don't, and the water piles up behind the dam. Maybe we're playing all-or-nothing, afraid that if we get an inch, we'll demand a mile—rather than allowing *some* of it in our lives, just a little, right now.

An old professor of mine once demonstrated to me that if I described a headache out loud—what color it was, what substance it was made of, what temperature, what it would say if it were a six-year-old, if it were a vessel, how much water it would hold—it would often diminish in intensity, sometimes going away altogether. If I could physically get it outside my body, translate it into meaty words or get it in writing, it didn't hurt as much. Perhaps the same goes for passions as for headaches. They're both a kind of pressure, and if we can release them a little, they don't hurt as much.

Just be careful not to turn a passion *into* a headache by forcing it to become a commodity, or a career, or something you can take to the bank. This can kill off a passion. I've heard countless stories from people who loved music or art or travel—until they made a job out of it. It is certainly a rousing idea to have passion pay the rent, but if you suddenly begin *depending* on a passion to make money or gain recognition or keep up with the Joneses, you add to it the emotional equivalent of someone leaving hot condensed breath on the back of your neck.

The point of passion is mainly to follow, to let yourself love what you love, to respect your hunger and obey your thirst.

THE FRUIT OF PASSION

Sometimes we follow a passion just for the following, just to be close to it, with no particular end in mind. I feel this way, for instance, about rhythm, a passion that feels like an implant under my skin measuring out a steady chemical command: Do it! I make rhythms everywhere. Every available surface is a come-on: I tap out paradiddles on countertops, coffee cans, pot lids, dinner plates, my knees, my chest, my skull. I percuss with the tempo of my turn signals, the cadence of mourning doves, the beat of backhoes backing up. I can't help myself.

Sometimes, however, through a passion, a very distinct vision takes hold inside us and insists on ripening into passion fruit. Some parents describe this phenomenon when they talk about pregnancies that gained a footing despite their most stalwart efforts to the contrary. "That kid wanted to be born," they'll say, "and there was no stopping him!"

Stephan Brown had such a passion, and a calling came through it like a blast through a trumpet. He wanted to create "a learning center" that would become a greenhouse for experiments in "reeducating people toward more holistic patterns of living with one another and with nature," a place in which to demonstrate an environmental and spiritual renaissance. The model for what Stephan had in mind was a place called Findhorn, a community in northern Scotland where he lived in the early 1970s, and which was to many people in the 1960s and 1970s what India was: a long way to travel to find out that it isn't so much a place as an idea.

Findhorn has been called many things—an ark, a planetary village, a training center, an educational foundation, a windmills-and-agrarian fantasy—but it was as a garden that it gained its almost mythic proportions. The garden was originally seeded in 1962 by a man named Peter Caddy, a clean-cut, fiftyish, former air force officer, and his wife, Eileen, who felt "instructed" (spiritually) to create a garden outside the village of Findhorn, in a climate dismally inhospitable to plant life. Within a few years, though, that garden bloomed riotously with fifty-six different vegetables, forty-two herbs, twenty-one fruits, and a growing community.

Scientists and horticulturists from around the world wanted to know how a garden of such unruly vigor could possibly flourish in those abominable conditions. Caddy told them: love, communion between human and plant kingdoms, attunement with devas—nature spirits. "Anyone who thinks he can achieve these results with normal organic husbandry," Caddy said, "let him try in the next sand dune."

After spending many years at Findhorn, Stephan returned to the United States. He began the slow process of nurturing the seed that had been planted in him at Findhorn and awakening to the call to start an educational center based on Findhorn principles. He needed to decide what it would look like, get a fix on its exact coordinates—the what and when and where of it—and perhaps most challenging of all, grow into it *himself,* into its true dimensions.

While experimenting with communal living, "looking for expressions for my vision, for what I wanted to see the world become," he pursued a career in real estate and land development and helped start up a mineral water company. He put together community-building conferences and gatherings for Findhorn alumni, and at each meeting ("the calling always gnawing at the back of my mind") he brought up the idea of starting a center. But it remained only an idea. "To re-create civilization in a microcosm, you can either take it on as a macrocosm—the political approach, which is an excellent way—or take it on as a microcosm and create a minicivilization, which is an awkward, stumbling, sometimes backward-going process of evolution, of trying to make civilization better.

"I recognized early on that what I wanted to do wouldn't in itself change the world. It's a drop in the bucket. But that's how a bucket gets filled up, lots of different drops. That helped keep me going." So did the fact that during those years two people he knew died young, and he understood that "if I put this off and wait until I'm older, what if I don't make it to being older? Then it won't have been done."

He also recognized that he had to become a community *himself,* had to establish a certain rough confederacy among the various and occasionally conflicting parts of himself, before he could create a community outside. "My visionary, for instance, wanted to keep my accountant in the closet, and vice versa." Passion had to enter into treaty with practicality. Too much practicality, he realized, stifles the imagination; too much passion and you lose your landing gear.

After ten years in a holding pattern, Stephan finally landed. In 1984, at another Findhorn reunion, he once again brought up the idea for a center, but this time the response turned from liquid to solid. Half a dozen people stepped up to him and offered their support. "I think there was a readiness in me that they felt. They said, 'We did it because we believed you.' Maybe I reached a certain point of maturity, of groundedness. It was the difference between being twenty-four and thirty-four. It was having ten years of business experience. It was passion finally meeting maturity and practical skills. I've learned that a calling has to be matched by fortitude. It's like entering into a committed relationship. If you're going to promise to be with someone, you'd better be in love or share a common purpose, because you know that being in a relationship is a difficult struggle. There has to be some higher purpose for it, otherwise you won't be able to maintain it."

It took that core group of founding fathers and mothers another three years to hash out a vision statement, to define their collective calling, and to muster their monies and resources, but what emerged is a thriving enterprise called the Shenoa Retreat and Learning Center in Philo, California.

In retrospect, he says, if anyone had told him at the beginning what it would take to make Shenoa a reality, he might not have done it. "I sometimes wonder if what I did was worth the price personally. The effect it had on my financial status, and how that directly affects my ability to help my kids through college. And in terms of time I lost with them, because Shenoa took a lot of evenings and weekends, time that will never be compensated. If I could have answered the calling in another way, and not exacted as much of a price, I might have."

There *was* no other way then, however, and it's fitting that today Stephan is a consultant to people who want to start up centers like Shenoa. He is committed to telling them, in the beginning, exactly what it will take.

"I meet with a lot of people who say they've got this great vision and are really impassioned, and I ask them 'What are you willing to do to make it happen?' I want people to really understand what's required. I'm really in their faces. I met with one group who wanted to start a rural retreat/education center. Highly efficient, professional people, management consultants, business people. I told them they were terrifically capable but that they didn't seem to have the passion. They were too comfortable, too complacent. I wondered if they had the motivation to create something better, and they understood that. There's definitely a trade-off between passion and security.

"Now I realize there's a risk here. It's possible I could discourage people who might otherwise have accomplished their task. But my hope is that if they're really determined, they'll regard my questions as a gift. People with real passion will endure. It's just that I've seen too many bandwagons go over cliffs, so I'm willing to take the risk.

"What I try to tell people is that this is a big decision. It's going to take you five, seven, maybe ten years of your life to really get it going, to where it's going to be self-sustaining. Are you ready to do that? If there's anything more that compels you, that calls you forth, then do that. Otherwise, it may not be the thing for you. Do it only if you *have* to do it, only if you feel like I did, that if I didn't do this, I'd spend the rest of my life regretting not having done it."

If like Stephan you also want to find a match between what your passions demand and what the world desperately needs, then you have to keep in mind, as theologian Matthew Fox says, that "if you get cut off from your passion, then where's your compassion going to come from?"

five

A W A K E N I N G

T O

D R E A M S

When I close my eyes in bright sunlight, I sometimes see a field so red it's almost black. It is filled with motion—waves washing across it, spirals of light like leaves rotoring toward earth, flash pops and novas.

I don't know what I'm actually seeing—electricity sparking through the muscles of my eyes, blood cells moving through capillaries, the vapor trails left by passing thoughts? But in reading these hieroglyphics, I see that I'm always in motion, always blooming inside with color, always filled with such goings-on: mad scientists at work, corps of engineers wielding lasers and paint buckets, dream sets being designed for the evening's performance.

The dark is a lively place. The storyline of our days weaves right on through it to the nightshift. Whatever our wild perplexities and appetites, whatever urgings circle inside us, as the poet Rita Dove puts it, "nosing the surface, hungry and mute," they are worked into tales when we sleep and dream, when we pass over the ink-dark isthmus into the Land of Nod. And we have to read those tales. Only then can we maintain continuity with the unfolding story of our lives and partake of the clayworks of making conscious-ness, making form out of what is unformed in us.

Dreams bubble up from the unconscious, which seems to contain an image of the way we're supposed to be. The unconscious works toward the expression of this potential the way a sculptor works toward releasing the statue held inside a rock. To ignore dreams is to hide the sculptor's tools, to tear out pages from our own stories, to drive with our tailpipes dragging on the ground. If we ignore dreams we cut ourselves off from the place from which calls emanate. Most spiritual traditions clearly regard dreams as revelations from the gods, the soul, the Big Soup, and consider the act of separating wak-ing life from dreams, the conscious from the unconscious, the same as tearing a plant from its roots.

Dreams, like all calls, point us toward what we need for growth, integra-tion, expression, and the health of our relationships to person, place, and thing. They point us toward a kind of equilibrium. They're the imagination at work while we sleep. They're meaning machines, and they *never* lie. "Dreams don't come true," says author Tom Robbins in his book *Half Asleep in Frog Pajamas.* "They *are* true." When we wish that our dreams would come true, we're really referring to our ambitions.

Dreams tell us how we *really* feel about something. They help us fine-tune our direction and ascertain our calls, show us our unfinished business, and remind us how much bigger our lives are than what we know consciously. In fact, dreams show us that consciousness itself is a scrabbling around at the hem of something so big it would short us out if we understood its true dimensions. I sometimes wonder: If I can possess such immense powers in my dreams, might I similarly possess powers beyond my imagination in my waking life?

Dreaming is about waking up. The unconscious often knows things we don't, things that in the broad daylight of consciousness remain invisible to us, just as the stars play to an empty house during the day when the sun is shining. Some things can only be seen when it's dark. Trying to solve our problems or make our way or get a grip on our priorities without the information that dreams provide, says Ann Faraday in *The Dream Game,* is like "a detective with only half the facts of a case."

Those who contend that they seldom or never dream are, according to sci-ence, wrong. Everyone dreams, and we typically have half a dozen dreams a night. The problem is that we forget most of them or lack interest in them. Carl Jung said that we're probably in a dreaming process continually, drawing up material from the unconscious even during the day, but consciousness makes such a racket that we don't hear it. We're missing masterpieces of metaphoric communication:

- You're trying to decide between following passion or security and dream of throwing a rock through the window of a bank, and then burying your briefcase in the backyard.
- You're unwittingly losing yourself in a job or a relationship and dream of losing your wallet with all your identification in it.
- You're following a call toward a very public life and don't realize your true feelings about sacrificing privacy until an anxiety dream shows the island you live on being towed toward the mainland.
- Someone with whom you're considering teaming up appears in a dream wearing costume jewelry and fake leather shoes.
- You need to be reminded that the spiritual ascent is not easy, so you dream of Jacob's ladder with the rungs spaced really far apart.
- You're postponing an important decision, and dream of "missing the boat."
- You're determined to write an autobiography, and have dreams of being naked in public.
- You're unsure whether you have the ability to handle what seems like an impossible calling, but then you dream about being able to breathe underwater.
- You're trying to decide whether to move to another country to work and receive a dream that tells you *exactly* what you should do.

This is what happened to Renata Ackermann in 1989. She was living in her native Switzerland, starting up a career as a therapist, when a group of people from the institute where she received her training in Zurich began making plans to start up a similar center in Portland, Oregon, and she began contemplating whether to join them.

She weighed her choices. On the one hand was adventure—living in the United States, being something of a founding mother, exploring "the bigger world," as she put it. On the other was risk—giving up her burgeoning practice in Zurich, her familiarity with the culture and the language, a place where "things were all set up."

"I kept wondering," she said, "how do you make a decision like that?"

Her therapist, who ran the institute in Zurich and was launching the enterprise in the States, told her that big decisions can't be made entirely consciously. They have to be informed by other realms, by contact with "something outside consensus reality." Wait for a dream or a sign, he told her, and just trust. You'll know, he said. "His advice made sense. The prospect of going to the United States was about going into the unknown, so it made sense that the decision would be made partly from that realm, too."

A few weeks later, Renata had the following dream:

"I was in a personal growth workshop, sitting across from my therapist, and we were meditating together. He said he was upset with me. He said he wanted me to give up my personal complexes, leave my personal history behind, and follow him to the United States.

"I suddenly woke up from the dream in the middle of the night and thought, 'This is it! This is the answer I've been waiting for.' And once I had the answer, I thought, 'Do I really *want* this answer?' "

The dream, she said, "Had the intensity of a nightmare, though it wasn't quite that threatening." At least not in the short term. Leaving Switzerland wouldn't be easy, and leaving "personal history" behind—which she took to mean "the way I grew up, the kind of role models I had, what was familiar"—wouldn't be an errand you could tack onto the weekly shopping list: pick up dry cleaning, buy stamps, get eggs and milk, drop off personal history.

Nonetheless, the dream brought a clarity to her deliberations that rang like a bell in the empty air, and within the year she left Switzerland and moved to the United States. "I've never second-guessed it. The clarity stuck. The dream was true."

S L E E P I N G   T H R O U G H   O U R   D R E A M S

In the weeks prior to losing a job early in my journalism career, one I was hanging on to primarily for the security and status, my dreams were splitting at the seams with portents of how I really felt about trading off integrity for comfort and a dollop of renown. Although I faithfully recorded them in my dream journal, I did absolutely nothing about interpreting them, and with good reason. It would have been like standing up in a canoe.

In one dream, I was handed a stack of hundred-dollar bills and later discovered that I'd been cheated: Only the top bill was a one hundred; the rest were ones. In another, I found a golden calf, deformed and chained to the ground. In a third, I was invited to the boss's estate for an extravagant pool party, but the pool was empty.

Now this is not, as they say, rocket science. The meaning of these dreams couldn't have been more obvious if it had been tattooed across the bridge of my nose. I was being invited to take a good look at what I was doing at that job and how I felt about being there. But because I didn't want to look I was completely shocked when I suddenly lost the job—the official reason, appropriately, was that "there isn't a fit." I shouldn't have been so surprised.

As if to confirm the validity, the *rightness,* of both the dreams and the eventual outcome, fate topped them off with an astonishing synchronicity. The Monday following my Friday dismissal from the job, I was supposed to interview the author of a book called *Starting Over: How to Survive the Loss of a Job.* That book was sitting on my night table when I got home, since I had planned to read it over the weekend. Needless to say, I did.

Dreams are a force to be reckoned with, so it's understandable why people sleep through them. The kind of self-knowledge they present is a commandment to live always tentwise, ready to move at all times, constantly in process. Fidelity to dreams means leaving the wild card *in* the deck while playing. It means wobbling the gyroscope, coming into occasional conflict with others, and admitting that we feel what we don't want to admit we feel. It also means accepting that dreams are more interested in the design and quality of our lives than in making us rich or famous.

Listening to our dreams, though, is an act of humility, a kind of genuflecting, and is thus unappetizing to some folks. It's conceding that there is at the very least *another* psychic reality—if not a deeper or greater one—than that by which we generally steer our courses. For people cemented to the rational and scientific, the linear and observable, the ego and the five senses, opening to dreams can be like suddenly realizing that your bathroom mirror is actually two-way.

Contrary to the rationalist hooey that dreams aren't *real* ("You're just dreaming"), dreams are very real. They convey real information, real impact, and real emotions, and they have real consequences if ignored. If we don't obey our dreams, we'll dream them until we do, or the unconscious will "dream up" other channels for their messages to come through, such as symptoms, neuroses, and compulsions. The more we're willing to sweat out our "nightmares" during our waking hours—whatever pursues us or where we feel like we're falling, lost, or trapped—the more likely we are to be free of them at night. As with anything we avoid, the more we ignore dreams, the more they take on the feel of an ambush, full of the sharp recriminations of whatever we've been avoiding. Sleep becomes a broken landscape we have to traverse, planted with trip wires and pocked with the craters left by other nights' dreams.

Dreams are only as dangerous as living, Faraday says, no more, no less. They're just a lot less familiar. Dreams are dark lakes in which each night we swim, and most mornings we don't even remember having been swimming. We glide into the water on our bellies, our spines fishtailing, breathing once again through our gills. We go primitive. All our conscious resistance dissolves like sugar in water, and we remember everything we claim to have forgotten because nothing is forgotten by the old gnome that sleeps in the soul.

In our dreams, we roam far south of rational and well to the west of Main Street. We wear the faces of fish, the beaks of birds, the tusks of animals who have answers buried in their fur and written onto the skin on their tongues. We hear them speak the unspeakable. By dawn we've climbed back over the stone wall outside the bedroom window and crawled into bed. When we awaken we find burrs clinging to our bedsheets.

W A K I N G   T O   D R E A M S

Members of a tribe in Malaysia called the Senoi put great stock in their dreams and gather each morning to share them. When they dream of being chased, they assume that whatever is chasing them is an ally rather than an enemy. So they turn and face their pursuer to inquire what the chase is all about—what the message might be that the pursuer bears.

This is the heart of dreamwork, of revealing the nature of the calls whose fins break the surface in our dreams, of deciphering the messages they bring. The challenge lies in turning around and facing whatever is there rather than running from it. It's like being chased by a dog, or a bear, or a big cat. The general rule is: Don't run! If you run from them they would consider you to be food, which could lead to a fatal case of mistaken identity.

If you're courageous enough to turn and face your pursuers, you're probably also strong enough not to get devoured by them. But you've got to be willing to boogie with the boogeyman. "I have come as a messenger of joy unto thee—why dost thou grieve?" reads the inscription carved on a temple in Chicago. They are the words of death, the king of the boogeymen.

Not all dreams, of course, are of this nature, but the principle is the same: There's gold in them thar hills. Still, it takes some nerve to study your dreams, the same nerve it takes to examine a firecracker that didn't go off. This certainly helps explain why dream recall is such a slippery affair. A part of us doesn't *want* to remember them *because* of the messages they bear, the things they reveal, the directions they point us in. The truth may set you free, but there's an even chance that first it will scare the daylights out of you.

❧

Dreamwork is a lot like dowsing, which a dowser of my acquaintance refers to as "the search for anything that can't be apprehended with the normal five senses." In attempting to divine our dreams, we're searching for a concentration of energy, a flow of meaning, somewhere to sink a well.

It isn't even necessary to understand dreams or mine them for meaning, writes Thomas Moore in *Care of the Soul.* Merely giving our attention to them, granting them their autonomy and mystery, goes a long way, he says, toward opening the portals. It shifts the center of consciousness from intellection to responsiveness. In fact, much of what determines whether we recall dreams at all is simply the amount of interest we pay them. "Let me treat every moment with reverence," says writer Bharati Mukerjee, "because I don't know what the mission of any of my moments in life is. That's why I'm not embarrassed to admit that I believe wholeheartedly in dreams."

Dreams respond not only to reverence but also to direct requests. You don't have to wait around for them to appear. You can draw them to you by petition. You can bargain with them. If you get in the habit of asking for dream guidance as you're dropping off to sleep, the minions of Morpheus will fairly beat a path to your door. Just be prepared to take dictation: Keep a pad and pen by the bedside. Promise the spirits that if they send you a dream, you'll write it down upon waking, even if that's at 3 A.M. Prompt them with specific questions. Ask for directions. Ask for clues. Ask what your next step should be. Ask for clarification of *last* night's dream.

Just get to your dreams before the world does. Write them down before you even get out of bed because the moment your feet hit the floor, you ground yourself, and the lightning energy of dreams disappears into the earth. The moment of awakening is make-or-break time in dream recall, and some finesse is in order. A dream is made of spiderwebbing. It's a journal whose pages are the pressed wings of luna moths. It tatters easily. So when you awaken, move as if you were paddling a canoe on a glassy lake, or walking across a room carrying brimming teacups.

As for the dream material itself, some of it is like junk mail. Only a small percentage is truly useful and worth slogging through. Some of it also comes in such a crazy mambo of images, vignettes, metaphors, and other psychic ephemera that trying to make any sense of it is like running down the street trying to grab the loose papers of a manuscript the wind has snatched out of your hands.

After you have something in writing that seems gainful, however, don't necessarily run with the first interpretation that comes to you. Brainstorm all associations you can conjure about the dream images or events, especially the most potent one in the dream. What words, ideas, people, memories, and feelings does it remind you of? Go with the one that elicits the most energy from you, that has the most *oomph*.

Avoid using a dream dictionary, an absolutist this-means-that approach to interpretation. Dreams are far too subjective for that. Water, for instance, will mean something very different to someone who almost drowned as a kid than it will to someone who feels more at home in water than the fishes. Sometimes we dream about drinking because we're thirsty, and other times we dream of drinking when we're *not* thirsty, which is an entirely different kind of thirst.

Since most dreams (though not all) seem to relate to something happening in present time, ask how the dream ties into your life right now. Where have you seen this particular scenario playing itself out lately? What is it trying to tell you? What is its central message? Ask how various dreams—of flying, falling, conquering foes, being unable to find something, having extraordinary powers, being chased—may be symbolic of aspects of your life. Before you settle on an interpretation, though, check the physical world first. If you dream your car loses its brakes, check your brakes. If nothing shows up, check where in your life you perhaps feel unable to stop or out of control. If you dream someone you know is dying, and they're not, then ask what this person *represents* to you—integrity, innocence, humor, playfulness, etc.—and thus what in your own life or personality may be "dying."

THE POWER OF RITUAL

I once presided over a good old-fashioned book burning. The book was mine.

I was sitting in my living room one afternoon when I heard a thump on the steps outside the front door. I knew exactly what it was: the sound of the UPS guy delivering from the publisher the first box of my first book. I carried it inside the way I imagine pharaoh's daughter must have carried the basket with Moses in it from the river. I stood in my living room staring at a copy of my first book with a combination of awe, rapture, and a bit of holy terror, the way parents first behold their children. The experience gave me a small appreciation of what pregnancy must be like. The overwhelming sense of anticipation. The feeling that after having waited for the better part of a year—in this case for the publisher to print it—I wanted the damn thing to come out already. I even felt the postpartum depression and a fearsome attachment.

That night I had a dream in which I was standing in front of an audience. On the table in front of me was a copy of my book, which looked like someone had put it through a meat grinder. The word *Obit* was written across the cover.

I woke up mortified and realized that I was desperately attached to the book and had to let it go. I was terrified of what the world was going to think of it, whether it would get good reviews, whether it would sell, and whether it would pay back its advance, thereby catapulting my work into that 5 to 10 percent of books that statistically make money.

The morning after my dream, I wrote an obituary for myself on the title page where I normally sign my name for people. Then I tore the book to shreds with my bare hands. I broke the spine over my knee. I cracked the cardboard. I tore up every single page. Then I burned it in my fireplace. It was an act that prompted my mother to declare that I was weird, though the experience proved to be remarkably liberating. It helped me let the book go out into the world to have a life of its own, and helped me get on with mine. It was an object lesson in something I have had to learn over and over as a writer and as a human being: let go. Let go of my writing from where it's held on the inside. Let go of controlling it as it's coming out onto the page—allow the stories to tell themselves. Let go of the comfort zone and take risks with it. Let my tender shoots of optimism go out into a world that wears big, dirty boots. And finally, let go of my expectations for the way I think it will all turn out.

It's appropriate that the word writers use to describe the act of sending their work out into the world is *submission.* It is, indeed, a kind of surrender. And my dream was a call to surrender. It was also a call for ritual, which is, I think, dreamwork's denouement. It's the way we bring our dreams out of a dream state and into waking life, into the here and now. It's the way to bring them from the abstract down into our muscles and body parts, our emotions and physical life. A ritual is an enactment of the dream *message,* of whatever change the dream is calling for. It's a way of taking a small step in that direction, making an outward sign of an inward intention. It's a little rite of passage.

There's an old belief in certain Christian denominations, Robert Johnson notes, that one is not praying unless one's lips move. This is an expression of the psychological truth that something physical has to happen to establish (to your unconscious especially) that you mean business, that your devotion to growth is real and not merely a high opinion you have of yourself.

If you dream of the necessity of choosing passion over security, for instance, you might ritually burn a one-dollar bill while entreating the gods of courage. If a dream points to the need to make a break with tradition, take a stick of wood and break it in two. If your dream shows you flying over obstacles, set up a series of rocks in the backyard, give them the names of your obstacles, and make broad jumps over them.

A ritual can be as simple, too, as putting a flower in a vase, making a circle of stones, burying something that represents an old habit, kneeling down in prayer, washing yourself in a river, anointing yourself with oil, visiting the zoo to spend some time with the animal in your dream, planting something, drumming or singing, feasting or fasting, making a mask, lighting a candle.

"I can light a candle because I need the light," says writer Christina Baldwin, "or because the candle represents the light I need."

six

THE
LANGUAGE OF
THE BODY

---

*"I have ceased to question stars and books; I have begun
to listen to the teachings my blood whispers to me."*

— HERMAN HESSE
PROLOGUE TO <u>DEMIAN</u>

At a writers' conference recently, a woman walked up to me after my presentation and shared something that people won't generally tell you unless they're fairly sure they'll never see you again.

"You know why I'm so fat?" she said.

It was apparent I wasn't meant to take three guesses, and in the dead silence that followed, several passersby turned to stare at her as thoughts scattered in my head like billiard balls after a break shot.

"It's because I have so many stories inside me that I'm not writing down," she said.

⁓

There is no science or philosophy I know of that can dispute a self-diagnosis delivered with that kind of clinical detachment and decisiveness. By virtue of her certitude alone, her statement carried (you'll pardon the expression) a weight of authority that was irrefutable. This woman knew that her condition meant something and what it meant. Her obesity was the mark of Jonah, the testimony of her flight from a calling.

She seemed to understand that within her body all the records of her rejected desires, deflected dreams, and frustrated creativity were piled up and pushing out from inside, tumid from neglect. Her obesity was the insignia of her struggle for authenticity. It was a treasure chest filled with undiscovered stories and bound, no doubt, with coils of ropy fear.

After working with thousands of patients, the psychologist Arnold Mindell, founder of Process Oriented Psychology, believes that symptoms are often dreams trying to come true and, furthermore, that the medicine is inherent in the symptom. If we ask our bodies what remedies they need—not just for the sake of curing our maladies, but also for healing our lives—they'll tell us. "Symptoms are purposeful conditions," he says. "They could be the beginning of fantastic phases of life, or bring you amazingly close to the center of existence, or be a royal road to the development of the personality. Anyway, there's no known method I've ever heard of that will allow you to avoid a message that wants to come into your life. Even right up to the moment of death, it will try to pop through."

Physician and surgeon Bernie Siegel, author of *Love, Medicine and Miracles,* agrees. "When you start looking for the message in disease, you realize that there always is one." Unfortunately, by following the great modern commandment of sickness—Get well!—we usually end up trying to eradicate our symptoms before finding out what dreams might be trying to come true; we kill the messengers before they have a chance to deliver their messages.

Like dreams, body symptoms present information of which we're unconscious. In a dream, this information comes as symbols. In the body, it comes as symptoms. Both mean exactly the same thing: signs! Sickness is a dream in the body, and symptoms are possessed of what the physicist David Bohm calls "soma-significance." They mean something. They have wisdom, metaphoric power, method in their madness. They are one of the languages the soul uses to get across to us something about itself. The word *pathology,* in fact, means the speech of suffering, the logic of pain, and in order to understand that logic, in order to speak to the wild imagination at work in symptoms, we must *bring* to it a certain supple and symbolic imagination.

If we suffer cramps or constipation or arteriosclerosis, for instance, in addition to tending the symptoms, we might ask in what way they're speaking to us about something blocked in our lives. If we have a hernia, is there some way in which we may be pushing too hard? If we're having insomnia, is there some part of us that wants to wake up? If we have diarrhea, is there something we want to run from? And so on, with all manner of irritations, exhaustions, pressures, congestions, itches, and even emotions, which certainly belong to the body: boiling the blood, quickening the breath, tensing the muscles, and over time etching themselves into our faces and physiques.

In the cosmology of the Iroquois, sickness is often the soul's way of indicating that something is *missing* in our lives. To the degree, then, that a body in pain is often a soul in longing, consider the following examples, which I've gleaned from medical research over the years, of people whose symptoms came to have very distinct meaning (to them!) and spoke fluently of something missing:

- A man suffering lower-back pain whenever he sits down experiences a complete reprieve of his symptom when he realizes that "I hate where I'm sitting" and quits his desk job to start his own company.
- A woman whose doctor says he can find no physiological reason for her internal bleeding says she can't help feeling that "I'm crying from the inside out."
- A man suffers a heart attack after having stomach cancer, which necessitated the removal of half his stomach, and concludes: "Eat less, love more."
- An adoptee, searching for his biological mother, is suddenly stricken with an inability to blink, and he says to the doctor, "If I blink, I might miss my mother."
- A woman miscarries and says afterward that she really had "no room" for a baby in her life.
- A man with cancer in his backbone says that he "was always considered spineless."
- A woman who has undergone a double mastectomy and complete hysterectomy talks about having "all my female parts taken out" at the same time that she is struggling with the split loyalties of pursuing her career and tending to domestic duties and motherhood. In the back of her mind, she says, is also the memory of her mother who "went crazy" taking care of five children and leaving her own career untouched.
- My own father, shortly after quadruple bypass surgery, cries openly in front of me—something I have never seen before—and tells me, "For twenty years I've wanted to hold you in my arms." After finally

doing so, amidst much manly blubbering on both our parts, he adds, "This is the medicine I've needed."

Right down at the cellular level, and right from the start of our lives, Bernie Siegel insists, our bodies know what we are to become. Consider, he says, that as the cells in a fertilized egg multiply, they soon reach a point when the subtlest indentations appear in the growing cell-ball, which distinguish the head from the hindquarters. Although this distinction seems to be lost on some people, nonetheless from this point on, if you take a cell from the head and place it at the hindquarters, it will migrate back up to the head.

"It knows what it is," Siegel says, "what it is to become, where it belongs." We can trust the body, he says, to bring us into alignment, and we can trust the soul to speak to us through the body. The soul is the plumb line, the polestar, the homing bird. It is the master storyteller who scatters stories around the body like apple seeds.

The body is not an obstacle to soul, as so many spiritual pilgrims would have it; it is not a mere skin to shed on the way to some incredible lightness of being. It is rather a channel to it, and the body's sufferings are "the midwife of very great things," as the Swiss physician and alchemist Philippus Paracelsus once said. "Decay," as he put it, "is the beginning of all birth, the beginning of the Great Work, that of spiritual transformation."

The alchemists—those mystical chemists who sought an elixir that would cure all ailments and worked toward this by striving to turn lead into gold—didn't, after all, try turning silver into gold, or copper into gold, or platinum, or any of the exalted metals. They worked instead on that bottom dweller, that plainest, basest of metals: lead. If there is a cure for what ails us, they were saying, it is most likely to be found in the common rock, in the philosopher's stone of our sniffles and backaches, our fevers and infirmities. At the very least, these are certainly more accessible to us than visions of gold and clouds with silver linings.

The body also provides countless examples of alchemy and transfiguration—of pain midwifing growth. Fracture triggers the engineering of a bone bridge between broken ends. Laceration invokes the gluey gods of coagulation. Burn and abrasion pillow the skin with blisters. Injury brings on healing. "Illness has always been of enormous benefit to me," says Alice Walker, author of *The Color Purple.* "I have learned little from anything that did not in some way make me sick."

PANDORA'S MIRROR

Several years ago, state educators in Lansing, Michigan, halted plans to teach a breathing exercise as part of a health course in kindergarten through the eighth grade, deferring to concern that deep breathing could promote "devil worship and mysticism."

I understand why they're afraid. As a child, I knew the power of breath. I knew that if I held my breath long enough, I could turn blue and pass out, thereby generating gales of attention. And I used it regularly, or so I'm told by my mother, who still describes it with the kind of dreadful fascination people typically reserve for reminiscing about floods and earthquakes.

Breath is life. It is the holy wind that carried the Word. When children begin to feel that this power resides within them, they become too powerful to control, too intuitive to frighten easily.

But Lansing didn't let the program through, thereby doing its part to prevent any swelling in the ranks of devil-worshipping kindergartners, and adding to the already colossal alienation people feel from their bodies. It is an estrangement that prevents us from honoring our bodies as the emissaries they are. Who, after all, wants to enter into intimate relationship, or even conversation, with any-body they were taught to rise above or ignore?

Besides, who knows what we'd find out about ourselves if we peeked into that Pandora's box? Who knows what we might discover our souls are missing, and who needs the grief? A lot of us prefer to treat the symptom rather than face the source. We would rather be cut open from stem to sternum than open our hearts from the inside out.

In addition to our appalling disaffection from the body, we also have a long and pernicious history of linking sickness with sin, of dressing our wounds with guilt and judging our illnesses as failures and evidence of general unworthiness. The cruelest question that is always present, even if unasked, in the presence of illness, said the anthropologist Ernest Becker in his book *The Denial of Death,* is "Why are you sick?" Or worse, "Why have you done this thing to yourself?"

This attitude is guaranteed to make a sufferer feel worse, and it betrays a kind of arrogance. It implies that we are masters of our fate to such a degree that we can not only create disease but also make it disappear by the ordination of sheer willpower and the *proper* sort of faith. We are not, I think, so much in control of things. We have not necessarily drawn to ourselves every-thing that happens to us, and not every symptom is a metaphor. There are bugs in the world, and they carry diseases. There's arsenic in the water and exhaust in the air. There are tragedies like pits that people fall into. There are accidents, wrong times and wrong places, floods and earthquakes. There is also no guarantee that healing our lives will cure our diseases.

Rather than using sickness as an opportunity to beat yourself up, or set off on a crusade to figure out why bad things happen to good people, better to try and use illness and pain for what they were designed for—to get your atten-tion. Understand that though you may not have created them, your soul may still be attempting to communicate something to you through them. We are not so much responsible *for* our illnesses, says author and Buddhist teacher Stephen Levine, as we are responsible *to* our illnesses. The question is not so much what to do *about* our suffering, but what to do *with* it.

Being responsible *to* an illness, he says, means being willing to relate to it, have a full-on experience of it, and investigate not just the pain but also your reaction to it. It means letting it communicate with you rather than merely trying to subdue it. Though that's certainly the natural reflex, it probably is an accurate mirror of how we resist *whatever* is painful and unpleasant in our lives, whatever doesn't go our way, whatever makes us feel out of control. It's a mirror to how we regard not only the physical but also the emotional symp-toms in our lives: our sulfurous marital fights, our obsessions with money or love, our wayward kids, our debts piled up to here, that low-grade anxiety running like a white noise through our days, the constant feeling of something missing. To say nothing of the symptoms scattered around the body *politic*.

This sense of responsibility cannot be soft-pedaled. It will try your most grim self-restraint, for instance, to lie in bed and just let sciatic pain be while it yowls at you. But there is knowledge and therefore power in following its migrations, plotting its geometry, and noticing how sometimes it burns and sometimes it vibrates, sometimes it spills boiling oil down the legs and some-times it spreads hot coals in the pan of the pelvis, and always it makes you feel so *vulnerable*. It would be so much easier just to grab a fistful of aspirins, wash it down with an immediate appointment at the chiropractor's, and get back to business as usual—which might be what landed you on your back to begin with.

Being responsible, Levine says, means asking not "Why am I ill?" but "What is illness?" Not "Why am I in pain?" but "What is pain?" It means seeking the *what* rather than just the *why.* The mind is so desperate for answers, and so easily settles for the simple and convenient ones, that it often ends up leaving completely untouched the deeper truths and deeper processes. It also routinely ignores the need for change, which is the unspoken petition of any illness. This can be the need for a change in priority or posture, a change in attitude, approach, or tempo.

Change may or may not ameliorate the symptom, depending on how long we've waited before making the change, but it can have a powerful impact on the course of not only an illness but also a life. For instance, among those who have experienced spontaneous remissions—inexplicable recoveries from "incurable" diseases—over 90 percent, Bernie Siegel says, first experienced major, and favorable, change in their lives prior to the healing: dramatic rec- onciliations, religious conversions, the admitting of long-denied truths, the removal of obstacles to a career or a marriage, the birth of a child or grand- child. These people, however, didn't make their changes in hopes of effecting such an outcome, but "to do things more appropriate to living than dying," as one man put it. Healing was a *by-product* of the change.

If our only approach to the body's deep cries is to clamp our hands over our ears, we have dismissed the dreams of the body. If we medicate our symp- toms away or get them "fixed" by the doctor, hoping to return to our lives and pick up where we left off without missing a beat, then we've missed the point of pain. Fortunately and unfortunately, though, the opportunity to grow will come around again.

ADDING   FUEL   TO   THE   FLAME

In trying to help patients become more responsive to the meaning of their illnesses, Arnold Mindell once made a startling observation that despite peo- ple's stated desire to alleviate their symptoms, they often did things to exagger- ate them instead. Someone with a bruise would press on it. Someone with a stiff neck would bend the neck backward to feel the pain. Someone with a scab would pick at it until it bled. Someone with eczema would scratch it until it was inflamed. They behaved as if they were trying to worsen their problem.

Mindell's experience with a dying patient helped him understand this seeming contradiction. The man, who was dying of stomach cancer, was lying doubled up in pain in a hospital bed. Since he had already been operated on unsuccessfully, the man was open to Mindell's suggestion that they try something new: deliberately amplifying the pain. Having described his pain as the feeling of something in his stomach trying to break out, he began increasing the pressure, pushing his stomach out until the pain was unbearable, and he yelled, "I just want to explode! I've never been able to really explode! I've never expressed myself enough."

This, of course, is a common problem, and not everyone who has difficulty with self-expression comes down with a tumor. But this man had become ill, Mindell said, and though he'd been given a very short time to live, he improved enough after his "explosion" to be discharged from the hospital and live another two years, during which he worked hard at expressing himself.

Interestingly, Mindell discovered in working with this cancer patient that just prior to entering the hospital, the patient had dreamed that he had an incurable disease and the medicine for it was "like a bomb." Mindell recalls, "I knew that his cancer was the bomb in the dream. It was his lost expression trying to come out, and finding no way out, it came out in his body as the cancer, and in his dream as the bomb. His pain became his medicine, just like the dream said." Due to this observation, Mindell has since come to believe not only that the medicine is revealed by the sickness itself, but that it is also often revealed by the dreams that come *during* the sickness.

We have a tremendous need, he says, to feel our pain, which is often the beginning of great awareness, and by amplifying it, by magnifying our symptoms as we'd blow up a photograph to make certain details more visible, or squeeze an orange to draw out the juice, we can press ourselves toward consciousness and breakthrough. We can encourage the soul to tip its hand, to reveal its meaning. We can release the spirit in the bottle.

Mindell did this himself once while on vacation in the Swiss Alps. He started coming down with flulike symptoms and soon found himself "shuddering and shaking from head to foot. But I decided to go with it, to amplify the experience, so I took off my sweater and shirt and walked outside and rolled around in the snow. I started yelling and dancing and jitterbugging, and while I was doing this I realized I was bored out of my mind with what I was doing at the time. If you're bored, it means you're not in contact with deeper processes that are happening, and in my case that deeper process was that I was very excited about the prospect of beginning to study physics and its connections with psychology, and wanted to start right there on vacation. Which I did."

That night he also dreamed that a shaman went into an ecstatic dance and discovered "the core of magic." Although Mindell doesn't claim to have discovered *that* yet, he says, "I *am* learning a lot about how physics and psychology connect, and the symptoms I had on that vacation were my first calling toward that.

"I also never did come down with the flu."

⚜

" 'The Fall,' the metamorphosis into physical suffering, is preceded by premonitions," says physician Alfred Zeigler in *Archetypal Medicine.* There are fair warnings, clouds on the horizon. You're bent out of shape long before your back goes out. You're burning up inside well before your ulcer appears. You want to run before your bowels do. You also want to catch these things before they become the size of proverbial golf balls and grapefruits. You want to amplify your symptoms before your body does. Like a child trying to get attention, a symptom will usually get louder and louder over time, the signal coming across with ever-increasing voltage and violence the longer you ignore it. Health, it seems, is largely the art of listening.

So pick a symptom and practice, Mindell suggests, perhaps starting with one that recurs, that seems to accompany stress and transitions, that flares up alongside fear. A nervous tic, a rash, an allergy, a certain kind of headache. The dull throb in your lower back, the ache that goes across the top of your shoulders, the tightness in your jaw. Draw your attention to it. Forget what you *think* is going on, why you have it, what it means and, again, just focus on the *experience* of it. Then add fuel to the flame. Tighten the cramp, exaggerate the tic, push on the pain, don't scratch the itch but let it itch worse, don't move to alleviate the back pain, but lie still and let it come.

At some point, Mindell says, a "channel-change" will likely occur. You'll flip, sometimes quite subtly, from feeling into seeing or hearing or moving or talking. "You might get an image of your symptom as a fire in your belly, a vise in your head, a knife in your heart. You might hear someone's voice in your head, or experience a memory, or start spontaneously moving." Now amplify this *new* channel. You might draw a picture of an image, talk to the voice in your head, write about the memory that got triggered, or do some movement or dance that captures the feeling. By doing so, you now have another way of understanding your symptom, a second opinion, as it were. You'll have a visual aid, a soundtrack, a written statement, a picture that's worth a thousand words.

PART FURY AND PART GRACE

In the spring of 1988, illness dropped like a meteor into Kat Duff's life, leaving a hole two years wide during which she rarely left her bed, slept twelve hours a day, and kept the door shut, the shades drawn, and the phone unplugged. Her worldly activities shrank to a radius of twenty miles from home.

Her illness began after a counseling session with a client, when she slumped exhausted to the floor and fell asleep. Waking up damp with sweat, her heart racing, she was unable to tell what time it was or where she was. She was diagnosed with chronic fatigue and immune dysfunction syndrome (CFIDS), a gray plague of exhaustion, constant fevers, muscle aches, memory lapses, fainting spells, disorientation, and an immune system so weakened it could no longer heal even a paper cut without hard labor. It was like a bad flu that never went away, and it did much to convince her that her body had a mind of its own, quite apart from the willfulness that she, "in the hubris of health," assumed was running the show.

One would think that such isolation and inertia would be not only frustrating in the extreme but also deadly dull. It was not. It was, she says, surprisingly interesting once she got up close, "in the same way that a desert landscape, under close scrutiny, comes alive." More than interesting, the illness seemed crucial, heavy with import. "It seemed like my symptoms were calling me, requiring me, to recollect and reorient myself." It was as if some pulling power, some coefficient of body and soul that was "part fury and part grace," as the writer Laura Chester puts it, was steering her toward self-realization, playing a tune for the cobra in her soul, "drawing old wounds to the surface," says Kat, "like a poultice, to bleed openly."

By necessity, she began to spend time with her body in a way she hadn't since adolescence. One day, staring at her face in the mirror, she noticed, for the first time, that one of her eyes was open and trusting, and the other squinting and suspicious, "as if the trunk of my life had been split in two." And it had. It was no coincidence, she says, that she came down with CFIDS after she remembered being molested as a child, working with the realization in therapy, and finally comprehending its truth. It was also no coincidence, she feels, that she suffered from a disease that weakened her immune system, which undermined her ability to cope with *invaders*. She was unable to ward off microbes, viruses, mold spores, and pollens; unable to hold off memories of the original breach of security in her life; unable to protect herself against something both her molestation and her disease had in common: "boundary violation."

The illness and the dreams that came to her during it aided her recovery from the sexual abuse by "taking me to deeper layers of my body memory, activating a cellular consciousness that remembers not only what happened, but also how to heal." The only remedy so far for CFIDS—rest—also provided a needed counterpoint to the hypervigilance that is one of the survival tactics abused children often take with them into adulthood. "Your defenses, your immune system, are up all the time, and after a while it doesn't know who's a good guy and who's a bad guy. It's reacting against everything. It gets stuck on 'alarm.' The disease broke down that resistance."

It also showed her, perhaps most importantly, how to trust her own perceptions, because sexual abuse survivors don't usually experience them as valid, having been told so often that something is different from what it feels like, that something is good for you when it's not. Relieved of the pressures of socializing, of the need to please anyone or put on a face, and being alone in a safe room in which she could think what she thought and feel what she felt, she learned "to stick closer to my own experiences, to what my body knows and feels, to notice whether a particular activity or person made me feel better or worse, and act on what I noticed."

Her illness was also "an antidote to the American way of life," of which she had wholeheartedly partaken and from which she so badly needed a break: the chronic busyness and extroversion that she came to see as precisely a kind of hypervigilance. From the vantage point of bed, she saw her own life as a time-lapse photograph of the path her car had taken in all its travels, as the accumulated skitter of a moth at a lightbulb. She saw her immense restlessness characterized so adroitly by the fact that she had moved every two years during her adult life, a condition of exile that the illness also cured. She has now lived in one place for more than twelve years.

"I doubt such pain makes us better," the philosopher Friedrich Nietzsche once said of illness, "but I know it makes us more profound." And for Kat, her frailty has brought her a solidity of self and a depth of understanding she never possessed before. In the book she wrote about her experience with CFIDS, *The Alchemy of Illness,* she said, "I feel as though I'm finally standing on both my feet for the first time in my life, as if the pale outline of myself has at last been filled in with color."

During her illness, she once had to turn down an invitation to participate in a meditation retreat because she didn't feel up to sitting for hours on end. She felt disheartened, wondering when she'd be well enough to resume spiritual practices. As she was falling asleep that night, however, she suddenly understood that her illness *was* spiritual practice, an opportunity to sit *zazen,* a way to employ the alchemical art of turning lead into gold. "I've come to see that I contact 'the divine,' or it comes forward most clearly to me, when I'm in my most human limitedness, whereas before I was seeking it by trying to be godlike, trying to transcend my humanness. It's an immense comfort to me that I'm closest to the divine by being closest to my own humanness and vulnerability."

THE SAFEST MEASURE

"I came to explore the wreck," the poet Adrienne Rich once wrote. "I came to see the damage that was done, and the treasures that prevail."

Having done so, having held our breaths and descended to the wisdom submerged beneath our sicknesses, how do we bring this treasure back to the surface? How do we integrate what we find in our symptoms into lives that are regulated by the hubris of health? In the last line of her book, Kat writes, "I hope I don't forget when I get well."

To that end, she has solemnly sworn that when she gets symptoms of any kind, "I give myself to them. I unplug from my duties and attend to them. I let them be a door that might open me to something bigger." For her, illness is to health what dreams are to waking life: the reminder of what is forgotten, the bigger picture working toward resolution. Although there's nothing inherently wrong with going to the doctor, it's terribly easy, she says, to rely on the powers of intervention available through medicine and technology. Though these can eliminate our symptoms, they can also take with them the deeper healing that might have taken place and "short-circuit a complicated system of suffering and meaning that's instrumental to life and consciousness."

We may short the circuit because our intuition tells us that the deeper healing called for by our illnesses will certainly be more difficult to effect than a trip to the apothecary, and possibly more difficult than the sickness itself.

Whatever it requires will likely be right at our limits, or what we perceive as our limits. Kat sees her own illness, for example, as requiring something new of her, a fuller response to her own gifts and powers, in particular writing. "My illness midwifed the writer in me. I think it was ready to come forward, and the illness was just about the only way life could get me to honor, receive, and assume that part of myself."

For Kat, writing turned out to be the dream trying to come true, as well as the medicine. Taking a risk to follow her calling turned out to be the safest measure, the healthiest choice for body and soul.

seven

T H E
T U R N   O F
E V E N T S

One of the shining qualities that heroes possess is the willingness to be educated by all things. They learn from the most impressive variety of people and experiences: the wise and the foolish; the obvious and the inconceivable; the living and the dead; the things they love and the things they hate; children and animals and the voluble energetics of nature; all the thumpings and all the bounties they earn from the world. *"Everything* nourished him," Henry Miller once said of Goethe.

Heroic people also understand that calls are not just inner experiences—passions, dreams, symptoms—but also outer. These come to us from the world and from the events in our lives, and whether they fling themselves at us like fastballs or follow us around and rub up against us like stray cats, they, too, require a response.

We, too, act heroically if we attempt to see the morals in the stories, the bones through the flesh. The events themselves, which may appear so ordinary, can take on the contours of signs if we give them meaning, and we do so when we pay attention to them. We look at what direction they're coming from and going in, who is caught up in them along with us, and how they're timed. We look for subtitles, listen for voice-overs, notice if insights detonate in our heads and if we ignore them. Chances are that sooner or later we'll be brought back to remembering that we ignored them. Too often we travel on cruise control, and the events of our lives flick by like white lines on the freeway, their lessons lost on us.

The things that happen to us are a kind of feedback, and interpreting this feedback is critical to knowing how to proceed. While working at a former job, I was so eager for feedback that I once made the following proposal to my boss, one I was certain he would accept: I was willing to take a $1,000-a-year *cut* in pay if he would agree to give me a fifteen-minute feedback session every two weeks. To my astonishment, and later my disgust, he declined, even after I presented him with studies showing that employees perform better with regular feedback. It was one in a long line of indignities that propelled me to leave that job and taught me a few things about the failures of leadership and imagination.

"Enter each day," Sam Keen instructs in *Hymns to an Unknown God,* "with the expectation that the happenings of the day may contain a clandestine message addressed to you personally. Expect omens, epiphanies, casual blessings, and teachers who unknowingly speak to your condition." Expect that through the right lens, all our encounters will appear full of thunderbolts and instruction; every bush will be a burning bush. Such encounters might include:

- An offer to collaborate with someone on a project that draws you in an entirely new direction.
- A sudden crisis that calls on powers you don't realize you possess but whose time has come. When a Japanese monk visited writer Gretel Ehrlich after she had been struck by lightning, he said to her, "You have always been so strong. Now it is time for you to learn about being weak."
- The loss of a job that pushes you over that edge you've been peering at for years.
- An illness or accident that reminds you of what really matters. The car accident that Harvard Medical School professor Joan Borysenko refers to as her "head-on collision with destiny" helped her take stock of her life and make some long-overdue changes, including leaving academia.
- The change your partner is going through—getting back into the job market, going back to school, struggling with a disease, retiring, desir-

ing more closeness or less—that becomes your own change, because
your partner's call automatically requires a response from you. During a
weekend seminar I taught recently in Texas, a woman raised her hand
and asked, "What should I do if the person closest to me is the person
most threatened by the prospect of my success?" Before I could formulate any sort of answer, another woman in the back of the room yelled
out, "Dump him!"

- A chance meeting with a stranger that sparks something in you. Early
  in psychiatrist Robert Coles's career, he met a six-year-old girl who
  was battling tremendous odds in attempting to attend an all-white
  school in the segregated Mississippi of the early 1960s. They became
  friends, and he was so moved by her strength that it helped redefine his
  own life's work.

- Some harrowing challenge is imposed on you. The German theologian
  Dietrich Bonhoeffer's imprisonment during World War II called him
  later to minister to others who were imprisoned.

- Something you witness that changes what you believe in or how you
  live.

- A tragedy that gives you your life's work and determines what it is you
  have to say to the world from that day on. Scores of organizations and
  support groups are started in just this way: Mothers Against Drunk
  Drivers, Parents of Murdered Children, Widow to Widow, Living with
  Cancer.

- One of the gross multitude of sufferings crying out to you from the
  world reaches out and touches your life in a personal way, and you find
  yourself responding.

- Any family reunion. However exalted we imagine ourselves to be in
  spiritual and emotional matters, we have only to spend a few days
  around our families to see how far we still have to go and what in particular we need to work on.

- Any strange occurrence. A woman I recently read about described how
  when she was nine years old she was saved from drowning off the coast
  of Oregon—by a seal. Later in life she returned the favor by working to
  save that species.

In whatever form these signal events come to us, they often seem to indicate a conspiracy, a "breathing together," a way in which events on the outside

and the inside work together and match each other. The event and our state of mind at the time become like the two eyepieces of a binocular microscope; they are both looking at the same subject, the same truth. If there's no match, there's probably no meaning and no call.

Or maybe the soul, like a shipwrecked sailor, uses every resource at hand to speak to us, shaking the world like a fruit tree in order to drop seeds into our lives. Sometimes they take and sometimes they don't. The events may reveal to us a bigger plan or they may just undo the plans we've already made. They can be subtle or they can be the equivalent of a slap across the face, a shock of sufficient voltage to jolt us out of our familiar lives and throw us right out of our shoes. Goliath 1, David 0. We're not so much called as commanded, conscripted, claimed. In no tradition are the gods timid.

John Graham found this out through what *Reader's Digest* calls a "Drama in Real Life," and the magazine wrote just such a story about the experience in which John was caught up, and called, back in 1980. *Reader's Digest* titled it "The Last Cruise of the *Prinsendam.*"

For fifteen years, John had been a self-described soldier of fortune, though his various and official titles while working for the Foreign Service included diplomat, political officer, congressional aide, UN advisor on Third World issues, and counterinsurgency and antiterrorist expert in Vietnam and Libya. He was also a strategic planner who met with other strategic planners in castles in Norway and summer homes in London, planning the deployment of NATO's nuclear missiles in Europe. "My job," he says, "was to deal with the political ramifications of killing tens of millions of people."

What he describes as "the gnawing"—the questioning of his own motives, the uncomfortable feeling that his life had no ethic—began in Vietnam in 1972 during what was called the Easter Offensive. The city of Hue, which was just below the demilitarized zone in South Vietnam, was being attacked by the North Vietnamese, and he was one of the State Department's men on the spot. The city, much of it burning, was terrorized by looters and had swollen to twice its normal size by the flood of refugees from other defeated cities. Most of the city's officials, police, and firefighters had fled, leaving the city in chaos.

John and a few other Americans took it upon themselves to try to pull some semblance of a working government together from the few officials who remained, including one minor bureaucrat whom they found in his underwear playing the flute as bombs exploded only a few miles away. John decided that the way to begin reestablishing order was to set up a firing squad to quell the looting. He stood in the mayor's office, pounding his fist on the table, yelling at the man to set up the execution poles to augment this plan. Suddenly his fist stopped in midair and a single thought barged into his consciousness: "This is crazy. Here I am screaming at one Vietnamese to shoot other Vietnamese so they can get together and shoot still other Vietnamese.

"I didn't give a goddamn for anything in that war," John now says, "including the aims of my own country, and these people meant nothing to me. I was just having my own personal adventure, being a mercenary, loving the feeling of being a big shot in the middle of a war zone. I had *always* tried to pretend that it didn't matter, that I didn't have any responsibility for the chaos and pain I was helping to inflict in the work I did. But standing in that office, it suddenly seemed incredibly irresponsible. Who was I to order the deaths of people for the sake of my own adventure, for the adrenaline rush? It was as if someone had hit me over the head with a two-by-four."

John eventually left the Foreign Service, and by 1980 he was in New York City with a failing political-consulting business, a failing marriage, a father who was dying, no money, and a collection of John Wayne war stories that were steadily losing something in the translation. He began searching for more useful and honorable ways to use his talents and adrenaline, and though he spent considerable time on the cocktail circuit strutting his "hazy ideas about doing the right thing," he didn't act on most of them. He said he lacked the courage.

The turning point came when a friend suggested he consider lecturing on cruise ships, which offered good money, prestige, and free travel. He jumped at the chance and in October 1980 boarded the Holland-America's *Prinsendam* in Vancouver, which was headed for Tokyo with 524 people aboard. Three days out of port, in the middle of the night in the middle of the Gulf of Alaska, 150 miles from shore, a fire broke out in the engine room. With the ship's band playing show tunes from *Oklahoma* and the captain wearing full dress uniform complete with silk scarf, the passengers began lining up at the lifeboat stations.

The rescue efforts, described in *Reader's Digest* as the greatest air-sea rescue in maritime history, began at dawn and dragged on through the whole next day. At sunset, with half an hour left before efforts would be called off on account of dark and a storm too violent to fly in, John was crouched in one of the few remaining lifeboats. He was with eight other men, and they had no engine, no radio, no lights, no flares, no fresh water, no food, and no cover in a typhoon with thirty-foot seas. One moment he was looking up at a thirty-foot wall of water and the next moment he was on top of a thirty-foot mountain of water. They were going up and down sixty feet between trough and crest every ten seconds or so, with a bathtubful of icy water thrown onto them at regular intervals. Everyone on board was vomiting and slowly dying of hypothermia, which John recognized from his days as a mountaineer. He figured he had three to four hours to live.

He also figured he had nothing to lose by praying, though it wasn't exactly his habit, as is evidenced by the kind of prayer he offered—an angry challenge to God to tell him why, when he was just beginning to turn his life around, he was going to be "snuffed out." God's answer, as translated by John, was: "Stop kidding yourself. All your ideals aren't worth a bucket of warm spit. You mouth them at cocktail parties, and people pat you on the back and tell you what a good fellow you are. But now you're lecturing on cruise ships, and if you get out of this one you'll lecture on another cruise ship or start another consulting business or skip away again from what your destiny is, from what will bring meaning into your life. And if you're going to continue doing that, then you might as well die out here. But if you want to get serious about your ideals, that's another matter."

John describes the exchange as "a stark, finger-in-the-light-socket moment with my Maker. I just looked up and said, 'Okay, I get it. I understand.' And at that instant—and I know this sounds like the ending of a bad movie—but at that *exact* instant, a Coast Guard cutter came crashing through this wild storm, headed straight for us."

After the last cruise of the *Prinsendam,* John headed back to New York City and, with the zeal of the born-again, began developing what he called "Change the World" seminars where he taught nonviolent ways to deal with conflict. "People thought I was completely crazy. I lost all my Foreign Service friends. But the important thing was that I finally had to exercise the real courage of my convictions, to undergo the embarrassment of feeling totally inept, the pain of losing friends, the very real fear of being up there without a net. But never mind that. I was doing it. I was setting the wheels in motion, making the brave decisions, not looking back. I was *moving!*"

Shortly thereafter, with the kind of uncanny fortune that so often seems to accompany the casting of one's lot with destiny, John met, fell in love and began collaborating with a woman named Ann Medlock, who was then hammering out press releases on a portable typewriter on her dining room table.

She was starting up an organization she called the Giraffe Project, which is dedicated to publicizing stories of people who "stick their necks out for the common good." John eventually became the executive director, working with Ann to move people to "courageous, compassionate acts." He also became a popular keynote speaker.

⤳

The power of like attracting like played a role not only in the outcome of John's experience but also in the very form it took. The extent of his avoidance was so great, the borders of his ego so well-defended, his need for status so entrenched, and his life itself so replete with violence, that an event of maximum amplitude was needed to bring him around. The two-by-four approach.

An affinity between a drama taking place inside us and a drama occurring on the outside indicates the presence of an immanent meaning. Movement is not far behind, *if* we are willing to be moved by our encounters, to be guided and persuaded and changed by them, and to ask of them, "What are you here to teach me?" Our experiences will then seem less like mere events and more like replies to the unspoken questions we put to the world just by living our lives. They will begin to seem as though they're happening not just *to* us, but *for* us, and the world will no longer seem so anonymous and random. It will be personal and purposeful.

THE CALL OF THE WORLD

That which oppresses me, is it my soul
trying to come out in the open,
or the soul of the world knocking
at my heart for its entrance?
— RABINDRANATH TAGORE

When I play the piano, I sometimes finish a piece by holding my foot on the sustain pedal and listening intently as the sound fades and eventually merges with the surrounding silence. When the last note is barely audible, there is a moment when I'm not certain if I'm still hearing the note or imagining it, whether it's part of me or part of the world.

No matter how hard I struggle to discern where I leave off and others begin, ultimately I find that there's no telling. I cannot convince myself that there *is* such a place. I cannot find a ramrod boundary line, only watery expanses, and in the diminuendo I'm always being carried out into the world. I grapple with a question once posed by the psychologist June Singer: "The space between us, is it a space that separates us or a space that unites us?"

The world continually reminds us that our calls both do and do not belong solely to us. Just as calls issue from our own bodies in the form of symptoms, they also come from the body politic, of which we're each single cells. Where an affinity of wounds connects us to others, where the world in its shocking condition touches our lives in a personal way, we can find ourselves responding to a call and turning from sympathizers to activists.

What we each determine is a fitting response is entirely subjective. One person might take on multinational corporations or federal laws or the plight of an entire race of people, another might adopt a child from the Third World, and yet another might simply sweep the street in front of the shop every morning. For some, all the activism they can handle in this life is in trying to heal their own souls, though by most accounts this *is* the work of the world. Contemplative nuns and monks, writers, and most artists serve the world best, for instance, in solitude. They touch the world most intimately when they're completely alone, conferring their medicine through prayer and painting, through writing books and working the beads. They may seldom see a soul yet be engaged in the deepest soul work, which simultaneously serves the greater community.

The world never stops calling, never stops acting as though it belongs to us, and its pain is always gathering force like storms offshore. It sends out flares the way we send signals out into space, always hoping that someone will come across them, will understand what they mean, will trace the calls. It shouts to us from the sickroom, from the cold calculus of the daily news, and from whatever we can't stand to look at and so avert our eyes. The world gets harder and harder to ignore as it gets smaller and its problems bigger, as whatever hits the fan gets a little more evenly distributed.

While working in the civil rights movement many years ago, Bo Lozoff learned the dangers of becoming sensitized to the world. When you recognize that the world has many faces and that sometimes it's the face of someone stricken and in pain, and other times the face of a Gorgon who can turn you to stone with a single glance, your heart can break in many places. In fact, the human heart is incapable of containing the world's suffering *without* breaking. Yet only by breaking does it make room for the world's suffering.

The trouble with trying to change the world, I once heard someone say, is that *weeks* can go by and nothing happens. Bo Lozoff learned that if we wait to tend to suffering until we've dealt with our own, we'll never get around to wiping away so much as a single teardrop of anyone else's. Find the form of suffering that touches you most, he says, find where someone else cries and you taste salt, and go there! He learned to follow the exhortation of Norman Mailer, who once said that "with the pride of the artist, you must blow against the walls of every power that exists, the small trumpet of your defiance."

The walls against which Bo Lozoff blows his horn typically have barred windows and are made of concrete that is several feet thick. Bo and his wife, Sita, are the founders and directors of the Prison Ashram Project out of North Carolina, which is dedicated to teaching prisoners to use their time for inner growth, their cells as ashrams, and to think of themselves as prisoner monks rather than convicts.

Having taken part in the civil rights movement and spent time in spiritual ashrams studying karma yoga, the yoga of service, Bo felt himself "primed for a way to serve." In 1972, when he was twenty-five, the world obliged, "though it was certainly different from anything I would have dreamed of doing." While visiting his brother-in-law, who was in prison in Indiana for a drug bust, they talked about a particular prison guard. "That guy," his brother-in-law said, "is the only human being who works in this joint. If it wasn't for him, I'd have been chopped meat a couple of times over. He's a righteous dude."

"I could feel the depth of admiration he had for this guy," Bo says. "The guard was a decent person, instead of corrupt or brutal. And that was the remark that went in deep someplace and started bothering me." On the drive back to North Carolina, he replayed their conversation over and over and kept seeing the image of the guard in his head. Twenty miles from home, he passed a sign by the side of the road: NEW FEDERAL PRISON BEING BUILT ON THIS SPOT.

He applied there to be a prison guard but was turned down. The warden, though, was interested in his ideas about yoga and meditation classes at the prison and asked him to put together a proposal. Within an hour he was making plane reservations for Bo to fly to Washington, D.C., to talk about it with the heavyweights at the Bureau of Prisons, and within a very short time, Bo and Sita were teaching in prisons all over the country—without degrees, credentials, certificates, or any formal training—and doing it because they were perfectly suited to provide something missing in the world. "You've got to stay open to the touch of madness in the world," Bo says. "You never expect the wild card, but it's there."

You also have to stay open to the possibility that what you think is the calling is only the foothills of a much larger mountain. "I assumed that being a prison guard was the calling," Bo says, "but it was prison ministry. It was offering something that's lacking in the prison environment—spiritual friendship—which is evident in the sixty to seventy letters we get every day from all over the world. If no matter what I had followed that first inclination to be a prison guard, then the Prison Ashram Project wouldn't be what it is, which is worldwide.

"All personal calls eventually become calls to service," Bo says. "All yoga becomes karma yoga at some point, and that's as it should be."

SYNCHRONICITIES

In the fall of 1982, toward the end of my eight-year tenure as a reporter for the *Cincinnati Enquirer,* I was given a most elegant job offer. Gannett, the company that owned the newspaper, was starting up what they were calling America's first national daily, *USA Today,* and they were comparing it, in the high-flown spirit of maiden voyages, to France's *Le Monde* and Russia's *Pravda.*

Gannett took a hundred or so reporters from nearly that many of its newspapers and offered them a kind of trial subscription. If at the end of four months the paper flew and you fit, you became a journalist in Washington, D.C., working for "the nation's newspaper." If it didn't fly or you didn't fit, you were guaranteed your job back at whatever paper they took you from. I leapt at the chance and considered it a mere technicality that I sublet my apartment in Cincinnati instead of closing up shop. It never entered my mind that I would be coming back.

When I did, I was despondent and began what a friend later referred to as my Blue Period. I had known for years that I was ripe for change and had thought the move to D.C. was it. But when I was sent back home due to a bad "fit," I felt knocked completely out of my saddle, lost and embarrassed, and I utterly lacked any answer to the question "Now what?"

A few days after returning, I was driving home from work listening to a song by the Eagles called "Desperado." As I pulled to the curb in front of my apartment, the last line I heard before turning the engine off referred to the queen of hearts, and as I opened the door and stepped out, there on the curb next to my left foot was a playing card: the queen of hearts.

I stood absolutely dumbfounded, wondering what fate could possibly be trying to communicate to me with such a gesture. When I mentioned the incident to a friend that evening, she said, with an extravagant quality of assuredness, that when you're on the right path, the universe winks and nods at you from time to time, to let you know. She also said that once you start noticing these little cosmic cairns, once you understand that you're on a path at all, you'll begin to see them everywhere. It's what happened, she reminded me, when I bought my Toyota and suddenly began seeing Toyotas everywhere, and when I started noticing sexism in the language and thereafter couldn't *not* notice it.

I didn't know I was even *on* a path, I told my friend, much less whether it was the right one. I simply found myself unable to make heads or tails of the episode and ended up filing it under Unexplained Phenomena, which for me include déjà vu, extrasensory perception, spontaneous healing, water witching, and certain incomprehensible acts of forgiveness.

Even more remarkable than finding that card was that over the next few years, as I searched for a sense of direction, I found *five more* queen playing cards in improbable locations, such as a sand dune in Oregon and a mountain wilderness in Colorado six miles from the nearest trailhead. It made *The Twilight Zone* seem like *Mister Rogers' Neighborhood.* Each time I found another queen card, the sheer unthinkability of the occurrence took another giant step forward, and eventually the synchronicities went so far beyond the laws of probability that I only barely hesitate to say it's *impossible* that there was nothing more going on than blind chance and dumb luck. Such an adroit arrangement of events and timing—such stagecraft—seemed orchestrated by something with wits.

Still, the phenomenon became more inscrutable with each find, though it also made more and more sense. A pattern—more, a passageway—emerged; the scraps of a treasure map began slowly fitting together. "To ascribe intention to chance is either the height of absurdity or the depth of profundity, according to the way in which we understand it," the philosopher Arthur Schopenhauer once wrote in an essay entitled, "On the Apparent Design in the Fate of the Individual," which gives away how *he* understood it.

I came to understand this rather profound administering of chance as directing me toward something that both my writing and my life needed at that time: more heart, less head; more intuition, less intellect; more confessing, less preaching; more of the inner life, the emotional life, the life of the senses; more listening, more following, more of what Carl Jung referred to as the anima, the force of the feminine in a man's life. The queen, of course, is the *archetype* of femininity—of powerful femininity—and I felt myself being compelled toward this energy by the kind of meaningful coincidence that Jung called synchronicity.

Synchronicities are events connected to one another not strictly by cause and effect, but by what in classical times were known as *sympathies*. This is the belief that an acausal affinity exists between events inside and outside ourselves—a cross-talk between the conscious and the unconscious, mind and matter, humanity and nature—all of which is governed by a certain species of gravity.

We have only to look at our own bodies to appreciate that such a rapport exists. Seven-tenths of both the human body and the planet Earth are composed of water. The whorls of our fingerprints are remarkably similar to those found in wood, shell, and bone. The bronchial tubes that fan out into our lungs look like river deltas when seen from above or like tree limbs as they divide into branches and twigs. Even our superstitions are evidence that in some primitive part of our psyches we all believe that we can influence the force that operates in synchronicities: We blow on dice, wear our lucky gym shorts to an important basketball game, and beseech Lady Luck for favors.

Jung believed that synchronicities mirror deep psychological processes, carry messages the way dreams do, and take on meaning and provide guidance to the degree that they correspond to emotional states and inner experiences—to thoughts, feelings, visions, dreams, and premonitions. For example, you're trying to decide whether to say yes or no to a particular opportunity, and while driving on the freeway someone suddenly cuts in front of you and you notice the bumper sticker: JUST DO IT!

Or you're struggling to focus your energies and not spread yourself so thin and scatter your interests and attentions among too many projects. While taking photographs one afternoon, you drop your wide-angle lens, and it shatters.

Or you're worried about the isolation of moving to a small town, worried that you'll be bored for lack of stimulation, wondering how you'll cope without a decent coffeehouse and the ability to get a pizza at 2 A.M., and a few days before leaving, while out on a hike miles from anywhere, you find a fortune cookie message: "You discover pleasure in your own company, and rely on your mind to occupy you."

Synchronicities can be, at one end of the spectrum, stupefyingly obvious: Allan Combs, coauthor of *Synchronicity,* relates the story of a friend who was trying to decide which of two women to marry. One of the women was named Julie. He then saw a license plate that read JULIE4U. A newspaper article I read several years ago told another such story, of a woman who was trying to decide whether to stay in her church choir group. While driving home from what she thought might be her last choir meeting, she saw an image of Jesus in a billboard advertisement for spaghetti, which she took as a sign that she was meant to say in the choir.

At the other extreme, synchronicities can be tremendously subtle: You've just made up your mind about a course of action when a small dark cloud, the only one in the sky, momentarily obscures the sun, or a door slams, or someone drops a book; you get just enough of a jiggle to give you pause.

Perhaps synchronicities, like dreams and symptoms, are happening all the time and we simply don't notice them until they reach a certain level of explicitness—which may be different for each of us. Maybe they have to shout and wave flags, splash their perfume around, and put on sequins and dance a hootchy-kootchy. In the Age of Information, a lot competes for our attention.

We derive meaning from "just coincidence" when an external event matches up with an event on the inside. It doesn't always. You might be sitting in a waiting room, for instance, reading a magazine article about George Gershwin, when the receptionist sticks her head out the door and calls for the next patient, a Mr. Gershwin, and as outlandish as this may seem to you, if it finds no hook on the inside, it's only an amazing coincidence and not a synchronicity. If it means something to you, however, then it's amazing *and* potentially instructive.

Synchronicities are instructive, Jung felt, because they seem related to the growth process he called individuation, which is the work of becoming ourselves and making ourselves distinct from our surroundings, from the grabby dictates of the collective and the expectations of others. One way synchronicities may do this, he said, is by reflecting—or perhaps projecting onto events in the outer world—something we already know but don't know we know: the authentic self as it's encoded in the soul. The queen cards thus act as signs for me to trust what my heart knows. The fortune cookie mirrors your intuition that the move is going to turn out all right. The JULIE4U license plate is an indication that you already know the answer to your dilemma. The Jesus-in-the-spaghetti becomes your way of seeing what you unconsciously *want* to see.

A synchronicity is a coincidence that has an analogue in the psyche. Depending on how we understand meaningful coincidence, it can inform us, primarily through intuition, how near or far we are from what Carlos Castaneda calls "the path with heart." Among shamanic cultures, says anthropologist Michael Harner in *The Way of the Shaman,* synchronicities are considered one of the signs of a certain fidelity to psychophysical fitness, "a kind of homing beacon analogous to a radio directional signal indicating that the right procedures and methods are being employed." Synchronicities can therefore help us follow the right paths and procedures, and following them can in turn bring on synchronicities. As chemist Louis Pasteur said, "Did you ever observe to whom the accidents happen? Chance favors the prepared mind."

In the movie *Grand Canyon,* a woman finds a baby. She believes this is a reply to an unspoken yearning inside her. When she tells her husband she wants to keep the baby, he is immediately overcome with a migraine. In frustration, she shakes him and says, "A headache is an inappropriate response to a miracle."

This was easy for *her* to say, since it was her miracle not his, but she had a good point. Synchronicities are minor miracles, little mysteries that point to a bigger one, perhaps a central one, of which we are a part. One of the prominent images in twentieth-century literature, says Mark Holland, the other coauthor of *Synchronicity,* is that of the wasteland, which speaks of the absence of mystery. "The wind crosses the brown land, unheard," wrote T. S. Eliot in his poem *The Waste Land,* "and the nymphs are departed."

In contemplating synchronicities, Mark says, "Don't just marvel at the laws of probability, but wonder at their meaning. They're there to remind us to think about what we're doing, to pay attention, but also to deepen the mystery of life. Ultimately, I think, a living symbol like this can't be reduced to intelligibility, and it's possible to get a bit harebrained about reading meaning into synchronicities, going symbol-hunting, trying too hard." After all, he says, synchronicities aren't entirely beyond the laws of probability, and a certain number of amazing coincidences are *bound* to happen in the course of life. We're amazed when we think of a friend and he suddenly calls, but we fail to consider all the times we thought of him in the past and he didn't call.

Still, Mark says, "The primary reality of synchronicities is emotional, not intellectual. The reason they're there is to make us feel something, and the feeling that our lives are rich and worth our reflection comes in part from our sense of the depth and mystery of life."

Perhaps synchronicities appear for no other purpose than to jostle our skepticism and open our minds to the existence of the inexplicable and the numinous in our lives, whether we believe in these dimensions or not. Some things can't be grasped with the mind but can only be cupped, as one would cup a palmful of water. Perhaps synchronicities help us reflect on the beauty and harmony in life, says author Milan Kundera, and if we're blind to them, "we deprive our lives of a dimension of beauty, because synchronicities are composed like music."

Maybe the most important thing synchronicities bring us is astonishment. How often, in the course of a day or a week or a month, do we find ourselves thunderstruck, flabbergasted at life, amazed by its finesse? Synchronicities are like the glimpse of a wild animal seldom seen, the discovery of an arrowhead or a geode, the return of your wallet by some Good Samaritan. Far removed from the mundaneness that seems to characterize such a vast portion of daily life, they help reconnect us to our awe. Given the tyranny of the commonplace, what a service!

Synchronicities remind us that the world is shot through with mystery and extravagant gesture, and that we ought to be amazed that *any* of it happens. We need only to look out into space to remember that life itself, the boisterous diversity and design of it, is utterly improbable. In the entire known universe, which covers considerable acreage by now, there isn't a single scrap of life anywhere else but here. Given that improbability is so basic to the world, synchronicities are really no more than reminders, emanations, sparks thrown up by a great fire.

A REALLY FIRST-CLASS UNIVERSE

To make sense of synchronicities, to be astounded by them, it helps to set aside the idea that the universe and our part in it unfold logically. We also need to reconsider the belief that what goes on inside us is entirely separate from what goes on outside us, that subjective reality and objective reality are unaffiliated.

In his book *Healing Words,* physician Larry Dossey presents abundant evidence from both anecdote and controlled laboratory studies of the existence and *importance* of what he calls nonlocal events. An example of a nonlocal event is the proven healing effects of prayer. When we pray, Dossey says, the mind takes leave of the body to which we believe it is bound and travels in both space and time to affect the health of another.

As long as 2,500 years ago, the Greek physician Hippocrates understood nonlocality. "There is one common flow," he said, "one common breathing. All things are in sympathy." The individual and the world, inner and outer, are like two mirrors set face-to-face; they reflect each other in an infinite number of ways. The calls we receive through synchronicities may simply be echoes.

Scientists, largely through quantum physics, are coming to the empirical understanding of something that mystics and medicine men, poets and priest-esses, and even a handful of mathematicians have known for millennia: The world is dynamic and its parts are inseparable. Seemingly random events in nature can correspond to events in human lives and be related to psychological processes. "Everywhere I turn," Freud once remarked, "I find that a poet has been there before me."

If inner processes can influence outer ones and draw synchronicities to us, then perhaps this is no stranger than the fact that outer events, such as the position of the moon and the stars, influence matters on Earth and in people's lives. Perhaps, too, both scenarios are presided over not so much by mechanical cause and effect—by a kneebone-connected-to-the-thighbone principle—but by some overarching coherence, some wink-and-a-nod affinity between the two. "A really first-class universe," says mathematician Rudy Rucker in *The Fourth Dimension,* "must include a mixture of both sorts of patterning."

Many human experiences are simply not explainable by straight cause-and-effect reasoning, yet they are ubiquitous—all forms of divination and psychic phenomena, spontaneous remissions, miracles, luck, and synchronicity. All of these suggest the presence of some agency beyond the bounds of normal probability, consciousness, and even belief. Ultimately the most useful question may not be why synchronicities happen or what causes them but, as Marie-Louise von Franz writes in *On Divination and Synchronicity,* "What likes to happen together in a meaningful way in the same moment? What tends to happen together in time?"

Causality itself is a fairly rough science, which I learned after an intriguing confrontation in a philosophy class in college. The professor was upbraiding a student who was late, yet again, to class. The conversation went something like this:

PROFESSOR: What caused you to be late?

STUDENT: My car got a flat.

PROFESSOR: What caused your car to get a flat?

STUDENT: I hit a pothole.

PROFESSOR: And what do you suppose caused the pothole to be there?

STUDENT: I guess the Department of Transportation didn't have enough money to fix it.

PROFESSOR: And what caused the Department of Transportation to be in such dire straits?

STUDENT: Probably the president cutting their budget.

PROFESSOR: So, you're telling me that the President of the United States caused you to be late to class again today!?

In the strictest sense, the "cause" of anything is lost in the maze of time, and no starting date can possibly be affixed to anything with certainty and without the risk of absurdity. "Doubt may be an uncomfortable condition," the philosopher and dramatist Voltaire once said, "but certainty is a ridiculous one."

No one has been able to fully explain synchronicity, so perhaps we should simply accept it as a wild card *and* an ordering principle, the height of absurdity *and* the depth of profundity, and as a crack in the door through which we can catch sight of the nymphs.

THE TRICK IN TRICKSTER

The paradoxical nature of synchronicities makes it fitting that the god most closely associated with them is Hermes, the trickster god in Western mythology. Known as Coyote to the Plains Indians, Maui to the Hawaiians, Krishna to the Hindus, and Edshu to the West Africans, Hermes is both clown and creator and possesses the paradoxical power both to order and undermine. He makes the cosmic consommé and then spits in the soup. He carries his genitals in a box on his back, eats his own intestines when they catch on fire, and yet he creates the world. He's a conniver but also a carrier of souls. He's the patron saint of overturned applecarts. He's the worm in Newton's apple, the *dog* in *dogma,* the *con* in *consequence,* the *nor* in *normal,* the *anal* in *analysis.*

Hermes is also the god of boundaries, transitions, and travelers. Those like Jung who have studied synchronicities consider them boundary events. These tend to cluster at points of transition in our lives and to accompany periods of transformation and emotional intensity: midlife, changes of career and changes of heart, shifts in gear, reversals of fortune, births and deaths both physical and psychological, travel, even meditation and prayer.

In *The Global Brain,* Peter Russell asserts that meditation and synchronicity are connected. The more you meditate, the more synchronicities you will find. The same is true with prayer. The British archbishop William Temple once said, "When I pray, coincidences start to happen. When I don't pray, they don't happen." One reason for this, says Russell, is that meditation and prayer carry ordinary consciousness out to its borders. While engaging in these activities we're in a sort of transition zone between consciousness and unconsciousness, which is where Hermes, that mongrel messenger god, carries out his daily mail runs.

Michael Talbot, author of *The Holographic Universe,* feels that synchronicities not only point to transitions and emerge from them but also tend to peak when the shift is just about to happen. They may even play a starring role in that shift. One of the classic stories in the lore of synchronicity is of precisely this nature: Carl Jung had a patient whose grimly rational approach to life was making it difficult for her to benefit from therapy. During one session, she related a dream involving a scarab beetle, which Jung knew from Egyptian mythology was associated with rebirth. He was just about to tell her this when he heard a tapping on the window, and when he looked, he saw a gold-green scarab beetle. He opened the window, and when it flew in he caught it in his hand, presented it to the astonished woman, and said, "Here is your scarab." It had the desired effect of puncturing a hole in her Cartesian balloon, and she commenced to respond quite favorably to the treatment.

The same pattern of synchronicity-preceding-change has occurred in my own life, and on one occasion it occurred in a manner strikingly similar to Jung's scarab story. Ten years after I found the first queen card, I was once again at a point of passage, a make-or-break time in the dual arenas of work and love. I felt called to make structural rather than just cosmetic changes that would redefine who I was, challenge some of the most fundamental habits of my life, and make most of my previous efforts at inner work seem like playing pattycake. Just prior to making some of these tectonic changes, I had the following experience.

The night before I was to fly to Austin to teach a seminar, I was reading about the Meso-American Indian belief in bats as symbols of rebirth. The next day, sitting by the river that flowed behind my hotel in Austin, near a place called the Congress Street Bridge, I witnessed one of the most extraordinary displays of urban wildlife in the world. Just before sunset, a million Mexican free-tailed bats, the largest colony in North America, began pouring out from beneath that bridge in search of food. For a full half hour they swarmed into the darkening sky in a torrent of hunger and energy and rebirth, and I sat there once again transfixed until the river turned a dark orange and the mosquitoes began to bite.

As I walked back to my hotel room, the bats were still ribboning down-stream by the thousands, and it crossed my mind that since the setting for this remarkable synchronicity was a bridge, Hermes must certainly have had a hand in it.

part three

INVOKING

CALLS

eight

THE
PORTALS OF
ART

Art therapist Rudolph Arnheim claims that the shape that most children from all cultures tend to draw first is the circle. Perhaps it's the shape of mother's face, the sun or moon, the dream of a nest. Or is it the tunnel at the end of the womb and their parents' mouths agape at their birth?

Art making, whether conjured by a stick in the dirt or generated by computers, is a primitive impulse, something we express instinctively. It draws out of us shapes, images, and memories that may not even belong to us personally but that we can use to fashion a self-portrait and to engage in the process of self-discovery that is so essential to the discernment of a calling. These pursuits are all presided over by the Muses—those daughters of Zeus and Mnemosyne, the goddess of memory who knew everything that happened since the beginning of time. Each Muse took her mother's memories and used them differently, to create verse, music, dance, song, mime.

We can use art to bring us in line with our callings. Through it we have access to timeless sources of wisdom in ourselves, deep drives, and memories of who we really are. "Art is an articulator of the soul's uncensored purpose and deepest will," writes Shaun McNiff in *Art as Medicine*. Through it we can make scale models and blueprints of our calls, we can see them in writing and in pictures, we can conjure up visual aids. Through art we can also reactivate the mind of the child within us, which knows what it knows with great simplicity and accuracy. The last time that many of us made art was when we *were* children. In most of us, an artist died young and an adult survived.

The last time many of us engaged in *play* was when we were children, too, when we derived pleasure not only from building up our blocks but also from knocking them down. Play is the springhead of discovery, the heart of art, the exploratory urge made manifest, and every utilitarian pursuit, as the philosopher Eric Hoffer once said (including the search for a calling), evolved from the nonutilitarian pursuit of play and tinkering. "Man as artist is far more ancient than man as worker."

Most of us, unfortunately, are good for a quote from the Protestant work ethic, but not so good at giving over an afternoon to fire up the imagination, sinking our hands into the prima materia, playing with paints or music, squeezing clay through our fingers, or making art not for self-discovery but for the sheer sensuous pleasure of it. This is why anthropologist Margaret Mead once said that education would never work unless it was based on art, by which she meant that *all* subjects should be taught in the spirit of exploration, imagination, and play. "We talk too much," said the poet and dramatist Johann Goethe. "We should talk less and draw more."

Some years ago, I sat down and divided a piece of paper into three columns and made lists comparing the characteristics of the three arts to which I have devoted most of my own creative energies: writing, piano playing, and drawing. When I was finished, I realized that the three lists were identical, that all these arts are leavened by the same ingredients: composition, tone, drama, color, surprise. They are all glass-bottom boats over the unconscious. They all render self-portraits and invite contemplation, they all remark on the need for balance between centeredness and eccentricity, and they all involve discerning priorities: what must be kept and what must be discarded, what must be left in and what left out, what's important to express and what's not important.

These three arts all pit the creator against the uncreated, against the sheer compulsion to make something new under the sun—a sound never heard, an image never imagined, a solution never thought of. They all teach that there is a process to any kind of creativity. There are certain steps to go through that cannot be short-circuited. Instant art, like instant intimacy, requires no real commitment. Like dreams, these arts all present information that's on the brink of consciousness. They demonstrate the true relationship between inspiration and perspiration and that, as Thomas Edison once observed, creativity (or a calling) is 2 percent illumination and the rest love and discipline. We are each Ulysses, lashed to the mast and ravished by the Sirens' song, and we are also his crew, ears plugged for safekeeping, bent over our oars and surely wondering who is the more bereft, Ulysses for having to hear the song or ourselves for being unable to.

All artistic practices, says writer Bharati Mukherjee, are "satellite dishes for hearing the signals the soul sends out," and each art form individually offers unique contributions to the work of discerning calls. Drawing and painting expand our ability to *visualize*. Writing helps us tap into the *stories* we tell about our lives. Dance increases our *range of movement* and shows us how we position ourselves and move through the world. Through drama we *act* on what we know.

Ultimately, creativity and discernment have much in common. They increase our ability to "draw out," to call into being, what didn't exist in our lives before. We do a rain dance, we say the magic words, we pull from Chaos a pinch of this and a dash of that, we take a lump of clay and breathe life into its nostrils. Just as sculptors often speak of *freeing* forms from stone or wood rather than creating them, we, too, through the artistic process, work to liberate the spirit trapped in matter, the soul implicit in what the alchemists called the *massa confusa* of our lives. We work—and ideally we learn—to separate our own calls from the background noise.

This is exactly why I began my own journal writing at the age of nineteen, and I have kept at it every year since. I was, at that time, contemplating making the first big decision of my independent young life—to quit the college that I hated even though I had financial aid and transfer to one that offered classes in journalism. I not only had to discern a calling, but I also had to contend with much background noise, including my parents' confoundment and the loss of the financial aid.

The writing in my journal—the hours of unabashed and occasionally runny and confessional writing and storytelling I did in the months before that decision—was, as Marvin Barrett describes in a memoir called *Spare Days,* like the logs kept by "the captains of derelict ships, doomed wanderers in the desert, mountain climbers lost above the timberline, men in lifeboats, or huddled, writing beside wrecks of one sort or another in some kind of wilderness." The writing and self-reflection helped me find my own voice in the wilderness, as well as clarity and courage. Keeping a journal mirrored my struggle and called me deeper into it. It was instrumental in precipitating the change I eventually made because the simple act of recording my behavior interfered with that behavior. It gave me a quasi-outside perspective on myself and the opportunity to make adjustments.

Through that first journal I discovered that although there's a social language I'm compelled to speak and often struggle mightily to make my own, there's also a private language, a way I speak only to myself. Each time I use it I strengthen my connection to myself. The journal thus became a safe place in which to rehearse my feelings before articulating them to others. But when I began it I was paranoid that someone might get his hands on it, so on the first page I wrote, "This is a personal journal. You can think about this or you can turn the page." On the second page, writ large, was a rather blunt expletive.

Initially it was unsettling to put my thoughts down on paper, unnerving to see them all there in black and white and to read thoughts I'd often kept private even from myself. My writing in that journal seemed at the time embarrassing and dangerous, though no more dangerous, I thought, than *not* writing it.

By beginning that journal I took on the fate of Scheherazade, the queen whose stories make up the *Arabian Nights.* She became, by choice, the wife of the sultan of Persia, who had decreed that every woman he married would be killed on the morning after the wedding. On the day of their wedding, Scheherazade began telling the sultan a story, but she stopped just short of the climax. The sultan agreed to let her live one more day so that she could finish the story. On the next day, she finished it and began another, and again the sultan let her live so that she could finish her story. After 1001 nights and 1001 stories, the sultan, who by now had fallen in love with Scheherazade, finally agreed to repeal his savage law.

I, too, felt that if I stopped writing, stopped telling stories, I would place myself in grave danger and would lose a critical connection to my own life. By starting that journal, I was initiating a conversation I must have sensed I would have to see all the way through. I was heading up the big hill on the roller coaster, taking on the sultan, peeking in Pandora's box, nibbling at Eden's apple. That which is holy is both sacred and taboo. The Ark of the Covenant and the chalice of the Holy Grail, for instance, are simultaneously sacred and forbidden. Self-knowledge, I think, is likewise holy, and art is perfect for the job of acquiring it.

Thomas Merton said that art attunes the soul to God. Because it brings us into present time and allows us a few blessed minutes or hours of self-forgetfulness where we are wholly absorbed and fascinated, the creative act is a version of what Abraham Maslow called peak experiences, and what others call mystical experiences. When we become immersed in any creative activity, we bring on ourselves a sense of rapt attention, of rapture, of departure from ego, from time and place. We see into the heart of things and get a glimpse of something that was previously hidden. In this way, the creative act is a mystical experience.

DRAWING OUT A CALL

When Anna Halprin was four years old, she first encountered dance by watching her grandfather pray. A Hassidic Jew, he prayed by singing, jumping up and down, and flinging his arms in the air. "He had a long white beard, and I thought he was God, and that God was a dancer."

The sight of her grandfather's ecstatic prayer filled Anna with the belief that dance was a way to pray, a way to connect with whatever was highest or deepest in herself, a way to call on the god that would one day call on her to become a dancer. Following her own creative spirit became a way to follow in the footsteps of God the Creator. D. H. Lawrence declared at the end of his life that art is, at its core, a religious activity.

Perhaps art was the *original* religion and was practiced to put us in sympathy with unseen powers and to invoke the spirits. Anna's mission is to take dance all the way back to the Stone Age, when art—the first art—was as much functional as aesthetic, as much religious as decorative. When the head of a university dance department, frustrated at the lack of a recognizable "performance" in one of Anna's modern dance pieces, wrote in a review that she had set the dance world back a hundred years, the critic obviously didn't realize how conservative that estimate was. Just as the first artists believed that drawing a picture of the animal they were hunting would somehow bring that animal to them or them to it, Anna believes that by invoking the arts we might similarly animate our own lives, call to us whatever is pressing for consciousness and wanting to be awakened.

The most important turning point in Anna's sixty-year career as a dancer propelled her into an entirely new sense of dance as a calling when she began in 1972 to use the medium of *drawing.* Many years before, she had developed a process she called Psycho-Kinetic Visualization, in which people "dance a drawing" by putting into movement the images that well up from the unconscious. By making pictures they are literally "drawing out" messages and giving momentum to them.

Image is psyche, Carl Jung said, and imagery is the language of the unconscious—whether that imagery comes through a drawing, painting, sculpture, or narrative, or a dream. This belief in a correspondence between imagery and the deep self mirrors the ancient belief that a soul could be appropriated by fashioning a likeness of the person to whom the soul belonged—making a voodoo doll, for instance, or even taking a photograph. To some degree, an image *does* capture soul, but more likely the soul of the person who *created* it. Anyone who has ever kept a diary understands the visceral dread that it will fall into the wrong hands and lay their souls bare. For this reason, some people make sure their personal journals are completely illegible to anyone but themselves. Therefore, writes Jungian James Hillman in *Healing Fiction,* "When I ask, 'Where is my soul, how do I meet it, what does it want now?' the answer is, 'Turn to your images.' "

Anna turned to her images and drew a self-portrait on butcher paper. It was a life-size rendition of her body, and in its geographical center, crouched in the middle of her pelvis, was a round, gray mass. It was a drawing she was unable to dance. Initially, she interpreted the mass as the symbol of an embryo, a scene of nativity, but she remained unconvinced by her own explanation because she refused to put it to the test: She refused to dance it.

That night, lying quietly in bed and staring into the dark, she realized that the drawing was trying to tell her something she wasn't willing to look at. The next morning she went right to the phone and called a doctor.

She told him about the drawing and said she wanted him to examine her precisely where she had drawn the gray mass, and when he did, he found colon cancer. She was both shocked and not shocked. During the years she and her dance students had been using the drawing-and-dancing process, they had discovered that premonitory images—drawings prescient of illnesses and accidents, of breakthroughs and transformations—were not uncommon.

Three years after a colostomy, Anna had a recurrence. She said she then knew that she would have to make "drastic changes" in her life. When the doctor began outlining another radical operation and suggesting chemotherapy, she turned to him and said, "Give me two weeks. I want a chance to try something on my own first." That something was another self-portrait, which she described as "the perfect picture of health. I'm young, brightly colored, with my hair blowing in the wind, full of vitality. I suppose I thought that if I drew myself as healthy, I would become healthy." But again, she couldn't dance it. "I tried, but it just didn't feel right, didn't strike a deep chord, didn't feel like me."

In a fit of frustration, she turned the paper over and drew another image of herself, this one "black and angular and angry and violent." It was a dark, stiff, masculine figure, heavily armored and helmeted, stabbing himself with a knife, the colors all black and red, with blood flowing into a bowl on the ground. This, she knew immediately, was the dance she had to do.

She did it in the company of "witnesses"—family, colleagues, and students without whom, she said, she couldn't have undertaken what turned out to be a physical and emotional ordeal. It was a volcanic dance of rage and purgation not unlike the dances of rage done for the purpose of releasing stored-up anger and grievance by tribes such as the Dagara in West Africa. At the end of this exhausting dance, Anna collapsed and sobbed. "I needed the witnesses there to encourage me to go through with it, to face my fear, to express parts of me I've never given myself permission to express—anger, grief, weakness, and vulnerability. They kept me honest, urging me to go deeper, reinforcing my sounds, calling out parts of the picture I needed to dance."

Only then was she able to turn over the paper and dance the healing image. And only then was she ready to go back to her doctor, whom she presented with one of the great surprises of his medical career: Over the course of barely three weeks, Anna's cancer had completely disappeared and has never returned.

For twenty years afterward, though, Anna withdrew from public performing and worked on some of those drastic changes, on trying to figure out what her next dance steps would be. She especially worked on "my definition of art;

why I danced, who I danced for, what purpose it served in anybody's life." She began searching for ways to make dance more "useful." She edged away from theater toward ritual. She moved into a liminal zone between art and therapy, between dance and healing, and in 1981 she began working with people—through dance and the "expressive arts"—who were confronting life-threatening illnesses such as AIDS and cancer.

Her work with patients is based on what she calls the Five Stages of Healing, which outline a process of "identification, confrontation, release, change, and assimilation" of wounds and loss, personal or communal. She developed "Dancing with Life on the Line," a five-day workshop with a hundred participants structured on the Five Stages, which culminated in their giving a public performance attended by over a thousand people in the San Francisco Bay area.

"I had never had an opportunity to do anything that was so bottom-line. This was the real stuff. This was what I knew I was being called to do with myself and my art, to work with real-life issues: living and dying, birth and aging, union and separation, illness and health. What that one drawing in 1972 released in me was very powerful, a major breakthrough, not just personally but artistically. It opened up a whole new range of possibilities for me as a dancer. I was now able to work with material that had to do with vulnerability and sadness and anger, and to work with the kind of people who inspire me most, those who are willing to face their life-and-death situations, to face what they need to face to move on in their lives, to give up their status quos."

᠅

Soul is closer to movement than it is to fixity, said Socrates, and loss of soul is the condition of being stuck—fixated on something, as the psychologists would say—and overcome by the downward-pushing forces that govern all moving bodies: gravity and inertia. The arts, being about creativity and therefore about change, are ideal for leading us toward movement, whether we do a dance with life on the line or oscillate between stepping up to a canvas and stepping back or go in hot pursuit of a calling.

It was a single image that moved Anna Halprin to redirect her life and her work, and it was a single image—a memory—that guided her back from her long moratorium on public performing. In her first performance in twenty years, done for her children and grandchildren, she reenacted her grandfather's ecstatic religious dancing.

THE GENIUS IN THE BOTTLE

I know a chemist who teaches enology—the study of wine—at the University of California. She has a hair-trigger gag reflex for the sort of impressionistic muddle that passes for common nomenclature in the wine industry, and whenever she attends a wine-tasting and someone begins waxing glassy-eyed about how this or that wine is "adventurous yet unassuming," "flushed with heroic tonalities," "light but perspicacious," or "confident with restrained aromatic notes," people always look to see her reaction. She tries to be nice. It isn't always easy.

"We need to demystify this thing," she once told me. "It's such a pompous affair. Consumers end up saying, 'God, I don't know what I want. I'm ignorant. I'll just have a beer.' "

The wine world reminds me a lot of the art world. Far too many people feel unqualified to create art, insisting that they're not "the creative type." But when we leave art only to "artists," we lose touch with our own artfulness, our own creativity and inventiveness, and block a portal through which great vigor and intelligence can make their way to us. We distance ourselves from art when we professionalize it, just as we disassociate from our own healing powers when we place responsibility for healing only in the hands of "healers." This creates a system in which *we* do all the suffering and healers do all the healing.

We all possess creativity, however, although we may not all have the courage to act on it. Even if you have tuned out your creative impulses to draw or write or make music, you still can't entirely amputate creativity from your life. At the very least it will find its way into your dreams and fantasies. When you go out into the garden and cut some flowers and arrange them in a vase with the yellows in front and the purples behind and the blues in between, you're being an artist. When you doodle while talking to your father on the telephone, you're drawing art out of the unconscious, which is where all art has its source. When you absentmindedly whistle while you work, you're making music. When you sit down to write a letter to a friend, you're writing. When you tap on the desk with your fingers, you're drumming.

If self-discovery is your intention in art making, if you want to draw out the calls that are embedded deep in your soul, then the more emphasis you put on formal standards of art and aesthetics, the less raw personality you will see in whatever you create. If you make discerning your callings your priority, then the "quality" of your creative efforts is determined by how *honest* they are, how true the expressions are to your inner experiences. It is not determined by popularity, or marketability, or technique, or talent. Think of yourself as having genius in the original sense of the word, which meant having a genie, a guardian spirit, which *everyone* possesses—even animals.

In 1980, a young Indian elephant named Siri was noticed making scratches on the floor of her enclosure with a pebble. Her keeper started providing her with pencil and drawing pad. He held the pad in his lap. Though not rewarded in any way, Siri responded by producing dozens of abstract drawings, scribblings, and doodlings. The keeper sent them to a journalist, who sent them on to various scientists and artists, including the painter Willem de Kooning, who, before reading the cover letter, exclaimed that they possessed "flair and decisiveness and originality." Upon learning the identity of their maker, he remarked, "That's a damned talented elephant."

If we're more concerned with virtuosity than with expression and spontaneity or more intent on technique than on emotion or more concerned with the end product than the process and what the painter Robert Henri called "the art spirit," we're going to suffer a certain self-consciousness around art. It's been shown that when people attempting to make art know that they're being watched, they feel cowed, and their art is less spontaneous and expressive.

Transcending self-consciousness about art making is an art in itself, even when you're completely alone. Yet it often seems that the more you know about art, the easier it is to be intimidated. For example, I'm in the habit of reading a series of books called *The Best American Essays,* which is published annually. Each volume is compiled by a different guest editor whose sole opinion determines what constitutes the "best" American essays that year. The essays themselves are not so intimidating, but the biographical notes about the essayists, which appear in the back of the book, often *are* intimidating. These writers invariably have titles like "The Edmund G. Fluckermeyer Distinguished Professor of Letters at Harvard University, author of thirty-five books, sixteen of them translations from the ancient Sumerian, she is currently working on a new book on the philosophical disenfranchisement of abstract art. She and her husband—a famous writer or painter—have homes in both New York City *and* Cape Cod."

We don't need to compare ourselves to anyone else in order to feel intimidated, however. Our own standards are quite sufficient to put us at what a young acquaintance of mine calls "the fuzzy end of the lollipop," especially if our art resembles something rendered by a first-grader. By first grade most of us were well into trading off spontaneity for conformity and had already begun putting the brakes on making pictures, telling stories, dancing around the room, and singing. So when we start up again, it makes perfect sense that we'd pick up where we left off.

In fact, we probably should. Just pick up an oil crayon or colored pencil and simply move it around on a page, see what emerges, see how it feels, see if you can keep your mental mitts off the process. Or wrangle with a lump of clay, which, being entirely tactile, is especially good if you tend to get marooned up in your head; shape it into an emotional self-portrait. Or take scissors to a stack of magazines and put together a collage depicting your state of mind or your hidden self or a composite of the person your parents would love you to be.

Or, as Deena Metzger suggests, write a paragraph every word of which begins with a letter of the alphabet, starting with *A*, going to *Z*—"*All big calls demand elongated fidelity . . .*" or "*A big corpulent dog eats fruit given him in jest . . .*" etc. Then write for ten minutes about some segment of it, a phrase or word that grabs your attention. Or take a mood and make it move. Find out what part of the body it wants to express itself through and then move like an animal or the motion of underwater plants, spin in circles, shout or growl, make horrible faces and scare the ghosts. Or take your camera and pick a theme—change, risk, nurturing, surrender, triumph, conflict—and head out for an afternoon to capture it. Or just take a doodle pad into your next staff meeting.

What we're after is letting the unconscious go on a roll with a paintbrush in its hand, or a hunk of clay, or a keyboard, and granting ourselves permission to speak from the heart. The more we can make explicit that which is implicit in us, the more familiar we become with ourselves, and the more material we make available to our art. We generate momentum, we tap into knowledge that's locked away in memory, and we refuse to wait for divine inspiration to strike.

The technique called *free association* abets this process of self-discovery. Developed by Sigmund Freud, it means any activity—spoken, drawn, danced, sung—that removes the censors from self-expression and allows images, impressions, or emotions to flow unhindered. Free association is about brainstorming, imagining, wool gathering, and the wilder and woolier the better. The motto of free association is "garbage is good."

In free associating, we learn to follow our instincts, says Naomi Newman, an actress with A Traveling Jewish Theater. Naomi considers improvisation (any kind of impromptu composing, whether in music, movement, or drama) to be excellent training for following our physical, sensory, and emotional impulses. "If you feel two impulses," she says, "go with the one that has the greatest risk for you. It will be by far the most interesting." Improvisation has helped foster in her the understanding that, in listening for calls, "the answers don't ultimately come cerebrally. You may discuss a call, contemplate it, weigh the pros and cons, and vacillate, but eventually you just *know*. You feel it."

Here's how free association works: Gather your tools—your charcoals or tape deck, your body or voice, your fingers suspended like bats over the keyboard, ready to drop into flight—and pick a subject, any subject, or formulate a question you want answered. Take ten minutes and begin to write, talk, sing, or dance. Don't stop, don't think, don't let the critic get a word in edgewise. (The critic's proper place is *after* creativity, not on top of it.) Follow your imagination wherever it goes as it breaks into a run and dashes up hills, down hairpin turns, through tunnels and thickets and mud, and into rabbit holes. If you reach a point when you say to yourself, "That's it. There's no more," keep going for another five minutes. Frustration is often an edge, not an ending. If you find yourself blocked, write or sing or draw a picture of being blocked.

When meditating it is easy to be distracted by a blizzarding confetti of noises, self-talk, and the general dither of daily life—the dog barking, the children screaming, the heater rattling, the planes going by overhead. Meditation teachers will usually tell you that distractions are not obstacles to the meditation; they *are* the meditation. So when the dog barks, you say to yourself, "Ah, the dog-bark meditation." The same goes for free association. Blocks aren't blocks to the creativity. They *are* the creativity.

The blocks arise for a reason, though, and free association is not some harmless parlor game. It excavates material from our edges and underbellies and has its glories and perils, such as creating images that don't correspond to the images of ourselves we present to the world, to our families or colleagues, or even to the bathroom mirror. Through free association, through art, we reimagine ourselves, and sometimes the background music is the sound of grind-

ing gears. "You have to be willing to invade your own privacy," writes art therapist Janie Rhyne in *The Gestalt Art Experience.*

But given half a chance, the unconscious will definitely associate with us,
and it is a genius. In keeping a drawing journal, which I began as a way to
encourage and chronicle my passage through a particularly arduous calling, I
have noticed that many of the pictures have some element in them that I was
completely unconscious of having drawn but that spoke volumes. In one
drawing, a man is pushing furiously against a boulder, inside of which is the
distinct image of a female torso, something I didn't see at all until people began
pointing it out, and now it's impossible to miss. In another, the eyes in an
angry face look not angry but sad and fearful, a little subconscious commen-
tary on the active ingredients in anger. In still another drawing my "shadow"—
which I imagined as a malevolent genie coming out of a bottle—wore a
grimace that bore a distinct resemblance to a grin, which provided me with a
startling revelation: He is as much my guardian as my ghoul, depending
entirely on whether I acknowledge his existence or not.

The drawing journal has taught me not only that we are all "creative types"
but also that we are creative deep down. Like dreams, creativity has a life of its
own, an immense imagination, and cannot be talked out of existence by a
mere act of will or forgetfulness.

WHAT   WE   HAVE   LOST

The making of consciousness, James Hillman has said, is nothing more
than the art of conversation, and unconsciousness is nothing more than letting
things fall *out* of conversation. If you were to listen to a tape recording of an
hour of therapy—the attempt at raising consciousness—what you would hear
is simply a conversation, a dialogue, really, between a person and himself or
herself, a powwow with one's own soul, dreams, symptoms, fears, ambitions,
and relationships.

Carl Jung often said that people rarely integrate anything told to them by
others, however, even those they pay dearly for the advice. "It is the things
given them by their own unconscious that make a lasting impression." For this
reason, he devised a form of dialogue he called "active imagination." It involves
the conscious mind deliberately striking up a conversation with the unconscious, with the parts that reside below the waterline, below the threshold of

awareness, and it takes place through the imagination, which Jung considered a liaison between the two. He also felt that active imagination is a surer route into the unconscious than dreams because the conscious mind is involved in imagination rather than asleep.

In active imagination, which can last an hour or a lifetime, we interact with images, voices, characters, our past or future, our work or talents or emotions. We parley with dream figures, real or imagined mentors, parts of ourselves, even with archetypes: the wise old man or woman, the warrior, the fool, the sleeping beauty or the sleeping giant. We tell it how we feel, inquire about how *it* feels, ask for advice, negotiate treaties.

Sometimes we forget that active imagination is supposed to be a dialogue, a matter of call *and* response, give *and* take. Some years ago, I thought I heard a call to write a book about midlife, though I was only thirty-seven at the time. When I mentioned the idea to an editor of my acquaintance, he said, "Oh hell, you're too young. You don't know anything about it yet, and by the time you do, you'll be forty-five and too full of despair to write anything."

I was incensed. I was going to prove him wrong, and I began by mounting an immediate defense. I had *intended* to engage the figure of Doubt in a head-to-head debate, via active imagination, but mostly what I did was sit at my computer for an hour and harrumph, creating a lengthy and indignant monologue that even included calling on expert witnesses like Dante Alighieri, who was thirty-five when he wrote the *Inferno,* which many consider to be Western literature's classic midlife story.

I invited barely a peep from the part of me that might have shared even a shred of the editor's skepticism, but when I stopped foaming at the mouth long enough to ask if he had any rebuttals, I, too, heard an earful. The outcome of the conversation was that I began questioning, and rightly so it turned out, what had appeared to be a true calling but was, in fact, merely the infatuation stage of a false one. The true strength of a calling seems to emerge only when the shadow does, and you get to see how you deal with *that.*

Since the unconscious isn't limited to verbal expression, the ways into dialogue with it are numerous. Any of the arts will do. You can write it down, talk it out, act it up. You can paint it, sculpt it, sing it, or dance it. In *Boundaries of the Soul,* June Singer relates the fascinating story of a "drawing dialogue" a client, Charles, had with an aspect of himself he called his ape-man, who seemed to be calling him to relinquish what Singer calls his "dry, superior, intellectual approach to life."

Charles sat at a table with pencil and paper in front of him and imagined his ape-man sitting next to him. He drew a triangle on the paper and put his pencil down. The ape-man picked it up, drew a circle around the triangle, and put the pencil down. Charles picked it up and drew a square around the circle. They went back and forth like this for some time, conversing with each other by adding shapes onto each others' shapes, until a mandala-like image emerged that was a combination of the two of them, a syzygy of their respective impulses.

Jung said that active imagination is not so much an artistic endeavor as "an attempt to bring people back to nature, because this is what we have lost." It can bring us back into conversation with our instinctual selves, our native intelligences, our indigenous urge to play with the elements, to paint with our fingers and scratch our names in rock, to draw circles and whistle to beat the birds. To Jung, nature isn't opposed to transcendence—it *is* transcendence. "The old wise man," he said, "is really an ape."

To art therapist Shaun McNiff, it's important not merely to converse with the wise man but also to record and contemplate those conversations, to tell creation stories about our art and about the acquaintances we make in making our art. When we tell stories about the images we create and how we created them, when we speak to them and listen to what they have to say, we release art's "expressive medicine," the aspect of art that, as Friedrich Nietzsche once said, is "a saving sorceress, expert at healing." Images come through us like children, McNiff adds, "and they inherit biological and psychic traits. But, like children, they also have autonomous lives and souls that quickly begin to influence and change, and even heal, the lives of their makers."

Such a healing took place in Daniel Saucedo's life when his writing instructor, author Deena Metzger, asked him one day, "Do you have a story to tell about your ethnic background?" His response: "There is no story. My parents are completely assimilated. We never talk about Mexico. It doesn't matter to us." The manner in which he insisted on the absence of a story, she felt, "sounded like an amputation, and I wanted to know about the missing limb." So over the next two years she gently prodded him to reconsider his claim of cultural neutrality.

Toward the end of that time, at a family gathering at Thanksgiving, Daniel discovered that his paternal grandfather, who came to the United States from Mexico in 1908 to escape the Mexican Revolution, had kept a journal of that period. He began the journal with the admission that he was lonely in America and that the journal would be his best friend—and it ended ten years later when he married Daniel's grandmother, who, he said, took over the role of the journal.

Daniel's aunt had kept the journal in a trunk in her house, but it was entirely in Spanish, which Daniel couldn't read. His refusal to learn the language was part of his denying that he was Mexican, which, he said, was "a socially incorrect nationality" in the 1950s in Covina, his white middle-class neighborhood in Los Angeles. Still, he was very excited by the find and persuaded a cousin to read it to him. During the reading the two of them ceased being cousins and became grandchildren. "By the time I found the journal," Daniel says, "I was ready to find the journal."

He was also ready to begin answering his writing teacher's question and began an outpouring of writing that Daniel came to call "the exploration of the grandfather," a way, he says, of easing into the issue of being Mexican rather than confronting it head-on. Since he had never known either of his grandfathers, he wrote about and conversed with an imaginary grandfather, a composite drawn from the journal and the stories he had been told about both grandfathers, which also reflected his own image of "the ideal grandfather."

Shortly afterward, when Daniel and his wife were looking for a place to take a vacation, she suggested they go to Mexico, perhaps even to the villages of Daniel's grandfathers. It would have fulfilled "the family dream" to go back to Mexico, he says, because "the American dream wasn't really my grandfather's dream. His was to come here for a while, wait until the revolution was over, and go back home." One way had led to another, however, and he had never returned. In the journal, though, was a piece of paper that everyone in the family called "the deed," which indicated that Daniel's grandfather owned land in Zacatecas in central Mexico, which may or may not have been sold by then. In spite of all his misgivings about being Mexican, Daniel wanted to find that land, "just to stand on it."

Daniel once gathered all his writing together and discovered that it's true what they say about writers: they really do write the same story over and over. No matter how many stories they write, their truth repeats itself, and as the writer Alberto Moravia once said, "They keep trying to perfect their understanding of the one problem they were born to understand."

For Daniel, two such stories seemed to weave themselves through everything he had ever written: "atonement and homage"—making reconciliation and paying respects—both of which were central to his exploration of the grandfather, his increasing awareness and appreciation of the fact that he was Mexican, and his eventual decision to make the trip to Mexico, to cross the border between "there is no story" and "there is a story."

Daniel's true calling may not even be the writing after all. Like any art, writing is really only the mode of transport. The true calling is whatever we hope to draw to us *through* our art, what we want it to bring us. Perhaps, as Daniel once wrote, our calling is "an unknown culture buried beneath the city we have been painstakingly excavating. That may be why some of our profound stories, in my case the forbidden stories, take so long to discover; they were so well hidden that we never knew they existed."

Traditionally, the role of storytellers in various cultures has been one of knitting the society together with stories, keeping alive the traditions, the memories, the myths and parables; the tales were used to do the teaching. Stories form connective tissue in the body of knowledge and in the body of the people. Daniel's story of his own heritage has had the same force in his own life. In remembering it, he is re-membering himself, bringing the scattered pieces back together, healing himself by making himself whole, which is what the word *healing* means.

By discovering that a hidden life existed, by being willing to follow where it led, and by "the intimate engagement with my imagination," Daniel has erased the stigma he felt about being Mexican. "I no longer have a sense of shame about it, which is a tremendous relief. Now when someone asks me my nationality, I don't say Italian, like I used to. It's become a great comfort to me. I'm even planning another trip to Mexico, this time in search of the grandmother."

THE BELLS ON INDRA'S NET

In her book *O Pioneers!* Willa Cather remarks that "there are only two or three human stories, and they go on repeating themselves as fiercely as if they had never happened before." She doesn't say what those two or three stories are, but nearly twenty years into my career as a journalist writing about human stories, and after a lifetime of living my own, I began wondering what stories, deep down, she was referring to—love, alienation, death and rebirth? I had begun feeling weary of the stories I was telling, of the who-when-why-what-

and-where of them, of the "struggle and pathos of our little local stories," as the psychologist Jean Houston puts it. I began feeling that I was missing something vital about Story, and didn't know what it was.

In a move that then seemed scandalous to virtually everyone I knew, and even to myself, I stopped reading the daily newspaper entirely, stopped listening to the radio, and canceled all eight of my magazine subscriptions. I entered a kind of seclusion from Story, a hermitage from the news, and practiced the kind of "media celibacy" the singer Rachel Bagby spoke of. To my great astonishment, I maintained this fast for years!

A sympathetic friend told me he thought I was "detoxing" from a lifetime of immersion in the prevailing zeitgeist, and indeed, I experienced the kind of relief I feel when someone's car alarm, which has been stuck in the on position for the last hour, finally stops. It was a blessed silence and spaciousness that, over time, helped me realize that what I was after was not just a sabbatical from the same old stories, but a nose for a different kind of news, the journalistic equivalent of a look at Earth from outer space, the chance to reempathize with the world.

I began to realize that beneath the stories of our lives are other stories, other lives, and great archetypal armatures on which all our individual stories are hung. I discovered dramas that are taking place in an arena so large that, by comparison, all our local stories, even all the news of the world, seem like the tempest in the teapot. I discovered myth, which is among the oldest art forms and the source of our original creation stories. In the sense that art is, as D. H. Lawrence said, a religious activity and connects us to what is greater than ourselves, myth is also among our oldest religious activities and is an excellent tool for linking us with our calls.

Myths, like dreams, are stories in symbolic language, in images, and although we have mostly forgotten this, they are stories we have been prepared to encounter from earliest childhood, when we were read nursery rhymes and fairy tales—the preschool of myths. Myths, too, begin with "Once upon a time"—meaning not just a time that once was but also this time right now, and all the time yet to come—and they speak about the country that in the old Russian stories is called "East of the Sun and West of the Moon," and for which, as P. L. Travers says, there is no known map.

Myth is not, as most people suppose, synonymous with falsehoods and fanciful exaggerations, as in "The Myth of the Middle Class" or "Ten Myths about AIDS," though it *is* a bit like fiction, in the sense that both fiction and myth involve stories that are not factual but that are true. They aren't literally true, but they are psychologically true. They didn't really happen, but they're happening all the time. Myths are the stories we create to help explain ourselves to ourselves. In fact, says J. F. Bierlein in *Parallel Myths,* myth is the ancestor of science: it's our first fumbling attempt to explain *how* things happen. It is also the forebear of philosophy and religion in that it tries to explain *why* things happen. Myth is also the earliest form of literature, preceding recorded history by thousands of years.

Myths are metaphors, analogies, stories that get at the heart of human behavior, at profound truths, universal themes, ageless patterns. They are, perhaps above all, stories of transformation: from chaos to form, sleep to awakening, woundedness to wholeness, folly to wisdom, from being lost to finding our way. They describe the stages of life, the initiations we all go through as we move from one level to another: child to adult, young to old, single to married, cowardly to courageous, life to death, death to life.

The Odyssey, for example, isn't just Ulysses's story, and *The Wizard of Oz* is not just Dorothy's; they are the accounts of anyone struggling to find their way home. *Hansel and Gretel* is not just the misadventure of a couple of children, but, among other things, it is a parable about being lost and devoured. *Exodus* is about *any* kind of deliverance from bondage. Myths also do not simply weave daunting stories and then leave us breathless and stranded. Like dreams and symptoms, they also suggest cures, clues, directions, solutions. They don't just diagnose, says Robert Johnson; they also prescribe.

Each of us is living out a myth whenever we are brought down by our fatal flaws (Achilles); our naive exuberance (Icarus); when our curiosities get the better of us (Pandora); when we're engaged in futile effort (Sisyphus); when we take the weight of the world on our shoulders (Atlas); when we're self-centered (Narcissus); when we imagine ourselves invincible (Superman or Wonder Woman); when we're undone by our own anger (Ahab); or when we run from a calling (Jonah).

In our contemporary reenactments, the battlefields can be quite prosaic. They don't take place on the islands of the Aegean or in the Land of Oz, and they don't pit the hero or shero against dragons or Cyclops or armies of flying monkeys. Instead they take place in our homes and offices and in our relationships to our loved ones, our careers, our rebellious teenagers, and our health. The outcomes are capable of making or breaking us as surely as did the trials of Ulysses and Luke Skywalker, of Dorothy and Goldilocks. But given that these conundrums have animated human stories ever since there were any, our own "local stories" partake of the mythic.

If you were to retell your own life story as a myth—as the most persistent theme in myth, which is the myth of the hero's or heroine's journey—you would become the hero or heroine, and your earthly struggles, rather than being taken so personally, would become mythic in scope, recast as plot twists in an epic adventure. The calling you seek becomes the treasure, the obstacles to your path become the tests of initiation you must endure, and friends become the hero's guardians. You would see the Big Picture of your life, the way it looks from the height of orbit, from the depth of the unconscious, from the press box on Mount Olympus where the gods sip mint juleps and watch The Game.

You would see it through the perspective of archetypes, those eternally recurring themes in the human experience, those symbols we were first introduced to in nursery rhymes and are continually reminded of in our dreams: the heroic struggle, the mother/daughter or father/son bond, the battle between good and evil, death and resurrection. You would also meet the entire cast of dramatis personae who have always populated myth and literature, art and religion and dream: the king and queen, the dragon, wizard, lover, fool, enemy, rebel, divine child, crone, and codger.

All of these archetypes emanate from what Carl Jung called the "collective unconscious," that communal costume shop of symbols, images, and themes. Myths are the best proof of the existence of this collective unconscious. Strikingly similar myths (creation myths, trickster myths, myths of the hero's and heroine's journey) have, throughout history, arisen *simultaneously* in Africa, Asia, Europe, the Americas, and the Middle East. The image of the dragon, for instance, appears in the myths of cultures as far-flung as the Egyptian, Iroquois, Polynesian and Anglo-Saxon, and has, for all of them, come to represent the conflict between earthly energies (the serpent) and spiritual energies (the eagle). Combined, they make a dragon, which typically symbolizes the struggle between these two parts of us.

All this suggests that myths grow not in the soil of any particular place but in the humus of humanity itself. We are not strangers to each other. We drink from different wells but from the same aquifer. A Hindu myth about the god Indra offers a beautiful illustration of this unitive principle. Indra once wove a net to encompass the world, and at each knot he fastened a bell. Thus nothing could stir—not a person, not a leaf on a tree, not a single emotion—without ringing a bell, which would, in turn, set all the others to ringing.

The anthropologist Mircea Eliade described myth as "the story of the breakthrough of the sacred into the world." To the degree we are each looking for the places where callings break into our lives as emissaries of the sacred, it would serve us well to take pen and paper and try reframing our lives as myths.

Begin by describing, in a word or phrase, the theme of your present search, i.e., your heroic journey. Remember, myths are about characters in the process of transformation. Is your theme "finding my calling," "taking on my power," "learning forgiveness," "from cowardice to courage," "saving the people," "letting go of the past," "waking up"? As you write your myth, have a particular challenge in mind.

Before sitting down to a session of free-writing, consider the following ingredients of the mythic hero/heroine's journey, offered with a tip of the hat to Joseph Campbell, who has done much to help us rediscover the power of myth.

- Hero/heroine: Are you a king or queen, prince or princess, space traveler, monk, prisoner, farm girl, fisherman, wild animal, or house cat?
- Ordinary World: Where do you start, from what familiar surroundings and landscape, conventional philosophies and established relationships?
- The Call to Adventure: You are confronted with a challenge, a dare, a problem to solve or adventure to undertake. The need for a change in the Ordinary World is announced by a dream, a stranger's appearance, a death or birth or illness, an inner urge, a knock at the door, or an inner voice, like the one the protagonist heard at the start of the movie *Field of Dreams:* "If you build it, they will come." Here the stakes of the game are established, as well as the ultimate goal.
- Refusal of the Call: You face the fear of the unknown, perhaps back away from the call, turn down the quest, hesitate and are temporarily lost. Even Christ in the Garden of Gethsemane balked, saying, "Let this cup pass from me."
- Allies: Anyone or anything that pulls you through the refusal and who then continues to inspire, provoke, teach, test, train, and protect you; anyone or anything that brings the sense of trust to your journey. This could be a person, place, or thing, a dream, a code of honor, a bit of magic, a power won on a previous journey. But as Dante discovered on

his sojourn, allies can go only so far, and ultimately you must go it
alone.

- Obstacles: Whatever thwarts you, from within or without. Whatever
  tests you, like the Sphinx that confronted Oedipus with a riddle before
  he could continue on his way; whatever helps you gauge your courage
  and stamina, your strengths and weaknesses. Though they may be
  demons and dragons, witches and warlords, powers that must be mastered or masters that must be overpowered, do not confuse obstacles
  with enemies. Often the journey includes a Supreme Ordeal, in which
  you face your greatest fear. Whether you are inside the Death Star or in
  the Wicked Witch's castle, you encounter here a physical or psychological life-or-death encounter, a moment of epiphany.

- Return: You come back from the journey visibly changed and, given
  that the word *hero* in Greek means one who serves, share the boons of
  the quest with "the people"—a new status quo for the Ordinary World,
  a higher order of functioning, a sacred marriage, a reconciliation, a treasure, a calling. The Return also typically includes a final exam, a last test
  to see if you've really learned the lessons of the journey or the Supreme
  Ordeal, if you've really changed. It is a last chance for the forces of darkness to strike back at the triumphant hero or heroine, as the evil Saru-
  man did against Frodo at the end of *The Trilogy.*

- Finally, remember that this is just an outline. Not all myths follow this
  structure to the letter of the law. You can add or delete as you wish.
  Things don't have to make sense or be in perfect chronological order.
  Characters can simply appear or disappear, things can suddenly just
  happen. Begin with "Once upon a time."

When we touch the mythic and archetypal level of the unconscious, Jung
said, it releases immense energy into our lives. It can express itself as a call and
hook us up to a more inclusive frame of reference—something bigger than
ourselves—which can be quite useful when we're searching for greater meaning in our lives. Touching this deep stratum can also help us appreciate the
sheer size of the human soul, which Jung conceptualized as an iceberg. The
one-tenth that is above water is consciousness, the nine-tenths below water is
the unconscious, and the ocean in which the whole thing floats is the collective
unconscious, in which myth swims.

Myth also taps into what the theologian Reinhold Niebuhr called "the permanently valid insights in primitive imagination," the venerable savvy of our ancestors, whose wisdom is brought through eons of time to us in the modern age (although every age was modern to those who lived in it). "Primitive doesn't necessarily mean simple or rough-hewn," an archaeologist named John Rick once told me. "We weren't just monkeys with hoes. We had books, but they were in our heads. We had skill and intelligence that was no less great than what we have today."

As if to prove his point, Rick once handed me a Stone Age spear that he had fashioned himself by knapping a five-inch chunk of obsidian, straightening a length of green wood by heating and bending it over a fire, gluing feathers to the end of it with boiled salmon skin, and finally binding the obsidian to the wood with strips of animal tendon. In this "primitive" spear, whose design was imbued with a native intelligence not to be underestimated, is the origin of knives and scalpels, the lineage of the blade from flint to metal to laser.

Ironically, this Stone Age technology, like myth, is being rediscovered. Magnified ten thousand times, the finest scalpel looks like a saw. Obsidian blades, however, which are made of black volcanic glass, are perfectly smooth, harder than metal, and their edges poised at a molecular level of thickness. This gives them the edge, literally, in allowing minimal tissue damage during surgery. Due to the efforts of a few diehard stone toolmakers like Rick, obsidian blades are now being used in brain surgery, and the technology, surgeons are finding, has never been improved.

Sometimes, Rick says, you have to take a step backward in order to move forward, and the answers to our questions lie not in the future but in the past. Sometimes the voyage is not so much about discovery as rediscovery, and what we seek is not something new but something old, "a treasure that was lost and has to be found," as P. L. Travers says, "our own selves, our identities. By finding this, we take part in the one task, the essential mythical requirement: the reinstatement of the fallen world."

nine

M A K I N G

P I L G R I M A G E

My father's favorite game to play with my two brothers and me when we were children was something he called the Alien Game, in which he was a visitor from another planet and we were his guides here on Earth. He would point into the sky, for instance, and ask, "What are those formations that move through the atmosphere?"

"Clouds!" we'd say with great confidence.

"Clouds? What are they made of?"

"Water," we'd all say at once.

"How does the water get up there?" he'd inquire, "and what holds it up, and why does it move?"

In no time at all it would become apparent to us Earthlings that clouds weren't the only things that were over our heads. Entire afternoons could go by as we pondered the mysteries of water and wind, and how it's possible that we can know so much and understand so little, that we can live with something every day of our lives and never really come to know it.

What the Alien Game taught me—and what I keep trying to remember—is to see with the eyes of a child, who, after all, is in most ways an alien to this world.

⚬

In searching out the mystery of our own callings, in trying to find answers to our most basic why-is-the-sky-blue questions of meaning and purpose, we, too, can leave our houses, go out under the clouds, and, with the guilelessness of children, simply ask those questions that seem obvious but often aren't—Who am I? What matters? What is my gift? What do I need to hear? What on Earth am I doing? We can also try to approach these questions as if each were an emissary from some Great Unknown, each itself a mystery, and any number of lifetimes insufficient to get us much closer than the outskirts of the thing.

Questioning is at the heart of spiritual journeying, of leaving home for a time to go on a retreat, pilgrimage, or vision quest, of removing ourselves from the duties and dramas, the relationships and roles that bombard us with messages that may be distracting or irrelevant or even destructive to our emerging sense of self, and that interfere with our asking for responses to our burning questions. In making pilgrimage, we're calling on God rather than the other way around. We're "crying for a vision," as the Oglala Sioux holy man Black Elk called it, the one that may reveal our true vocation, our real name, our purpose; the one that may come as a dream, a fantasy figure, a voice in the head, an animal encounter, an overpowering emotion, a sudden inspiration or surge of creative energy, a chance meeting out at a crossroads. We're practicing the art of following calls because spiritual journeys, like calls, involve a break with everyday life.

"I went to strip away what I had been taught," Georgia O'Keeffe said, describing her retreat to New Mexico from New York City in the 1920s, "to accept as true my own thinking. This was one of the best times of my life. There was no one around to look at what I was doing, no one interested, no one to say anything about it one way or another. I was alone and singularly free."

In taking a walkabout, in leaving home and the distracting fusillade of activities that often keeps us from ourselves, what is in the background becomes foreground, what is overlooked has the chance to get looked over, what is waiting in the wings is given an entrance cue. We ask for a calling and the faith to follow it. We go a'courting. We stand beneath the balcony and croon. We cry out with the longing we feel. We drop our handkerchiefs.

We may or may not get an answer, but what's important is not to cease asking. Perhaps we mispronounced the question, or our timing wasn't right. Perhaps we received an answer and didn't recognize it, or perhaps the answer we heard wasn't the one we wanted to hear, so we ignored it. Maybe we need to travel still further on our journey, around the next turn in the road, over the next pass, into the company of someone we have yet to meet.

Pilgrims, says theologian Richard Niebuhr, "are persons in motion, passing through territories not their own, seeking . . . completion or clarity; a goal to which only the spirit's compass points the way." Sometimes that motion is religious and sometimes secular. Sometimes we design our own journeys and sometimes we follow in the paths of those we revere: pacing the garden Jesus paced, sitting beneath the tree where Buddha saw the light, praying in the chapel where Merton prayed, visiting the house where Shakespeare wrote *Romeo and Juliet,* walking the same streets of a village in Mexico or a shtetl in Russia that your own grandfather once walked.

Sometimes we journey with the body, on a long walking meditation or a bicycle trip through the Holy Lands, and sometimes with the mind, as Joseph Campbell did early in his life by holing himself up in a cabin for five years and doing nothing but reading, which the Hindus call *ynana* yoga, the search for enlightenment through knowledge and the mind. Our approach depends on our primary way of experiencing the spirit. Sometimes we make the journey entirely in private, in solitary retreat or solo vision quest in the wilderness, and other times in crowds, like the great pilgrimages—to Mecca, Benares, Rome, Jerusalem, and Compostela in Spain—which resemble enormous migrations.

Simply taking up a bedroll and hitting the road won't generally suffice to alert the forces of enlightenment, however. They require that you do more than just move around. Whether we go to the Ganges or Graceland, maintaining a spirit of observance and self-reflection is key. We must be intent on spending time searching for soul, moving toward something that represents to us an *ideal*—truth, beauty, love, perspective, strength, serenity, transcendence, sacredness, whatever.

Without this intention, our pilgrimages are only vacations, our vision quests are struck blind, our retreats are not also advances. We're merely tourists and window-shoppers or curio seekers. Perhaps we're even escapees, people in flight rather than in quest. Something like a Law of Spiritual Enthusiasm seems to dictate what sort of response we get to our inquiries, intents, and purposes and to highlight the importance of being earnest. The hungrier we are to learn and be guided, the more we're taught and the more we *allow* ourselves to be taught. We can't fake it, though. The gods and our own souls know when we're being sincere and when we're just smiling and saying cheese.

Spiritual journeying, whether we walk around a holy mountain or sit in a single place on a five-day meditation retreat, is about interior or exterior movement *toward the deep self.* A geographical journey is symbolic of an inner journey for which we long.

CROSSING OVER

In Hindi and Sanskrit, the word for a *pilgrim site* means a ford, a crossing place, a point of transit. People seem most inclined to take spiritual journeys at just such points in their own lives. These journeys are rites of passage, rituals we enact to help us cross over into maturity of one kind or another. Historically, the crossings take place at birth, puberty, marriage, the entrance into secret societies, the creation of a shaman, the passing of seasons, and death. Without these rituals, without actively honoring that we change in dramatic ways, the passages of our lives can become impasses.

Spiritual journeys follow what Robert Atkinson in *The Gift of Stories* calls the "sacred pattern," the same three-fold progression of separation-initiation-return as rites of passage and heroic myths; the same process of surrender-struggle-recovery common to twelve-step programs; the same architecture of beginning-middle-end as storytelling. We open a door, step across a threshold, and return through it from the other side. We leave an old life behind, experience a life transition up close, and receive its thorny wisdom, and then head home and hope to follow through on whatever we learned.

Rites of passage celebrate the passage, the initiation, the processional of a single spirit toward transcendence, the revelation of the sacred to the initiate— not the separation or the return. The threshold crossed is not a line but a *region* in time or space, said the anthropologist Mircea Elide, who coined the term "rites of passage" at the turn of the century. Making the passage is not actually as simple as walking through a doorway but more akin to passing through a tunnel, across an ocean, through a pregnancy or bereavement, through a dark night. Jung felt that the process of individuation is the result of a series of such initiatory ordeals, all of which begin with an act of rupture, of separation and thus separation anxiety.

Whenever I spend nights in the wilderness, I'm aware that as long as the fire is high and crackling with percussion, and the conversation lively, I feel at ease. But as soon as the fire dies out and darkness and silence envelop the camp, the beasts of the night come in for a closer look. I listen apprehensively to their bodies moving nearby, and sleep fitfully. This is why I usually plan my camping trips during full moons—I want the night-light—although this once thoroughly backfired when, while camping in the backcountry in Yellowstone, my night-light cast the shadow of a huge bear on the side of my tent. Light doesn't eliminate the fear of the dark. It only eliminates the dark.

Being *alone* out there, moon or no moon, is the challenge of undertaking a vision quest, which typically involves spending a few days and nights alone in the wilderness, crying for a vision and sometimes just crying. A mouse scrabbling around in the underbrush becomes a monster or a maniac; you're beset by a quality of loneliness akin to Christ's experience in the Garden of Gethsemane, and you're ready to ditch your faithfulness for the furry warmth of the herd.

When our very distant ancestors from nearly every culture invented this form of spiritual journeying, they understood that it was a potent ritual of initiation for those making the passage from childhood to adulthood, from ignorance to wisdom, or for those searching for their place in the scheme of things. They understood that one must be tested, that death must precede resurrection into a new mode of being, and that even ritual or symbolic death is frightening. They understood that nature is the master guru in matters of death and rebirth, that the entrée into enlightenment comes with a side order of holy terror, and one must have the appetite for it. Even something as seemingly simple and harmless as meditation can be quite fearsome simply because you're alone with yourself in the dark.

The experience of the holy, says Sam Keen, always involves trembling. Quakers quake, Shakers shake, dervishes whirl, prophets stand knock-kneed before God. The myth of the hero/heroine tells us that we must come face-to-face with our greatest fear before revelation and triumph can occur; that the thing we most fear is the thing we must do. Thus the vision quest, the rite of initiation, reveals, as Eliade said, "the almost awesome seriousness" with which archaic peoples assumed the responsibility of receiving and transmitting spiritual values and guidance.

Joseph Campbell once said that "where you stumble, there is your treasure," referring to a story from the *Arabian Nights* in which a farmer's plow catches on something in the dirt, and despite much struggle he can't dislodge it. He finally stops, digs in the ground, and discovers that his plow has caught on a metal ring attached to a door, through which is a passageway leading to a treasure. Wherever our most primal fears reside—our fears of the dark, of death, of being devoured, of meaninglessness, of lovelessness, or of loss—chances are good that beneath them lie gems of wisdom and maybe a vision or a calling. Wherever you stumble—on a tree root, on a rock, on fear or shame or vulnerability, on someone else's words, on the truth—dig there.

Nature, in general, is central to many spiritual journeys. Historically, vision questers often dug a hole in the ground and lay there, waiting for a vision, and pilgrimage sites and retreat centers are often located at places of great natural beauty. Nature is a proper setting for a return to ourselves, our source, our place of origin. It is the place where the world was created, where our ancestors came from, where they spoke their first words and spoke with the gods who taught them the alphabet. By going "back to nature" we are, in a sense, returning to the garden, to the place where we were contained within nature's wholeness, as John Sanford puts it. We were not separate from the divine, from whence our visions and calls emanate, but in right relationship to the larger forces, as well as to our own senses.

We also realign with nature not merely as wilderness but also as the source of the *super*-natural—the scene of Creation, the landscape of myth, the stomping ground of the gods: Pan in the forests, Poseidon in the seas, Demeter in the plants, and Artemis in the animals. We need to reclaim our supernatural and mythic imaginations, Sanford says, to cultivate the ability once again to look up into the night sky and see there not just an undifferentiated swarm of stars, but the heroic contours of Hercules, Pegasus, and Andromeda. We need to recapture the vision of our natural selves, remember our native wisdoms, reinherit the wind. And we can begin by seeing our own lives from the vantage point of the woods out beyond town, the mountains into which no roads lead, the rivers which once *were* our only roads.

Many of us are afraid of nature in part because it's so inscrutable to us, so rife with the unknown—so full of capriciousness and food chain activity—and in part because we've demonized it. Hell has traditionally been relegated to a place *within* the earth itself, under our very feet, at the center of our world, while heaven is in the unreachable reaches of space. We've come to associate hell with the earth and heaven with the ethers.

Whether or not spiritual journeys involve an excursion into nature, they are formidable because all rites of passage necessitate that we leave our old selves behind, leave the trappings of identity and status, and move to a place where no one knows or cares who we are. Like the pilgrims on the hajj to Mecca, who are required to wear the same tunic, in taking to the road we wear the cloak of anonymity, the prospect of which may fill us with a certain dread or, if we're lucky, relief.

For these and other reasons, many spiritual teachers recommend guides for extended meditation retreats, vision quests, and pilgrimages deep into nature. It is useful, and occasionally critical, to have the guidance of someone who has gone this way before you, who knows the ropes, is familiar with the psychological and physical terrain, can help prepare you for what you might encounter, and who provides the motivating element of leadership. Beyond that, feel free to design your journey to suit yourself, drawing on any practice that keeps you focused on your goal. Make music, sing songs, paint pictures, write in a journal, practice yoga, walk all day in the wilderness, or just sit still. Pray, read holy books, or stare fixedly out the window. Abstain from talking or sleeping or socializing, or fast to remind yourself that you're hungry.

"You are ceremonially free," says Stephen Foster in *The Book of the Vision Quest*, "to bury, burn, smash, change your name, bathe, vow, draw blood, cut your hair, heap stones, chant, rattle, dance, sing, tie knots, light a candle, go nude, make gifts, use incense, pray, kneel, meditate, nightwalk, paint yourself, or behave in any other way that is meaningful to you."

THE BURNING QUESTIONS

In the story of the quest for the Holy Grail, the hero, Parsifal, must ask the right question, in this case "Whom does the Grail serve?" Only by surrendering to his curiosity is he able to help heal the king and the kingdom. He doesn't actually need to secure the answer himself. He only needs to ask the question.

Spiritual journeys, like stories, have at their core a central question—as do our lives—and if we understand not even the answers but merely the questions that animate our own journeys, we've understood a lot. "Curiosity, no less than devotion, makes pilgrims," the English poet Abraham Cowley once said, and like pilgrims to Delphi, we must come bearing questions, with the hope that the meditations, contemplations, dreams and rituals of our journeys may offer some answers. In any case, we need to know what we're looking for, and by having a clear question, we are halfway to getting an intelligible answer. Questioning is a prerequisite to change and innovation, and without it there is no discovery.

What question is at the heart of your pilgrimage and your life? What question were you put here to understand? We're after questions that do not arise solely from the intellect but from a crying need to know, an existential thirst, a deep mystification. We pose these questions, as the writer Jack Matthews says, "with the dumb hope that there may be gods that exist in the silence of time who in their own inscrutable ways will respond secretly and cunningly to our most honest expressions, assuring us that the ideas that riddle and beguile us are true and beautiful and worthy of our attention."

We may have questions about a call we seek: What is my purpose? To whom do I belong? What can I believe in? Who are my teachers? What is the name of the dragon in my life? What changes must I make? How can I use my talents? How can I serve the world? Where am I going and how can I get there? Or we may have questions about calls we've already received: How do I make community? How do I learn to forgive? What conditions foster cooperation between people? How can healing and laughter be combined? How can conservationists work *with* business rather than against it, to protect the environment? How does the mind influence the course of disease? How can I raise compassionate children?

Nothing shapes our lives so much as the questions we ask, says Sam Keen, who himself wears a small silver question mark on a chain around his neck. Imagine, he says, how different lives would be if they were propelled by the question "How can I serve others?" versus "Where can I get my next fix?" Or "How can I be the most authentic?" versus "What will the neighbors think?" Or "How can we balance ecology and economy?" versus "How can we make the most money?"

The writer Annie Dillard once observed that "the way we spend our days is the way we spend our lives." The way we live our lives also depends on the questions we ask.

Fran Peavey has a daily meditation practice during which she asks herself a single question: "What can I do to help the earth?" Her life is both the testing ground for that question and the response to it. She calls the answers she receives "promptings," and she has followed them into the most unorthodox arenas and unexpected pilgrimages.

The most consistent answer she's received to this question over the years has been simply "Listen!" In order to serve herself or others, the prompting instructed, she must first listen—to needs, longings, sufferings, secrets, dreams, and demands.

The first time she heard this was in 1963. She was working at Roosevelt Junior High School in San Francisco, where a third of her students were black. Two weeks into her first year there, she realized she knew nothing whatsoever about being black, so she went to the local NAACP chapter and told them, "I'm teaching your children, and I don't have any idea what their life experience is like." She asked them to teach her about black history and the worldview of black kids. Once a week, after school, she had what she refers to as her "black lessons." Her tutors took her to people's homes, workplaces, and churches, and she asked them what their lives were like, what they wanted their children to learn, how school had been for them, how those who were parents felt when they visited their children's schools for open-house night. "When you wonder about a group of people who are different from you," she says, "find someone from that group and ask them to teach you."

This experience, and the continued practice of asking her question, helped give Fran the courage to take on an even bigger listening project a few years later, one that had many of the elements of a pilgrimage. She decided that in order to serve people properly as a social activist working to prevent nuclear war, she had to know a little more *about* people. So she sold her house, paid off her debts, and with some of the remaining money bought a plane ticket around the world. She asked friends to send her the names of people she could talk to and stay with, and she planned to go only to those cities where she had four or more contacts. Since she also wanted to talk to people at random, she came up with the idea of sitting on park benches all over the world, holding a cloth sign that said AMERICAN WILLING TO LISTEN, and for four months, she did just that; she traveled, sat on park benches, and listened to people talk about their lives. It was, she describes, "one of the scariest ideas I've ever had."

The journey began in Japan, and it took Fran several days before she got up the nerve to carry out her plan. Finally, one day, she unfolded a two-by-three-foot cloth sign, lay it on the ground in front of her bench, and waited. "Time passed. People came over, sized me up, and walked away. I tried to smile pleasantly, all the while thinking, 'This is a bad idea. I've spent a lot of money and the plan isn't working. I'm making a fool of myself. This is a mistake.' "

Half an hour passed before someone finally sat down next to her, a man in his thirties, and told her about some of his concerns: the border war between North and South Korea over control of rubber trees; the investment of massive amounts of Japanese capital in China; the extent of consumption and consumerism in Japan and other developed countries; even his views on the relations between the sexes. His wife was part of a women's consciousness-raising group, and he and the other husbands felt envious of it. They had tried to start their own, but it fell apart, and he was disappointed.

As Fran's confidence grew and her fears ebbed, people began *lining up* to talk with her, and "it showed me how little I knew about the world. It occurred to me that I might have to go on interviewing full-time for the rest of my life to get any sense of what was going on in the world." This is practically what she's done. Her listening project, which she writes about in her book *Heart Politics,* has become a continuing practice, "a kind of tuning up of my heart to the affairs of the world. I hear the news differently now and act with a larger context in mind. I hold myself accountable to the people whose lives I have seen, and carry with me some of their pain. It does not weigh me down."

Nor does her daily practice of setting aside one hour, from four o'clock to five o'clock in the afternoon, during which people come to talk with her. "I don't charge them, but I ask that they each bring a rock. The green rocks go into the bathroom upstairs and the rest go out into the rock garden. Perhaps looking for the right rock helps them focus on what it is they're looking for, why they're coming to see me. They ask questions, most frequently, 'I want to help the world. How can I plug in?' They often think they need to have big ideas, but I encourage them to start small, otherwise they can get a spiritual hernia."

This condition can assail anyone who goes at questions as if they were bench-pressing, who insists on answers with a kind of "gotta have it" attitude that tends to set up resistance and desperation in them, and who forgets that answers can easily devolve into dogmas, which, as D. M. Dooling, the founder of *Parabola Magazine,* once said, leads to "the degeneration of search."

Instead of demanding clear-cut answers, it is better to hope for visitations, images that might linger like alpenglow in the mind's eye, a flood of lyrics or music, a voluminous and eloquent silence, a surge of electrons in the brain that illuminates a vision or a dream. The deep questions may not have singular answers but multitudes of them. The principles of brainstorming have taught me that even the questions ought to be framed as if this were the case. Rather than asking "Who am I?" we might ask, "In how many ways can I be myself?"

Rather than asking "Where is my place in the world?" the question might be better put, "In how many ways can I experience a sense of belonging to the world?"

It is also better to cultivate patience than premature answers, although most of us seem to prefer *any* kind of answers to none at all. We don't like having to wait for answers, and we certainly prefer answers to questions. A therapist of my acquaintance, Winifred Kessler, once conducted a communication seminar for couples, during which, contrary to custom, the women spent one whole day making declarative statements while the men spent the day asking questions. The result: The women were energized, the men were exhausted. One reason for this, Kessler said, is that those in authority (usually men) make statements, and those not in authority (usually women) ask questions, and it's more energizing to be in authority, to be *an* authority.

Questions can be exhausting and also occasionally dangerous. In some countries they're fatal. But the biddings of personal evolution and conscience, especially as they impress themselves on us during a rigorous spiritual journey, often require that we question everything we—and often others—hold dear: our standards for ourselves, the purpose of life as recorded in the gospel of parental and social instruction, and the most fundamental priorities by which we've led our lives. This can have the most valiant vision quester whimpering for a night-light and explains why Black Elk often referred to the vision quest as "the lamentation."

As a frequent lecturer and teacher, I am sometimes appalled at the consistency with which people say, "I know this is a stupid question, but . . ." Personally, I think there are no stupid questions, though there are often stupid answers. What I hear in this ubiquitous statement is a common anxiety that attends the quest for knowledge: the fear of being shamed for the lack of it, or the want of it. Unfortunately, this fear is often warranted. Questions are not always welcomed, and many of us *have* been shamed for our inquisitiveness, either outright or insidiously. We have all had the experience of asking a question and having others quickly change the subject, or "ahem" at us in polite company, or tell us we think too much, or turn stiffly back to their chores as if they never heard us ask, or send us from the table or down to the principal's office.

Most of us can probably remember the effect of asking a certain question of a certain person who didn't want to be asked: the time you asked the nuns how Christ could possibly have been resurrected when he'd been dead for three days and there was a large stone covering his grave. The time you asked your doctor to explain every test result in detail. The time you asked your mother while she was entertaining the ladies of the auxiliary how babies are born. The time you asked why Daddy drinks so much. There are also the questions we don't even want to ask *ourselves,* for fear that we may not be able to come up with an answer, or that we *may* find the answer and then not be able to erase it from our minds.

In ancient China, it was common to engrave questions on bone or tortoiseshell, then fire the piece and read the answers in the pattern of cracks caused by the heat. In taking a spiritual journey and posing our own deepest, most blood-borne questions, we fire them in the amplified heat of solitude and silence, and we shouldn't be surprised that cracks appear. At some level we know this is the purpose of the journey, and in our keenest moments, says P. L. Travers, "We ask our questions knowing that there is nothing to be gained, only a purpose to serve, and seeking not so much to find as to be found."

CIRCLING THE ANCIENT TOWER

When your ship, long moored in harbour, gives you the illusion of being a house . . . put out to sea! Save your boat's journeying soul, and your own pilgrim soul, cost what it may.
— BRAZILIAN ARCHBISHOP HELDER CAMARA

Lake Superior is an inland sea. It is the largest lake on the planet, more than 1,200 miles around, and one of the most volatile, capable of whipping itself into a frenzy of thirty-foot seas, and it is famous for its shipwrecks. It is also one of the coldest. For most of the year, the water temperature is in the midthirties, about as cold as water can be without turning into something else. During the "hand test," Ann Linnea found that she could hold her hand in the water for only nine seconds.

Kayaking around the lake would be the most dangerous thing she had ever done.

The idea had first come up five years earlier, when Ann and Paul Treuer, a longtime friend, bought a couple of used kayaks. After their first exhilarating runs on the lake, he said, "I bet we could kayak around this whole lake," to which she replied, "Yeah, right." Nothing would have come of it except that that little seed dropped into fertile soil, "the part of me," said Ann, a former

National Forest Service naturalist and marathoner, "that always wanted to do one long wilderness adventure."

As the years went by, it would also be nourished by another part of her: "I knew, vaguely, that I was approaching the end of some kind of life cycle, the life my parents lived, the life I thought I was raised to live: wife, mother, home, good citizen. I wondered, Is this the fullness of what I can be doing? I wanted to reset the course of my life, to come to clarity about what the gift is I'm supposed to return to the world, and I thought the trip could teach me. The question that I brought with me, and kept asking over and over, was 'Am I doing the most I possibly can with my life?'

"My purpose was to find a purpose, to find the deepest courage in myself, to look for the extraordinary growth, not just the ordinary, day-to-day growth, which is certainly valid, but it was the kind of incremental journeying my whole life had been about. I wanted to step outside of that, to really open the door wide, which is why I liked the symbolism of Lake Superior. It was so wide I couldn't see across it, couldn't see what was on the other side, and that was just the magnitude of change I was inviting. To grow beyond the expectations we're raised with is a radical act, but one I felt was necessary to claiming my full self."

The trip Ann and Paul eventually took in the summer of 1992 was, as Ann described it, "a self-designed midlife rite of passage, which I chose to make rather than it choosing me, and I chose an arena in which I was the most skilled, comfortable, and inspired." She chose kayaking because "I learn best by using my body, by moving until I have insight." She chose a wilderness trip because "all my life I have sought wild places for good counsel." And she chose Lake Superior because "it was really important to me that the journey take place in my own backyard, rather than someplace exotic."

On the day they were planning to leave from Duluth, Minnesota—Ann's home—they stood by the shores of Gitchee Gumee, as the Ojibway Indians once called the lake, and considered the judiciousness of starting out in thirty-mile-per-hour winds, four-to-seven-foot waves, and a small craft advisory that certainly included crafts such as Ann's seventeen-foot sea kayak, *Grace.* They'd managed worse storms, but they worried about the message such a departure might send to their already fretting families: They would be taking unnecessary chances.

Her parents were slightly aghast that she could leave her children, a third-grader and a sixth-grader, for the whole summer. Her husband couldn't understand why she had to be gone so long (over two months). One friend wanted to know if they had really considered the dangers, and another pointed out that if no woman had ever circumnavigated the lake, there must be a good reason.

"There weren't many people who said, 'Oh, that's really a great idea.' In fact, there were none. It was very tough being on the receiving end of not only my own doubts, but everyone else's. It's really hard to stand in your own truth when everybody around you is telling you, 'Why don't you just keep things the way they are?' "

They did postpone their trip a few days, hoping for better weather, and meanwhile suffered "the disappointment of remaining put when one is ready to leave."

When the weather didn't break after several days, they decided to head out anyway. The forecast, according to their weather-band radios, was for strong winds, low clouds and fog, four-to-seven-foot surf, and a small craft advisory, which, though they didn't know it then, would become the weary refrain for much of the trip—the coldest and wettest summer in a century.

⚜

Although modest, the currents move counterclockwise around Lake Superior, and Ann and Paul were heading clockwise, against the currents, because they wanted to hit the wildest stretch of the lake, the north side, early in the trip, and because "it just felt right," and because it was symbolic. They were also, unbeknownst to them, following a very ancient pilgrimage tradition, that of circumambulating a holy site in a clockwise direction.

At a deep level, we all associate journeying with circularity. We buy *round-trip* tickets, whether our actual trajectory there and back is circular or not, as if we recognize that every journey is essentially a journey toward ourselves, a circling around some mysterious core of life that we can glimpse only while moving, just as it's easier to see through a screen while moving your head back and forth. Every trip, then, and especially one undertaken with sacred intention, is the enactment of a pilgrimage, a mirroring of the planets that wheel around the sun, the clock's arms swinging around time's center, dancers carrying their streamers around the maypole, oxen turning around a well, drawing up water.

Even the word *pilgrimage,* in some languages, refers to this circling. The expression for it in Tibetan, for example, is "to turn around the place," a place that is often referred to as a "center." The word *hajj,* the journey to Mecca that every Muslim must make at least once in his or her life, comes from an old Semitic word meaning "to go around, to go in a circle." Whether it be around a person, a shrine, a temple, a lake, a mountain, a country, or even, as some have done, around the world, a simple mathematical principle defines the purpose of circumambulation: by drawing the circle, we define the center. By circling the lake, Ann was turning around the axis of her one desire: to locate her own center and to know it from all sides.

The circle, Carl Jung once said, is the classic symbol for wholeness, or God, and the circular path an analogue for the way toward it. We are always being drawn toward it, says June Singer, and yet "to fly straight into it would be like a moth darting into a flame or the Earth hurtling itself into the center of the sun," or a kayaker taking a hard right and heading straight for the center of Lake Superior. So we maintain an orbital tension, close enough to feel the heat, but not so close that we burn our wings. We can do no better, said the poet Rainer Maria Rilke:

> I am circling around God, around the ancient tower
> and I have been circling for a thousand years,
> and I still don't know if I am a falcon, or a storm,
> or a great song.

And yet, because we have the image of wholeness imprinted on our souls, a deep impression where the ancient tower once stood, we are, in a sense, always at the center, always in Benares, dipt in the Ganges, always in Jerusalem, wailing at the wall, slipping notes to God, touching our remembered glory.

At one point during Ann's voyage, she glimpsed the center. One evening about a third of the way into the trip, she stumbled onto the ruins of an old stone altar, a miniature Stonehenge, whose rocks were stacked ten feet high on a narrow terrace above the shore. In the presence of the indigenous, she saw a vision of her own life that she described as "fleeting, like a deer startled at the edge of a clearing who quickly disappears into the safety of brush. But I know I saw it." *It* was an image of herself as "finally able to embrace spirituality in everything I did." Actually, she was ready to *re-embrace* spirituality. Earlier in her life, she had had an unabashed relationship with what she calls "spirit." In junior high school, she once wrote a vocational paper about being a missionary, and her parents told her "don't get so carried away with the religious stuff," a comment she unfortunately took deeply to heart. She got the message that in order for her passion for spirit to be accepted, she would have to temper it. "It wasn't until I went around the lake that I returned to that pure passion for a spirit-filled life, and felt encouraged to follow it."

That would mean, among other things, taking a step away from the schools and environmental education centers where she had taught for many years. "I always had to be very careful about how I presented ideas about spirituality. But I was really ready to bring spiritual presence—meditation and prayer, open discussion of spirit and mystery—into my work in a way that was uninhibited. That was probably the biggest truth I discovered on the trip: I wanted to have the courage to make spirit be at the foremost of everything I did."

Thomas Merton said that a hope is built into our psychology that we may somehow find our way back to "the source and center of religion, the place of revelation and renewal." Ann Linnea's grueling rite of passage in the wilderness, a journey of more than 1,200 miles and sixty-five days, long stretches of which were spent entirely alone after she and Paul decided to take different routes, and the daily practices of keeping a journal, prayer, ritual, and asking for dreams enabled her to find the coordinates of her own center, to find her way back to her deepest courage, the courage to "live beyond a focus on safety and security," to reset the course of her life.

Her return also involved a difficult period of transition, during which she had to try to translate the level of physical courage she learned on the trip into the emotional courage she needed to make the changes. The toast she made with Paul on the last day of the trip, with a bottle of Kahlua passed between them, was most appropriate: "To a damn good trip and a damn fine friend, and for the courage to deal with all that lies ahead," part of which was the realization that, as she put it, "the most vulnerable time for new truth in our lives is immediately after its discovery."

The next day, in flat, calm seas, they returned to twenty-six people waiting on the beach in welcome and quickly realized that they had made no provisions for the transition back. Paul, for instance, began teaching at the university within two days of returning, a culture shock of no mean proportions. Ann, who had "no intention of simply slipping back into my old routines," wished she had talked more with her family and helped them understand "that I'm going to come back tremendously changed, and not to expect me to go back to business as usual. I also wish I'd called a circle of friends to meet with me every few weeks in those first months, to give me a chance to share what I'd learned, and help me re-enter."

Part of re-entering involved dealing with a few basic physical matters and brushing up on some lapsed social skills. Her sense of hearing had become so keen that all phone ringers had to be set to mute for weeks. Her sense of smell was so acute that she couldn't walk down the street without being besieged by the smell of the neighbors' garbage cans. She had virtually no ability to engage in small talk. "The inevitable question, 'Did you have a nice trip?' left me dumbfounded, unable to speak. I was really out of sync with people."

She had also hoped, on returning, that the trip would help reform her marriage of twenty-two years, which she described as "unemotional, businesslike, and efficient." Her intention on returning, she says, "was to work hard to strengthen my family and marriage, to try and include more emotion, more spirit and passion. But clearly there wasn't room for that. What I needed was not what he needed, or wanted."

Nine months after the end of the trip, Ann removed her wedding ring, which didn't come off easily, and said to her husband, "It feels to me that we're moving into a different kind of relationship here, and it's not about a traditional marriage." After another nine months of working hard to make the transition from marriage partners to friends who wanted to continue raising their children together, and of unraveling some of their entwined roots, Ann and the children moved to Whidbey Island in Washington State. Ann cofounded, with a friend, a seminar and teaching business called PeerSpirit, whose motto, fittingly, is "in service to the circle," and whose three guiding principles are that leadership rotates, responsibility is shared, and ultimate reliance is on spirit.

AVOIDING THE BENDS

Ann's experience in making the transition back home is instructive of a critical phase of the spiritual journey—the return. While you were out there circling around the ancient tower, those you left behind were doing the dishes, feeding the baby, and going to work as usual. In other words, they were *not* on retreat, so they can't possibly know what you've seen or heard or felt, and they want to know, or maybe they don't. Either way, it's important to be sensitive to this on returning to the Ordinary World.

While away from it, you've been removed from many of the normal laws of human exchange and conduct, the imperatives of time and obligation, sometimes the comforts of home. You've been on the road, in the wilds, under a spell, deep in the tropics of meditation. You've drunk strange brews, spoken in tongues or not at all, walked around inside yourself. You've climbed a mountain, slept out under the stars, breathed rarefied air. You've been accountable to no one, worn the same clothes for four days on end, and had the bathroom all to yourself.

Re-entry is a sort of decompression, and like returning from a deep-sea dive, it's best handled slowly. If you move too fast, you endanger yourself and your experience. In fact, it's one of the simplest ways to sabotage a spiritual journey. On the last day of a vision quest I took into the Trinity Alps in Northern California some years ago, one of the guides, Jay Wood, warned me that whatever promises I made to myself during the journey, whatever insights I gained and intentions I set, I would need to defend them against the tendency of life to level all uprisings, to stomp my enthusiasms back into low relief.

Be careful, he said, lest I twist an ankle going back down the mountain, get into a car wreck on the drive home, get sick or get into arguments with others. Beware of impulses, however unconscious, that might trigger a panic of retreat back to the relative safety of the comfort zone. He reminded me that after big openings often come big closings. After highs, lows. After breakthroughs, breakdowns. Being part of a couple, I knew this one by heart: Intense fights often follow intense intimacy.

I know one smart individual who, upon returning from a vision quest, simply went out to a movie with his wife and saved his tales of adventure and metamorphosis for the following day. My own guide's admonition, which was astute and saved me from a bundle of trouble, ended with his suggestion that I "post a guardian at the gate."

Orpheus would be a suitable choice of sentry, and his story is instructive here. Orpheus, whose lyre, it is said, moved even the stones to follow him, lost his wife, Eurydice, to the bite of a snake. Bereaved, he went to the Underworld and tried to persuade Hades to let her return to life. His music and lyrics were so beautiful that all punishments were suspended for the day. Tantalus forgot his thirst. Prometheus's liver was given a rest. Sisyphus just sat on his rock and listened. Hades relented and granted Orpheus's wish, but on the condition that while leading her to the upper world, he not look back at her until they had passed the portals of the Underworld. But just as he reached the outlet,

Orpheus, in a moment of forgetfulness or doubt that Eurydice was still following him, looked back, and she instantly disappeared.

If you forget that you have changed while on your journey, that you come
back followed by another whose spirit you sought, that you made promises
that must be kept, and that there are conditions to your transformation, you'll
jeopardize your mission. Know that your vision will follow you back and must
be incorporated into your life and the lives of those you know. The best way to
communicate your experience to others, says Foster, is not to talk about it but
to live it. "Vision, if it is anything, is your life story in action."

ten

MEMORY'S VITAL SECRETS

The writer Toni Morrison once described how the Mississippi River had been straightened out in places to make room for houses and livable acreage, and how occasionally the river will flood these places. Flood is the word they use, she said, "but in fact it is not flooding; it is remembering. Remembering where it used to be. All water has a perfect memory and is forever trying to get back to where it was."

People, too, have perfect memory for some things, and one of the purposes of reviewing our own histories, Morrison says, is to remind ourselves of where we were before we were "straightened out" and paved over. Personal recollection can help us remember what we already know, and the healing properties of memory and imagination, which of course are blood relations, can help us recapture our natural curves. History is a story, and the telling of deep stories is the doing of soul work.

Our past is intricately woven into our calls, and we can learn much about those calls by casting the occasional glance backward. The past tells us what has passed on to us and what we're attuned to because of it. It tells us what wounds might be calls in waiting, what business is unfinished. It tells us what footprints we follow, what legacies and dynasties we're driven to carry on, what damnations we're driven to transmute, even what wrongs we feel compelled to right, which is what the journalist Marvin Barrett was propelled by when, as a young man, he made a solemn vow.

The catalyst for that promise was a tragedy that took place on an Iowa summer afternoon in 1928, when he was eight. His three-year-old brother, whose hand he had been holding only a moment before, was suddenly struck down by a car on the avenue they had been warned repeatedly to avoid, and his lifeless body was from that moment on "inescapably forever mine." It was that afternoon, he would write fifty-five years later, "that drew me to religion, made it inevitable that at twenty-two I would dedicate my life to God. Nothing short of that dedication could set that afternoon right."

For many writers and artists, the themes that predominate in their work also dominate their memories. To some degree, this is true for all of us. The past shapes our visions, which in turn define what we'll see and what we'll seek. The past contains hints about "the deeper-than-conscious goals toward which the movement of our lives is trying to take us," as Ira Progoff says, that thread that has always alternated between being visible and invisible, between surfacing and diving.

The past reminds us of our struggles with our destinies and can often inspire us to remember that "the great thing existed and was therefore possible, and so may be possible again," as Nietzsche put it. The past reminds us that we've not only risen to challenges before and taken on daunting calls but also occasionally stepped into the ring with a prizefighter and not been utterly undone, even if we haven't prevailed. It shows us what wisdom we've wrested from experience and what powers we've earned for our troubles. For many of us, the past also contains the records of a diaspora, the scattering of our life's purposes and integrity, the strewing of our priorities, the way we've wandered out of earshot of whatever is calling to us. Recollection is a way we can, again, re-member ourselves, gather what's been dispersed, and in the process perhaps throw off a few curses.

In recollecting the past, you needn't compile an exhaustive account of your life, although some explorers, such as Carl Jung, Carlos Castaneda, Nikos Kazantzakis, and Buddha, have gone over the details of their entire lives in the service of self-knowledge, in Jung's case twice. You can narrow your sights and

still see a lot. You can focus just on "developmental" areas like childhood, adolescence, middle or old age. You can remember what took place in the arenas
of schooling, spirituality, relationships, creativity, or work life. You can even
write your autobiography, as Deena Metzger suggests in *Writing for Your Life,*
through the history of your relationship to trees.

You can also enter into dialogue with the forces that formed you. You can
talk with your father or mother, with the house you grew up in, with the
biggest decision of your life, with your most powerful conviction, or with the
ghost of whatever saint has hovered near you all your life. I once talked with
Elijah, the spirit of freedom for whom my family always reserved a chair and a
glass of wine during Passover celebrations, but who, at least to my untrained
eyes, never seemed to come; I asked him what it takes to be truly free.

In *The Mystery of My Story,* Paula Farrell Sullivan recounts the experience
of a man who wrote a lengthy dialogue with his old algebra book, realizing in
the process that what had deterred him from entering medical school was his
fear of math. He also discovered that this option was still open to him, this call
still called to him, so in his forties he quit his job and went to medical school,
following what Robert Frost called "the road not taken."

By opening the inactive file, says Progoff, we may discover the lost opportunities of our lives. Though some of them are dead, others are merely dormant. We might remember the times we held off fateful encounters with the
truth, avoided dealing with something we have never since been able to shake,
or suffered a crisis whose message completely escaped us. We may see the times
we followed the path of reason rather than intuition, the path of least resistance rather than the *right* way. We may remember unfinished business and
decide that we can find meaning in finishing it, possibly even revelation.

In the nineteenth century, Progoff describes in *At a Journal Workshop,* a
group of archaeologists discovered an ancient Egyptian tomb in which lay a
portion of a tree. Embedded in the wood was a seed, which they planted,
merely to see if anything would happen. They never expected that after three
thousand years the seed would grow—but it did.

❦

However we recount our personal histories, whether we conjure them
through writing, drawing, audiotaping or videotaping, we go to them not for a
bland reportage but for a literature of the person; not for the view through a
knothole—which is often the perspective we get on our present lives from

inside them, from present time—but for the panorama. We go to them with the understanding that, as Einstein said, no discovery was ever made except by those who were willing to lift their noses off the grindstone of details and take in the big picture, the one that shows us our lives have patterns every bit as distinct as those that land takes on when seen from the air. They have substance, forward momentum, designs of their own.

Not everyone feels this way about their past, of course. For some people, history isn't so much a gold mine as merely a mine shaft, "the nightmare from which I am trying to awaken," as the character Stephen Dedalus said in James Joyce's *Ulysses*. For others, history is synonymous with that most hated class in high school, that intellectual equivalent of leftovers. This may be especially so for minorities who don't see themselves represented in the history books because history belongs to the victors. We, too, may look back at our personal histories and have a hard time finding our own truest selves represented there. We may see nothing more than the chronicle of a passage through time, of the roles we played and the things we did and a life lived on other people's terms.

Still, if we go to the past at all, we go to it as one would to scripture, myth, or a guidebook: to find out how we should live, because as the writer Thomas Carlyle wrote, history is "the true epic poem and divine scripture." We go to it like miners, or detectives, or maybe penitents seeking absolution. We go to it to validate our lives, to prove that "I am the man, I suffered, I was there," as Walt Whitman wrote in *Song of Myself.* We go to it to ask our questions: What matters? What has always been there? What answers does my past reveal about the questions that are central to my life? What have I found myself saying to the world over and over just by the act of my life? What has been foreshadowed? What have people been telling me all my life?

We don't ask "What is the meaning of life?" but "What is the meaning of *my* life?"

We might also ask if our memories are to be trusted, knowing that the past is a game of telephone, losing and gaining something with every telling, and that any history depends on where you stand, on which side of the sword or the pen. It depends on your position relative to the throne, on the weight of the grudges you bear, on not just what happened but how you *felt* about what happened. Six people standing around a statue will report six different views. Four people witnessing an accident will demonstrate the laws of relativity. Three people growing up in the same family will each have different parents.

Memory is imprecise; it misinterprets. It is utterly averse to certainty. In some ways, we don't have direct access even to our own past. We stand on one side of a barrier and it on the other. Our view of the past—and the future—is clouded by ignorance and emotion. We approach it peering through frosted glass, with imaginations on fire. Memory, a child once explained, is "the thing I forget with."

Recently, a sizable number of people questioned in a large survey thought Chernobyl was a ski resort, DNA a food additive, and protons something you put on salad. An awful lot of erroneous information floats around out there and in our heads, and when we loop-de-loo into childhood, it pays to have a healthy skepticism for even our own cherished notions. We need to cast a discerning eye not only on the stories we tell about ourselves but also on the stories others tell about us.

Facts are not always facts. If George Washington never chopped down a cherry tree and Galileo never dropped weights off the leaning Tower of Pisa and Sir Isaac Newton wasn't inspired to discover gravity by an apple falling on his head, then maybe we ought to reexamine a few of the legends in our own lives, pull a few statues from their pedestals. Maybe it's also not true what others told you about how you should live and what's important to pursue, about your capabilities and what you'd ever amount to. Maybe they didn't *really* know what was best for you. Approach your own history with the eye of a revisionist, scalpel at the ready.

Remember, too, that it isn't necessarily true that we remember what's important to us and forget what isn't. "We forget all too soon the things we thought we could never forget," Joan Didion once wrote. "We forget what we whispered and what we dreamed. We forget who we were."

TAKING STOCK

When those who had lost their homes in the 1992 fire in Oakland, California, were asked by interviewers what they grabbed first on their way out the door, most of them said "my photo albums." We may say that the past is dead, that it's irrelevant and the present moment all that matters. But it isn't true. The past is alive and full of pertinence. The past matters.

Why else are we so keen on raising the *Titanic,* on plundering the graves of kings, unwrapping mummies, and knowing the birthdays of rocks? Why else would we risk our necks to save our photo albums? We want to remember who we are and how far we've come, how we lived and what was central to that life, what we've gained or lost, and how we survived or didn't. "We want to know what is in the trunks and lockers we lug forward through time," says the writer Lee Abbott, "what vital secrets they can be sprung to reveal." Hoping to find its den, we want to follow the tracks of time to where they disappear in the undergrowth.

We also want to know what the past can tell us about the present and the future because our past begs the question inherent in any history: Does it have a goal?

History answers with sly winks. Historians say that history doesn't necessarily repeat itself, that history isn't necessarily fate, but that the future can still be inferred from the past, that stories naturally contain clues. They insist that the study of history offers not certitude but only diagnostic skill, and that the best qualification of a prophet is to have a good memory.

Sometimes history makes us wiser, and sometimes it only teaches us that we've learned nothing from it, and we still believe that we can go about our lives as if they'll never be interrupted. In fact, I've heard it said that the best way to make God laugh is to proclaim your five-year plan. History is, above all, the story of change, and it's riddled with the unexpected: the upset decision, the sneak attack, the iceberg dead ahead, the confoundment of the elements, the unforeseen intervention, the sudden change of heart or mind. History and callings teach the same need for resilience.

People who have near-death experiences often report that part of the proceedings is a life review—conducted in an atmosphere of impeccable compassion. The past is vital to the future, and there's a bond between where we've been and where we're going. Death is a threshold experience, as are callings, and it's not uncommon for people to take stock before proceeding.

John Kotre once took stock at a threshold in his own life that demanded he be clear about what he was being called to do with his work and his marriage. The core of that life review was the memory of a pair of white suede gloves that his father once talked about and that had belonged to his grandfather, whom he never met. He has also never actually seen the gloves but always pictured them lying on top of some old clarinets he once found in the musty attic of his grandmother's house. Their memory helped him at a critical moment in his life and, as he put it, "confirmed the path."

When John was thirty-five, he taped the life history of his parents. Ten years later, in counseling with his wife, he was encouraged by the therapist to look at his family history to help him puzzle out how to proceed with his marriage of twenty years. John had become involved with another woman whom he loved. She eventually became his second wife, but for the sake of "the integrity of the counseling," he stopped seeing her.

John, himself a psychologist at the University of Michigan at Dearborn, went back to the tapes he made of his parents' lives and heard there something he hadn't heard the first time around, which, he says, "brings up the question of our interior state of readiness; what are we waiting to hear? I must have been waiting to hear something about soul."

What grabbed John's attention was a story his father told about his grandfather, who in his native Hungary had been a musician in a military band, and who was touring Europe and composing before he was twenty. When he came to the United States in 1912, he found that there were far more musicians than there were jobs for musicians, and after a year of struggle he gave up his music and got a job making bricks. After some time doing this kind of work, his hands could no longer fit into the white gloves he had worn when playing the clarinet. After brick making, he took a job shoveling coal. John's grandfather gave up his music, gave up what his father called his "whole soul," for bricks and coal, emblems of the practical life, elemental and down-to-earth, the stuff of building houses and making electricity and moving trains.

When he put away his clarinet, he did so for good, not ever turning back lest his soul turn to stone and crack down the middle. And when he listened to his own children practicing the piano, he would sometimes bolt upright in his chair and cry out in German, *"Falsch!"* False. He was reacting to a wrong note, but he may just as likely have been crying out about the life he had chosen.

"When I listened to the tapes again," John said, "when I heard the story of the white gloves, I did so with great relief, because I knew I was to go ahead and choose life over a deadening sense of responsibility. Now I hate to encourage divorce, or lack of responsibility, but in my life that's how things worked out. The memory of the gloves confirmed my decision, cleansed me of guilt—which in many ways is a good emotion; it makes you think twice—and connected me to a kindred spirit. Over the years, the memory has also returned to ease my way through the kind of deaths that permit life, such as separating from people I love or people I work with in order to pursue my soul. The gloves tell me what to do: Stick to the soul!"

He applied this advice not only to his marriage but also to his work. "One of the most moving and humbling parts of this experience for me was that although the gloves exist only in my mind, I know that they fit me and nobody else. I'm the only one in my family with slender fingers like my grandfather's, and an artistic temperament. It makes me think of Cinderella, and of the symbol of gloves—something about how they *fit*. I'm the one who was supposed to pick up those gloves and carry on what my grandfather wasn't able to carry on, which was art. I don't want to be a clinical or scientific psychologist, which I've been, approaching people's lives abstractly and statistically. I want to bring out the art and soul in my work, be a psychologist who makes portraits of individual lives." This is something he has increasingly done, recording people's life stories and putting them into books, audio programs, and even a public television series called *Seasons of Life*.

"It's been eighty years since my grandfather put those white gloves aside," John says. "If only he knew how much they have mattered."

W H A T   H A S   A L W A Y S   B E E N   T H E R E

Years ago, I spent a couple of days on a horse farm outside of Lexington, Kentucky, during foaling season. One night I stayed up well past midnight, helping birth a horse, pulling her gently by her front legs from her mother's belly. The stable manager told me that horses are usually born after dark because they need to be ready to move with the herd in the morning. It's an instinct that's as old as the dawn horse fifty million years ago and hasn't changed, even though there's no herd anymore to move with in the morning. Within one hour that wobbly foal was up on her feet.

We all have patterns fixed within us in the same way, designs we can't scribble over or erase. By going back in time, we can find what is timeless in us, what is enduring and not just ephemeral. We discover that we aren't just a particle but also a wave that starts far out at sea.

Calls fit into these patterns, and they grow out of them. In a sense, patterns *are* calls. They are what we've always felt the compulsion to do, for better and for worse, whether it's to say a certain thing, create and re-create a certain experience, serve a certain cause, or solve a certain problem. They are where we've worn footpaths to and from issues in our lives. The dream that won't go away is a call, as is the symptom that recurs, the section of the bookstore you always go to first, and the lesson you've endlessly had to learn or are intent upon impressing on your children. The thing people have been telling you all your life is a call, along with the kind of partners you continually attract, the things you repeatedly fight about with others, and whatever subject you can speak about with invincible authority, the emotional place about which you can unequivocally say, "I've been there!"

Ever since the writer Madison Smartt Bell was a boy, he found himself quietly inserting "he said" and "she said" into his friends' conversations, "as if I were to be life's narrator." That's a call. Ever since the Bishop Elmer Cleveland was a boy, playing church with his sister and friends, he'd always be the preacher, standing up in a little wagon and preaching. That's a call.

In discovering such patterns, people who feel they don't have a call may be surprised to find not only that they do but that they always have, and that they've been responding or reacting to it for much of their lives. While some calls come and go, others are lifelong projects, especially those that involve the wounds we inherit, for there's no end to the work of learning to love or forgive, deal with anger or fear or trust, figure out intimacy. Either way, we're thrown like yarrow sticks, and by consulting the past we can find patterns in the configurations.

Vocational counselors encourage people to take inventories of their personal values, their most beloved pursuits, their strengths and weaknesses, the major events in their lives, the activities in which they feel most at home, the things they believe absolutely, and the things they were told to believe absolutely but don't. They're after patterns and the calls concealed in them like subliminal messages. They understand that any change that fails to take into account the firmly established forces in your life—the great loves and hates, the unremittant beliefs and values—is likely to founder.

Sharon Matola does what she has always wanted to do. She follows her love of animals wherever it leads. By doing so, she has cultivated an enviable kind of success: a match between who she is and what she does. She runs the only zoo in Belize, a country that essentially *is* a zoo. The mahogany capital of the world, it is the only English-speaking country in Central America, 60 percent of whose land is still rain forest. If that were transposed on the United States, there would be solid forest from Chicago to San Francisco.

The story of how she ended up there began as far back as she can remember. She grew up in a row house in Baltimore City and regularly made the rounds visiting the dogs in the neighborhood, all of whom she knew by name. She kept worms as pets and often returned home at sunset with skinned knees and a jar full of butterflies. When her parents moved to the suburbs, she struck up a friendship with a squirrel, whom she tamed with peanuts, teaching him to sit on her knee.

"I was always enchanted, *thrilled,* with animals. All the books I read were about animals. All my friends were animals. I didn't hang around with kids very much, wasn't very social as a child. I didn't have a friend until I was twelve, and that was her wanting to hang around with me, not the other way around. I love the wildness and spontaneity of animals, and how responsive they are. They can sense things in people much more than people can sense things in people. I've walked around the zoo with people who are not fond of animals, and the animals will keep their distance. They'll respond to those who are fond of them. I have a lot of respect for any organism with that kind of sensitivity.

"I become very bored around most people. My mind wanders. I don't stay focused. I feel more comfortable in more beastly environments, and out in the bush. I'm not motivated by what motivates most people."

When Sharon was sixteen, she planned to run off to an island off the coast of Maryland and survive in the wild for a week, but her parents found a survival knife in her room and ended that scheme. "I always wanted to be an explorer. I remember drawing treasure maps as a kid, making mysterious passageways out of nothing, mostly my imagination, and going through people's backyards as if they were jungle paths. To be a real jungle explorer is a dream come true."

It started coming true after she graduated from high school and joined the air force, where she attended jungle survival training school. Part of the curriculum involved being dropped off in the middle of a jungle in Panama, which, once again, thrilled her. It was strange and familiar all at once. It was home and yet far from home. It was nothing like the city and the suburbs. There were no signs, no streets laid out with geometrical precision, no lawns straining for a dainty approximation of a golf course manicure. It was simply *alive,* and Sharon was completely in her element. "I loved it. I didn't want to leave."

She did leave, though, and over the next few years had stints as a researcher at the Mote Shark Research Institute in Florida, an assistant to a Romanian lion tamer, and as an ichthyologist classifying fish off the coral reefs in Central America. She got a degree in biology from New College in Florida, and while pursuing a master's degree in mycology (fungus), she answered an ad in the local newspaper for "tall white women" to be exotic dancers in a traveling Mexican circus. Given her previous experience working with the lion tamer, she was also given the lion and tiger acts. She would switch from her dancer's outfit—red sequined bikini, eyelashes out to here, a feather headdress, and silver high heels—into her gold lamé lion tamer's outfit.

Back in the States after a year of the gypsy life, she received a letter from British conservation filmmaker Richard Foster, whom she knew through an acquaintance, asking her to manage the captive animals used in one of his documentaries. He enclosed a round-trip ticket to Belize.

During the filming, Foster received a telegram from his film company in London, advising him that funding had dried up for the project. Before he left for another assignment in Borneo, he asked if Sharon would take responsibility for getting rid of the animals, which had become her wards and her friends.

Getting rid of them meant either taking care of them, which Sharon had no money to do, or killing them, because releasing them would have had the same effect, only slower. They were animals—jaguars, pumas, boas, tapirs, crocodiles, spider monkeys, toucans—donated to the film largely by locals who had kept many of them as pets. They knew only captivity and wouldn't have survived in the wild. With what she describes as "zero planning" and a state of desperation, Sharon threw herself into saving the animals, who were then housed in crude wire-mesh cages on a primitive plot of land thirty miles from Belize City. She was once again in the middle of the jungle, in survival mode.

With not a little irony, she painted a sign that read BELIZE ZOO and stuck it by the side of the dirt road that serves as Belize's main east-west artery. Then she paid a visit to her nearest neighbor, a bar and restaurant three miles down the road called JB's Watering Hole in the Middle of Nowhere. She told the proprietor that if his customers ever got bored, to send them down to her zoo. Whether it sat well with JB or not, his customers began paying visits to the new zoo, and word spread.

Soon she had daily visitors: schoolchildren from all over the country, for whom a trip to Sharon's zoo is now part of their yearly agenda; tourists making detours from their visits to the local Mayan ruins and the diving sites offshore; British soldiers stationed in Belize (formerly British Honduras) who heard about the zoo through Sharon's local environmental radio show on British Forces Radio and Radio Belize; members of the Ministry of Education; the Australian filmmaker Peter Weir, who contracted to use some of the zoo's animals in his movie *The Mosquito Coast,* starring Harrison Ford; even Prince Edward of the House of Windsor, who, on a visit to Belize, let the tea get cold at a capital luncheon while he sneaked off to see the zoo.

To support the zoo, Sharon has done whatever it took, from raising and selling chickens, which she sold to restaurants and coastal resorts—riding her Kawasaki 650 motorcycle into town twice a month for two years, carrying eighty pounds of plucked chicken in a backpack—to making forays into the jungle of international fund-raising, which has netted the zoo unexpected rewards. An architectural firm in Seattle donated a master plan for the zoo. The Hershey Foods company donated money for a jaguar exhibit. The Arco Solar company provides the zoo with photovoltaic cells for its energy needs, making it both the world's first sun-powered zoo, and one that's being studied as a model by other developing nations, as well as an exemplar of Third World conservation efforts. One woman she met at a zoo conference in the States, who shared Sharon's vision, even quit her job in Atlanta, sold her house, and moved to Belize to help set up the zoo's education program, demonstrating how one person's passion can become a call for others and serve them in the most inadvertent ways.

Today, though the zoo has 125 animals of forty-eight native species, a staff of twenty-two, a thousand acres, and an operating budget of nearly half a million dollars, Sharon still says, "It's an absolute miracle that it worked. It's been a survival situation for the animals *and* for me. If I stopped pedaling the bicycle for even a moment, it all just stopped. We came close to closing many times and having to end the whole operation."

What kept her going, she says, was her lifelong "sympathy for the animals" and seeing the looks of amazement and wonder on the faces of the Belizean children, who reminded her so much of herself. "The sacrifices I've made are nothing compared to the contribution. I'm very glad I did this with my life. As a matter of fact, the happiest people I know are those who are following the same likes they had when they were children."

THE BOTTOM OF THE ICEBERG

INTERVIEWER: If your house were on fire,
which object would you take with you?
JEAN COCTEAU: The fire!

I once saw an eagle drop like a stone into the blue-green water of a bay in the Sea of Cortez. For the better part of a minute, he thrashed around violently on the surface, rising a little and then, it seemed, being yanked back down, sometimes nearly underwater. Finally he rose, clapping his wings loudly against the water, and lifted out a fish almost as large as himself, carrying it off to a cliffside nest.

Whatever lives beneath the surface will usually put up a fight to stay there, and this goes for some of the wildlife we're likely to encounter in diving into our own pasts. We're up against that which doesn't want to be remembered and wants to remain anonymous, invisible, mute, to cover itself with dirt and leaves and hide while the posse gallops by. We're up against whatever we've rejected throughout the run of our lives; the parts of us that split off and went tumbling away; our unlived life; the animal that sleeps at our doorstep.

These unlived parts can include "negative" qualities, such as anger, fear, weakness, aggression, vanity, idealism, lust, laziness, tears, everything we were instructed not to talk about because it was too embarrassing and too private, all the ghettos and back alleys of our psyches. The unlived parts of ourselves can also include "positive" qualities, like power, leadership, trust, compassion, commitment, sensitivity, sexuality, creativity, faith, exuberance, and the contents of that 90 percent of our brains we haven't figured out how to use.

These rejected parts include whatever wasn't loved, respected, and accepted in us by ourselves or our parents, teachers, peers, religion, and culture. Carl Jung called it our shadow. Robert Bly calls it "the long bag we drag behind us." In it are all those qualities that were disapproved of by the people whose approval we needed in order to survive, or believed we needed.

Here's how Bly explains it: When we were one or two years old, we had a 360-degree personality. Energy radiated from all parts of us. But as soon as our parents began saying things like "Can't you be still?" or "Sit up straight" or "Quit running around" or "Don't be smarter than the boys" or "Don't touch yourself there" or "Don't talk to strangers" or "Boys can't be dancers," we started stuffing parts of ourselves in the bag in order to assure an uninterrupted flow of our par-ents' love and approval, even if it was only measured out by the eyedropper.

We then responded the same way to our teachers, our cronies, our col-leagues, and our culture, and by the time we were twenty or so, our pie was reduced to a sliver, and a terrible wealth of talent and soul was imprisoned. In becoming "civilized," we became brutish, tyrannical with our energies, and fas-cist in our repressions. We had no choice, however. It was our soul's way of protecting us, the only way we could make our way through.

In whatever we rejected, though, is something that a part of us *wants,* and there lies a calling that we should follow, if only for the sake of completing the jigsaw and healing the past. We want that anger and that creativity, and the creative power that anger can be if we learn how to use it. We want those tears that swab the soul. We want access to the top of our lungs, where the shouts and the holy hosannahs are, the whoops and wails and hullabaloos—not just the bottom of our lungs, which is reserved for whispers and polite conversa-tion, for things said under the breath.

If calls take us toward what we most deeply want anyway—authenticity, integrity, the full complement, the uncut version—then shining a light into the shadow is part of our deliverance to that outcome, part of our passage. "Everything rests on the awareness that a hidden life exists," the writer Joy Williams says.

In any case, we're going to need all the help we can get in following our calls. We're going to need every resource at our disposal, including some of those we've previously disposed of. We're going to need our self-interest to admit that something is missing in our lives, and maybe our despair to moti-vate us to find out what it is. We're going to need our blind faith to trust that what we hear *is* a call. We're going to need our stubbornness and righteous anger to stand up to the resistance from within and without. We're going to need the hermit in us to separate from the culture of conformity. We're going to need our insanity to do what might seem insane. We're going to need our spontaneity and impulsiveness or we'll never make the jumps. We're going to need our power to push us through, and our joy to celebrate at the feasts.

A D R A G O N   I N   T H E   C A L C U L A T I O N S

Ignoring these needs isn't the ticket. If we don't go to them, if we don't occasionally arrange the lighting so that our shadows are cast forward where we can see them, in all likelihood they'll come at us from behind. They'll lodge themselves between our intentions and our achievements, thumbing their noses at our attempts to get them off the playing field. They'll become the downstairs neighbors who bang on the ceiling with a broomstick while we're busy having a party.

"It does not do you good to leave a dragon out of your calculations if you live near him," J. R. R. Tolkien once said.

Jung considered it a foregone conclusion that whatever we're unwilling to face in ourselves, we'll be forced to confront in the outer world, that our past doesn't obediently stay in the past, and that our lives will conspire in a hundred ways to call us toward those very things. What we most want to run from we'll end up running toward and drawing to us, the way sharks are attracted to thrashing bodies.

"The material I was determined to elude has claimed me," the writer Pat Hampl once described, "while the subjects I wished to enlist in my liberation—fat novels about love and betrayal—have spurned me." For example, when she started college at the University of Minneapolis, she lost no time in dumping the Catholic world her parents had so carefully constructed for her. This is why she chose to go there. "I understood that many people had succeeded in losing their religion at the university." For decades she considered it a shining achievement that she had eluded the nuns. Result: She spent the better part of five years writing a memoir about growing up Catholic; the protagonist was a contemplative nun.

Hampl also felt vaguely ashamed that her Czech grandmother couldn't write English, "that she was who she was at all. An immigrant is a quaint antecedent at a distance. Mine was too close for comfort. The shame was real, disloyal, mean. Result: She came and got me and became the heroine of my first memoir."

There is no walking away from our shadows or the radioactive elements of our past, anymore than we can walk away from an angry partner and expect him or her to not still be angry when we come back, anymore than we can shove unpaid bills in a drawer and expect the electricity to stay on, anymore than we can pour poison into the ground and not expect it to come up through the fruits and vegetables. There's no *away.* There's no *out,* as in throwing the garbage out, no trash icon, no abort function. Like the Earth, our psyches are closed systems.

You can't, for instance, convince yourself one clearheaded and optimistic day that you no longer feel any fear and that you will sit right down and do Something Important, without expecting that your shadow, unable to stomach the hypocrisy and, in fact, feeling genuine fear, will turn on the television and order out for pizza, or discover some ancient and unfinished project that suddenly seems in immediate need of resurrection, or insist that you couldn't possibly get a lick of work done with your office looking the way it does.

We end up going to our shadows one way or another. Either we take them on willingly and attempt to work them into something useful, or at least manageable, or we splatter them onto others—"projecting," as psychologists call it. For instance, if we're frustrated with ourselves for not following a call, we often become frustrated with others who aren't following theirs, or envious of those who are. The most expedient way to recognize shadow is to look at what we project, because what we can't admit or abide in ourselves, we'll find, even seek out, in others; it is what we despise in people, or envy, or worship, or become obsessed with; whatever manners we associate with devils and saints.

Ursula Le Guin's book *A Wizard of Earthsea* addresses projection beautifully. In it, a young wizard named Ged accidentally releases a demon into the world in practicing some sorcery. The book revolves around his attempts to reconcile this situation. At the end, he confronts the demon and realizes that the only way to gain control over it is to say its name, which is his own.

"Name the pain," theologian Matthew Fox says. By naming our demons we diminish their power over us. We reform them from demons back to daimons. Daimons were the origin of demons. They were divine spirits, demigods, intermediaries who passed notes back and forth between gods and humans. The Latin translation of *daimon* is soul. As such, they can be either creative or destructive, depending entirely on whether we receive them or reject them. By negating them, we turn them into angry spooks, consigning them to what the poet John Milton called Pandaemonium, the capital of hell, and an apt description of what happens in the human psyche when our guides are driven underground, when a force as powerful as the shadow is scorned.

Some traditions still carry on the notion that noontime is actually dangerous because at this time the shadow—being identified with the soul, and the soul with life—grows smallest, meaning that life itself is threatened. Conversely, says James Hillman, the ancient root of the word *happiness* is eudaimonia, or a well-pleased daimon.

Since shadow is largely what was unloved in us, and in some cases with good reason, reintegrating these parts will mean attempting to love them as if they're strangers who might be gods—but it's still critical to keep our wits about us. Loving our own cruelty or rage or vengefulness or narcissism is different from identifying with it or giving it license. Treating the devil with respect is not the same as worshipping the devil. Dealing with the shadow demands the ability to deal with paradox: Shadow must be loved *and* changed. It is intolerable *and* it is in us. The enemy is also an ally, or as the novelist Isabel Allende says, "A scary cellar acts as a stimulus to the imagination," which is why she hides, in her own basement, "sinister surprises" for her grandchildren: a plaster skeleton, treasure maps, trunks filled with pirate disguises.

Myth is full of examples of the dualistic nature of the daimonic:

- Pluto, the Roman name for Hades, god of the Underworld, is also the god of wealth.
- Mars, the god of war, was originally the god of agriculture and the life force.
- Pele, the Hawaiian goddess of volcanoes, represents a destructive force, but also one that actually creates new earth.
- The wicked fairy in *Sleeping Beauty* was a wise woman angry at not being invited to a royal bash given in honor of the newborn princess.
- Lucifer means light.
- The Minotaur, the bull-headed beast who lived at the center of the labyrinth, was named Asterion, which means star.
- Ninety percent of the shadow, said Jung, who coined the term, is "pure gold."

In her book *When the Heart Waits,* Sue Monk Kidd describes a conference she once attended, during which participants were given a sheet of colored construction paper and asked to tear it into a shape that represented their lives. While these were later being pasted on a bulletin board to form a large collage, someone came around with a glass bowl and collected the scraps of paper everyone had torn off and intended to discard. The jar was then placed on an altar. Only by gathering up this "confetti of scars and torn places," Kidd says, only by embracing it and setting it on an altar, can we begin to transform it.

The philosopher G. I. Gurdjieff followed a similar instinct during the time he led a spiritual community in France, which included an old man whom no one liked. The man was irascible, unkempt, fighting with everyone, and helping no one with the chores. One day, fed up with how he in turn was treated, he left for Paris, to everyone's relief. Gurdjieff, however, followed him there and offered him a considerable monthly stipend if he would return to the community. When he did, everyone was appalled and became more so when they discovered that the old man was now being *paid* for his incivilities while the rest of them were paying quite a sum to be in the community.

After hearing their complaints, Gurdjieff said, "This man is like yeast for bread. Without him here you would never really learn about anger, irritability, patience, and compassion. That is why you pay me, and why I hire him."

Such solutions utilize what I've come to think of as bicycle psychology: If you're falling, you turn your wheel *toward* the fall, *into* the skid. If you're losing traction with the ground, you turn in the direction of the loss. We do not become enlightened by imagining figures of light, Jung once said, but by making the darkness conscious, though at the risk of some audacity I would add that doing some of the former might come in handy during bouts with the latter.

The body's own immune system operates on this principle and shows us that the skill of transforming darkness through embrace is one that comes quite naturally; it is one we know in our cells. The body routinely "turns not-self into self," as the author Neil Douglas-Klotz describes, merging with invading enemies and making them part of the body, part of the whole. We can thus use whatever pulls us down to help pull us back up, the way rockets use the gravity of the planets to fling themselves deeper into space.

We acquaint ourselves with the shadow and the past in which it leaves its tracks, however, in order to become aware of as much of our experience as we can, to have as much information as possible to draw on for our journeys. We are not just hauling whatever is in the catacombs up into the light of day and cataloguing it, as if for some museum exhibit. We need to go bodily down there through therapy, art, journaling, active imagination, bodywork, etc. and spend some time just mucking around and getting to know the place. We're *meant* to stick our noses in this deep strata. "It's common sense," Annie Dillard once wrote. "When you move in, you try to learn the neighborhood."

The story of the Garden of Eden is a good case in point. Why would anyone have planted there a "tree of the knowledge of good and evil" without expecting—without intending—that the locals would take an interest? It's the Original Setup. It's like leaving a bunch of children alone in the house and telling them not to look in the cookie jar. Or telling Pandora not to look in the box you gave her as a *gift*. We weren't provided with curiosities for nothing, the neighborhood is out there for the exploring, and it stands to reason that we're going to stick our hands in the cookie jar, reach up into the tree, open the box. And we should.

Danger lies not so much in the shadow itself but in panic; in the acute anxiety that grips some people when confronted by some of the material there; in the fear of losing their footing in the conscious world because of what they find in the unconscious; in the fright that we rightly feel, Bly says, "when we see the shadow of an ape pass along the alley wall."

If you're at all worried about being overwhelmed by your past or your shadow, reckon with it in a caretaking situation such as therapy or a therapeutic workshop. You can't just pull the contents out of the bag like you're pulling feathers out of a pillow, at least not without psychological readiness and considerable emotional effort, as well as some grounding: a solid relationship or two, a work life, a community or support group, some stabilizing routines, and a life with which you're not already overwhelmed.

Above all, says Thomas Moore, take it easy. "The shadow is a frightening reality, and anyone who talks blithely about integrating it as if you could chum up to the shadow the way you learn a foreign language, doesn't know the darkness that always qualifies shadow."

Why should we only honor those who die on the field of battle, the poet William Butler Yeats once asked, when we can show as much daring, as fierce a courage, in entering into the abyss of ourselves?

WHAT DOES AN ANGEL WANT?

The last place you'd think to look for a hero is among the downtrodden, the weak and dispossessed—what good, people once asked, could come out of Nazareth?—yet it's the stuff of cliché how often it happens just that way, that the least likely is the most likely to succeed: Jesus, Cinderella, Parsifal, the Ugly Duckling.

The last place we might think to look for a calling, too, is in the abyss, yet it often turns out that calls are echoes coming out of the chasms in our lives, the concentric rings spreading out from where something heavy was dropped into the pond, the shock waves from concussive events whose big bangs sometimes split our lives into B.C. and A.D., into marking time as that which came before it happened—the accident, the illness, the divorce, the tragedy—and that which came after it.

In such a place, Lee Glickstein found his calling. "I was called by my misery," he says, which he describes as the colossal frustration of not being able to express himself because he was "tragically, excruciatingly shy. I didn't know how to be heard. I bottled everything up. I had so much to say and didn't even know what it was, because my means of communication had been so stifled growing up."

He portrays his family, especially his father, as "listening impaired" and himself as someone who had a lot to say, but for whom it was dangerous to say it. He was teased and told to shut up. He was ignored and humiliated. "It was dangerous to be myself. Just imagine someone with a big voice coming into a family where there's no one to listen. Until I was forty-five years old, I felt incredibly frustrated. I knew I had a contribution to make, something to say, but I didn't have a voice. I remember hours and hours of pacing back and forth, saying, 'I can't believe it, I can't believe it—maybe this was a kind of prayer—I can't believe this is my life. I can't believe I'm not doing something. I can't believe I'm forty and I'm a typist.' I felt desperate to participate in the world and humiliated at being left out."

His own desperation turned him toward the dusty backwater of his past, and he was determined to find what he felt was the gift at the heart of his defining wound, determined to confront himself with it through therapy.

Not all suffering, to be sure, is redeemed with gifts and talents—sometimes people who grow up in sick families are just crippled by it—but the cold truth about turning a wound into a gift, if that is its nature, is that first you must feel it. You've got to be willing to go back and re-encounter the grief of it, starting with the brute fact that you got a bum deal, that justice is beside the point, and no one's going to make it up to you. The past can't be changed, only your attitude toward it can.

Psychologist Jean Houston says that one way toward holiness is by being punched full of holes by life. She stresses that wounding is an age-old training ground for teachers and healers. In order to discover what is trying to be born in you from your wound, what gift or call might be pressing for delivery, however, you need to stop reciting the small story about it—the particulars, the details—and tell the larger story. "Tell the tale anew," she says, "this time with the wounding as the *middle* of the story."

As you begin to retell your story, consider that Winston Churchill, one of the world's most eloquent orators, was dyslexic and stuttered as a child, as did the actor James Earl Jones. When aviator Charles Lindbergh was a boy, he had frequent nightmares about falling from a high place. Robert Peary, the first man to reach the North Pole, and Manolete, considered the world's greatest bullfighter, were both fearful, timid children who clung to their mother's legs.

Psychology would say that Manolete became a great bullfighter as compensation, but perhaps, argues James Hillman, Manolete *knew* he was a great bullfighter even at nine years old, that his fate was to stand in front of thousand-pound charging bulls, and of *course* he held on to his mother. It's not that he was inferior. He had a great destiny (assuming that you consider bullfighting a great destiny), and his guiding spirit, which understood the true proportions of his gift, was simply working to protect it so that it wouldn't emerge before he was strong enough to carry it.

Instead of seeing a childhood illness that keeps you bedridden and isolated as the cause of your later becoming a writer or a monk, says Hillman, how about imagining the call arranging for the illness, so that you might practice for your later work. Instead of seeing children who stutter or cower or are excruciatingly shy as having developmental problems, consider that they may have some great thing inside them, that their symptoms are protecting a gift which, as Houston suggests, "burgeons like a night mushroom beneath a protective cover of fallen leaves."

At the least, this approach recasts victimization as preparation, handicap as training. "The puzzle," Hillman says, "then becomes not 'How did I get this way?' or 'Why did this happen to me?' but 'What does my angel want with me?' "

In Lee's case, his angel wanted him to know that there was something beyond his wound, beyond his definition of his misery, and that if a boy who clings to his mother's legs can become the greatest bullfighter in history, then another boy who had a big voice in a family with small ears and lousy reception, who was completely tongue-tied, could become a public speaker and eventually teach others how to listen and how to be heard. His angel wanted him to know that once he had touched the wound in himself, he could bring healing touch to that same wound in others.

The turning point came when Lee began co-leading a professional brainstorming group in San Francisco called the Brain Exchange, through which he realized that he was trying to create the kind of environment he himself needed in order to find his voice. The steadfast rules in brainstorming are no criticism and all ideas are welcome. When Lee then turned his attention to creating what he refers to as Speaking Circles^SM, he took those criteria with him as the heart of the work. In fact, instead of teaching people how to speak, he taught the group how to listen, and the speaking seemed to take care of itself.

In a Speaking Circle^SM, each participant takes the stage and the microphone to present a spontaneous, five-minute talk. Afterward, the only feedback permitted is positive. Lee's theory: People already know what their shortcomings are and have had plenty of opportunities to be reminded of them. Besides, a lot of critical feedback is inaccurate anyway, more a reflection of the person giving it than the person receiving it. People *really* need to hear about their strengths. "Once you start to be heard with absolute positive attention, even if it's only for five minutes a week, you'll start to say everything you need to say."

The only drawback was that Lee was teaching what he needed to learn, but he was not submitting himself to the process that he had created for his own benefit. At one point he noticed that he was making a living teaching people public speaking, but his students, not Lee himself, were making the quantum leaps in their ability to express themselves; he was standing up only long enough to present the ground rules.

Then one day when several people didn't show up for one of the Circles, someone suggested that Lee get up and participate. "I went up there and was just as scared as anyone doing it for the first time. But when you get into the unknown, into that awful place of maybe falling apart in front of a group, or not knowing what you're going to do when you're the center of attention, and when people keep telling you you're okay anyway and you keep surviving it, you begin to realize there's something beyond any way you've ever seen yourself. I now get up every Wednesday."

So does Lee's father. It began when he attended one of Lee's public lectures and Lee introduced him to the group as "the man who made this work necessary." His father, who is eighty-five and regularly attends Speaking Circles^SM, stood up and said that he is also the man who made this work *possible,* but that in any case it's never too late to learn to listen. "My father," Lee says, "is now my student."

☙

The word *history* means to learn by inquiry, and in turning toward our own histories with inquiring minds, with curiosities sufficient to the immensity of them, we can help ourselves heal. We can even be shown a calling. In turn, by following the calls we're shown, we can sometimes heal the past and can go back to it in order to remember ourselves, to pull ourselves together into a more solid form.

The past shapes us, but by following the deep calling to heal ourselves and throw off old curses, we may be able to reshape our response to that past and perhaps even the way in which we remember it. Sometimes we're called to move backward so that we can move forward with a greater sense of ourselves, and with greater confidence.

part four

SAYING

NO

TO CALLS

eleven

FLIGHT TO TARSHISH

"No, no," cried all the evil spirits. "Sleep, sleep, sleep."
— ABORIGINAL STORY

I was standing in the kitchen when I saw the dust devil hurl itself around the corner of the house, spraying the windows with sand and grit as it flew, headed for the open garage. There hadn't been a single breeze all day; it came out of nowhere. The next thing I heard, a few seconds later, was a loud expletive, and then silence again, the whirlwind evaporating into the blue sky as instantaneously as it came.

I opened the inside door to the garage but couldn't see through the cloud of brown dust to the other side, and from somewhere in the middle of that cloud I heard a disembodied voice swearing.

My partner, Robin, had sequestered herself in the garage-studio to paint, after coming home infuriated about an incident that happened between her and a few faculty members at the graduate school she was then attending. I had rarely seen her that outraged, and only later did she remember that a "subtle voice" in the back of her mind was telling her that she was, as she put it,

obsessing, hanging on to her umbrage well past the point of diminished
returns—a voice that was calling her to let go of her anger.

It took a daimon snapping the end of his towel at her to shake the rage
from her, but it worked. The dust devil was like a violent replica of her angry
mood, and it shook her up, drained the adrenaline from her, and freed her
from being caught in her own drama. "I was afraid that if I didn't let go," she
said, "I might draw worse negativity to me."

Having seen the *deliberation* with which the elements seemed to single out
her studio from all the possible landing sites in that enormous desert, Robin
was convinced that she'd brought that little storm down on herself, and I'm
inclined to agree. It was as if, by her refusal to listen to that voice in her head,
she somehow reached through a barrier that normally separates the real and
imaginal worlds and called down the Furies.

"We are an integral part of higher, mysterious entities," the playwright
Vaclav Havel once wrote, "against whom—or which—it is not advisable to
blaspheme."

Robin had profaned a call with a snub, however subtle and for whatever
good reasons, and brought a storm down on her own head. In doing so, she
was acting out a personal version of the archetypal drama we all provoke when
we say no to our calls. It's the same story made famous by Jonah, patron saint
of refused callings, and someone who understood better than most why natural disasters are referred to as "acts of God."

I was indirectly introduced to the full story of Jonah by Robin's father. On
my bookshelf I have a copy of the pocket-size Jewish Bible he was issued by the
United States Army in World War II. One day, struggling with the ill effects of
an unanswered calling of my own, I flipped it open randomly in search of
guidance, as I often do with books, and my eye fell directly onto the opening
lines of the story of Jonah, that bird in flight, caught between heaven and
earth, between saying yes and saying no. Jonah, fleeing to Tarshish with grim
relief, was running for the last place he thought God would ever look for him,
though God is always turning over stones.

Jonah was called to preach to the people of Ninevah and refused because
he presumed himself to be both an incompetent preacher and yet an expert
judge—he insisted the Ninevites weren't worth saving. So he went down to the
docks and booked himself passage on a ship sailing in the opposite direction
from Ninevah, to Tarshish. God, however, was not amused, nor fooled. He
sent a storm down on the ship, not so much as punishment but as an earnest

appeal for a more affirmative response from Jonah. But Jonah, despite being the strongest sailor of them all, the one who could subdue the storm if he chose, by taking responsibility for his part in creating it, chose instead to avoid dealing with it by going to sleep in the bottom of the boat, going into a state of what's referred to nowadays as denial, which only made the storm angrier.

He regained consciousness only when roused by the captain, that spirit of wakefulness, who confronted him with his responsibility for the mounting calamity. Jonah then proved himself to be a man of considerable courage. He confessed that he was to blame and offered himself as a sacrifice, telling the frightened crewmen that throwing him overboard was the only way to make the storm subside. Being decent and disbelieving sorts, however, they ignored his advice and rowed harder for shore, thus becoming unwitting accomplices to the crime, getaway drivers. When the storm took a violent swipe at the main mast, they changed their minds, tossing Jonah overboard and into the belly of the whale, who delivered him three days later to the shores of Ninevah and unceremoniously spewed him onto the beach, a changed man.

THE JONAH COMPLEX

"I'm very brave generally, only today I happen to have a headache."
—*Tweedledum in Lewis Carroll's* Through the Looking Glass

The psychologist Abraham Maslow calls spiritual and emotional truancy the Jonah Complex: "The evasion of one's own growth, the setting of low levels of aspiration, the fear of doing what one is capable of doing, voluntary self-crippling, pseudo-stupidity, mock humility."

No matter how sophisticated or ingenious the avoidance, Maslow says, it is still a cheap adaptation to the implorings of personal evolution, and it is reminiscent of a dire old joke about two clerics who are the first to witness the return of the Messiah. When the younger one frantically asks, "What should we do?" the older one tells him, "Look busy."

"The guilt of Jonah," says Arthur Koestler in *The Act of Creation*, "was that he clung to the trivial, and tried to cultivate only his own little garden."

If it's any consolation, so does almost everybody when confronted by a calling, at least initially. Everybody, to some extent, backs away from their authenticity, settles for less, hobbles their own power, doesn't speak when spoken to in dreams. Everybody occasionally ignores the promptings of the soul and then the discontent that ensues, trying to distract themselves by counting their blessings, all the reasons they ought to be happy with their lot in life, content with things as they are, things that may once have been be-alls and end-alls but that lost their intoxication after five years, put them on automatic pilot after ten, and became a prison after fifteen.

We all have a part of us, forever incalculable and arch, that simply fears change and reacts to it with a reflexive flinch, the way snails recoil at the touch and birds bolt for the sky. And a calling is a messenger of change, a bell that tolls for thee, and it brings on the fear that frightens away sleep. There's no guarantee that change will be a change for the better.

Resistance is not only universal but also instinctive. It may be contrary to the open-mindedness and resilience we would prefer and that seem so necessary to getting through life with a measure of grace, but it's still involuntary. Our brains are wired for it. For one thing, in the course of an average lifetime, trillions of bits of information pour into our brains through the senses, and if we didn't tune some of them out, our circuits would fry. If we didn't respond to change with some resistance, every incoming stimulus would set off an outbreak of reflexes that would put Pavlov's dogs to shame. If we had no impulse toward caution, our curiosities would probably kill us. We'd probably step out of the car at the safari park.

Resistance is critical to the health of the immune system and to mental health, where it assumes the form of defense mechanisms, which can protect us against the possibility of being overwhelmed by the boogeyman of sudden change. It's hard to give up a symptom that's so useful.

Given, too, that we each invest years, decades even, in our own status quos, we're naturally loath to part ways with them, and the harder-won the status quo, the less inclined we'll be to risk getting grass stains on our pants. Most of us, Peter Marris says in *Change and Loss,* are conservatives that way. We seek to conserve the meaning of our lives, that is, whatever means a lot to us. We're simply trying to protect our investments: the skills we've spent years honing, the relationships we've stuck by, the way we relate to our past and our future, the things we believe about ourselves, whether they're true or false. Our worst fear, he says, is that our notion of who we are and what we are might tip over into anarchy.

One of the grave difficulties in following a call is that it may feel utterly and hopelessly at odds with whatever we're trying to conserve, and this is always a moment of crisis, which means to separate, meaning that a call is asking us to separate from something. No wonder we try to ignore it. A calling is an interruption and often an untidy thing; it is a rope strung across the road at chest level.

A calling also wears the face of chaos, a word meaning to gape, and it's with just such a countenance that we sometimes hear our calls and what they require of us. Sadly, chaos has come to have only a pejorative meaning: disorder and confusion. But in the Greek creation myths from which the original word comes, chaos is that pure potential from which all things and all beings emerged, what author Deepak Chopra calls "the field of infinite possibilities." In the Bible, chaos was simply the condition of the Earth before creation, before the great formlessness was molded. It's also the condition we must each pass through, repeatedly, until the end of our days, if we're faithful to our calls and the creations that they invite.

A calling will also make us wonder if we're good enough, smart enough, disciplined enough, educated enough, patient enough, and inspired enough. We especially question ourselves if we believe calls to have been sent directly from God, because then the pressure mounts. If we're afraid of failing, we're afraid of failing not just in our own eyes but also in God's. If we extrapolate from our experiences in the human arena, from life in a family, at school, on the job, even in bed, and remember the times when failure brought ridicule, disappointment, anger, scorn, or punishment, then we might naturally imagine the worst for failing *God*. Historically, the reaction typically elicited in those who were chosen for a divine calling wasn't pride and shouts of hurrah but fear, awe, and humility. Even Moses, on being called to free the Israelites from Egypt, said, "Who am I . . ." to do this thing?

This becomes even more disquieting if we add to it M. Scott Peck's idea, from *The Road Less Traveled*, that the endpoint of our lives, at least for those who postulate a loving God, comes down to "a single terrifying idea, the single most demanding idea in the history of humankind: that God wants us to become Himself (or Herself or Itself). God is not just the source, but the destination of evolution." If we believe this, Peck says, "it would demand from us all we can possibly give, all that we have, our highest levels of consciousness and loving activity, the constant push toward greater and greater wisdom and effectiveness, self-improvement and spiritual growth. It's no wonder the idea is repugnant: It brings us face-to-face with our own laziness."

It also brings us up against our sense of limits. Calls often seem immoderate, beyond our abilities or our wildest dreams, beyond what we believe possible, and immoderation is contrary to most spiritual wisdom. We balk, but it makes perfect sense that we should be called to go beyond our limits, say André and Pierre-Emmanuel Lacocque in their book *Jonah*, because, after all, the One that calls us is beyond all limits. The requests are thus perfectly in character.

Still, if the Greek philosopher Heraclitus was right when he said that the journey from human to God is akin to the journey from ape to human, then who can blame us for falling ashen at the thought of striving for godhood, when it's clear that the journey from ape to human was long, arduous, and spectacularly unlikely.

⋅⋄⋅

The final banana peel in our path is what psychologists call the superego, that mass of prohibitions we carry around in our heads, that hall monitor in the mind. From the superego's point of view, even the highest calling can seem like nothing more than an unruly impulse, which prompts the superego to flood us with anxiety, guilt, or panic.

We thus have an impressive arsenal of defense mechanisms—denial, distraction, repression, projection, procrastination—whose job descriptions are to prevent attack by the superego. They do this by blinding us to the kind of impulses—and callings—that trip the superego's alarms, and by misrepresenting the threat of those calls, making them seem more costly and inopportune than they are, so that we'll avoid them.

We don't actually have to *move* toward a calling to trigger a panic attack, either. Merely thinking about it will usually suffice. During a psychology class in my first year of college, Professor Turner announced that he was going to call on someone to come to the front of the room and engage in some activity that was likely to be embarrassing, though he wouldn't say what it was. He then stalked slowly up one aisle and down the next, his hands clasped behind his back and his black wing tips squeaking, looking from side to side at each student as he passed, deliberating at agonizing length about who his subject would be, while the ultimate adolescent nightmare took hold in a roomful of young minds.

After interminable minutes of this, he returned to the front of the room and confessed that he had no intention of actually picking anyone. He just wanted to introduce the day's subject matter: the power of suggestion. He then asked us to describe what went on in our bodies as he prowled the room, and we told him about our tight breathing, knotty stomachs, sweaty underarms, and frozen postures. A few confessed to having prayed.

In a creative writing class that same year, I was informed that a good piece of fiction will pit the protagonist against his or her greatest fear and rawest inner conflict. A calling will do the same thing. When we refuse a call, we're stuck, and we're stuck for a good reason. As long as we're conflicted, our story won't be complete, and we can't unrestrainedly follow the call. The hell of it is that we protagonists would rather choose chronic anxiety over acute confrontation. We'd rather dither for years than contend with the live wires of painful self-awareness and move *through* the resistance. We fear what the calling may ask of us, its consequences and responsibilities, and this fear of doing shows up as a fear of knowing.

Granted, the conflicts are often formidable, the fears intense, and sometimes they exist precisely to make us think twice—is it a true calling, are we really ready, is there something we've forgotten, an angle we haven't considered, a skill we haven't honed, a part of ourselves we haven't consulted? Maybe the conflict is with another calling, or a previous commitment, or somebody *else's* calling. Maybe the conflict is between two competing beliefs: for instance, "you can do it" versus "no you can't."

Maybe the conflict is with a stony taboo that has to be broken before you can follow a calling, as in the case of those who feel ashamed of their calls and whose response to them begins and ends with the words "Real men don't," or "Nice girls don't," or as in the case of a woman I know who's gaining recognition in her field and whose mother recently told her, "Don't you dare do anything that will take attention away from *me.*"

Maybe you feel called to finally heal your relationship with such a mother, but what stands in your way is a wall of rage, or a well of sorrow so deep that when you drop rocks down into it you never hear them hit bottom. Maybe the hostilities are between the urge to honor ourselves and the fear of losing others, which is a primally terrifying choice, and one that most people settle—as they have since they were children—by giving up on themselves and choosing approval rather than authenticity.

What happens then, says Maslow, is that "our center of gravity is in 'them' and not in ourselves. And what has been lost? Just the one true and vital part of us: our own yes-feeling, which is our very capacity for growth. This is not life, not *our* life. It is a defense against death."

Whatever the impediments, it's best not to resist the resistance. This only keeps the drama going. Best not to try talking yourself out of it, or letting others try to talk you out of it, or attempting to brainwash yourself with affirmations. It can even be dangerous trying to tear your defenses away or to force confrontation with them. People can crack. Besides, it's contrary to the outcome you want, which is to *open* to change, to follow the *Tao te Ching*'s advice to roll up your sleeves without bearing your arms.

"I know *I* change more effectively," social activist Fran Peavey says, "when people work *with* me to overcome my resistance, rather than banging me over the head and saying, 'Change! Change, already!' "

If resistance could be plucked from us like a bad tooth, Carl Jung once said, "we would have gained nothing, but would have lost as much as thinkers deprived of their doubt, or moralists deprived of their temptation, or the brave deprived of their fear. This would not be a cure. It would be an amputation."

⁂

There are just as many reasons *not* to follow a calling as there are to follow it, and both good and bad consequences either way. You just need to figure out what decisions will assure that when your life flashes before your eyes, it holds your interest. Resistance blooms naturally in the presence of change. You will encounter resistance in *all* attempts at ascendance, physical or spiritual. I think an acquaintance of mine summed up the fearsomeness of callings quite neatly when he said, "You shall know the truth and it shall make you nap."

The theme of the sleeper and the sleep that precedes awakening is age-old in the heroic journey-tales of the world: Rip Van Winkle, Sleeping Beauty, Snow White, Brunhild in her magic slumber, the Hindu king Muchukunda, who slept until brought around by Krishna, and of course Jonah in the bottom of his boat.

If our resistance to a calling doesn't take the form of outright refusal—whether it's a quiet withdrawal from life or an obstinate stomp on the ground with a puff of dirt for an exclamation point—then it often puts us into a state of suspended animation, a kind of emotional agnosticism in which we neither confirm nor deny the call but live in a netherworld of maybes. I met someone in this condition at one of my retreats in Oregon a few years ago. For five days she sat in the doorway, with two legs of her chair poised inside and two legs outside the conference room.

By doing this, says Eric Maisel in his book *Fearless Creating*, we avoid the anxiety of saying yes and the guilt of saying no, though it isn't a state of calmness and equilibrium but of tension and maddening equivocation. Prolonged, it is soul withering and bone dissolving. "It is vital," he says, "that you clearly hear this deadly, silent 'no.' This damned seven-eighths 'no' that can steal decades from your life."

In order to say yes, Maisel insists, you must first say no more forthrightly, must know precisely where you stand. "Better to be frankly disappointed in yourself that the 'no' is so loud than to be bitterly disappointed in yourself after decades of secret no-saying. Let yourself have the 'no.' Learn to hear it. Learn to say it. Hate it, but hear it."

Remember, though, that resistance is also a *good* omen. It means you're close to something important, something vital for your soul's work here, something worthy of you. "If it feels safe, it's probably not the right path," Mark Gerzon says in *Coming into Our Own*, "but if it scares you, it probably is." The degree of resistance, too, is probably proportionate to the amount of power waiting to be unleashed and the satisfaction to be experienced once the "no" breaks through to "yes" and the call is followed, once you allow your passion and faith to wash you overboard and carry you to the shores of Ninevah to be expelled in a pool of ambergris.

WAITING GAMES

I have spent my days stringing and unstringing my instrument while the song I came to sing remains unsung.
— RABINDRANATH TAGORE

I long ago discovered that boredom is characterized by restlessness, not listlessness, and by activity, not the lack of it. This is why we refer to it as "climbing the walls." The bored are fidgeters, doodlers, and daydreamers. So are procrastinators, who are further distinguished by resistance that often masquerades as quite frantic activity, even workaholism, not as laziness, which is popularly associated with procrastination. Workaholism is a perfect disguise because it's one of the few socially sanctioned addictions. It may be just another way of going to sleep in the bottom of the boat, but you can put it on a résumé.

The louder the calling, the more energy you need to use to outshout it, the more energy you exhaust in doing so, and the less energy you have left over to pursue the call itself—which may be precisely your unconscious objective. I suspect that all the energy you have bound up in resisting your own potential is more energy than you'll need to reach it. It takes as much energy to fail as it does to succeed.

The strategies of restless noncompliance, both conscious and unconscious, are legion:

- Hiding behind the tasks of discernment. By analyzing a call to death and picking apart all its varying implications and by poring over calculations that would put an actuary into a coma, we lose all the heat from the heart through the head, as if we had been in the bitter cold without a hat.

- Waiting for the Perfect Moment. Waiting for just the right combination of time, money, energy, education, freedom, and the ideal alignment of the planets. For most people, says professional public speaker Rosie Perez, "The refrain goes, 'It's one for the money, two for the show, three to get ready, three to get ready, three to get ready . . .' "

- Telling yourself lies. For instance, I have responded to several different calls with the same fish story: "I can't afford it." I can't afford to take the time or spend the money or learn the skills; can't afford to get off the hamster wheel even momentarily, lest my life come to a grinding halt. None of it was ever true, though. The truth was "I *won't* afford it." I won't reprioritize my life, won't make sacrifices, won't disrupt my family, won't forgo eating out in restaurants for six months to be able to buy myself the education I need.

    Telling myself repeatedly that "I can't afford it" only grinds into my subconscious a message of self-imposed limitation. It's an abdication of my desires, a surrendering of my power to outside influences like money and time, and it is the emotional equivalent of a rap on the knuckles at the cookie jar.

    A young man studying to be a monk in Germany once visited me when I lived in San Francisco. I asked him which of his vows he found the most difficult to honor, imagining that he would say celibacy or silence. He said that, without a doubt, it was honesty.

- Choosing a path parallel to the one you feel called to, one that's close enough to keep an eye on it but not so close you're tempted to jump tracks. You become an art critic rather than an artist, a schoolteacher rather than a parent, a reporter rather than a novelist.

- Attempting to replace one calling with another because you don't like it, your parents don't like it, it doesn't earn enough money or prestige. Perhaps you're called to work for the poor, or you were trained as a white-collar worker but feel called to do blue-collar work. Instead you try to substitute something else for it, hoping that a more lucrative or prestigious or secure pursuit will appease the spirits that gave you the call.

- Immediately turning a call into a Big Project, thereby intimidating yourself into paralysis.

- Self-sabotage. You feel called to go to art or medical school but are so afraid of finding out you don't have what it takes that you "forget" to mail the application until after its deadline has passed.

- Distracting yourself with other activities. You suddenly become inspired to finish old projects you haven't thought about in ages.

- Playing "sour grapes." You believe you won't succeed at a calling or will suffer unduly for it, and so you try to convince yourself that you don't want it anyway. For example, you're called toward a vocation for which you feel unqualified, so you tell yourself that the job you have now isn't really so bad after all, at least you *have* a job, and besides, work isn't everything. Or you're called to enter a relationship you're afraid will end as badly as all the others, so you go on a fault-finding mission or throw a fit, in order to create safe distance.

  Maybe you're called to blow the whistle on your company's nefarious activities, but you also have a family to support, so you tell yourself that risking your job for a principle is for saints and suckers. Or you're called to have a child, but are terrified of becoming the kind of parent your parents were, so you tell yourself that the world doesn't need any more children. "The danger is not that the soul should doubt whether there is any bread," the novelist Simone Weil once wrote, "but that, by a lie, it should persuade itself that it is not hungry."

- Trying to make yourself unworthy of a calling, hoping that God will decide you're not the person for the job and take it back. This was the strategy used by a man whose story I ran across in a fascinating book entitled *God's Yes Was Louder Than My No: Rethinking the African-American Call to Ministry.* His name is Arthur Kemp, and when he was a boy his family predicted he would be a preacher, a prophecy he was determined to put the lie to. Therefore, when he was stationed at an army base in New Jersey in 1952 and heard a voice tell him to "Go feed my sheep," and heard it twice more within half an hour, and when he recognized it as a call to the preaching ministry, he decided to follow in the footsteps not of Jesus but of Jonah.

"I had been taught," he said, "that if you're going to be a vessel for God, you've got to be a fit vessel and you've got to have good behavior, good morals, good ethics. So I determined that I was going to be the worst possible human being you could be, to make myself unfit to be a minister." He wasn't a drinking man then, but he started drinking. He wasn't a gambler, but he began gambling, and drug dealing, and pimping. He wasn't a fugitive, but in a spiritual sense he became one. "I just became a dyed-in-the-wool rascal, with the avowed intention of not responding to that call."

By 1959, after years of living the low life and the high life simultaneously, he bottomed out, lost as much self-respect as a person can lose without looking in the mirror and seeing nothing, and took to living on the streets and sleeping in fourth-rate hotels. He decided to move to Los Angeles, and on the way there he stopped in Columbus, Ohio, to visit his parents. The visit turned into an extended stay. He began showing up at church on Sundays again, and three months later, when his mother asked if he'd accompany her to a prayer meeting, he went. Just as the pastor was making his closing remarks, Arthur felt "a sudden flush of heaviness in my heart, as if I was carrying the weight of the world on me," and he broke into uncontrollable sobbing.

Nobody understood what was happening to him except the pastor, who said, "I know what's wrong with him. He hasn't told me, but I know what's wrong with him." And then Arthur blurted it out: "I've got to preach," he said. "I've got to preach, I've got to preach." And the pastor said to him, "I know it, and you're not going to have any peace until you do."

It took Arthur another fourteen years to get a bachelor's degree in religious studies, working part-time, going to school part-time, and supporting a family. His first pastorate was in a country church in Ohio, and his last, from which he retired recently, was a Baptist church in Akron called Mount Olive, named, fittingly, after the place at which the Ascension is said to have occurred.

THE STRENGTH WE HAVE AND
THE STRENGTH WE NEED

For the better part of a decade, I told myself that if only I had a nice fat chunk of time to write what I really wanted—which at that time was personal essays—I'd do it in something more than the fits and starts that generally characterized my pursuit of that calling. Such a dispensation of time seemed unlikely unless I could buy it, however, and financially speaking I was a "frustrated writer," a term that is, I think, largely redundant. What most writers earn, the author Rita Mae Brown once observed, is a sum not exactly designed to reassure your mother.

Then I got an offer I couldn't refuse. An advertising agency in California, whose sole clientele were lawyers and law firms and seemed to have more money than certain countries' Gross National Product, asked if I would write a book for them on the brave new world of advertising and marketing in the legal profession. Historically, attorneys have looked down their baronial noses at these activities, an attitude that in the modern marketplace is the entrepreneurial equivalent of wearing cement shoes. It wasn't a subject I would have chosen on my own, but the project would take me only two months and buy me eight, thus helping me realize one of the great writerly dreams: to have a nice fat chunk of time paid for in order to write whatever I wanted.

I have always believed that money costs too much, that the price people are willing to pay to have it is far too steep, and my decision to take such a "commercial break," in terms of the classic dilemma of selling out, seemed at first personally treasonous. I felt soiled, as if I were cozying up to the devil rather than being the martyr for purity that I imagined myself. I felt I was taking a condemnable departure from the calling. On the other hand, I told myself, there's nothing unconditional about the Muses, and I considered the trade-off a bargain, the proverbial one step backward in order to take two forward. Besides, I thought a dose of wage slavery would do wonders for my appreciation of freedom, which it did.

When the project was finished, though, so was my long-held excuse for not following the call to write essays: that I couldn't afford the time. When I finally had the time, what occurred to me with merciless clarity was that I had been fooling myself. Lack of time wasn't the obstacle and never had been. It was only an excuse, beneath which was a sorry succotash of emotional conflicts, most of which boiled down to feeling personally and professionally inadequate.

I was appalled at this realization, not merely because the *cliché* of it offended me, but also because I had secretly cherished the presumption that others had been born to fill the quotas of people with low self-esteem. I wasn't supposed to be one of them.

The following revelations began to dawn on me, in rapid and nauseating succession:

I feared that in writing those essays, I might find out I wasn't the person I imagined myself to be. Not writing them kept me at a safe distance from the possibility of such a discovery.

Some of the stories I wanted to write would necessitate that I awaken sleeping giants that I didn't want to disturb. In order to write with any authority, I would have to relive some of my past.

Some of the stories were about things better left unsaid, things that would blatantly disregard the admonition of my elders, who had taught me that if I had nothing nice to say then say nothing. My proclamations would not be welcome everywhere. Unlike the articles and how-to books I'd written previously, essays, being in the first-person singular, would require confessing rather than preaching.

I was suffering, too, from what the composer Stephen Nachmanovitch, in his book *Free Play*, calls "the fear of ghosts." This is the impotence that comes over us when we compare ourselves to our own heroes, whether they are parents, teachers, mentors, or, as in my case, the geniuses in my own field and the heroic image of my own ideal self. In contemplating the size of these gladiators, in weighing "the strength I have against the strength I need," as the poet Phillip Larkin once wrote, I came up with a negative balance and so shrank from the challenge.

Finally, I hated the thought of being a beginner again, especially after years of building up my journalistic skills to the point where I had some mastery of writing articles and was finally earning enough to give me something worth stealing. On more than a few occasions, when the calling to write essays began breaking through my resistance like damnable green buds through cement—in dreams, fantasies, symptoms, synchronicities, slips of the tongue, and a constant and ineradicable irritation with my writing—I threw the workaholic's

version of a tantrum: I worked double time on the articles, hoping to steamroll
the new calling, hoping to prove the worth of the status quo. This approach
failed miserably.

⚬

In the aftermath of these and other revelations, I felt flattened and decided
that this wasn't the mood in which to launch any new enterprise. In this stand-
still, I was afraid I might be tempted to pitch headfirst into another project
and scuttle my promise to use the eight months to write essays. So I took a
retreat: five days alone in a cabin whose adobe walls radiated silence, in a desert
whose expanse might remind me to think big again, or at the least whose simplicity and beauty might remind me of what is enough.

Ghost Ranch is a retreat and conference center near the isolated village of
Abiquiu in northern New Mexico, and it was made famous when the painter
Georgia O'Keeffe moved there from New York City in the 1920s. A more perfect setting for a desert retreat is difficult to imagine. It's a place where evolution takes off its skin and dances around in its bones, where every step I took
up or down in elevation moved me fifty thousand years in time, where the
sheer enormity of the space in every direction made my arms involuntarily
spread out from my sides, as if I needed to physically expand in order to take it
all in, and where I was reminded that great beauty goes unappreciated every
day in the world. Red rock mesas and stone spires rise a thousand feet from the
desert floor and play handball with the thunder, which is all that disturbs the
cavernous silence of the place. It is a quiet so penetrating that the faintest mur-
mur of the mind sounds like a cannon going off.

No wonder artists have loved it here. Ghost Ranch specializes in perspective, which I find to be one of the primary benedictions of retreat, and here it
is impossible to ignore.

Every day on my long walks I saw thunderheads piled high and plumed
with light, their bottoms gray like anvils, gray like the soles of Zeus's feet.
Every day I was reminded that Zeus juggles planets and asteroids, and if he
sneezes a comet shower is born over the desert, while I juggle a single earthly
life and can barely keep my breath. While the universe blasts out from ground
zero at unimaginable speeds, I work to build my résumé and lower my mort-
gage. While stars a thousand times the size of the sun explode and form nebula, I sit in a small lighted window at the edge of an immense desert and write
in my journal, putting small squirrely lines on pieces of paper.

On my third night there, I had a luminous dream. I was on a bicycle at the top of a hill, with a playing card stuck in the chassis that clicked with every passing spoke, every click representing a generation. I started down the hill slowly at first. Click: my own generation, gone. Click: my father's World War II generation, gone. Click click, picking up speed, my grandparents' immigrant generation and my great-grandparents' from Russia, gone. Click click click, faster and faster, generations lost in antiquity, invisible ancestry whom I'll never know; who they were, where they lived, whom they conquered or who conquered them, where they died, where their bones are—all gone. Click click click, the climate and the land changing, continents moving, mountains pushing up and wearing down, oceans pouring in and out, ice ages advancing and retreating, the card now slapping the spokes in a whirr, sounding like a cicada outside my window on a summer night.

I finally stopped my bicycle at the bottom of the hill and saw a man lying naked at the entrance to a large cave. He woke up from a drowsy sleep, stood up, and walked into the cave.

The next morning, standing at the bottom of an enormous mesa outside my cabin, I had the realization that I and my entire generation, my whole civilization, in fact, are going to be one thin layer of sediment in the side of a cliff someday. Yet precisely *because* it makes a flyspeck of a difference whether I write my essays or not, somehow this frees me up to write, to follow the calling, to do whatever I want, because there is no failure. Or rather, failure is already assumed. I'm going to die and be a million years dead, and anyone who might possibly judge me for my pursuits and mistakes will be a fossil right next to mine in that cliffside.

Our lives, the poet Tom Absher describes in his book *The Calling*, are like the garments washed by a peasant woman in a river. She wades into the shallows and holds each garment in the current, letting it fill with water and take on dreamy human form. Likewise our watery selves are composed briefly, then withdrawn. That is enough.

⁓❧⁓

Infusions of perspective like this are one thing when sitting beneath the soles of Zeus's feet and quite another when sitting in your own living room. One of the great challenges of such lessons and retreats is keeping their fires burning once you return home. "Even if some wise person soothes us by setting our toothache in a perspective of light-years, galaxies and spiral nebula," says the poet Howard Nemerov, "the toothache continues to hurt as though it has not heard. Toothaches can sometimes be dealt with by dentists, but never by philosophers."

I found myself up against the task of keeping perspective when I returned home, but I was greatly aided by an experience I had on the last night of my retreat. It was early evening, raining lightly, and I was lying in bed with the covers pulled up to my chin. As the day had progressed and the thought of going home and making good, or no good, on my promise silted up more and more of the sweet empty spaces the retreat had managed to scoop out of my normally fitful mind, I became increasingly tired.

Although it was barely seven o'clock, I alternately drifted off to sleep and then back to consciousness, off to sleep and back to the sound of dripping, the clock ticking, the heater cracking as its metal expanded and contracted while going on and off; back to a piercing anxiety. For nearly half an hour, I tried to decide whether to let myself fall into slumber or get up and write or read or meditate, and only days later did I realize that this struggle was not merely one of whether to doze or not to doze but whether to be or not to be.

Eventually, I felt myself drooping into insensibility, the sounds around me fading and becoming indistinguishable, my lower jaw falling open.

Then suddenly I was awake, as if someone had knocked on the door. Suddenly my eyes were wide open, and the sleepiness passed over me. Sounds came back into focus, the room seemed brighter, and in one single motion I pulled the covers across me and swung my body into a sitting position on the edge of the bed. I looked up at the ceiling and then let my head roll from right to left in a slow arc that made my neck crack and pop.

I awoke with the feeling that what had roused me was my own tongue slipping into my throat and momentarily blocking off the air, just as Jonah's slipping into the mouth of the whale was the beginning of his *own* deliverance back to his calling. It was as if my tongue—that carrier of stories—didn't want to slip into the dark, disappear down a well, go backward and down instead of forward and out into the world.

I got up and started writing. It was well past midnight when I stopped, well past ten when I awoke the next morning to the smell of sage and wet desert. The next eight months were some of the best and—juggling asteroids—some of the hardest of my work life.

PLAYING   SMALL

I have two friends who are very tall and tend to stand with a slight stoop, a slump at the shoulders, as if they're constantly trying to fit under low doorjambs. Both of these men have, at different times, told me the same thing about being very tall: They're afraid to stand up completely straight for fear of intimidating people with how big they really are.

We decline the invitation of our callings because we feel inadequate to the task, but the opposite is also true: We're afraid of our own power. "Our deepest fear is not that we are inadequate," says author Marianne Williamson. "Our deepest fear is that we are powerful beyond measure. It is our light, not our darkness, that most frightens us. But our playing small doesn't serve the world. There's nothing enlightened about shrinking so that other people won't feel insecure around you."

Ron Jones can vouch for that. He relates a story about his father, who was a musician at heart but who worked for thirty-five years selling televisions, refrigerators, and glassware in a department store in San Francisco. One day he was told that the store was closing. In those days there were no golden parachutes or retirement benefits, and when they asked him if there was anything they could do for him, his only request was to have the chair he'd been sitting in all those years. They *sold* it to him.

"He brought that chair to my house on his back one day," says Ron, a writer and storyteller, "and placed it in my living room and told me about all the years he had sat in it, and then he made me promise that I would never sit down in that chair, ever. It's in my living room to this day, and I never sit in it. I just tell the story, and the lesson my father passed on to me through it: Don't sit down in life. All through your life you're going to be asked to sit down, to conform, comply, and compromise, and it can be very deadly if you get in the habit of doing that. Be leery of the price of conformity, my father told me. Stand up, create things, do things."

"Nothing so upsets the Bishop," Joseph Chilton Pearce wrote in *Evolution's End,* "as the rumor of a saint in his parish," and nothing so upsets those in power as when those who are not in power suddenly realize that they've been sitting down when they could be standing up. Actually, *whatever* position you've settled into is the one others have gotten used to, and they're likely to feel unhinged when you change positions, question authority, disregard conventions, strike out on your own.

What happens when a martyr stops making sacrifices? When a pleaser stops pleasing? When a true-blue friend changes color? When a whisperer suddenly shouts, or a screamer suddenly whispers? What happens when you change whatever it was in you that others had come to rely on? In the heaving tectonics between you and others, what were once ocean bottoms or flatlands by a sleeping river now rear up into mountain divides, sometimes flung at a ninety-degree angle from their original positions. What were once floors are now walls. What was once concord is now discord. What was once acceptance is now rejection. A calling can have a tragic dimension.

In addition, we *ourselves* may not take so kindly to our own power. Although fearing power is kind of like fearing wealth, and it's a little hard to get sympathy, power does have its dangers. For one thing, taking on our power can shatter our perceptions of our own limitations, and without those perceived limitations—not enough time or money or talent, a bad back, too many other responsibilities, someone standing in our way—there are no longer any reasons to hold ourselves back. And as Giraffe Project executive director John Graham put it, that is "moth-to-the-flame stuff."

Say you believe, for instance, that you can't follow a calling to teach classes in your area of expertise because no one will be interested. Yet you follow the prompting anyway and the first class fills up. Now you're going to have to wonder what *other* limiting beliefs you might need to update. Perhaps these include a belief that you're not good enough to teach, or there's no money in it, or it's only a matter of time before you're exposed as a fraud. As your excuses begin falling away, you begin taking the risks you'd always thought of as terrifying. Your life isn't so predictable anymore, and you start to find out who you really are, which is always a bit of an acquired taste, always a bit nerve-racking.

THE STRAW THAT BECOMES GOLD

Obstacles do not limit us only because we *believe* they do. We do not refuse our calls only because we're stubborn and fainthearted. Some limitations—poverty, imprisonment, disease or disability, being responsible for children and aged parents, geographical isolation, lack of any education or any talent—are very real obstacles and exceptionally difficult to surmount.

Sometimes we're robbed of our calls by the fate into which we fell head-long at birth. "In a tenement in Bangladesh," Jean Houston writes in *A Mythic Life*, "I look into the eyes of a child so bright with intelligence that I know that given other circumstances she could be just about anything she chose to be. Here, however, her future will consist of being married very early, constant childbearing, a strong possibility of being abused by her husband, disease, and early death.

"In a desiccated field in West Africa, I found a farmer's boy who could build bridges between spirit and matter, a scientist of the first order, a Renaissance man. But I knew that he would spend his time on Earth as millions of his forebears have, straining his life away behind a plow. They are everywhere, these children of so much promise with their hungry spirits that will not be fed."

When I first heard the taped interview with my great-aunt that was made for the audio collection at the Ellis Island Museum many years ago, the story of her life in Russia at the turn of the century and her emigration to America, I was dumbfounded at how primitive my family's life had been only two generations ago. It was a story common to immigrants: dire poverty and constant persecution. Seven people and their chickens and ducks all lived in a one-room house with no running water or plumbing, with a dirt floor onto which, on the Sabbath, they sprinkled sawdust and considered it the height of luxury, and clothes that had to be washed in the river by hand, even in the winter, which in Russia is no mean thing. In addition, they were so insular that they didn't even speak Russian, only Hebrew and Yiddish; they didn't speak the language of the country in which they had been born!

Under these circumstances, the notion of following a call seems out of place, almost impudent, a thing of privilege. Perhaps to some degree it is. They did, after all, have food, clothing, shelter, and a tribe to whom they belonged. As the singer Billie Holiday once remarked, "You've got to have something to eat and little love in your life before you can hold still for any-damn-body's sermon on how to behave."

Still, my great-aunt's parents felt a calling to come to the United States in order to become educated and have religious freedom, and they followed it. They were exceptional in their motivation and magnificent patience—my great-aunt didn't see her father from the time he left for America, when she was three, until she was nine, when he could afford to bring her and her siblings across. Their limitations became their strengths, and their strengths and their sacrifices became the opportunities *I* have that I so often take for granted.

❧

In a class on improvisational theater, I was instructed to enter into dialogue with another actor using only two words, *please* and *no*—I took one and she took the other—and I was astonished at the number of ways we found to express such a limited theme, the seemingly infinite variations on inflection and body language.

Limitation can impede growth, but it can also induce it. In environments with little water, plants developed spines. People who lose one of their senses often find that the others are heightened. The smaller the animal, the more fruitfully it multiplies, and the colder the clime, the beefier the inhabitants. The more you compress a spring, the more strength you build in it. The brain is confined to a nutshell, but look at its *reach*. The entire universe, we're told, was once squeezed into a space too small to see, but the explosion it triggered is *still* taking place. The poet e.e. cummings, while incarcerated in a French jail cell during World War II, wrote a book called *the enormous room*.

"It may be that when we no longer know what to do," the writer Wendell Berry once said, "we have come to our real work, and when we no longer know which way to go, we have begun our real journey. The mind that is not baffled is not employed. The impeded stream is the one that sings."

So it may be with the impediments to our own callings—hunger speeds the plow. When you can't buy solutions, you invent them. Criticism can teach you to rely on your own intuition. The job you hate can pay the bills while you go to night school. Childhood trauma can set you up to do your work in the world. Personal tragedy can propel you to start up an organization to help others who have suffered the same fate. Parents who were negative role models for following your passions may motivate you to rebel against them. A competitor may end up being someone you team up with. Two competing calls can, over time, come to benefit each other.

The writer Anne Tyler, for example, once described that having children initially put a drag on her writing but in time inspired it. "They slowed down my writing for a while—in the beginning I was drained; too much care and feeling were being drawn out of me. But eventually when I did write, I found I had grown richer and deeper because of them, and had more of a self to write from."

We all have limitations, but what matters is how we convert them into our own creations. They're among the raw materials for composing a life. They're the straw that can be woven into gold. Pianists wouldn't think to judge themselves because their hands have only five fingers each and not six or eight—you work with what's there. We shouldn't unduly begrudge our own limitations but find the destination in destiny.

Limitations are just about *all* that the artist Joe Sam had when he started out in life. His first art projects were papier-mâché sculptures made of old newspapers and spit, mobiles made with wire hangers, and collages assembled using strips of lead-based paint that peeled off the walls of his apartment when it rained. Those were the only kind of art supplies he could find in the Harlem tenement where he lived. The circumstances of Joe's early life were not designed to encourage artistic initiative, but he did have, he once told me, an unshakable "indigenous spirit" and a schoolteacher who took a personal interest in him.

Today Joe is a successful collage artist living in San Francisco, and though he has no formal art training, the National Endowment for the Arts, which once awarded him a sizable grant, called him one of the country's most important black artists. Joe's acclaimed work includes a series of mixed-media pieces he calls *The Black West*, chronicling the life and times of the black cowboy who, like Joe himself, improvised an identity from whatever was at hand.

Anyone can make headway in life with a heap of resources—money, time, all the right tools and all the right contacts, a sustained round of applause and intact self-esteem. But creative artistry really demonstrates itself in the absence of these resources.

A calling *itself* is a limitation, and this explains why some people choose not to follow it. By following a call, we narrow our choices, and we close doors we may never be able to reopen. We're naturally afraid of losing our freedom of choice. This may be especially so for those who were brought up with the old Lutheran model of callings as "stations" in life that were preordained rather than chosen. That can sound an awful lot like a caste system meant to discourage independence and any move from one station to another, such as changing jobs or marriages or hometowns. Going against one's station was for generations considered an act of insubordination, and exercising one's free will and self-determination was considered secondary to a God who appoints those stations.

If we don't ever choose, however, freedom is just an illusion, an idea in the mind. If you're standing at a crossroads, with paths going off in all directions, you have, in theory, great freedom. Until you actually make a choice, freedom is only potential energy, energy in abeyance, in waiting. As soon as you head off in any one direction you've not only limited your freedom but you've also given it a body in motion rather than a static body. You've turned the potential energy into kinetic energy, energy in use, freedom that you're now exercising with every footfall.

Any creative act is the ideal place in which to practice, and witness, this trade-off between choice and freedom. When you write, for instance, you define a world and a reason for it; you define a theme, a setting, maybe a set of characters and what direction they're all going in. But by creating, you also destroy. You narrow your focus. You sacrifice the whole for the part. You perish the thought, at least for now, of other roads you might have taken, other stories you might have told, and when you're done you've fashioned not only a life but also chronicled a death, ghosts and all.

THE OPINIONS OF OTHERS

I was sitting in the grand ballroom of a fancy hotel in downtown Albuquerque, at a lunch for four hundred, fighting the urge not to scream as the conference keynote speaker droned on and on at the podium. He was reading, word for word, from a voluminous stack of notes. Standing absolutely motionless, he occasionally flicked a glance up at the audience in that utterly perfunctory manner that some public speakers seem to believe passes for eye contact. Meanwhile, four hundred grown-ups were playing with their silverware and doodling in their notebooks.

About two-thirds of the way through, having exhausted an entire month's worth of patience and stoicism in one sitting, I did something I've only done two other times in my whole life, and then only when I was sitting in the back of the room: I got up and walked out. This time, however, I was sitting in the very front of the room, directly in front of the podium, and I had to weave my way through a maze of tables and past countless staring faces, before I made the exit.

It took me an absurdly long time to work up the gumption to do what I should have done an hour earlier. I was so deeply employed in worrying that others might think I was rude or impolite, however, and so hamstrung by the misguided idea that I need to protect others from feeling bad, that my brain took an excessively long time to register that I was not the one being inconsiderate, the speaker was, and that I can't protect people from themselves.

I can only take care of myself, though I'm occasionally disgusted at my tendency to abandon even *that* responsibility, to ignore my own instincts—to say no to the calls I hear—in order to safeguard the approval of others, which I imagine is essential to survival. It isn't. A friend of mine once reckoned that in the course of life a small number of people will like you, a small number will dislike you, and the vast majority won't care one way or the other.

The small number of people that constitutes our individual circle of acquaintances exerts a disproportionate leverage on us, and the stinging nettles of their rejection and disapproval are often more than we care to tempt. All we want from them, all we ever wanted, is their love and approval, but when it comes to being true to ourselves, this very need for love turns against us and becomes the vehicle of our subjection. To ensure the continued flow of their esteem and attention, we adjust ourselves to fit whatever status quo *they* deem most favorable, paying, in the bargain, a steep price in individuality and power. "Fears about yourself dig into your ability to do your best work," say David Bayles and Ted Orland in *Art and Fear,* "while fears about what others will think of you compromise your ability to do your *own* work."

This is a most visceral fear and is rooted in the vulnerabilities of childhood, in the implied threat of abandonment if we didn't toe the party line. It is a hard fact, passed down through virtually every kind of human community, that compliance is rewarded and failure to comply is punished. What we risk in running afoul of conformity is what the psychologist Albert Ellis calls "the scandalization of others."

Imagine, for instance, with what sort of equanimity your partner and children would greet the news that you feel called to quit your job, thereby eviscerating the lifestyle to which they've become accustomed; or your parents that you plan to marry someone of another race or faith; or your friends that you're going to adopt children with AIDS, as a woman I know has done, five times.

Imagine wanting to be a gardener or a carpenter in a family that is disdainful of making a living by manual labor or that considers a golden tan de rigueur, but not if you acquired it at work. Imagine you're a woman who feels called to be a minister in a religious community that doesn't believe God calls women to be ministers. Naturally, people are going to treat you like you're blowing your nose on their prayer flags and spitting in their holy water. Naturally, you're going to think twice about following that call.

᪥

Michael Hall thought twice, and then a third time, and a fourth and a fifth about following his calling. At first, he thought maybe everyone was right when they told him he was crazy for quitting a $150,000-a-year law practice as well as a spectacular house on the water out on eastern Long Island, with a dock out back and a swimming pool. He gave it all up because of an "inner nudge" to move on, a shadowy feeling that he was selling his soul by continuing to practice law. He kept seeing an image in his head of a house in a desert somewhere, and a new line of work that was a complete mystery to him. After two years, three scouting trips across forty states, thirty thousand miles of highway, and six hundred pages of journal notes, his vision would take Michael, his wife, and their two children out to Santa Fe, New Mexico, where he took up writing and searching for "something bigger and better to do with my life."

When Michael announced his intentions, however, he began a long process of working through not only his own fears but also those of others. People were scandalized, "and I was afraid not just of what they were going to say, but, perhaps worse, what they were going to keep to themselves." It seems they kept little to themselves, though. His father, who shared the law practice with him, yelled, "Are you crazy? What are you running away from?"

"Nothing," Michael said, propping himself on top of his desk so he wouldn't feel quite so small, and trying to act less defensive than he actually felt. "I just don't belong here anymore."

His father attempted to dissuade Michael by telling him just how good he had it, enumerating all the perks of a high-rent lifestyle and economic freedom. When that failed to impress Michael, his father bellowed, "What are you going to the damn desert for? It took man thousands of years to get out of the stupid desert."

Only a handful of times had Michael seen his father that angry. "His religion was Logic, though, and my decision was obviously illogical to him. I might as well have told a fifteenth-century monk that the Earth was round and not the center of the universe."

In quick succession, he heard similar refrains from friends, family, and colleagues. His mother told him to "leave well enough alone." A cousin asked, "How can you leave your family?" in a tone of voice Michael describes as "more accusatory than inquisitive." His cronies at the Kiwanis Club said it was fine to move if your company moves you but not if you just up and leave the job and the money behind. A friend declared that "You're always *looking* for something," as if this were an indictment. Another denounced him as being a "malcontent."

One of the frightening prospects of saying yes to a calling is that you may find out who really supports you and who doesn't.

During the process of extricating himself from his practice and dealing with the fearful projections of his friends and family, Michael began reading, with no little irony, eighteenth-century pioneer journals. He hoped to get some idea of what others who had preceded him in heading west had struggled against. What jumped out at him were passages like this one: "July 11, 1852, passed fifteen graves, made thirteen miles. July twelfth, passed five graves, made fifteen miles. July eighteenth, passed four graves, made sixteen miles." From the time Michael first announced he was leaving to the time he actually left was roughly a year, "and it was a *long* year."

The year could have been considerably shortened if Michael had presented the idea to his family differently. In presenting your calling to others, it pays to recognize that the response you get is greatly affected by *how* you tell them about your calling. It depends on what you choose to say or leave out, your tone of voice, whether you present the information in a language they can understand, whether you anticipate their reactions, and whether you start with the easy customers and work your way up to the hard ones, not the other way around. All of these communications will affect the messages that others give you about your calling.

Michael's approach was, unfortunately, the opposite of a wise grafitti message I once ran across: "A closed mouth gathers no feet." For one thing, he tried too hard to make his family understand something he barely understood himself—his reasons for leaving. In fact, he would take another seven years to figure out what his inner nudge was a call to *do*, which was "to be on television," as he put it. (Today, he hosts a television program on the local PBS station called *Meet the Masters*, in which he interviews "living role models." He says that he wouldn't have found this work had he not been willing to move *first*.)

Michael also tried too hard to defend people against their own discomfort and tried to explain it all in a language that they derided as "cosmic." He didn't understand that he was an astronaut and that there are stretches of the journey to outer space and back in which the traveler is completely out of touch, in which communication is impossible. Still, he says, "Nothing obsessed me more than making them understand. I craved their support and approval, and I was willing to make an idiot of myself to get it. I guess I succeeded beyond my expectations."

Michael also fell into a trap common to those who make dramatic spiritual breakthroughs or changes in their values and priorities: They turn around and judge negatively their former lives and anyone who still inhabits it. "Though I didn't know it at the time, my attitude was, 'You guys are misguided and I've found the light. I'm stepping toward freedom and you're not.' I kind of laid a trip on them."

When he began to disengage from his old life, Michael didn't understand that he was unconsciously rejecting his own family and friends by rejecting their values. He was going against much of what "the system" holds sacrosanct when he deliberately decided to earn *less* money and step *down* the ladder or off it entirely. He didn't understand that his father was losing not just a business partner but, as Michael said, a best friend, and that he wasn't feeling so much angry as abandoned.

He didn't understand until years later why a couple with whom he and his wife had been friends for ten years never spoke to them again after finding out they were leaving. "They were constantly bemoaning their situation in life, and our departure must have held up a mirror they didn't want to look into." He didn't understand that when his wife's mother said to her, "How could you do this to me?" what she was in part saying was, "How could you take my grandchildren away from me?"

When others protest our changes, it's not that they don't want us to change; they just want us to change to meet *their* needs, not our own.

"I didn't realize that though their reactions really hurt me, *they* were also hurting, feeling threatened, and couldn't communicate that. It took me years to realize that's what was going on. Had I been able to see that at the time, it would definitely have eased the situation. If I had just said to my father and mother, 'I know this must really be confusing,' it would have made a big difference, but I never said that. All I said was, 'It's just something I've got to do and if you don't support me I'll do it without you,' and I drove off into the sunset with my head down. If I had it to do again, I'd be much more compassionate with my family. I'd do it without the judgmental attitude and cockiness."

As is often the case, a blessing was hidden in the conflict. Michael realized that other people's reactions and interrogations had exacerbated the conflicts he himself felt. He tended to fight against *them,* write *them* off, blame *them* for holding him back, when all they were doing was holding up a mirror that *he* didn't want to look into. Though their cross-examination freighted him with "huge self-doubt," it was also an invigorating slap in the face. "I couldn't go into denial. I couldn't run from the questions. I had to think about it: Why *am* I doing this? *Am* I running away from something? *Am* I crazy? It forced me to be really sure, really conscious of my decision. It ended up serving me."

"I have learned silence from the talkative," Kahlil Gibran once said, "tolerance from the intolerant, and kindness from the unkind. Yet strange, I am ungrateful to these teachers."

T A L K I N G   T O   T H E   W A L L

Professor Turner had it coming.

After his tutorial in the power of suggestion, we students in his psychology class devised an opportunity to show appreciation in kind. We tailored it to the subject he was teaching us at the time, classical conditioning. Most people know about conditioning by way of a famous experiment conducted by the Russian physiologist Ivan Pavlov, whose dogs were taught to salivate at the sound of a ringing bell.

Taking advantage of Mr. Turner's habit of pacing back and forth while delivering his lectures, we concocted the following experiment: Whenever he walked toward the window, we very subtly adopted postures of boredom. We slouched, fidgeted, doodled, we stared vacuously into space. Whenever he walked toward the door, we assumed positions of interest. We sat up straighter, began taking notes, and fixed him with our keenest scholarly expressions.

By the time that day's class was over, we had Mr. Turner glued to the door, and I could only have been more pleased had he begun to visibly salivate when the bell rang signaling the end of class.

It is astonishingly easy to condition someone, and by extension, to *be* conditioned, without a single word being spoken—everything done in pantomime. If it took us barely forty-five minutes to condition our *psychology professor* with a new set of behaviors, unbeknownst to him, imagine the effect on us of a *lifetime's* worth of conditioning, of domestication, regarding what direction *we* should take in life. Imagine the effect of the thousands of messages, spoken and unspoken, that have been knitted into our minds ever since we came squawking out of the womb, and which we took on like hand-me-downs, regardless of whether they fit us or not. Think of all the unconscious trespasses that have been visited upon us in the name of love and education, in the name of God. Together, they form a kind of hypnosis, whether true or false, positive or negative.

If we look only to others to show us who we are, however, then the reflections we'll have of ourselves will always be distorted a little, like our reflections caught in other people's sunglasses, in dark windows, fish-eye lenses, or the sides of teakettles—the light always a little refracted and the image never quite true. The atheisms within us, says theologian Frederick Buechner, "are not so much denials of whatever is godly in the world, but denials of people telling us what to believe, what to do, what to think."

If each such encroachment were a brick, the size of the wall they'd build over the course of all those years would have anybody talking out loud to themselves in no time. I recommend talking to the wall. Acquaint yourself with exactly how you're conditioned to say no to yourself.

Part of the wall runs through our personal history: the admonitions of our Jewish or Catholic or Muslim ancestors; the convictions murmured to us by our Russian or Spanish or Chinese forebears; the worldview we inherited by growing up on the plains, in the mountains, by the sea; the secrets our families hid from the neighbors and what those secrets told us about what can and cannot be said or done or hoped for in life; the map we were each given to follow by the economic class into which we were born.

Part of the wall parallels whatever was unlived in our parents' lives, the thwarted or abandoned ambitions that they passed on to us to remedy and compensate for—"do what I could not do." This legacy places us in an impossible situation because the sword imbedded in the stone can only be removed by the person to whom the sword belongs. When we attempt to carry our parents' unfulfilled lives, we squeeze out our own. Thus we're forced to become failures, says psychologist John Sanford, if only because by becoming a failure we can free ourselves of our parents' domination and perhaps find something of ourselves.

Handwritten on the wall are "conventional wisdoms" that can easily wring the life out of our attempts to respond affirmatively to our calls: you can't do *X* without an advanced degree; voluntarism counts for little on a résumé; relationships on the rebound never work; retirement is death; art equals poverty; "back to the land" is quaint but unworkable; something is wrong with you if you don't want children; whatever you do, you need money.

The principles of conformity are perhaps most deeply imbedded in our institutions. Being the keepers of tradition—family, religion, academia, law, government—they are naturally hidebound. People entrenched in these institutions are equally conservative, and the more entrenched, the more evangelical their insistence on stability and order, and on others following suit. Unfortunately, says Stanley Milgram in *Obedience to Authority*, individual conscience and initiative diminish when people are brought under the dome of a hierarchy, and they learn quickly who pulls the strings and who dances and that deference is the only acceptable, appropriate, *comfortable* response to authority.

In an experiment Milgram conducted, he found that in a contest between the voice of authority and the voice of an individual's own conscience, authority typically prevails, and to a dismaying degree. Just as the light of our cities obliterates the light of the stars, so the weight of other people's authority can blot out the singularity of our own.

In the study, subjects were asked to oversee others who were learning to perform a task and to administer an electric shock every time the learner made a mistake. The subjects were to increase the voltage with every mistake until the shocks were clearly at a dangerous level of 450 volts, which is considerably more of a shock than you'd get by sticking your finger into a light socket. Though no shocks were actually given, and the learners were actors who feigned suffering, the experimenters insisted that each subject continue giving shocks until the end of the experiment, despite their concerns that they were causing the learners harm, and despite the learners' sometimes vehement protests, which occasionally reached the point of agonized screaming.

Still, 60 percent of the subjects obeyed orders to the end, and their moral concerns became focused merely on how well they were doing their duty, not on what they thought of that duty. "The demise of a sense of personal responsibility," Milgram says, "is the most consistent consequence of submission to authority."

His experiment ably demonstrated the lengths to which people—good people, moral people, people who think of themselves as upstanding and compassionate—will go to obey authority, how much compliance they'll display before stopping the show, however contrary to their own desires, and how difficult it is to break rank without feeling disloyal.

In order to understand what we're up against in defying the voices of authority, Milgram says, picture someone who represents authority to you. Someone who you respect, someone older by a generation, someone you would refer to as Dr. Charles Clark or Professor Gaines or Father Dominic. Now imagine that the next time you encounter this distinguished individual, you are going to address him or her by first name or even a nickname. "Good morning, Charlie." Note the discomfort you feel from breaching this etiquette. Now imagine going beyond a breach of decorum and acting contrary to your mother's canon laws, your father's dogma, your boss's standing orders, your department's rules. Imagine reaching for your religion's forbidden fruit.

In a scene in an old Woody Allen movie called *Everything You Always Wanted to Know about Sex,* a man and woman are making love, and he's having difficulty . . . summoning the necessary enthusiasm. The camera takes us inside his head, where we see a mission control room not unlike the bridge on the Starship *Enterprise,* and a lot of concerned-looking technicians who can't figure out what's holding up the mission. Suddenly two burly bodyguards drag in a half-crazed priest who they claim to have found holed up in the cerebral cortex, where he was turning up the guilt reflex. The priest is shouting, "Blasphemy! Sex between unmarried people. Blasphemy! Blasphemy!"

The point is, we're not going anywhere with voices like that shouting mutinies in our ears. If we don't confront them, if we don't even consciously *hear* them, they will end up authoring our own undoing.

By the time we're old enough to start shaving, we barely even need anyone to tell us what's "appropriate" behavior and what's not, what to do and what not to do, which calls to answer and which to ignore. By that time, we've largely taken on the job ourselves, internalized the messages, become the Voice of Authority, the Bell Ringer. We hear a calling, and a horde of caveats and commandments latch onto it like antibodies on an invading bacteria. This self-censorship is all done very quietly, though, in the muffled blood and the dark unconscious, and we only see its effects in our personal abdications of power and responsibility, in the ways we turn away from our calls, and in the regrets that rise up from our lives like heat, in waves.

D O G   L O G I C

There comes a time in the life of most families, says Fred Chappell, a professor of literature at the University of North Carolina, when a child begins to assert the need for independence and frequently fixes on the one means to achieve it that his parents cannot abide. "Anything but that," they'll say. As Chappell describes it in *My Poor Elephant,* "We want you to be happy; you're free to do whatever you want to do. Except become a rock musician, or an artist, or a hang glider, or a homosexual, or a soldier of fortune, or . . ."

Or a writer, which is what Chappell wanted to be. Not only did his parents not want to hear what he wrote, they also didn't even want to hear *about* it. When he sat at his old Royal typewriter, whose clattering could be heard all over the house, visitors sometimes asked what the noise was. "Oh, that's only Fred working on his typing," they were told. "Their embarrassment was just that acute," Chappell says. "I wasn't trying to write. I was learning to type. Typing was a useful skill that might come in handy someday. Writing was impractical. These were the tag-end years of the Depression, and it was imperative to be practical."

This kind of message gets into you and is very hard to get out. Maybe the only way to do so is the same way you'd extract a fishhook: backing it up a little before pulling it out. First, you become aware that there is a fishhook imbedded in you, and then you re-examine those messages, look for their origins, rewind and play back parts of your childhood and try to understand—and this is critical—whose messages they were and what kind of people gave you these messages.

Apply dog logic: Don't look at where the finger is pointing, look at who is pointing the finger. Whose voice of authority comes blaring through your head with advice and admonitions about how you should respond to your own callings? Whether these people are dead or alive, ask yourself what motivates their advice and their lives. What are their stories? What are their values? What chips do they carry on their shoulders like epaulets? Ask yourself if you believe what they believe, value what they value, operate the way they operate.

We want to find the stories beneath the stories we're told, the agendas hidden behind the advice, and we want to flush them out like beaters driving game. We need to do this so that we can take others' counsel, however well meaning, with the proverbial big grain of salt. We need to reformulate our relationship to these voices of authority, as well as to our own. In Chappell's case, it was vital for him to understand that his parents' message grew out of a Depression mentality that made impracticality, as he put it, "worse than heresy, thievery, and some kinds of homicide."

You might tell a co-worker that you're going to follow your dream to leave the company and start your own, and she may tell you you're out of your mind in this economy, and what a great opportunity you'd be throwing away, and won't you miss all this, when what she's really saying is "I can't believe you're leaving. You're my only friend at this crummy job," or "I'm envious, but I'm too scared to do anything about it myself."

You might tell a friend that you're finally going to move, and he may play devil's advocate with you, though a little too heavy on the devil and a little too light on the advocate, and come across as combative and disapproving, when he's really feeling frustrated with his own lack of *movement*.

You might tell a colleague, as I once did, that you've set aside four months to put together a business proposal and forget that his response—"Four months? Hell, I knock those things out in a weekend"—is based on the kind of projects *he* works on, and yours is very different, and *you* are very different.

Maybe your gift or your call is tormenting to your mother or father, who scorns it but who had the same gift or the same call and never honored it. Maybe they felt that their cherished security in life is founded precisely on their refusal to honor their gifts, and so, lest they tear themselves down the middle with grief and regret, they tout the security and not the gift. Or perhaps they tested the waters briefly themselves once and found it too cold, so they attempt to pass this wisdom—the water is too cold, stay out—on to you.

In fact, until a son can see his father and a daughter can see her mother as just another woman or just another man who had children and dreams that did or didn't come true and who struggled with personal demons, he or she does not really grow up, and is unlikely to forgive parents for their misdirections and criticisms. Until we understand someone's history, we can understand neither that person nor on what they base their own voices of authority.

⁓

All this dog logic is really just the work—and it *is* work—of finding out where others end and we start. Perhaps this work is no more than remembering what we have always known.

A few years ago, a friend of mine, Clare, told me of an interaction she had with her then five-year-old daughter, Jennea, who wanted to do something Clare didn't think advisable. "Jennea, honey," she said, "I wouldn't do that if I were you." To which Jennea, with absolute innocence and certitude, replied, "But Mommy, you're *not* me."

At one point in our lives, even if only for a short time, we all knew the boundaries. We all knew what was ours and what was theirs and that in addition to being connected to others we are also separate. I wish I could say I've discovered a surefire way to rekindle that quality of innocent certainty, but I can't. I do know that it is something to which to aspire.

M O S T   V A L U A B L E   P L A Y E R

I have a $10,000 bill taped to the Rolodex in my office. It was given to me by the five-year-old son of some friends. He taught me a critical lesson in the economics of self-worth and the part self-worth plays in how we refuse our callings.

I first met Christopher at the front door of his house, outside of which, piled in a corner of the portico, is a collection of rocks in the shape of hearts, several dozen of them, as large as hubcaps and as small as dimes. Standing behind his parents, he wore tiny bright red cowboy boots, a red baseball cap, and thick, round glasses. One hand was on his hip, a pose his father describes as "ready for action."

During that afternoon he showed me his secret hiding places, and we played baseball in the backyard. I let him win 15–7, even though I was hankering to slug a few balls over the roof, take him to task for making up rules in midgame, and running the bases in a halfhearted circle that barely extended beyond the pitcher's mound.

Later, as I was saying good-bye to his parents in the kitchen, he ran in carrying an envelope stuffed with play money, sat down, and very exactingly filed through it with his fingers, as if walking them slowly across a tabletop. He pulled out a $10,000 bill—the largest denomination he had—and handed it to me, saying, "Here. This is for you. For playing baseball with me, and being my friend."

In the moment of hazy self-consciousness that came next, I gave it back to him, mumbling something about it being only a baseball game and not worth ten grand, but thanks anyway. He looked puzzled, and I felt clumsy and wished the moment would pass. He went back into the envelope and pulled out two $100 bills and handed those to me. I was about to turn them down, too, when Robin whispered in my ear that it was a gift and I should accept it. So I did.

That night, as I was undressing for bed, I emptied my pants pockets and found the two $100 bills, and the first thing that went through my mind was, "Dammit. I could've had $10,000. How did I end up with only $200?"

I was keenly motivated to find out because within a few weeks I would have to put a price on my head for writing that law book for the advertising agency in California, which had the potential of being the most lucrative project of my career. I had never taken on a project like it before, however, and didn't know what I was worth, and the incident with Christopher didn't seem like a very promising omen. It was a call to think big, which is exactly what I needed at that moment, and I turned it down, and if I was declining the advances of a five-year-old, I began to wonder what tactical blunders I might commit at the bigger bargaining table at which the adults play?

When it comes to all the reasons for saying no to a calling, most of them seem to pale when compared to the issue of basic self-esteem, that core regard for ourselves, that part of us that knows exactly why we should be here tomorrow.

Sometimes, it isn't even that we consciously *say* no to our calls but that we're stuck in a position of negating ourselves. Our calls are just swallowed up in the same black hole as all our soul's other petitions. The very self that receives calls is injured, fouled with surrender, lamed by the injured souls who raised us and their poor estimation of *themselves*. The central message we received was a no rather than a yes, and that's what we carry. A woman I once knew in Cincinnati carried a particularly virulent form of this message: When she lost 100 pounds from her 450, and could finally fit into a dress with a waist, she was told by her mother that she looked like a streetwalker.

The beating heart of self-esteem is the feeling that we're acceptable *as we are*, without having to *earn* it. When it comes down to a crunch, self-esteem is what tells us that despite all our misgivings about ourselves and our callings, despite all the obstacles and the self-abuse, despite the odds, we know we can do this thing! We know deep down that we can do it, and all the contrary opinions are just strangling vines and rust.

Ironically, it's a *function* of self-esteem that we resist our callings. Resistance is about self-preservation. We're protecting ourselves from imagined harm, the threat of pain, the experience of feeling bad about ourselves. "It is love, not hate, that underlies self-defeating behavior," writes Roy Baumeister in *Escaping the Self.* "Our love of self is so great that it becomes intolerable to let ourselves be seen in a bad light. When events threaten to cast us in a bad light, the first impulse is to turn the light off."

Elevating self-esteem, though, is among the most difficult work there is. The term "self-esteem" is tossed around with such cloying abandon that it has effectively been gutted of meaning and is often represented to be something we can turn on with the flick of a switch. Our deeper intelligence tells us, however, that the lack of it is a monster at the heart of the soul, at the heart of the world. Filling the void requires courage and damned hard work. Healing wounds to our self-image cannot occur if we don't admit the wounds exist, if we don't take the hot waters of self-scrutiny and take up the plow to work new furrows into the brain. We also cannot heal without understanding that healing not only involves our own hard work but also requires retooling the apparatuses of human relations: child raising, education, religion, relations between the sexes and the races. In other words, self-esteem is not just individual work but also cultural work.

The difference between saying no and saying yes can be contained in a split-second decision—take the $10,000 or leave it—yet arriving at the point of being able to *make* that decision can take a lifetime.

The question "What am I worth?" is far more than a financial question, and answering it demands far more than a cursory look at what the market will bear or what the competition is charging. The answer isn't just a function of what your parents thought you should receive in your allowance, what the fast-food joint you worked for in high school paid a hamburger flipper, or what the newspaper was willing to bid for a cub reporter. The answer also depends entirely on whom you ask. To a chemist, our bodily components, boiled and centrifuged, are worth a few bucks in trace minerals. To a five-year-old who has no one to play baseball with in the backyard, I suddenly attain Most Valuable Player status.

Christopher's bountiful gesture was a way of saying that what is most valuable, what he was willing to pay top dollar for, is *intrinsic,* friendship and time spent. He got me to thinking along the same lines. First, however, he tripped a wire inside me and slung out the shrapnel of memories, of the times I unwittingly marked myself down.

Flashback: I'm home from college for Christmas break, winding up a visit with my father that could best be described as an attempt by two warring nations to maintain trade agreements. I'm standing alone in the front bathroom, staring down at five twenty-dollar bills I'd splayed out on the counter, debating whether to take them or leave them.

Moments earlier, my father had peeled them out of his wallet and, with gangsterlike dexterity, folded them twice with one hand as he gave them to me and whispered, "Go buy yourself something." It was an act I always took to be one of remorse on his part, for not being around more and for the way things turned out. Money was *often* the currency that passed for love and hate and communication between us, and as I stood in the bathroom just before leaving, I was bitter about feeling bought off, yet I was greedy for the money.

At the last moment I snatched the money off the counter and pocketed it, flung a sour look into the mirror, and walked out of the bathroom as I put on my coat.

Years later, as I prepared my pitch to the advertising agency, this and other recollections of times I'd sold myself short kept surfacing: my decision to attend the college that offered me financial aid rather than the one I really wanted to attend; not quitting my job at the newspaper sooner; falling into relationships I didn't want because something seemed better than nothing; all the times I told myself "I can't afford it" when I could; all the times I tried to win my parents' approval, or heaped regrets on myself for decisions that were over and done with, or clamped my hands over my ears when my life was playing my song.

These past experiences orchestrated my conduct with Christopher, prompted me to turn from his friendly call, to black out to the possibilities it hinted at. It also lent a tremendous performance anxiety to my deliberations about what to charge for writing the law book. The day before I faxed the ad agency my pitch, I was back at Christopher's house. It was my birthday, and Christopher's father, Dan, gave me that $10,000 bill, which he knew had obsessed me ever since I had let it slip out of my fingers. This time I accepted it.

I asked for five times the amount of money the ad agency had hinted it was prepared to pay, and twice the amount of time.

I had a contract within a week.

To this day, I still have taped to my Rolodex that $10,000 bill, which has

on it the picture of an Indian chief with a great hooked nose. Although it says
NOT NEGOTIABLE across the top, it reminds me of a tender negotiation with
myself that helped me re-evaluate my life.

In retrospect, I've probably gotten more "value" from that play money
than from most of the money I've earned in my life for services rendered. It
was certainly more valuable than the $200 check from a magazine that was in
my mailbox the afternoon I returned from meeting Christopher; money that
went right out the door to pay an overdue phone bill. I was able to spend that
money but not enjoy it, and so it didn't seem any more real than Christopher's.
It was money that did *nothing* to remind me that I have a friend somewhere
who would gladly show me his secret hiding places, who knows the true value
of friendship, and who has money to burn.

twelve

B   R   I   N   G   I   N   G

D   O   W   N

T   H   E   S   T   O   R   M

A key is made for only one purpose. To fit a lock. Not just any lock. One lock.

Anyone who feels made to do one particular thing in this world but is unable to do it becomes, in a sense, an unreconciled key.

Eric was such a person. I first met him when he agreed to let me interview him for a magazine piece I was writing on sex-change operations. I was unprepared, however, for the beautiful blonde who answered the door wearing a low-cut black dress, spiked high heels, and pink fingernails. In a husky voice, the blonde introduced herself as Erica. I was even less prepared for the turn our interview took an hour later when, as I tried tactfully to broach the subject of what Eric's body looked like halfway through the mandatory preoperative year of hormone treatments, he said, with considerable sobriety, "Would you like to see?"

Stripped, Eric was a chimera, a sexual sphinx, the top half woman, the bottom half man, an object of wonder even to himself and one of astonishment to me. In a moment of lapsed journalistic objectivity, I blurted out, "Jesus!"

All his life, Eric said, he had felt alienated from himself in a deeply existential way, felt that the gods had somehow mixed up their kits, because whenever he looked in a mirror he expected to see a woman but kept seeing a man. All his life he felt like a spy, moving unnoticed through all the intimate realms of boyhood and manhood—locker rooms, bathrooms, dorms, clubs, fraternities—trading men's secrets, speaking their language, sharing their idiosyncratic society, and yet living in a no-man's-land, in a body that was all wrong for his spirit.

༺༻

It is not, in my estimation, an undue stretch to say that if we are living lives that are all wrong for our spirits, and if we say no to the calls that could put that spirit to rights, then we, too, like Eric, are lost souls. If the earth calls to the apple and it doesn't come, it tends to rot on the tree. If a panther is confined to a cage, "a great will stands stunned and numb," as the poet Rainer Maria Rilke once observed. If the timorous heart is too fearful of failure and loss, too panic-stricken to relinquish the status quo, we won't be propelled through the door. We'll remain outsiders to our own selves, and the air around us will fill with the smell of something burning on the stove. In the Afghani tongue, the verb *to cling* is the same as *to die*.

A calling is not something we can turn down as we turn down the page corners of a book so that, at our leisure, we can pick up where we left off, *if* we pick it up. No rituals can hold off the gods who deliver calls; no sleight of hand can distract them from their appointed rounds; no amount of double-talk will confuse them. We cannot refuse with impunity. Neglected gods devolve into demons whose pitchforks are made for moving bodies around and who are inclined to get our attention by shaking us until our teeth rattle in our skulls. "If you bring forth what is within you," Jesus said (The Gospel of Thomas, verse 70), "what you bring forth will save you. If you do not bring forth what is within you, what you do not bring forth will destroy you."

Eventually, our feelings of inauthenticity and restlessness, our envy of others' successes, our panic at the passage of time and our own reflections in the mirror, all become like tombstones—they remind us of where someone is buried—and we will measure our fear of death by the distance between our desires and our actions, between the life we want and the life we have.

In space travel, the escape stage, during which a rocket has to break away from Earth's gravitational pull, is considered the most unstable stretch of the journey, the most stressful on the rocket's system. So with us, the attempt to shake the gravity of our spiritual home turf is possibly the most perilous stage in encountering calls. Breaking away defies the forces of nature and shakes the works. Occasionally, there's hell to pay.

When we say no to our callings, then the Force of Completion, which is the soul's resolve and is faithful to us even when we're unfaithful to it, fires up its furnaces and begins working toward our conversion. The inducement of choice is typically suffering. "The voice of eternity within us demands to be heard," the philosopher Søren Kierkegaard said, "and to make a hearing for itself it makes use of the loud voice of affliction, and when, by the aid of affliction, all irrelevant voices are brought to silence, it can be heard."

We struggle against nothing so hard as coming-to, the author Saul Bellow once wrote, the work of busting the spirit's sleep, and "suffering is about the only reliable such buster-upper, though there is a rumor that love also does the trick."

If we don't attend to the soul, Thomas Moore adds in *Care of the Soul,* it will come to us in the form of symptoms, which he describes as "pathological art forms"—the dark blues of depression, the rhythms of arrhythmia, the architecture of ulcers. Not coincidentally, several years ago the American Medical Association found that most heart attacks occur around nine o'clock on Monday mornings. This undoubtedly has something to do with what most people are doing at around nine o'clock on Monday mornings, which is going back to work, or more precisely going back to work they don't like, to lives that are ill-matched to their spirits.

It's not poisonous to do without something we really want, the writer Doris Lessing claims. "What *is* poisonous is to pretend that the second-rate is first-rate," to pretend that you like your work when you know you're capable of better, to pretend you love what you don't, or don't love what you do.

A few years ago, while driving back home after teaching a college class I no longer wanted to teach but kept doing because I had convinced myself that "I couldn't afford" not to do it, I noticed a twitch in my neck. Over the course of the one-hour drive, it became more and more pronounced until it was a constant, painful tic, accompanied by a roaring headache. Eventually I pulled over to the side of the road and brought my full attention to it: a sharp up-and-down motion of my head, as if I were furiously nodding yes to something.

"Yes!" I yelled inside my car and exaggerated the tic. "Yes!" I yelled louder, my head bucking up and down epileptically. "Yes! Yes! Yes!" I screamed, my head a hammer pounding nails. "Say yes to my life! Say yes and move on!"

By the time I pulled back onto the highway, the symptom had completely subsided, and the headache was not far behind, though my neck ached for two days afterward. I never returned to that class.

As Augustin De la Pena wrote in his book *The Psychobiology of Cancer,* the bored brain is one that is isolated from proper stimulation, from a healthy flow of information and imagination, and it can send messages to various body parts to initiate processes to augment that flow, to make us aware of the world again. Disease, he once told me, is sometimes a mechanism to rectify a lack of interest in the world, increasing the probability of novelty right at the cellular level. Understimulation, of course, is entirely relative. One person could be bored at an amusement park and another could keep perfectly busy in a strait-jacket. But whatever the case, the brain will take matters into its own hands.

By symptoms I do not mean only medical symptoms (symptoms, says James Hillman, "do not belong first to disease, but to destiny"). The corrosive effects of avoidance also exact their toll on our emotional lives. Consistently choosing safety over adventure, brakes over accelerator, no over yes, and consistently preferring to be a passive observer rather than an active participant in our own lives can readily bring on anger and remorse, sorrow and frustration. We direct these emotions inward at ourselves or at those we claim to love, those who have to live with us but cannot say yes *for* us. Not honoring ourselves is fatefully tied up with not honoring others: our children and partners, our communities, the natural world. All of them suffer from our passivity and detachment.

When we sleep, we do not sleep alone. Some of the great myths—Sleeping Beauty, for example—speak about the truth that when we sleep, all around us also sleep. We live in a wasteland, a dormant kingdom, and when we awaken, all around us also awaken. But if we do not redeem our passivity, it can easily turn into a stifling inertia, a vast, flat plain between life's highs and lows.

Our good nature, our regard for ourselves, and our health are all bound to be compromised, the author Anne Morrow Lindbergh once said, "if, day after day, you do the opposite of what you desire, you say the opposite of what you believe, you allow yourself to be pushed and pulled where you do not want to go. There is no impunity for mocking authenticity in this manner. The most exhausting thing in my life is being insincere."

Mocking authenticity turns blessings into curses, but the vigilance required to *keep* doing so insures that we will bring storms down on ourselves. In the 1950s, experiments with monkeys demonstrated that the constant guardedness needed to ward off harm is as dangerous as whatever the harm might be. The monkeys worked six-hour shifts, pressing a button to avoid getting electric shocks. They performed admirably, avoiding all but a few shocks. But after three weeks, most of them died—of ulcers.

We often expect that saying yes to a calling will bring down the curtains, shock us with its demands and its sacrifices, but the constant anxiety we bring to the ramparts to defend the status quo is worse than the threat that lies beyond them. "All the time I'm not writing, I feel like a criminal," Fran Lebowitz once said. "It's horrible to feel felonious every second of the day. It's much more relaxing actually to write."

T H E   L O G I C   O F   W A K E - U P   C A L L S

Alarm clocks have probably contributed more to arousing the working class than the *Communist Manifesto,* but there are far more agreeable ways of being roused in the morning than by the typical alarm clock, which is to the sleeping nervous system what a rocking chair is to an unsuspecting cat.

The alarm clock I bought as a concession to my nerves and my general disposition, and which cuts down on profanity in the house, goes off with a quiet beep that increases gently in volume and never goes beyond the decibel level of a civil conversation. It is also motion sensitive, so a magisterial wave of the hand anywhere within half a foot of it will turn it off. This I greatly prefer to the jangling finale my old clock meted out to what, in most cases, was a decent night's rest. It brought a bitter end to the succor of sleep and made a harsh demarcation between night and day.

It is stupefying to me how many people prefer to wake themselves up in such a raucous manner. Maybe they don't even notice. The great majority of people appear to have cultivated, with seeming nonchalance, the ability—worse, the willingness—to live with uproarious noise pollution. Housing developments are built right alongside major freeways. People picnic under the flight patterns of airports and in the shoulder lanes of highways. Where I live in Tucson, the National Forest Service leases a chunk of land at the mouth of the most popular canyon in town to a gun club and shooting range, whose presence can be heard miles into the wilderness. To my mind, it nullifies the whole point of setting aside national park land.

The ability to tune out the tumult, though undoubtedly useful if you have to live in it, exacts a toll. The kind of obliviousness it requires dulls our senses, and it's no wonder it takes a loud and strident noise to get people's attention and rouse them from dormancy.

Such is the logic of wake-up calls.

Wake-up calls are simply calls that have become desperate to get our attention. They generally start as polite requests, gentle taps on the shoulder, whispers in the ear, and they escalate to rude shoves and barbaric yawps only after we have repeatedly ignored them. Our souls will speak as softly as possible, but as loudly as they have to. Sometimes calls are Muses who dab perfume gently on their wrists and their necks and anywhere else they hope to be kissed, and sometimes they're Harpies spraying their smell around enough to scare the werewolves.

At that point, they become crises that often alter our lives so dramatically that we have no choice but to change, and we then do our mightiest just to cope. The sociologist Gordon Allport calls this the power of the fait accompli. The done deal. The career disaster that has the effect of blowing a hole in your hull below waterline. The accident or illness that changes everything. The partner who leaves you for someone else. The case of burnout that lands you in the hospital. The addiction that lands you in the courtroom or the newspaper.

Some kinds of change can *only* be set in motion by a strong-arm tactic, otherwise the forces of habit and fear and laziness are just too stubborn. Perhaps wake-up calls should even be considered alternative rites of passage for people who no longer have them. They are the means by which new powers and patterns can break into consciousness and new stages of life can be attained. In any case, there's no sense blaming the messenger. If responsibility is the ability to respond, when we do not respond to our calls, we put them in the position of having to come after us, in the same way in which my partner, Robin, has to come after me when I neglect my share of the housework. It appears that *she* is the problem, the pursuer and tormenter, when really I am the problem.

I suspect that those who experience wake-up calls usually discover, in hindsight of course, that they had received plenty of warning before the poop hit the propeller, but they chose to disregard it. A lot of divorces and diseases and dismissals from jobs probably don't come as a complete surprise to those who suffer them. Fights and infidelities, or a morose silence, fall over a relationship well before the word *divorce* ever splits the air. Children show us in countless ways that they need our attention well before they get mixed up with the law. We begin taking little chances at a job when we just don't care anymore—extralong lunches, leaving work early, filching from the stockroom, sick days from which we come back with a tan. They are indications we're probably not long for the job.

Granted, some wake-up calls are *not* a function of neglecting calls—natural disasters, mass job layoffs, parents suddenly coming to live with you, the suicide of a friend, a sudden empty nest, the death of a child—but whatever the case, we're drop-kicked into consciousness, even if only temporarily, and we either use the experience or we don't. Either we understand that the point of the experience is to reorient us and recognize the call in the calamity, or we attempt to drive ourselves deeper into the status quo, the old equilibrium, and thereby miss the point entirely.

Wake-up calls, however, change the bottom line. What seemed important before doesn't now. You have a new set of priorities. When you get sick, work takes a backseat. When your kid gets in an accident, your previous concerns pale. When someone you love dies, whatever you failed to tell them that you wished you had often becomes a top priority in your *other* relationships. When *you're* dying, when you turn that sharp corner and suddenly realize not only that there is *an* end but that this is also *the* end, all your obsessions with security and status and time spent doing anything other than what you really want to do, or must do, often seem ludicrous.

These realizations often come to us in shattering moments, when our sustaining habits are pulled violently from us and when the demand for a new way comes hard up against the armies of the old. We figure out that no amount of business-as-usual will stop the inevitable from happening. Not that we can't rebuild, but first there's a shattering and the need to acknowledge that we're in shock.

Whether a wake-up call becomes a boon or a bane depends on what we're willing to learn from it and whether we're willing to be moved by the experience. The outcome depends not on how strong we are but on *how* we're strong. Not just any kind of strength will suffice in the face of a wake-up call. Physical strength may be virtually useless, a strong will may only make things worse, and the ability to withstand pain may work against us. We may instead need to call on the strength to surrender.

THE PRIMAL NECESSITIES

The higher brain that we so proudly hail as that which "separates us from the animals" houses those most human of qualities: self-reflection, creative thinking, intellect, computing, reason and the will to ignore it, poetry and paranoia, all our philosophies and all our fears of death. This part of the brain is called the neocortex, which means new bark. It is the outermost layer, not the trunk, of the brain and is built onto the chassis of a very ancient brain shared with the animal kingdom, and programmed over the course of tens of millions of years of evolution. Its intelligences are primitive and contain the instincts for physical survival, the regulations of the body, and our basic awareness of the environment. It is also the habitat of intuitions and emotions, and all dreaming, night or day.

The old brain also lodges our most elementary aversions and attractions, our most basic sniffing-the-wind sense of what to move toward and what to move away from. Here the primitive in us is far wiser than the "higher animal." It knows, for instance, that relatedness is critical to life. It knows that intuitions are meant to be trusted. It knows that when following our noses, keeping the body in balance, and honoring the essential tropisms of desire, everything we need to know we learned in the Paleozoic.

Callings are essential in this same way and reflect our most fundamental necessities and instincts, the primitive "I want!" of the soul. By moving against our calls, we move against ourselves. We mistrust our deepest intelligence and run out of the bunny hole when a hawk is flying overhead. No wonder we get wake-up calls. Thank goodness for such a mechanism, although gratitude is not generally our first response.

Kathleen Dusek kept ignoring a primal necessity for community, for relatedness to something larger than herself. She describes "the core of my starvation" as an immense isolation, both physical and spiritual. It took not one, but *two* wake-up calls to pull her out of it.

From 1977 to 1983, Kathleen had been a travel documentary filmmaker living in Los Angeles who spent half the year filming and the other half traveling around the United States, Canada, and Europe, presenting her films to

audiences of sometimes thousands at universities and theaters, science acade-
mies and art institutes, even the National Geographic Society. Her life from
the outside appeared to be tremendously glamorous, and it was certainly that,
but her life was also, as she says, "miserable."

The itinerary of airplanes every day and hotels every night and the repeti-
tiveness of having to present the same film sometimes hundreds of times were
growing exceedingly tedious. Her relationships had been rendered essentially
inert by the constant travel, so a corroding loneliness set in. "I was incredibly
isolated. I couldn't keep relationships going with men, I had no community, I
had wonderful friends scattered all over the world, but I saw them maybe once
a year for a couple of days.

"I also felt alienated from myself, and though I kept getting signs that I
needed to begin looking into the spiritual side of my life—through people
I met, situations I'd get thrown into, books and tapes people insisted I read—
I would have nothing to do with them. I was given the opportunity again and
again to start down that path, but I kept refusing. I simply would not go."

It took an accident to get her going. It happened when Kathleen was filming a documentary on the Orient Express, which travels from Paris to Istanbul,
a few days before her thirty-second birthday. It was early summer, midafter-
noon, and the train was moving at thirty miles an hour as it clattered through
the Turkish countryside on the outskirts of Istanbul. One moment, Kathleen
was leaning over the shoulders of some men standing in an open doorway
between two cars, filming a group of children running through a field, and the
next moment she was falling.

At first, everything moved in slow motion and in absolute silence as she
tumbled through space, feeling the wind on her body, feeling surprised. Then,
as if the movie suddenly sped up again, the ground came rushing up to meet
her. She saw the train roar past her, its whistle screaming, her body somer-
saulting on the cantaloupe-size rocks lining the railroad tracks. Her life also
flashed in front of her eyes. In the distance, she heard the train screech to a
stop as someone pulled the emergency brake.

Conscious throughout the entire event, she suffered a concussion and frac-
tured skull, torn ligaments in her left shoulder and had substantial tracts of
skin flayed off and contusions everywhere. Amazingly, she left the hospital in
Istanbul after only one day, though there was no sound reason for this and no
medical logic. She was out of her mind and just happened to live through it.

She spent a week in a Hilton hotel before flying to Paris for "an emotional breakdown," and then on to the Alps for solitude. During all that time, she says, "I got very quiet, but I still refused to look at what it all meant."

Six weeks later she flew back to Los Angeles and discovered that just because she had gotten a wake-up call didn't mean she would necessarily wake right up. "Life was telling me to get off the track I was on," but while she was forced to admit that no wasn't the answer to the question, she was still not able to say yes. When the lights suddenly go out, you're thrown into total darkness, and only gradually do your eyes adjust until you can see better. Initially, you are often paralyzed, disoriented, even panicked. *Crisis* is Latin for "to decide," and when in a crisis, you still have to *decide* to wake up. You can make all sorts of changes but still not wake up, which is what happened to Kathleen.

Although she began exercising and losing weight, bought a new wardrobe, and made superficial changes in the way she related to people, "It was all outer action, not an inner shift. I didn't understand that the changes needed to come from inside. Mostly, I chose to go on as before. During a writing exercise, I wrote, 'There is a place in my brain, a wall, that I cannot get beyond.' " Nonetheless, at least she was attempting to change. The accident transformed a longtime despair, a chronic sense of being stuck, into a catastrophe that at least had some *movement* to it.

Throughout this outer process, Kathleen did have one glimmer of real awakening, however. For the next year, she began to *notice* when opportunities were being offered to her to create a sense of community and to open her spiritual life, and she began to notice when she was turning them down. She understood that the accident was "a great prophetic sign of a coming opening."

Unfortunately, she needed another wake-up call to bring on that opening, and it happened on the same train! Eleven months after the accident, she was back on the Orient Express to finish shooting the footage she'd missed the year before. On the last night of the trip, she had an affair with a Frenchman and became pregnant.

"I panicked, I absolutely panicked. I was terrified, depressed, suicidal. I felt invaded. I'd always had a hard time turning over control of my life, in any way, to others, including God, and the pregnancy made me feel incredibly out of control, and vulnerable. It felt like a life-or-death situation. Years before, I remember thinking that the only thing I would never want to have to make a decision about was whether to have an abortion or not. It was my most fearful scenario, and there I was, in just that situation. In fact, I did make a suicide attempt, but in looking death in the face—again—I realized I really wanted to live."

A few days after returning home, Kathleen punched a hole in that mental wall she had been unable to get beyond and reached through it. She opened the phone book, looked under Psychologists, closed her eyes, and stabbed with her finger. Shortly thereafter, she submitted to an abortion, an act that, aside from the moral conundrums it held for Kathleen, proved to her that she could take on her most fearful scenario.

"The biggest decision I had to make at that point," she says, "was deciding to tell myself that I was a good person, especially in the face of having had the abortion. So I took on the simple act of repeating to myself 'I'm a good person,' and though I didn't believe it, I began saying it hundreds of times a day. It was the first time in my life I ever said something good about myself. It was a quantum leap of choice. It was the first tiny chink out of that wall."

Kathleen spent much of the following years in what she describes as "recollecting myself. I realized I had chosen an isolated life because I was terrified to get close to anyone. I kept avoiding my spiritual life because I felt victimized by the Christian God of my youth, and I believed that if I started opening to myself, anger was going to come up and the whole shebang would come apart. I also realized that the call toward a spiritual life was largely about healing my low self-esteem, and for me that meant connecting with God rather than *working* on my self-esteem, because as soon as I found I wasn't separate, that I was part of a whole, part of everything, I felt better about myself, and didn't feel so alone."

While traveling in North Carolina during those ensuing years, Kathleen saw a picture in her mind of herself sitting at a computer, which she didn't even know how to operate at that time, and writing a book. In her hotel room one night, she couldn't sleep, so she picked up the Gideons' Bible, that was sitting on the night table. "Okay, I need a sign," she said aloud, whereupon she opened to this passage from Jeremiah: "And the Lord God said to Jeremiah, 'Write the words I have spoken to you in a book.' "

Today, Kathleen is writing a book and working on performing theatrical monologues, "my little modern myths," she calls them, whose theme is "expanding our realms of possibility." This includes a few of the possibilities she herself thought inconceivable only a few years before: having community and a fully flowering spiritual life.

"To my amazement, I now live next door to my parents and can actually feel love for and from them, whereas ten years ago I could feel only anger and blame. I'm also totally involved in the community here [she now lives in Cornville, Arizona], have a tremendous group of friends, am active in the local film festival and in lobbying in Phoenix for different civic issues. I'm really in the world, for the first time."

THE   BENEFITS   OF   AVOIDANCE

When we say no to our callings, we're like the blind, who can keep forever intact their inner visions of the way things look, the ideal and the real never confronting each other. We can keep intact our fantasies of how talented we are by not putting our talents to the test, of how indispensable we are to a company or a community by never leaving it, of how safe and secure we are by just staying put.

There are payoffs to saying no, benefits of safety and security, that we receive in not having to face fear and limitations, and there is a lot to be said for safety and security. When we fear something, we don't reach out and risk, but when we don't reach out, we *also* don't get burned as much (though we reinforce the fear). "Habit is habit," Mark Twain once said, "and not to be flung out the window, but coaxed downstairs a step at a time."

For a lot of us, refusing our own impulses is desirable for the simple reason that it feels familiar. One of the most confounding human habits is that we continue to do what hurts us just because it's familiar, it's the pattern we know, it makes us feel *at home*. It reminds us of what our original home life was like, an almost physical memory that is of magnetic—of gravitational—power. We swing back to it again and again, obviously not learning something we need to learn. We repeat to ourselves the same criticisms our parents leveled at us. We distract ourselves from our desires with the same diversions—food, money, a quick change of subject—*they* used with us whenever we cried out. We adopt the same addictions our parents used to cover up their own passions and pains. Sometimes we find ourselves repeating the relationships our parents had to work and to love, patterns we swore we'd never emulate, and the awful realization that we ended up emulating them anyway can itself be a wake-up call.

The psychologist Rollo May touches powerfully on this subject in *Freedom and Destiny* when he discusses the phenomenon of "imprinting," in which newborn animals—mostly birds, a few mammals—will follow whatever creature, or object, they first encounter, thinking it kin. He described having seen a full-grown duck following a rabbit around because that was the creature to which it originally got imprinted, even though the annoyed rabbit routinely turned around and bit the duck to drive it away.

Even though we don't *enjoy* feeling stuck and frustrated, or living with unworkable situations and nagging desires, when we refuse our calls, we may still benefit from saying no when there are rewards for conformity. We can, for instance, congratulate ourselves on being stable, reliable, faithful to our responsibilities, obedient to our faith. Eldridge Cleaver, in his book *Soul on Ice*, remarked that for many people it's perhaps better to "choose the trivial," to maintain in their affairs a certain superficiality. That way, "The scars are not too deep and no blood is hacked from the soul."

Escaping from ourselves is not all bad and is even essential to the flowering of some of our highest ideals. Spirituality and love are both based on the urge to escape the self, to melt I into Thou, to experience transcendence. The term "ecstasy," so common to the literature of love and religion, means to stand outside oneself. But transcendence and ecstasy are not to be confused with avoidance and feeling relief. The benefits of the former are substantially different from those of the latter.

We might benefit from asking ourselves exactly *how* we benefit from flight. As Barbara Sher puts it in *Wishcraft*, we need to understand what our emotional investment is in the belief that "it can't be done." For every part of us that wants to follow a call, there is an equal and opposite part that doesn't, and that part is served by our stasis. It's one of the laws of physics: If you were to stand on a skateboard and throw a ball forward, you would roll backward. This idea of equal and opposite actions is, in fact, part of philosopher Ken Wilber's definition of the human shadow. He claims that shadow is the exact opposite of "whatever you consciously desire, like, feel, want, intend, or believe."

If you desire consciously to succeed at a calling, there are also unconscious parts of you, Wilber says, that don't want to succeed. If you succeed, for instance, that very success will probably demand more and more of your time, time not spent with your family or friends, and part of you knows you're going to hear about it. By not following the call, you keep such conflict at bay. If you succeed, you may be burdened with your and others' expectations of *continued* success. By ignoring the call, you avoid the performance anxiety. If you succeed, you're likely to draw increasing attention to yourself. If you don't want the scrutiny, all you have to do is just say no.

What all this tells us, Wilber says, is that some part of us *wants* every fear, symptom, and neurosis we possess. Some part of us has perfectly sound reasons to play a leading role in creating and perpetuating them. Rather than fighting them—and ourselves—Wilber recommends that we use active imagination and compassionate listening to reflect on these parts of us and seek to understand them.

H I T T I N G   B O T T O M

Escaping to Tarshish, our belongings bundled at the end of a stick, we could just as well be leaving a trail of bright blood or paint, or arrows on the ground where every footstep falls. We could just as well be confiding to every passing stranger our destination, as readily as people seem to see it in our eyes. Our painted dreams, our accusing consciences, our bodies in flight, all remind us that the earth is still round, and that even if we run in the straightest line, we're still running along the circumference of a circle that will eventually carry us back to where we started.

Maybe we *need* to run. Maybe only by running can we find out that Tarshish isn't a refuge but just someplace we'll have to walk all the way back from, because the work is *here*. Maybe running is part of the work, the part that makes us finally bow to the storm, realizing, as Jonah did, that God will not simply pocket the affront.

Maybe at the end of our running, we'll even feel contrite or desperate enough to finally say yes instead of no. Maybe it's the only way to find out that there's no escape. We resist but cannot find release. We can turn our backs, but we do so on a tiger. Running gives us the illusion that we're outdistancing something, but only children really believe that if they cover themselves with a blanket they're invisible.

Francis Thompson wrote in his poem "The Hound of Heaven":

> I fled Him, down the nights and down the days;
> I fled Him, down the arches of the years;
> I fled Him, down the labyrinthian ways, . . .
> I sped . . .
> From those strong feet that followed, followed after.

One of the unsung benefits of refusing our callings is that, like Kathleen Dusek, we may hit bottom. The bottom may be the best thing to hit us because, after all, we can go only *up* from there. Progress isn't only a forward perambulation; it works backward as well. Going backward can be going forward. Procrastination and resistance can be part of the path, part of what helps plunge us into a predicament that can serve to awaken us. In other words, there may be a certain *rightness* to our chariots swinging so low.

"It was certainly true for me," says speaker Lee Glickstein, "that being completely stuck was part of my path, and maybe I couldn't have gotten unstuck any sooner than I did. But until I was forty-five years old, I thought I was the laziest person in the world. I was totally frustrated, totally undisciplined, and not willing to pay the price of following my call. I had to get to the low point, I had to hit bottom, before I was desperate enough to act."

"When in doubt about where you are meant to be," a Buddhist saying goes, "look down at your feet."

The very despair that can ensue from refusing a call can be our greatest ally in coming to terms with our destiny, with the demand to face our lives. When people hit bottom, Rollo May says, when they hit ultimate despair, which he describes as "a desperate refusal to be oneself," they can more easily surrender to "eternal forces," and this is the dynamic in all authentic conversions.

The connection between despair and joy is so vital, May says, that the ancient Greeks devoted one of their central myths to it: Persephone and Demeter. In her grief at having her daughter Persephone abducted into the underworld by Hades, Demeter, goddess of the harvest, went dormant. The land bore no food, and famine spread like germs in a preschool. Finally, Zeus, king of the gods, ordered Hades to let Persephone go, but before he did he gave her six pomegranate seeds, which she ate. In doing so, she sealed her fate: She had to spend half of every year with Hades.

Thus, whenever hell's ferryman takes Persephone across the River Styx to see Hades, it becomes fall and winter, and when she returns, it becomes spring and summer. The story reminds us that the descent into despair is followed by the ascent of joy, which, says May, "is stronger than Demeter would feel had the sorrow not preceded it." So it is with all resurrections.

May also points out that people's interest in the descent is far overshadowed by their interest in the ascension, and it is a lopsidedness that works against them. There is scant attendance, for example, at observances of Good Friday, marking Christ's death, but mobs attend Easter Sunday services, which mark his return. This is symptomatic of our refusal to acknowledge that death must precede rebirth, that despair is act one of a two-act play, and that our refusal to heed a calling may in fact be the initial phase of following a calling.

W H E N   S A Y I N G   N O   I S   T H E R I G H T   C H O I C E

Another of the surprises of saying no to a call is that not everyone who hesitates is lost. Had Jack Meanwell, for instance, said yes to his calling *when* he wanted to, he wouldn't have been able to do it the *way* he wanted to. So, although he didn't plan to do so, he waited twenty-five years to become the abstract painter he'd always wanted to be.

After returning from World War II, Jack lived in Windsor, Ontario, working as a commercial artist. His father-in-law had, at the time, a one-person coffee company in Cincinnati and offered Jack a partnership and a 40 percent interest in a business with a negative net worth. He also offered fifty dollars a week. Jack was earning thirty-five.

Although he felt he could paint on the side and did for many years, he often got sidetracked by the arguments of practicality. The work of keeping a business from going bankrupt, a house from falling down, and a wife and child in decent spirits often kept him away from his painting for years at a stretch.

Twenty-five years is a long time to be doing something when you'd rather be doing something else, and sometimes Jack thought to himself, "If you're in something for twenty-five years, you're in it for life." Yet one of the things Jack discovered during all those years is that callings aren't fragile, and they don't give up. *You* may give up. You may throw up your hands in disgust and despair, but the search party will not retire.

Jack's turning point began to take shape when he took on a partner himself. Now the owner of the Wallingford Coffee Company, Jack hired a man who lived, ate, slept, and breathed the business, and he expected Jack to do the same. Whenever Jack had an art show or a mention in the paper, his partner became angry, "furious that I wouldn't give that up to work twelve hours a day instead of ten."

In 1972, his partner sent Jack a certified letter: "Either buy me out or sell out. You have ninety days to make your decision." If Jack had decided to buy him out, "I'd have been working for the bank for the next ten years, paying off what I would have had to borrow to buy him out. And kiss the dream of being a painter good-bye. I thought I might never have another chance like this at my painting, and I was at an age when it still made sense to go for it."

He also realized that at that point in his life, the call demanded that he wake up in the middle of the American dream: a picture postcard life with three children, a house in the suburbs, a station wagon, a family dog, and a $60,000-a-year job (in 1972 dollars). But at fifty-three, Jack, "always the safe, conservative, orderly, no-waves type," sold his fifty-fifty share of the business, divorced his wife of twenty-seven years, took custody of his fifteen-year-old daughter, became a painter, and moved into a small studio in the artists' section of town, which all fits neatly into a run-on sentence, but it reflected a decision that was "awful and harrowing, like jumping into a freezing cold lake. I had a tremendous amount of indecision, not just because the coffee business was booming, which made it very hard to get out. The ninety-day deadline helped," and, as he put it, "it also appealed to the heroic in me."

Jack knew full well what some people would say, and he also knew that people do not need paintings to help them wake up in the morning. His decision also put him up against gallery owners who would look at his paintings and say, "Look, Jack, if you put a little Indian village here in the corner, we could sell it." After twenty-five years, however, this "no-waves type" obviously felt a little more at home in the surf, largely because by the time he finally took on his calling, he was in a much better position to make it happen. He had been able to build up his skills, his portfolio, his contacts, and his bank account, and he could comfortably and securely raise a family.

Jack also had twenty-five years' worth of business skills and had learned a few things about how a product sells, which taught him how to navigate in an art world where gallery owners often seem to believe that genius flourishes best in penury, and the market for abstract painting is often small enough to fit inside a hobo's handbag, with room left over for sculptors and poets. Eventually, Jack was earning several thousand dollars for a painting, whereas in the beginning he would trade a painting for a tank of gas.

Had he gone into painting right out of art school, as he had wanted to, the struggle would likely have crushed his spirits. The waiting and the strain of keeping his painting career at arm's length for twenty-five years might also have, but it didn't. In fact, by the time opportunity allowed him to make good on his calling, he wanted it like a man who has been forced underwater wants a lungful of air.

Sometimes we don't know until much, much later whether a course of action is right or wrong, and whether saying no to a calling might turn out to be the best decision.

A C A U T I O N A R Y T A L E

The story *Beauty and the Beast* tells us that love can change what is beastly in us into beauty. Underneath this obvious interpretation, though, is the hint of another story, the dark possibility that lies at the heart of the happy ending: the tragic fact that a beast can die untransformed. If we don't love our lives, if we don't leave home and follow them deep into the forest and give ourselves over, the beauty can become stuck in the beast. We can reach a point of no return, beyond which we simply no longer have the life left in us to follow a calling, and we end up cataloguing with sad precision the passing of our days, the withering of the rose.

If the story ends this way, one final benediction remains. It can serve as a cautionary tale for others, for future generations, for those who look to us for an example. Like our children.

My father used to have a chemistry laboratory of Frankensteinian proportions in the basement of our house, and it was emblematic of one of the saddest facts of his life: His greatest passion had been relegated to the basement. He was a businessman who should have been a scientist. But he had bowed to his father's pressure to enter a family business that stretched back to the turn of the century.

Only in that basement laboratory did my father's calling ever really come to life, and by the time I left boyhood, he had abandoned it.

His calling had taken root temporarily in one other place, however—in my elementary school. I think it significant that my own fondest memories of him are when he would sometimes come with me to grade school in the morning and be my show-and-tell, the mention of which actually appeared in his obituary in the *New York Times*.

After the other kids had displayed their pet turtles and dead black beetles, or the handful of autumn leaves they'd grabbed on their way in to school that morning, my father would draw the blinds, lay a sheet of aluminum foil on a table, and from an old apothecary jar pour out a cone of green powder half a foot high. Then, with a huddle of spellbound fourth-graders peering over each other's shoulders to get a look, he'd light a long wooden match, wave it under his chin for ghoulish effect, and touch it to the top of the cone, which would erupt in a simulated volcano, right there in the middle of Mrs. Doer's classroom.

I compare this in my mind to the times when I went to visit *him* at the factory, where he had two desks. One was a big government-issue gray desk right out on the sprawling shop floor where his factory workers called him by his first name. The other was an ornate oak desk big enough to play several rounds of golf on, and which completely dominated the quiet back office that was his father's, and before that his grandfather's.

Whenever I visited him at the factory, he would lead me into the back office and motion to a green vinyl couch against one wall. But rather than joining me on that couch, he would position himself across the room, in a high-backed leather chair behind the desk, and, palm over fist, look at me over his bifocals. Mounted on the wall behind him was a shield and two crossed swords. It was all very imposing, but it really wasn't his desk, and the scene often struck me as a bit theatrical.

That desk and everything else in his factory—including that moat in the back office between desk and couch, the space that seemed to grow as I grew and followed my own calls, which I suspect he found galling and commendable all at once—was sold out of the family when he died because neither I nor my brothers wanted to sit behind it. A man's desk is a mirror, and I just couldn't picture myself in it. I couldn't picture him in it either, though he tried mightily to play the part.

One of the consequences of my father denying his call is that somehow it became a fire that has driven my *own* life. His no became my yes, and I struggle to follow my own callings in part as a way to keep my father coming to show-and-tell, to conjure the image of him in his laboratory in the basement, to try to rectify his misbegotten decision, though really I know better.

There is a force in me that is determined to honor the imperatives of my life, and I trace it to my father, who, in the year he died, said this to me: "When the brass ring comes around in life, kiddo, you'd better grab it, because it may never come around again." Knowing what he was really saying, I felt it was the saddest thing I'd ever heard.

part five

SAYING

YES

TO CALLS

thirteen

T H E

D I G N I T Y   O F

D A R I N G

Three kinds of souls, three prayers:
1. I am a bow in your hands, draw me lest I rot.
2. Do not overdraw me, I shall break.
3. Overdraw me and who cares if I break!

— N I K O S   K A Z A N T Z A K I S

The first time I met David Roche, my face froze involuntarily into a blank stare, a chink in decorum with which he undoubtedly has a weary familiarity. David has a striking facial disfigurement, and as we stood at the front door of my house, where he and his wife, Marlena, had come to participate in one of Lee Glickstein's Speaking Circles^{SM}, it took me an egregiously long moment before I recovered from my fumble. I then was able to proceed with the usual social amenities of shaking hands, introducing myself, and ushering them in.

While a small, portable stage and video camera were being set up in the living room, lights and microphone arranged, and chairs pulled in from the kitchen, I marveled that he was here at all. I couldn't help noticing that his wife was beautiful; she had a dancer's bearing and stratospheric cheekbones.

Lee introduced the evening by saying that while it is common belief that the most prominent fear people have is that of dying, in fact it has been shown that the number one fear is of public speaking; the number two fear, he said, is that of dying *while* public speaking. So when David volunteered to go first, I was doubly astonished and imagined a light sweat breaking out on a roomful of foreheads.

I adopted a supportive smile as he loped onto the stage, grabbed the microphone, took a deep breath, and without missing a beat, said, "I was born with a face that's a gift from God. Not the kind of gift you rip open exclaiming, 'How exquisite. How did you know?' More like, 'Oh, you shouldn't have.' "

There was a moment of lunar silence in the room, and then my fictive smile broke into an unexpected laugh made up of equal parts surprise and relief, and I flicked a sideways glance at the others to gauge my reaction. It was unanimous.

David's gift is that his shadow is on the outside, and he has no choice but to deal openly with it. He cannot pretend, as so many of us do, that it doesn't exist. And if people are going to stare—which they do everywhere he goes—he figured he might as well make the most of it. His gift, his wound, has thus become his calling: "to remind people of what they already know," he said. "That it's okay to be flawed."

His calling has also necessitated that, as Lee puts it, David "talk his walk," that he be willing to devote himself to the risk taking that *must* be undertaken if a calling is to be affirmed. Author Gail Sheehy calls this "the master quality of pathfinding," of confronting the challenges of life creatively. David takes risks every time he steps up onto a stage, which he does for a living! A public speaker, entertainer, and stand-up comic, he does one-man shows at theaters and clubs and keynote speaking for national medical conventions attended by five hundred people.

"The best works," said French author and architect Fernand Pouillon, "are those at the limits of life. They stand out among a thousand others when they prompt the remark: 'What courage that must have taken!' "

Courage, of course, like risk, is absolutely relative. What is courageous to one person may be fainthearted to another. Risk is whatever scares *you*. It is the threshold we are required to cross before we can lean down to our passions lying dormant and kiss them awake. The double entendre of *threshold* is fitting. A threshold is a place of passage, a portal through which we pass from here to there and from known to unknown. But it also means a measure of endurance. If we can increase our threshold for crossing thresholds, then we can transcend some of the limits of life, and we can change our lives in the most prodigious ways. If a worm can grow wings and become a butterfly, can reap a complete change in physical form, from one creature to an entirely other, what then is possible for us?

There is no shortage of answers that are simple to declare and complicated to execute for how one gets *hold* of such courage. John Graham insists that all answers share at least one commonality. "There is a very clear link between courage and the degree of meaning in someone's life; the sense, at a really deep level, that you *know* why you do things, you know what your life is about. Most fear is fear of the unknown, but when you can answer this root question of what your life is about, that root insecurity is dealt with, and dealing with it makes it so that no fear is as bad as it was before. The more meaning, the more courage, and the less fear."

In climbing up onstage David risks that which we all risk when we honor the demands of a calling: We risk going beyond the limits we've set for ourselves toward the primitive fears of rejection and failure that are attached, like barnacles on a rock, to the idea of risk. We go toward the shadow sides of ourselves, which we try to hide even from ourselves—the timidity and indecisiveness, the fear of change, the fear of being a beginner. We move toward the possibility of flawed efforts at risk taking, and we don't like flaws. "God mend thine every flaw," goes a line from "America the Beautiful."

The courage it takes David to talk his walk, flaws and all, is the same courage it takes any of us who look straight into the dark gate of whatever is unknown to us and know that our fate lies in there, that our lives won't be complete and won't make sense until we go through. A calling is not so much something in our path as we are in *its* path. In following it, we exercise the courage to leave behind what we have for what we don't, what we are for what we could be, and to take on challenges compared to which even depression and torpor might seem preferable. It is the courage to step past the point of no return, to acknowledge that all our mightiest refusals are mere resistance. At some point, we have to stop preparing and jump, realizing, as philosopher Ernest Becker says, that "beyond a given point we are not helped by more knowing, but only by living and doing in a partly self-forgetful way."

The first time David tried public speaking, his subject was politics, and the venue was a public bus in downtown San Francisco. The instant he opened his mouth he discovered he was no longer in Kansas anymore. For ten days he tried summoning the courage to stand up, to quit clearing his throat and start speaking, and when he finally did, someone heckled him, yelling out something that roughly translated to "Shut up and sit down!"

In the blur of self-consciousness that followed, David walked to the back of the bus where no one could see him, but on the way there, he recalls, an old Irish lady grabbed his hand and said, "You did just fine, young man," whereupon she turned and yelled at the heckler.

We love to quote the philosopher and poet Goethe who said that "whatever you can do, or dream you can, begin it. Boldness has genius, power, and magic in it." But we forget that he also said, "To put your ideas into action is the most difficult thing in the world." The poem in the head is always perfect, Stanley Kunitz once remarked. The challenge comes when we try to convert it into language. This is especially so when we discover, as we often do, that saying yes to a calling requires not just one act of heroism and risk taking but a prolonged period of action that can stretch into years.

I occasionally find myself in the position of advising others who feel called to leave employment for self-employment (having done it myself), people for whom this departure is the source of endless daydreams and sleepless nights. And rightly so, for this is Scary Stuff. It requires letting go of deep familiarities—a mind-set, a lifestyle, perhaps a trade. I heartily do *not* recommend that people just up and quit their jobs, unless the prospect of financial ruin and emotional turmoil is preferable to the emotional and spiritual death they're experiencing at work. As Henry David Thoreau once said, "The mass of men lead lives of quiet desperation, but it is a characteristic of wisdom not to do desperate things."

Many times I myself came a hair's breadth away from quitting my job out of desperation and was stopped only by a stubborn survival instinct. More frequently, I was talked out of it by someone who knew better, who knew that if I attempted to begin self-employment without preparing for the rigors of that business, as well as starting a new venture in the emotionally shell-shocked aftermath of quitting a job in desperation, that I would likely drown. One friend, an environmentalist, pointed out that sudden transitions in nature are usually catastrophic: eruptions, earthquakes, flash floods.

The skill that seems most essential for such leaps is a certain feel for *ripeness.* It is having the patience to abide the growing season and develop a subtle sense of touch and the understanding that whatever the outcome of risk, of letting go of the tree, the point is always the moving on of life. Whether fruit is eaten by a passing animal, harvested on a farm, or simply melts slowly into the ground on some back acre of a forest, the fat, succulent demand is always for more life.

The move from employment to self-employment is one of life's dramatic thresholds, so I encourage people to offer an obedient bow to the gods of time and the harvest, and to give this transition the attention and patience it needs. I do not even consider it extreme to wait five years or more to phase out one way of life properly and phase in another. Your outer circumstances need time to be readjusted, as do your inner ones: the mind-set of being employed; your attitudes toward responsibility and self-management; and your attitudes toward discipline and the definition of success. All take great draughts of time and sustained risk taking to rework themselves. Meanwhile you need the courage to wait, which can be wearisome work that resembles nothing so much as sitting up nights with a feverish child.

RISK AND REFUGE

Have you really lived ten thousand or more days,
or have you lived one day ten thousand or more times?
— WAYNE DYER

The very act of risk taking sets up an antagonism with the established order of things. In creating lives based on our callings, we may have to break the rules, disappoint people, part ways with colleagues and friends, refashion our marriage vows, head against the prevailing winds. Occasionally the risks are mortal. For some people, their calls have brought them into very real lines of fire: threats, jail, excommunication, loss of community, rocks thrown through the living room window, crosses burning on the front lawn. Jesus promised those who would follow him only three things, says writer Marty Babcock: "That they would be absurdly happy, entirely fearless, and always in trouble."

To keep our balance amidst the troubles that ensue in taking risks, some measure of order and safety is critical, just as one arm of a drawing compass swings free only because the other one is anchored. Some useful anchors to have when following calls include money in the bank, a Plan B to fall back on, a support group, and people who believe in you. When someone who is about to take a leap is reminded by even a single loved one that he or she will be loved whether the endeavor flies or flops, it makes it easier to leap and *much* easier to flop.

To give himself a sense of stability, David, for instance, plans out, to the detail, significant portions of his day, especially the first five minutes after awakening: what he will wear, what he will do in what order, which cup he will drink from at breakfast. He says he is following the admonition of Gustave Flaubert, who counseled, "Be regular and orderly in your daily affairs that you may be violent and original in your work."

Risk taking should not become a theology, however. Sometimes it is merely a disguised form of escape or a kind of repetition-compulsion in itself—a blind urge to prove our wills superior, to refuse to be scared, to idolize the river gods who personify eternal change. Sometimes hanging in there, or exercising creativity *within* the status quo, is the better part of valor.

Before taking a leap, establish whether a particular status quo in your life is a monument to the fear of change, and whether the risk to which you're attracted is a function of sheer restlessness and ennui. Nothing is inherently wrong with either status quo or restlessness, but if you're taking chances and making changes just for the sake of not standing still, your actions may be more about running away from something than moving toward something. Motion is not necessarily progress any more than noise is necessarily music.

᠅

Elsa Buchner, at the age of twenty-two, heard the call of adventure and made a vow: Every five years she would stop whatever she was doing and do something different. For more than fifty years, she has done just that. She has worked in accounting, magazine production, advertising, sales, business consulting, and the jewelry business, to name a few. She has written musicals. At age fifty-five she traveled across Europe with a knapsack on her back, and she got married at seventy for the first time. At the start of each venture, she marked her calendar for five years hence and, true to her word, moved on— though she says she is making an exception for her marriage.

"It's easy to succumb to tradition and security," she says. "In fact, I do get terribly attached to things and am quite sentimental, so all the leavings have been painful. But it's part of adventure, and there's so much I've wanted to do in life. Security is certainly wonderful to have, but not at the price of inertia. I'll have plenty of that in the grave."

Elsa believes that if you love something you must let it evolve. To obey means to hear, so if you are obedient to your own heart, the leaps you take in allowing your life to unfold are not so much risks as responses. It is challenging, Elsa says, to decide what responses you are willing to make to your life and how much risk you are willing to take to assure that your life turns out the way you want it to. You don't want bumper stickers on your car that say "I'd rather be sailing" or "The worst day fishing is better than the best day working."

Elsa believes in preemptive change—you strike first before it strikes you. She has also allowed herself to be moved to adventure by her convictions, and Warner Brothers once offered to buy the movie rights to one of those adventures. She had been living in New York City, running a jewelry business when, one day, a friend called from Arizona and told her about an Indian tribe that owned a troubled gemstone mine. Unscrupulous buyers were paying them a fraction of what their stones were worth. Could Elsa help?

"I thought it odd that chance had thrown that opportunity at me, because I was interested in gems, had a marketing background, hated injustice, and felt an affinity with Indians [her father had grown up on a Chippewa reservation in Minnesota]. It felt like fate, so I said yes."

That yes led to her setting aside her business in New York, spending her own savings and borrowed money, and going to live in a trailer on the edge of an Indian reservation in Arizona, where she would help the San Carlos Apaches set up a development plan for their mine. The tribe's medicine man, who had invited her, had also admitted to mistrusting white people. So when Elsa arrived in Arizona, she says, "The medicine man tested me many times to gauge my level of commitment. For instance, he kept me waiting for three days before meeting me. But I just waited and used the time to learn more about the project. There was no backing down. You play the game to the ultimate. You risk doing the great thing."

Elsa's great thing turned out to be great for the San Carlos Apaches, too. With Elsa's help and commitment, they were finally able to set up a successful gemstone business.

Perhaps risk boils down to a simple equation, Elsa says: Is the payoff worth the pain? When the payoff is worth it, keep taking pains. When it's not, stop. Or, to borrow a bit of cowboy wisdom: When your horse dies, get off!

PAYING   HOMAGE   TO   PAN

He who trembles is not bored.
— STENDHAL

In myths and folktales, those places beyond the cozy confines of the village are typically populated with figures of dread and danger—ogres, dragons, half-men, shape-shifters. One of the most familiar of these is Pan, the cloven-hoofed, classical god of forests. We ought to approach risk with the deference and forethought with which we would approach Pan, who instills panic in anyone who blunders into his domain. To those, however, who dedicate their first fruits to him, who respect the role that the unknown and unseen have in any undertaking, he is far more benign, even beneficent.

Intelligent risk taking, then, means giving a tip of the hat to Pan before stepping foot in his forests. It means entering with no illusions and knowing that your endeavors will always be attended by the conflict between the voices of despair and faith, whose concussive debate will pit your soul against your mind in a boxing ring. It means knowing you must follow your heart even in the face of heartbreak and courageously contend with whatever spills from it when it tips. It means knowing that whatever you harvest by taking risks— new freedom, new love, success, power—you will also suffer loss, and that loss is a skill.

When I was a child, I loved generating a stomach-dropping arc on the swing in my backyard, going high enough in both directions that the chain slackened momentarily. I would then let go of the swing at the forward end of this giddy parabola and becoming airborne, floating, flying out over the world, and land in the sandbox. I felt this sensation in my throat, my solar plexus, and my groin simultaneously, and I still do whenever I must let go of what is famil-iar and fly out over the unknown. Letting go demands what the writer Mar-garet Atwood calls "an almost physical nerve, the kind you need to walk a log across a river."

I have great faith in starting small with risks, though, and starting in your own backyard. "Where you are, and one step," as David puts it. No rule says you have to tackle a call in one jump. Nor does a call have a single right answer. A call asks us to *create a response,* and even a diminutive one is still saying yes. The point is to move *toward* it, however humbly. Take small risks and record your impressions; keep field notes. Vary your daily routine slightly. Ask the waiter to take back an undercooked hamburger. Privately engage in some activity at which you typically feel inept: music, art, singing, writing. In an argument, don't defend yourself. In the grocery store, buy something you've never tried before.

At the trailing edge of the rudder on some large oceangoing vessels is a smaller rudder. It is used to move the big one, which moves the ship. The application of a small amount of energy can have a dramatic effect, which goes for our responses to calls as well as the risks at the core of those responses. Do *something* that inches you toward your calling and you'll probably trigger a great deal of useful information. Walk down the road a *little* ways and see how the vision, the dream, the energy, hold up. Try things out for an hour, a day, a week, and ask of each action: Does this take me toward or away from what I want? Whatever the gesture, though, however modest, do it wholeheartedly because, says Eric Maisel, "a less than belligerent commitment is a curse." Any ambivalence in responding to a calling has the same results as ambivalence in personal relationships: The constant draft coming in through the back door will sap your strength.

In heeding a call, the idea is to gain a sense of accomplishment—of *movement*—early in the game because the sooner you do, the more likely you are to keep going. Position yourself to win, for the same reason that spiders build their webs near porch lights—that's where the action is.

Small risks, of course, are always in danger of staying small, and practice can easily devolve into procrastination. There is no end to the rehearsals we can make, the questions we can pose, the experts we can consult, and the classes we can take. At some point, we have to leap. "You cannot cross a chasm in two small jumps," the British statesman David Lloyd George once said.

Fear of course is the great goblin of risk taking and has been since human life first winked on. In myth and literature, for instance, whenever dragons appear, no matter what names they go by, they are all fear, and we encounter them at every stage of the quest: every threshold, every turning point, every crossroad. Fear, like a dragon, is determined to hang on to life. Fear is a signal that you're close to something vital and that your call is worthy of you. Even so, taking risks may make you feel like you're building a house of cards while fate holds its breath.

Fortunately, you do not have to be fearless to take risks. You don't have to have all your proverbial ducks lined up, or even to feel good. These are not prerequisites. Yet most of us will still approach risk with the usual baggage of emotional anxieties about failure, rejection, and humiliation—enough to warrant a personal bellhop. Bilbo Baggins expressed the common approach toward fear and risk neatly in *The Hobbit*, at the beginning of his own epic journey: "We're just plain quiet folk and have no use for adventures. Nasty disturbing uncomfortable things. Make you late for dinner. I can't think what anybody sees in them."

Actress Naomi Newman captures another aspect of our relationship to risk when she says, "If we wait until our hands stop shaking, we will never open the door," and we must. We may not cease being fearful, but we can cease to let fear control us. Furthermore, she says, since there's fear and suffering in life whether or not we take on adventures, whether or not we follow our callings, we might as well suffer in the service of our dreams.

"Only to the extent that we expose ourselves over and over again to annihilation," wrote philosopher and psychotherapist Karlfried Graf Durkheim, "can that which is indestructible arise within us. In this lies the dignity of daring. We must have the courage to face life, to encounter all that is most perilous in the world."

FIRE WALKING

Although small steps in honor of our callings are in danger of remaining small and ceremonial, they provide us with just the practice we need to move on to bigger steps and eventually leaps of faith across those chasms we cannot cross in two small jumps.

One spring morning in my late twenties, I found myself sitting in the back of a six-person raft on the Gauley River deep in a gorge in West Virginia. Gripping my paddle with white-knuckled fingers as we rounded a bend, I heard the thundering roar of a rapids known as Pure Screaming Hell. Above the din, our guide yelled out that if we wanted to walk around it, now was the time, because in another thirty yards there'd be no stopping.

At twenty yards, my thighs and stomach trembling, my attention fixed on Hell approaching fast dead ahead, I thought about why I was there at all. Although the ostensible reason was simply adventure, I had only enough time to realize that the subtext had something to do with the conversation I'd had with a friend who'd recently returned from one of those fire-walking workshops whose sole purpose is to convince you that if you can do *this* you can do anything.

At ten yards, the water around the raft began to bellow, I began to hyperventilate, and boulders loomed up on both sides, blocking any chance for exit. I turned around and saw the guide crouching in the back, screaming for us to paddle hard right, hard right, harder *harder!* Then his voice was completely drowned out.

The river dropped out from under us, and we dropped with it, suspended for an alarming moment in midair above a swirling hole eight feet deep. Only the back end of the raft even touched water at all. And then everything was a chaos of bodies and supplies slamming against one another, oars being ripped out of our hands, and the raft buckling in two like the sides of a board game. Two men spilled out into the boiling water, their faces a still life of fright.

Suddenly I heard the guide's voice from somewhere above and behind me: "Forward, forward! Paddle forward hard, hard! Don't let it suck us back in." Behind me was a wall of dark green water veined with coils of white foam. Between it and us was a fuming trough, where the water was turning back on itself as it poured over an enormous boulder. Earlier in the day the guide referred to these troughs as sleepers. "You get caught in one of those," he had said, "and that's where you're gonna sleep."

It had happened to a kayaker the day before. A group of six of them had just put into the river below the dam, and a hundred yards downstream, at the first rapids, one of the women in the group yelled. We looked over and saw her pointing to a large rock midstream. It had a good-size sleeper beneath it, and all the other kayakers were converging toward it with panicky speed.

As we stared at the spot on the river, the tip of a blue kayak shot out of the middle of the sleeper and was sucked back under. "He's being Maytagged down there," was how our guide assessed the situation, and there was not a single thing anyone could do about it.

A moment later the kayak was ejected from the sleeper and floated belly up downstream. Two of the kayakers raced toward it and flipped it over. Empty. Twenty minutes later someone turned off the river.

The Gauley is dam controlled, with three sluices big enough to drive semis through, and through which icy water from the bottom of a lake thunders onto the rocks below, like giant waterfalls turned on their sides. Someone must have gotten to the dam operator, and he simply shut it off. Within minutes, the level of the river dropped to almost nothing, as if entire seasons had been condensed. Only then could the kayaker's companions pull his battered, lifeless body out from beneath the rock.

Our guide conjectured that the kayaker was probably working above his level and made a fatal lapse of judgment or attention or both, but we were nonetheless left feeling extremely grim when he added that this rapids was nothing compared to what was downstream.

❧

By now, only four of us out of six were left in the raft, and we were all paddling wildly in our attempt to climb out of that hole. The river was shouting obscenities in our ears while the guide was trying to shout over the river, "Hard, hard!" A second later, we slipped over the edge of Hell and into Hell's outwash, paddling fiercely to catch up with our overboard crewmen.

A few days later I returned home wearing the coveted "I survived the Gauley" T-shirt, feeling that if I could do that, I could do anything. Until I got back to work, however, I didn't understand the real reason I had gone.

"So, you've conquered the Gauley," a colleague and fellow river rafter exclaimed, clapping me on the back. "What do you do for an encore?"

"Quit my job!" I said.

FALLING   UP

When I was graduated from journalism school, rather than heading back home to New York and ending up as another college graduate driving a taxicab or working for an exterminating company, I headed for the Midwest, to Cincinnati, Ohio, which seemed at that time like the far reaches of the galaxy. I had a week to drive out there and get a place to live before punching in Monday morning at a job on a magazine.

I pulled into downtown Cincinnati on a late August day when the final game of the 1976 World Series was being played, during which the Cincinnati Reds beat the New York Yankees. I parked my car, with its conspicuous New York license plates, in front of a restaurant and went in for a late lunch. When the game let out and the streets filled up with fifty-five thousand exuberant Reds fans, some loose cog from the Big Red Machine decided it would be a testament to his regional pride to slash the two back tires of my car and write in red lipstick on my windshield, "When you're hot, you're Reds hot!"

It set me back not only eighty dollars for two new tires but also emotionally. Was this an omen? Was coming out here a mistake?

My decision to cross the River Jordan and move to Ohio had felt like a calling, and landing a job there like a confirmation. So I naturally expected all the requisite blessings. Since I was meant to go, I assumed I was also meant to succeed. But my unexpected run-in with the locals literally and symbolically took the air out of my tires.

Although we may have our hands firmly on the wishbone, there is an even chance that in taking any risk we'll encounter setbacks, which most people refer to as failures. Yet if we see life as an experiment in which there are no failures, only results, our interpretation of those results will determine how successful we feel. For instance, if you pitch an idea to someone and it's rejected, you can conclude either "wrong person" or "lousy idea." Someone once asked Albert Einstein which question, among all his inquiries into the mysteries of the universe, is the most important question to ask. He responded: "Is the universe a friendly place or not?" How we interpret the results of our own lives— and thus how those lives unfold—is largely a function of how we each answer Einstein's question.

Had I answered it no, I might have reconsidered my decision to move to Ohio and might have felt ganged up on by the forces that be. But I said yes, and the incident became an example of what mythologist Joseph Campbell describes as the task of the hero/heroine learning the rules of the unknown land into which he or she has stepped. One does not park a car with New York license plates anywhere near the Coliseum during a World Series game between the Cincinnati Reds and the New York Yankees.

Campbell calls these experiences "directive crises," and Gail Sheehy refers to them as "falling up." They are setbacks that set us up for ultimately life-enhancing lessons: course corrections, insights, a better grip on our strengths and weaknesses, even valuable delays. They must not be impulsively prejudged. As in a Dickens novel, accidental encounters and happenstances often turn out to be formative events, but we realize this only in retrospect. So we must ask of setbacks, "What are you trying to tell me?" and "Where is my life attempting to go?" and "How might this be a plot twist that I won't understand for another two hundred pages?"

Risk taking will also be considerably more palatable if we approach it with a Grand Scheme in mind. Take it for granted that our lives have meaning and purpose. A sense of meaning can carry us through the most incredible hardship. Understand that the outcome, whatever it is, will contain a quality of rightness that will be as difficult to explain as to deny.

It is unfortunate that so many of us wear garlic wreaths around our necks trying to ward off the presumed evils of failure. An advertising executive of my acquaintance once described a curious phenomenon that has helped change my own attitude toward failure. After the agency's employees attend sales or productivity seminars, he said, business actually falls off for a month or two afterward. After a while, he figured out what was happening: In picking up new ideas and techniques that challenge our old habits, we venture beyond the approaches that previously worked. But the new behaviors don't come naturally at first. Before they become second nature, the extra effort shows up as a dip in performance. In the long run, however, the new skills make us more productive, and we begin to experience the alchemical conversion of risk to reward.

The commitment to stretching beyond our comfort zones demands the willingness to take one step backward in order to take two steps forward, and it is a peculiarity of successful people that they're able to tolerate sometimes extended periods of uncertainty and still hang on to their faith. They also tend to make room among their anticipations for the unexpected. They make room to fail. They have some money in the bank and some people to fall back on. They give a nod to the vagaries of Murphy's Law, and risky propositions *need* a few fail-safe mechanisms just as cliff-dwelling birds lay pear-shaped eggs so that when they roll, they do so in circles and not over cliffs.

For most of us, the reasons why we're so cautious and averse to risk have long since been plowed under by time and forgetfulness. How we each approach risk, interpret failure, and answer Einstein's question, however, is greatly determined by the behavior that was modeled for us while we were growing up: what we learned about taking risks, making changes, and about loss and failure and security and hope and faith. It is determined by what was given to us and what was taken away; by the assemblage of abandonments and blasphemies that defined our formative years, and that we've shouldered into adulthood; and by whether our fledgling attempts to explore life were cherished or not. In order to move forward, we may have to take a step or two backward and remember or relive those experiences and see them for what they were. We may need to see our parents as the flawed and uncertain people they were and make some kind of rough peace with how it was.

Family, though, is only one among many institutions—education, religion, government, law—that schools us in continuity rather than change. Evolution itself has also hardwired us to avoid risks, to seek security, to transform novelty quickly into habit, to jump at the slightest sound. In a manner of speaking, we all have our fight-or-flight buttons stuck in the on position. Yet evolution is also constantly creating. "Whatever there be of progress in life," Henry Miller once wrote, "comes not through adaptation, but through daring. The whole logic of the universe is contained in daring, in creating from the flimsiest, slenderest support."

This logic is also contained within each of us in quite a visceral way. Almost all predators have eyes that face forward, whereas the preyed upon, those who survive primarily by escape, have eyes on opposite sides of their heads. We are, in other words, creatures of initiative. Ultimately, we are creatures of both initiative *and* caution. Human life is, in some sense, the chronicle of a land animal caught between its desire to sprout wings and fly and to retrace its steps back into the sea.

LEAVING THE BIRDCAGE

Your life mirrors what you put into it or withhold from it. "When you are lazy, it is lazy," say the authors of *Art and Fear.* "When you hold back, it holds back. When you hesitate, it stands there staring, hands in its pockets. But when you commit, it comes on like blazes."

There are damages inherent in risk, but there is also recompense. Though you may lose composure when you stand before a group and speak, you may also discover that you *are,* after all, someone who is capable of public speaking. If you're panic-stricken in the face of conflict between you and others, and yet rise to an occasion and confront someone, you may lose a few nights' sleep, but you may also lose your terror of it. You may even find that your very acuteness around conflict makes you the best sort of negotiator—that your wound is, like David Roche's, your gift. If you're afraid to test your wares in the marketplace, to send your delicate shoots of optimism out into an indifferent world, and if you do it anyway, you risk losing your innocence, but if you sell, you gain confidence that cannot be had in any other way.

And if you discover that, indeed, you *can* partake of your callings, you *can* act in accordance with your deepest values and passions, you *can* have what you so desire, you are then faced with another task: having to revise your beliefs about what is and is not possible for yourself and the world. Not revising theories to fit the facts is not only bad science but also skewed perception.

An old joke in psychoanalytic circles illustrates this need to protect an established self-image against the blessings of growth:

A man goes to a psychiatrist convinced that he is dead. Unable to help his client shake this delusion, the psychiatrist says, "You've heard, haven't you, that dead men don't bleed?"

"Yes," the client replies.

The psychiatrist then takes a pin and pokes the man in the arm, making him bleed. "What do you say now?" he asks.

"Well, what do you know," the client says, "dead men *do* bleed."

The desire to protect ourselves from change probably does more harm to the flowering of human life and spirit than almost any other choice, but it is imperative to understand something about security: It isn't secure! Everything about security is contrary to the central fact of existence: Life changes. By trying to shelter ourselves from change, we isolate ourselves from living. By avoiding risk we may feel safe and secure—or at least experience a tolerable parody thereof—but we don't avoid the harangues of our consciences. It's almost axiomatic that the important risks we don't take now become the regrets we have later. In fact, I was once told that if I'm not failing *regularly*, I'm living so far below my potential that I'm failing anyway.

The more time we spend locked in our studies with our slippers by the desk, our books arranged alphabetically on the shelves, and our pencils sharpened just the way we like them, the less time we have to frighten ourselves with the uncertainties of the road and the anxieties of adventure. We can comfort ourselves with the thought that if none of our fantasies come true, then at least neither will our fears. Hidden deep in the clockworks of the heart, though, is the beneficent fear of living life, as Henry Miller once put it, without ever leaving the birdcage, and we need to touch that fear.

Outside the cage, the sun is roaring with fission, arching through the blue sky. Wild winds flap the flags and fill the air with the sound of songs caught up in ecstasy and longing. There is life in its fleshy and toothsome grandeur, all the spill and stomp and shout of it, all the come and go of it, all of it on the one hand waiting for us to act, and on the other rushing down the hourglass.

fourteen

SACRIFICE: THE SHADOW IN THE CALLING

Faith contains a certain ferocity, an unspoken demand that to maintain it we part ways with comfort and give up something we have for something we want. We may have to relinquish the precious commodities of time and energy, or something that represents security to us, or simply whatever internal resistance stands in our way. We may have to cede our intractable self-doubt or the false composure, the bliss of ignorance, bred by living unconsciously and avoiding risk.

Faith will eventually ask of the faithful, "What are you willing to give up in order to follow your call?" Sacrifice, says Thomas Moore, is "the shadow in the calling." It reminds us that we pay a price for every choice and that life doesn't hold still. It constantly gives over this for that; it wears down its banks and changes course; it's a propeller that spins so fast it only *appears* to be solid, but you don't dare try and grasp it.

To insure fertility, farmers and shepherds traditionally yielded up their first fruits to the gods. To help educate people about wildlife, zookeepers cage a certain number of animals in hopes of saving the bulk of them. In teaching children to listen to their own voices, we need to let them weigh *ours* along with their own. In order to receive guidance, we have to relinquish being the knower. In order to be planted, says writer Michael Ortiz, we have to be buried.

We may have to dismantle what we've built up with our own hands and abandon that which we've committed to with our most earnest intentions. We may have to unloose what seem like the very girders of our lives, and we ourselves must do the undoing, must discover that we're both the priests and the lambs, both the ones who wield the separating knife and the ones who bleat.

Sacrifice is not solely a human undertaking. It is also a natural process, the endless conversation between the chicken and the egg, between night and day, between the seasons, each giving way so the other can bloom. It is the price we *all* pay for growth.

❧

After two years of maddening indecision and the escalating entreaties of my partner, I finally agreed to move a few years ago, for the first time, from the city to the country. Or more precisely, from San Francisco to a desert in northern New Mexico surrounded by the silence of interstellar places and nights so black that I remembered a childhood fear of the dark.

The night before we were to fly there to begin house hunting, I had dreams of falling and spent the night flopping around in bed like a fish on a dock.

Flying into Albuquerque, the plane hit a trough of air that pitched two glasses of water from the tray table into my lap and brought my lunch up to mid-esophagus. The airplane's wings flapped like the arms of a man fighting for balance on a tightrope. In the airport, I saw a man wearing a button that said "Welcome to New Mexico. Land of the flea, home of the plague." We later learned that some of the state's outlying areas—not far from where we were headed, in fact—have a problem with fleas that carry the bubonic plague, which killed a fourth of the population of medieval Europe.

As I headed for baggage claim, I heard in the back of my mind the words of the poet Rilke reminding me that the purpose of life is to be defeated by greater and greater things, and I had the uneasy sense that I had come to the right place.

I had a hundred reasons not to move—101 including the fleas—and a hundred reasons why I had to. Among those I was able to articulate to inquiring and skeptical friends and family were that I needed a place where nature lifts up her skirt and dances, where the cost of living is somewhat more hospitable to a freelance writer, and where there are no job opportunities for traffic reporters. I was less inclined to try to explain that I wanted a place where what is of value is not advertised, where there are no guardrails, where I might find an answer to the question, "Is this all there is?"—and because my partner wanted to move and I didn't want to lose her.

Beneath all the reasons and rationalizations was also an undefined yearning for change. I knew in my marrow that it had something to do with surrender, which nature, and midlife, excel at teaching.

&

For a long while, living in the wilderness was overwhelming. During the first few months, I slept twelve hours a day and barely left the house for more than a few hours at a time. The scale of the mountains, the sky, the horizon—everything—made a mockery of my sense of perspective. The hundred-mile visibilities seemed to double the size of the world, making me feel very small. The passage of time, which was marked not in the human scale of weekdays and weekends but in epochs, argued that even the mountains are mortal.

The perverse silence of the place kept startling my reptilian brain into idle chatter. The Indian and Spanish cultures felt alien. Hail was the size of marbles; flash floods were capable of carrying off children, livestock, and large appliances; and thunder sounded like gunshots going off next to my ear. In this stretch of the wild west, the majority of STOP signs had bullet holes in them, whereas in the Bay area, they were more likely to be spray painted with phrases like "the arms race" or "in the name of love" or "faking orgasm." Moving there from the city felt like coming out of a movie theater in the middle of the day.

I wrote to a friend that I felt like a coward in the face of such grandeur, which accused me of my own impotence and stripped me of the hubris that I had developed from being a city dweller surrounded by the man-made my whole life. It is easy to imagine yourself king of the hill when only the rumor of death instructs you otherwise.

Jacques Cousteau once remarked that when you enter the ocean you enter the food chain, and you do not necessarily enter at the top. When it snowed in New Mexico and the land filled up with paw prints, I, too, saw clearly what my relative position is in the colossi and that I do not have tenure. I followed bear tracks for a mile along a mountain fire road and mountain lion tracks on the mesa running like a dotted line between the junipers. I saw blood on the snow and was left hyperventilating by the sound of rustling.

I suppose that feeling out of control made the incident with the magpie so unnerving. I was sitting at my desk one afternoon several months after moving, staring out the window at columns of thunderheads while the wind pounded on kettledrums outside. Suddenly a bird flew directly into the window with a bony thud and bounced off, leaving a clump of feathers stuck to the glass.

I stood up reflexively. A meadowlark lay stunned on the ground. At just that instant a magpie, three times the meadowlark's size, barreled down from a nearby tree and pecked the small bird to death as it flapped around helplessly. When it was dead, the magpie took it in its beak up to a low branch of the apricot tree, set it there, and flew off.

I stumbled outside, horrified, wondering what act of carnage I had just witnessed—was it the end of a chase, some violent spasm of territorial impera-tive, or was it a mercy killing? I felt my sense of vulnerability in being there at all deepen in that moment.

Four days later that clump of feathers was still stuck to my office window like a suicide note. I was still rattled, not just by the violence or the suddenness of it, but more because I didn't understand what it meant, and this reminded me of what I gave up to move there. It is something that all sacrifices on behalf of a calling require, whatever their particulars: the need to let go of what is familiar for what is not, to relinquish full jurisdiction over our lives and let fate have a greater hand in them.

A few days before I left California, for instance, I walked slowly through and around my house, a fixer-upper I had lived in longer than any since child-hood. I realized how intimately I knew it and how bad I felt at leaving it. I knew how many seconds it took the bathroom faucet to make hot water, where to step to avoid creaking the wooden floors when I was up at 2:30 A.M., and how stiff a wind it took to drive rain into the broken storm window upstairs.

I knew which tree the vultures most favored for roosting, which trails in the surrounding hills would be muddiest after a rain, and the names and tem-peraments of every dog in the neighborhood. I knew which week during Sep-tember the robins would fly in to gorge themselves on the pyracantha berries near my front steps, and that during that week I'd sweep those steps of bird droppings twice a day. I knew that if I heard rustling in the vicinity of the pampas grass in the front yard, it would be Boozie, the neighbor's big, dumb dog of indeterminate genus, and I knew exactly where to rub Boozie's chest to paralyze him with pleasure and make his back left foot twitch.

And I knew that starting in a few days, by choice, I would be a stranger again, would have to start learning all new coordinates, the habits of all new birds and beasts, find my way around unfamiliar territory, and figure out what the signs all mean. I remember walking along a dirt road near my new home in New Mexico a few days after arriving and being barked at furiously by the dogs at a farmhouse, and feeling *hurt* by it. "We're going to be friends someday," I yelled, jabbing my finger at them. "You just wait."

I tried to distract myself from my insecurities with the one activity that has always conferred on me a sense of meaning and control over my life—my work—but failed miserably. It was like being bitten by a rattlesnake: I panicked and ran, which only caused the poison to travel faster through my system. That panic-stricken way of working also felt painfully familiar, only now, with the deserts and the distant mountains standing as indictments of my restlessness and commotion, it also felt laughable and damnable, the emotional equivalent of a bad appendix—vestigial and possibly fatal.

In the city, such frenzy was reflected everywhere and seemed normal. Not so in the wilderness. There is more grace in a living acre of ground than in the lives of most people, including mine.

The magpie incident pushed me deeper into a sense of loss and fragility, of not knowing, which I didn't like one bit. Perhaps it was growing up in a culture that doesn't know the difference between uncertainty and anxiety, and to which mystery is something to be solved, not serenaded. Perhaps it was coming from a family of sleuths. My grandfather used to be a detective, and my father frequently read to me from a book of "minute mysteries," and I had to figure out whodunit. I thought that almost anything could be figured out and would yield to sheer determination.

But life and the natural world are not just more minute mysteries to solve, and not everything can be figured out. I am no closer to feeling secure in the world for having lots of answers. Making peace with the questions seems the better bet. After all, life doesn't end with an answer, but a question—what next?—and it *certainly* ends with a sacrifice—the hero always dies.

In the months after I buried the meadowlark, I chose, quite uncharacteristically, to stay in suspense about what had happened to him, when one phone call to the ornithology department at the University of New Mexico could have settled the matter, as well as my sense of disquiet. But I didn't call. I wondered.

One afternoon I even spent several hours speculating on the lives of birds—their compulsions and their conspiracies—as I watched a group of gray juncos outside my house repeatedly flock to the ground, peck for seeds, and suddenly, as if on some invisible cue, explode into flight in every direction like shrapnel from a grenade and then regather slowly on the ground like fallen leaves.

A few days later, while shoveling snow, a flash of falling black like a chunk of obsidian caught my eye and my breath. A magpie, perhaps the same one, dropped toward the ground like a stone from some unseen place, and at the last possible second flared its wings.

Then one day I stopped wondering. I called the ornithology department at the university and ended my little murder mystery. Magpies, the young woman told me, are thievish and opportunistic and will take advantage of an injured bird for the sake of an easy meal. That, she said with great certainty, is what I saw.

I hung up feeling oddly disappointed, not in the cruelty of nature but in the cruelty of certitude. The knowing, that is, put an end to the wondering, which in many ways was far more entertaining and instructive. In it, there was room for imagination and discovery, for the *quest* implied in *question*. The truth, it seems, did not set me free.

In hanging on to the familiar, I have what is familiar. But in letting go, in moving into the unknown, I have no idea what comes next. Life becomes a cloud rolling overhead, changing shape moment by moment like a moving Rorschach. It's a gargoyle, then a fish, then a serpent, and there's no predicting what it will be next. It's a hawk, a dancer, an airplane, a buffalo, an archer, and the only thing I know for sure about it is that I am, like the magpie, resourceful, and like the meadowlark, vulnerable.

B R I N G I N G   T H E   M O U N T A I N
T O   M O H A M M E D

He who mounts a wild elephant goes where the wild elephant goes.
— R A N D O L P H   B O U R N E S

In the story of Jonah, magnitude is a recurring theme. God, Ninevah, and nature—in the forms of the ocean, the storm, and the great fish—are all portrayed as enormous and all-encompassing. There's a good reason for this symbolism, as well as for Jonah's natural impulse, which, like our own, is to run like hell, when what he needs to do is submit.

He needs to make a sacrifice, the aim of which is always to forge a link with whatever is bigger than ourselves: a calling, God, nature, humanity, community, the future, the force of fate, our own intuitions, some greater good. Sacrifice is a kind of healthy denial, denying ourselves something we want for the sake of something we want even *more*.

If we didn't devoutly believe that a greater good would be served and that we'd gain something in the bargain, we probably wouldn't make sacrifices. The prospect of what may be gained in pursuing a call needs to outweigh the loss sustained in attempting it. If we can convince ourselves that though our loss may be significant, it is still a small price to pay for the possible blessing, we've cleared a high hurdle in following a call and can get on with it. Even the act of leaving your home or your job, of relinquishing your security or status, can then be seen as worth the chance at a more authentic life, a clearer conscience, a deeper connection to soul or God or others. The scales tip in favor of sacrifice, and the odds tip in favor of a payoff.

Nonetheless, sacrifice, like prayer, can easily devolve into a kind of petitioning in which we're secretly attempting to dicker with the deities: I'll do this if you'll do that. Though the point of sacrifice has always been an *exchange* of favors, it's probably best to concentrate on the give rather than the take, which is not the part we have any control over.

"Keep away from saying 'I will do *X so that Y* will happen,' " cautions writer Deena Metzger, "so that I'll be happy, or make money, or be recognized. Cause-and-effect is the narrowest way of seeing the world, and your goals then become conditional. Don't negotiate with the gods. Just offer yourself, 'Thy will be done,' without knowing the outcome."

The original Hebrew word for *sacrifice* meant to bring nearer. By making our offerings, the mountains will come to Mohammed. Sacrifice, like gift giving, creates a bond. Sacrifice is the signature of a contract, a covenant between two parties who need each other for some purpose. We need the gods to bring us our callings, and they need us to bring them off.

꙼

Bringing *ourselves* nearer to making a sacrifice is another matter. Self-preservation, not sacrifice, is the biological imperative. Sacrifice is also a naturally sensitive subject for recovering Catholics, adult children of martyrs, and anyone who has spent substantial portions of their life sacrificing their own needs for those of others and are ready for a change. To them, sacrifice comes freighted with an emotional charge that repels them.

In making sacrifices for a calling, and thereby paying homage to something bigger than ourselves, we're admitting that there *is* something bigger than ourselves. This is no mean concession for people who don't believe in the existence of the soul, or who cannot answer the question "Who turned on the lights?", or who believe themselves to be the center of the universe. For some people habituated to being in control, the idea of relocating the center of gravity from the ego to the soul, from themselves to something bigger than themselves, the idea of *following*—which is required by a calling—can be an untenable form of vulnerability. For them, *following* means following orders, following behind, complying. It brings with it a demotion from being the Mover to being the Moved and the sudden realization that your own leadership role is actually most like the role of a tugboat. It *is* a considerable sacrifice to surrender the sense of personal hegemony, the assumed position at the top of the chain of command.

Sacrifice *is* a demand of the soul against the ego, a demand for renunciation that the ego will *still* try to turn to its advantage, as when we hear ourselves being proud of our sacrifices, arrogant about our humility; and this will likely continue right to the end. The actress Naomi Newman captures this adroitly in a line from her play *Snake Talk:* "Mommy, Mommy, look how good I'm dying."

Preparing for sacrifice can be greatly abetted by the making of *ritual* sacrifice, a symbolic surrender that has the psychic effect of turning over the soil in preparation for an actual sacrifice. It is a way of practicing, of testing out our emotional reactions, of priming the unconscious. Changes do begin to happen simply from the enactment of a ritual; the inner vision begins to take on form.

A calling requires action, decision making, change. We may break a stick in half to symbolize our intention to break with a tradition or a person, but unless we also put our asses on the line and concretize that break with real action, the power of our resolution can erode into wishful thinking. Breaking a stick is not breaking with tradition but a demonstration of intent. Although intent is powerful, we still need to follow through with time spent at the grindstone. We still need to work with the back and legs and voice.

Sacrifices in the service of a calling take many forms:

- In order to share your work with the world, you will have to yield some privacy. Sharing is an act of communication, and the circuit isn't complete until you give it to someone.

- If you want to collaborate with others, you will need to share power, which can be a stinker because you also have to let go of control.

- If you aspire to peace, you will have to sacrifice your own projections, stop making spittoons of other people—making them receptacles for your untidy judgments—and stop imagining that you could cast the first stone with impunity.

- In attempting to heal your insides, you may have to put a halt to what comes in from the outside. In her book *Revolution from Within,* Gloria Steinem relates the story of a "man junkie," a woman who, in the service of learning to feel "whole on her own" without a man, went cold turkey for five years, turning down all invitations from eligible men. No sex, no romance, no addiction, no adrenaline binges, no withdrawal.

- If you want to leave a company for the relative freedom of self-employment, you must forsake the momentum and financial resources of an established institution and take up the slack created by your own time-management sins. That is, *you* now pay for extralong lunches, leaving work early, talking to friends on the phone, hanging around the water cooler, coffee breaks, clock watching, indiscriminate wastes of paper and supplies, and those sick days that were really paid vacations your company didn't know it was giving you.

- In order to help loved ones, you may need to let go of trying to rescue them. It may twist your heart up and frustrate you to no end to stand by while they fumble the ball, to contend with the awful truth that love cannot conquer all, that you can't do it for them, and sometimes the best you can do is hold their hand while they suffer. Love isn't like pulling someone from a burning car or saving him or her from drowning. The drama of a loved one's need is much more complex than that and demands that you weigh right action from wrong action, support from sabotage. There is love that enables and love that disables, and only a torturous judgment call determines which is which.

- To follow the principles of your religion, you may need to forgo some religious trappings and trade ten easy steps for one difficult step. As Garrison Keillor once said on *A Prairie Home Companion,* "Give up your good Christian life and follow Christ."

- To focus on a creative project, you necessarily must set aside other commitments. While writing her novel *Opening Nights,* Janet Burroway kept a journal, part of which was published in *The Writer on Her Work, Vol. I.* At the beginning of that journal she writes, "I have been stripping everything carefully away for several weeks to clear myself for the ceremonial undertaking of the commitment. Got rid of classes, turned down student summer projects, wrote overdue letters, called the producer and told him not, after all, to consider casting me as Lady Bracknell in the Tallahassee summer production. Entered into a no-appointment frame of mind that has even made me unwilling to say I'd appear at the beach or the dock at a given hour."

- If you aspire to spend more time with your family—or time together *as* a family—you could start by putting the televisions in the garage for a month.

- If you feel compelled to create a healthy relationship, you may need to sacrifice time that you might have spent building your career, time that you may not be able to make up but that may present you with the lesser of two regrets in the end. Though power tends to win in the struggle between power and love, love tends to have the last word. J. Paul Getty, who sacrificed his marriages on the altar of power and prosperity, said this late in life: "I hate and regret the failure of my marriages. I would gladly give all my millions for just one lasting marital success." He wouldn't, of course, while he was busy *making* those millions, but priorities naturally change as we get older, and it's easier to see our sacrifices for what they were.

O U R   W I L L   B E   D O N E

On John Amodio's desk is a *Far Side* cartoon that he says sums up, for him, the struggle between higher calling and bottom line, the struggle that's at the core of any sacrificial equation. Some poor fellow is standing in front of two doors, one labeled DAMNED IF YOU DO and the other DAMNED IF YOU DON'T, and the devil is poking him in the back with a pitchfork, saying, "C'mon, c'mon, it's either one or the other."

This is how political life often feels to John, the assistant secretary for resources for the State of California, someone who early on understood that sacrifice would be a constant factor in fitting his own calling into the world, which is "to serve as an advocate for the extraordinary natural forces that do not have a voice outside of people representing them." Nothing about a calling is sacrosanct, and John developed an ongoing dance of compromise between himself and that calling while still a student at Humboldt State University in Northern California.

In the mid-1970s, John joined the fight to expand Redwood National Park, to protect it from the erosive effects of the logging taking place at its boundaries. He did this at a time when you risked life and, so to speak, limb just to sport a Sierra Club bumper sticker on your car.

John had become the principal spokesperson for a local community group, which asked him to go to Washington, D.C., to represent their concerns at congressional hearings on the fate of the park. Some members felt that he should take a *bus* there and back rather than fly because, in their opinion, it was more environmentally responsible and cheaper. The group had been given very short notice about the hearings, and timely decisions had to be made. John flat-out refused to take a bus.

"It was a very minor thing, but it crystallized for me that some compromise on the solely idealistic set of actions needed to be made in order to pursue the greater goal, to keep our eyes on the prize. In some ways, it was a choice between doing what I loved or being effective, but to me the value of being in D.C. sooner rather than later, the tactical advantage, the need to enter more frankly into the way in which the game is played, outweighed the expense of flying there and the greater resource consumption required by flying."

By making that sacrifice, John joined a long line of activists who have similarly discovered that politics is built on compromise and that the more idealistic they are, the more insulated and isolated they become. Activism is a kind of warriorship in which, as John puts it, "You can't avoid getting dirty, you're not above the fray." He also involved himself in the classic trade-off of having to work *within* the very system he's trying to change and *with* the very people whose values are contrary to his own, with the "Establishment."

How much can we sacrifice the ideals of a calling without effectively neutering it? How much can we fiddle with the particulars, bend it to fit the dictates of practicality and effectiveness, and balance it with other people's lives and agendas without compromising it down to its skivvies? How much tinkering can a vision endure until it no longer resembles your vision, until it no longer has the running jump it needs to clear the trees at the end of the runway?

Of this much I'm certain: Calls are not immutable. Certainly there is "Thy will," but there is also "my will," and together they make "our will," and it's the only way things get done. Compromise, after all, means promising *together.*

If you're even *worried* about the prospect of "selling out" your calling, this is probably a good sign. It means you believe you have something worth protecting, perhaps even something worth selling. What makes for too much or too little compromise is entirely subjective. No one can ultimately judge whether you're selling out but you. The course of action you take to shape your calling depends on your values, your aspirations, and the nature of your calling.

I've run across this drama of compromise repeatedly in my own profession. For some writers, working at a job, any job, is selling out; for others a day job provides the only way they can afford to keep writing. For some, selling out means writing a "popular" book when they'd rather write a scholarly one; for others, selling out means bending to professional disdain and writing a scholarly work when they'd rather share accessible material with a wider audience. For one writer, it's doing public relations for a nuclear weapons contractor; for another, all's fair in love and work. For one, it's having children instead of a writing career; for another, it's having a writing career while his or her children are eating alphabet soup for dinner every night.

Principled decisions you make to support your calling lead you toward, rather than away from, what you really want to do, however circuitously. They support your goals rather than sabotage them, and they don't make a shambles of your integrity or anyone else's. I once overheard someone say, "The successful artist is someone who continues to make art and isn't more than 50 percent bitter about the rest of life."

There is a difference, says writer Michael Ventura, between compromising and selling out. "Sometimes you're gonna maneuver, you're gonna give a little, you're gonna dance, you're gonna duck, to stay alive. You don't wanna be a dead or even a penniless hero without a very good reason. But selling out means accepting the goals and the tactics of the society as your own, as a way of life, when privately you don't agree with that way of life at all."

Whatever our choices, we have to be willing to renunciate "the infiniteness of our aspirations," says Edward Whitmont in *The Symbolic Quest,* for the sake of bringing those aspirations into being at all. If we don't have the quarter needed to ride the bus, he says, and we're not willing to break a twenty, we won't be able to board the bus. Any endeavor contains more desires and possibilities than you can carry to fulfillment. Something's got to give.

John, for instance, wanted to finish school in natural resources management, but he dropped out when he was offered the directorship of the North Coast Environmental Center, following Mark Twain's admonition not to let school get in the way of his education. Another necessary loss involved surrendering his desire to avoid getting involved in the political process, and all the unpleasantries involved in making public policy, which he had once held in disdain. "There's an old expression that you don't want to see how your sausages or your legislation are made, and I certainly felt that way. But if it took becoming a sausage maker to follow my call, I was willing to do it."

John always wanted to live "a simple and quiet lifestyle," preferably in the country, preferably vegetarian, but he pulled up stakes on those ideas, too, when he moved to Washington, D.C., to be a lobbyist for the Redwood National Park campaign, where he became what he calls an "opportunivore, someone who works for a nonprofit organization, earns a pittance, and makes meals from whatever appetizers are served at receptions hosted by the well-heeled."

Eventually, John moved to Sacramento, where "the game" is played, at least in California. His friends comforted him by saying, "Well, at least it's *close* to a lot of nice places," but it wasn't close to the redwood cathedrals in which John first heard his calling, and with which he maintained "as spiritual a relationship as I've ever had.

"I began to lose my connection to the place—nature—that I was working to defend, and that was a genuine sacrifice. Working in Sacramento came at the cost of losing close access to the redwoods, which were now too far away to get to regularly. But when I became almost debilitated by the effort, overwhelmed with distress and anger at the political process, I'd find my way there and get rejuvenated. I'd put on a backpack and hike to my favorite spot in the redwoods, a place called Emerald Creek, and just being in that place, which is so sacred to me, just sleeping there helped discharge much of my hostility. I'd become filled with the power that anyone who's ever been in the old growth forests cannot deny exists, and hike back out with renewed energy and clarity of purpose, and clarity in a strategic sense. Going there helped me work out the age-old struggle between being engaged in the world and being detached. I've never really succeeded in being all that detached, I keep choosing to be engaged, but going to the redwoods really saves me."

Back in Sacramento, however, John eventually crossed a line that some of his colleagues found unpardonable: He went to work for "the enemy," the Republican governor, Pete Wilson. "I didn't think of it that way, but many others did. A number of folks I'd thought of not just as colleagues but as friends were very quick to write me off. It was personally very painful. They thought I was becoming a government bureaucrat.

"At first I, too, thought, 'Yeah, right, working for a Republican.' But the more I thought about it, and the more I talked to my more pragmatic environmental peers, the more I thought this would be an extraordinary opportunity to help shape a substantive environmental platform. So when Wilson decided to make the environment one of the top three issues in his gubernatorial campaign in '89, and asked me to come on board, I said yes. I realized that I was more of an environmentalist than I was a Democrat. Besides, in the political arena, bipartisanship is not only valuable, it's essential, and as with natural ecosystems, the more diverse the community, the stronger it is.

"Without question, I can also say that though there have been times when I had to do some serious soul searching, I've been able to contribute to bringing about some breakthroughs I wouldn't have been able to bring about from the outside, and the sacrifices I've made have yielded the greatest sense of meaning to me, and accomplishment, and satisfaction."

This includes the satisfaction of, among other achievements, helping to save eighty-three miles of wild river, all that remained untouched of the entire Tuolumne River in California, and being instrumental in adding nearly fifty thousand acres to Redwood National Park. These campaigns were staggeringly complex, took several years each of commitment to something that was no sure thing, and taught him much about the nature of sacrifice.

If we only want to feast on the big ideas and the grand schemes and are unwilling to give our time and energies to seemingly small and limited tasks, to the thousands of baby steps needed to carry off our high concepts, then we will make little headway. Any calling requires a certain affection for drudgery. "Mundane" tasks simply refer to the earthworks needed to shape a world, and boredom doesn't necessarily mean you picked the wrong path. "Opportunity is missed by most people," Thomas Edison once said, "because it is dressed in overalls and looks like work."

We're led to believe we should aspire to society-page lives, that callings and adventures are by definition dramatic, and that what is great is visible from the next galaxy—all of which are pure horse puckey. Living out a calling may mean living an unspectacular life, a life of quiet ministry, steadfast backstage work, politicking without reknown; it may mean a life unknown to fame. Even the highest calling entails the unremarkable tasks of licking stamps, stuffing envelopes, and tacking up flyers. It asks that we do our homework, sweep the front porch, sock away pennies, and knock on wood.

SURRENDER AS VICTORY

Much of the pain associated with callings comes from avoiding them, from not surrendering to them. However much sacrifice may be involved, much of the pain we feel in surrendering to callings actually comes from our *anticipation* of the pain and not from the actual capitulation. Once we do surrender, we often feel a sense of great relief, and just as often we are bewildered about why we didn't do it years ago.

We mistakenly equate surrender with defeat and sacrifice with annihilation. We bring to our renunciations the same panic and anxiety—"Oh God, I can't give *that* up"—that we often bring to our deliberations about intimacy, the fears of being devoured and overpowered, of giving our lives away. Granted, parts of us *are* broken into smithereens in the process of following our calls and experience real compromise and real suffering, but this is not defeat any more than a flower suffers defeat by going to seed. Furthermore, says theologian Frederich Buechner, "What's lost is nothing to what's found, and all the death that ever was, set next to life, would scarcely fill a cup."

In the religions, myths, and psychologies of the world, surrender is envisioned not as defeat but as liberation, and sacrifice typically precedes a resurrection. It's about swapping something temporal for something transcendent, about turning suffering into victory. It explains why God proved merciful once Jonah finally took the plunge. It explains why the feast days of the Christian martyrs—those extremists for liberation—are celebrated not on their birthdays but on their death days, because that's when they were considered to have been truly "born." Like evaporating water, we give up an earthly bond in order to rise.

Historically, that which is sacrificed is also venerated. It is, as the word *sacrifice* itself suggests, "made sacred" and not simply tipped over the side and done away with; sacrifice is not merely a means to an end. Many sacrifices were made on altars, which elevated whatever was placed on them. By making sacrifices, we honor not just what dies but also the *act* of death, the skill of dying, by which we also honor the ultimate fact of life, the way the game is played: we get and we give, we win some and we lose some, and life is the trapeze act we perform between the two.

Whatever we have to give up to follow a calling is, in a sense, giving its life for our benefit. We sanctify it by recognizing that we wouldn't be able to liberate ourselves to follow that calling without it being sacrificed. Gratitude, of course, is less of a stretch in hindsight, once we've safely negotiated the passage and can look back and see how critical it was to our unfolding. If we can let go of the trapeze platform and make our necessary surrenders, we may be liberated, but if, while still suspended in empty air, we can say "thank you," we're damn near enlightened.

ॐ

Although surrender is not defeat, the unwillingness to surrender *is* defeat, and one reason we're often unwilling is that we can't abide one of the corollaries of sacrifice, which is that every sacrifice involves some suffering. Our avoidances of sacrifice demonstrate that we're afraid to suffer. But the degree to which we're *able* to bear suffering is largely determined by the degree to which we intend it to happen. If we don't volunteer for it, we are more likely to turn bitter about it.

Ideally, sacrifice is performed in full consciousness, not in an altered state of impulsiveness, momentary revelation or rapture, or workshop high. In the story of Abraham's call to sacrifice his son Isaac, he was given three days to mull it over, to understand the meaning of it, to contend with his own contrary desires, and presumably to come down from any fervor of religious compulsion, toward which he was already considerably prone.

By refusing to make sacrifices, we defeat our own purposes. Our most desperate hopes elude us, and we spend our lives merely catching sight of their heels disappearing around corners. Late in life, we may find ourselves trying to buy our souls back from the devil or striking desperate deals with God. No amount of security, accomplishment, or busyness will distract us from the knowledge of what we gave up. No amount of success, money, food, sex, or booze will take the place of the offering that needs to be made. There are no substitute sacrifices, no cheap adaptations, no cosmetic changes. If the status quo has got to go, working double-time to prove its merit will not appease the soul, which is no fool. If you feel restless about using your talents and attempt to assuage that restlessness by constant travel because you figure that the antidote to restlessness is *motion,* you're playing a shell game with the gods, who can see through stone.

If a sacrifice doesn't put you out, doesn't hurt a little or even a lot, it's probably insufficient to bring on the changes you're after. If your partner is crying out to you for attention, giving up the occasional golf game probably won't suffice to call your relationship back from the brink. If you feel called to share your art or writing with the world, but you show it only to friends and family, you're not stepping all the way up to the plate. If your body is telling you it needs more exercise, then taking the staircase up to your second-floor office instead of the elevator is little more than a symbolic gesture, faint praise, a plastic Jesus.

"It's true that heroes are inspiring," says writer Jeanette Winterson, "but mustn't they also do some rescuing if they are to be worthy of their name? Would Wonder Woman matter if she only sent commiserating telegrams to the distressed?"

THE LOVE OF SACRIFICE

One day a few years ago, while I was living in Santa Fe, I called up the dog pound and asked if they were interested in volunteers. I wasn't interested in swabbing the decks or pushing paper around or fund-raising. I just wanted to play with the dogs. I wanted to come in once a week and go from cage to cage giving tummy rubs, throwing a stick around with them out back, giving them each a fistful of the little Milk-Bones they keep in a jar at the front desk. The woman told me to come down anytime I wanted.

It isn't just that I love dogs and hate to see them suffer. The animal that appears most frequently in my dreams is the dog, and when they yelp in their sleep, I want to know what *their* animal dreams are. I sleep with my wrists curled the way dogs do and shake my head when I step out of the shower. Before I sit down on the grass I sometimes walk around in tight little circles, a holdover, I've heard, from when dogs were wild and would tamp the grass before lying down. I have a complete repertoire of dog imitations. I'll play with complete strangers' dogs on the street and have absolutely no recollection of what the people looked like.

After a month of volunteering, I noticed that from week to week the cast of characters changed. I learned that a week is about as long as most of the dogs stay at the pound. Half of them will find homes and the other half (up to four hundred dogs a month) will wind up in the landfill. I pictured their bodies suspended in the ground in whatever positions they landed in after they were thrown and covered over—some running, some sleeping, some stretched out, others curled. They would be found in these positions in another thousand years when a road is built, or a temple.

We love, knowing that it ends, that those we love will die. Here, then, was some instruction in the kinetics of following a call: We need to give it all we have on one level and surrender completely to the way it is on another. "Why love what we will lose?" the poet Louise Gluck asks. "Because there is nothing else to love?"

After finding out about the landfill, I continued to love the dogs as eagerly as before, but now I never knew for which of them it would be the last loving they ever got.

Sacrifice isn't something we do once. It prompts our following a call, but it is also a component of living out that call. It is an ongoing state of mind, a string tied around the finger to remind us that as long as we continue turning around on the mortal wheel, we need to let go of life as much as we need to hang on to it.

The love we feel for the calling makes the difference between being at peace and not being at peace with the sacrifices we're called to make. Love turns them into something almost akin to blessings, where others might see only horrendous sacrifices. I came to understand this lesson in a most visceral way through my acquaintance with a remarkable woman named Alita Henri. For thirty-five years, she served as foster mother and in loco parentis for more than 550 children, and that was only by *her* estimate. According to one of her own seven kids, it was a lot more than that.

The oldest was eighteen, the youngest a few months. They stayed for a week at the shortest and twenty-two years at the longest, and at one point twenty-five children lived at Henri's Children's Ranch at the end of a long, winding dirt road outside Tuolumne City in the foothills of the Sierra Nevadas. Each child also had an animal, something of his or her own to care for and be loved by unconditionally. So there were also goats, guinea pigs, cats, dogs, birds, chickens, and sheep.

Alita's first foster child was Wiley, a neighbor boy of alcoholic parents who was fixing to run away to Arizona to become a cowboy. He was really headed for San Quentin when Alita asked his parole officer if Wiley could move in with her and her kids. It was all off the cuff—no money or even permission from the state. Alita just saw something in the boy that no one else could see. "He wasn't a bad boy. Just a boy in a bad situation."

So was one of the next children Alita took on. Social workers found Stevie hiding under a table in his parents' house in San Francisco, biting and snarling like a dog. "They said he was mentally deranged. They said he had 'intents to kill.' My God, he was two years old." This time the authorities went to Alita and said that if she couldn't help him, no one could. "And let me tell you, I had to chip all the emotional scars off that little boy, he was so hardened. When I picked him up in my arms, he was like a board. But when one of those social workers came back a month later, he was a real little boy, not an animal, and two years later he was adopted."

What other people insisted would take months or years, or couldn't be done at all with the children, usually took Alita a few days. "It was love. They knew I loved 'em. I was never too big to say 'I love you.' And I loved 'em like they were mine. If I couldn't feel like they were mine, I couldn't do anything with 'em. And the kids did what I asked. I never said something more than once or twice. In the beginning, every one of them would test me out, see if I'd stick with 'em when they did their worst, and when I did, they felt safe. I was made for children. I'm like a Pied Piper. I seem to draw children to me. When I go to schools, kids run up to me and just ask to be held."

The first time I met Alita, I understood why children respond to her that way. I got hugged three times and kissed twice, was fed lunch and cookies, and saw in her eyes the reason for her success with children: complete acceptance.

Her love is not even remotely possessive, either, which has helped her cope with the need to surrender on roughly 550 occasions, because Alita has not been permitted to know where any of the children went after they left her care. I once asked her whether all that caring for so many children and their menageries, and all that letting go, felt like too much of a sacrifice. "Sacrifice?" she said, as if I'd offended her by the question. "No! It's been the greatest privilege of my life."

fifteen

ARIADNE'S
THREAD

The naturalist Milton Olsen once observed that when geese travel the blue lanes of sky on their migrations, each bird flapping its wings creates an uplift for the bird following it, and by flying in **V** formation, the whole flock gets over 70 percent better mileage than if each bird flew solo. When the lead bird, which doesn't benefit from these physics of cooperation, gets tired, it rotates to the back, and a new lead bird takes over. If any bird falls out of formation, it is quickly reminded of the dynamics of drag and the importance of getting a little help from its friends.

✢

Years ago, I interviewed Richard Bolles, who wrote *What Color Is Your Parachute,* probably history's best-selling book about job hunting and career change. When the conversation turned to the subject of being self-employed, he said that self-employed people can hire out just about any skill, even, to some degree, discipline; you can get someone to call you every week and help keep you on track. But the only trait you cannot hire out, he said, and without which you'll "die on the vine" is the willingness to ask for help. Self-employed, he insisted, doesn't mean you're out there all by yourself.

Similarly, although our calls are our own, nowhere is it written that we must pursue them alone. Attempting to do so can make us feel as if we're stringing beads without tying a knot at the end, without having the help of other people to secure the far end of Ariadne's thread and keep us from slipping away.

Resourceful people gather their resources, send for provisions, and join forces, whether they need help in pulling themselves through their own resistance, carrying the torch through the dark places on the journey, or letting go of one calling for the next. They aren't above asking for help and seeking allies whether they need a loan, a contact, advice, or material support. From the first threshold to the last, they understand the need to draw on whatever will point them toward aliveness and illumination, toward fulfillment of the call. Any calling can be undone alone, but not all of them can be *done* alone. Callings are plays with other players and many gods in the machinery, panoplies of cause and effect, and calls call us into community.

If you were called to Ninevah, you'd need your own feet to begin the journey, to carry you to the docks and away on a running ship. But you'd also need crewmen to row, a captain to fix positions, stars by which to fix them and God to blot them out, taking them by storm. You'd then need the captain's wake-up call, the storm's accusing finger, the crew to toss you overboard, and the whale to carry you in its hollows back to the beach. You'd even need the people of Ninevah, unrepentant and scoffing, to help carry you through the streets on foot and on orders. All of them are players. All of them help you complete the calling.

In other words, even if we refuse help, we're still "helped" to come around. Many hands, seen and unseen, will guide us toward our destinations, though more roughly than we wish. Help is inherent in the call, and we either seek it and have a hand in the proceedings, or we refuse it and are pushed from behind by the soul's tough love.

Ideally, we make ourselves anchorites and tether ourselves to whatever will help anchor our callings in the world. We begin with awakening to them, and, as Sleeping Beauty told us, a single kiss at the right moment may be all it takes. I know several people who were asked in college (by someone who wasn't a guide until the moment they spoke up) what the hell they were doing in engineering or medicine or philosophy when it was so abundantly clear that they were artists or teachers or scientists, that they had a knack that wasn't handed out to just anyone.

We moor our callings in the world by seeking the aid of anyone or anything, says James Hillman, that will help us touch the common ground so that we can reach for the uncommon ground. This aid can include the basic advocacy of friends and mentors; the elementary vigors of health and physical strength; the steadfastness of certain practices and beliefs; and the stability of *place*, of staying put somewhere for a spell, which gives us solid ground on which to pivot.

We may be helped by many things: dreams or intuitions or just inexplicable faith; the solace we reap from books; the support we gain from our participation in any group whose members are working toward awakening and self-remembering; the memory of a father or mother, the part of ourselves that never went to sleep; or simply the remembrance that life is short and death is long.

People who understand the struggle involved in following a call may provide encouraging counsel that helps overcome the drag of inertia and fear because they've struggled successfully with their *own* callings. You don't want advice from a "Do what I say, not what I do" type, but from those who are busy with calls of their own. They understand that when we talk about a calling, we're speaking of an encounter with divinity, with the deep soul, that must be honored. These people are most capable of propelling us into the greatest strides in growth and the profoundest changes in the course of our lives because they've witnessed and esteemed what is deepest in us. Even if we've cried wolf a time or two before, they also love us robustly, bear no major grudges against us, and take us seriously.

The help we need may simply be the added backbone of our own affirmative inner work—meditation, prayer, therapy, active imagination, or self-talk designed to seed the brain with messages of confidence rather than of pessimism. To some degree, success is a numbers game. We're after the kind of momentum bred by a team effort, which can generate the considerable energy needed to escape the gravity of self-doubt. A speed of 25,000 miles per hour is needed to escape the pull of Earth; 133,000 miles per hour to quit Jupiter; and 1,368,000 miles per hour against the sun. The bigger the home planet, the greater will be the pull of the past and the familiar. The greater the exertion required to pull away, the greater will be the need for a little help from your friends.

RAGGED INDIVIDUALISM

The slope of the beach appeared to drop off steeply about ten feet out from shore, but when I ran down the beach and dived in, I discovered, a little too late, that it was only the *illusion* of depth. In fact, it was merely the sand changing color from light to dark. I landed hard on my elbows in that bright water of the Gulf of Mexico, my legs flipped indecorously over my head, and I both heard and felt an ominous sound somewhere between a crack and a tear.

I spent the next month flat on my back, lying on a hot grill of torn ligaments. I filed my stories to the newspaper from the floor of my living room, which slowly began piling up with empty pizza boxes, dirty clothing and dishes, books and papers, and an odor most commonly associated with locker rooms. One day, several weeks into this prostration, a friend came by unannounced and peeked in the window. When he tapped on the glass, I craned my neck and saw, framed by the dirty windowpane, an expression that roughly translated to "What the hell is going on here?"

When I told him, he was genuinely angry with me for being too stubborn to call him, or anyone, for help. I hadn't told any friends of my accident, hadn't called anyone to come cook me a meal or do a load of laundry or go food shopping for me or rub my spasming back muscles or even just say "There, there."

"What the hell are friends *for?*" he scolded as he began picking up pizza boxes and dirty clothing. "What were you *thinking?*"

I was thinking of my pride. I was thinking that I didn't want anyone to see me in that condition, laid up, flat out, down on the mat, not even someone who was in a *support* group with me, as this friend was. From this I learned that a part of myself needed to be in control at all times, hated to be vulnerable, and prided itself on being independent. I was afraid to test the tensile strength of love and friendship, afraid it might give out under too much strain, afraid even to find out how much was too much. I was afraid, just as my father was afraid when he insisted I not fly to New York to visit him after his heart attack. Like an idiot I listened to him, and only much later did he admit that he should have told me to come, that he was, as he put it, "being the Stoic, not wanting you to see me that way." He used to call me "a chip off the old block," and rightly so.

The refusal to ask for help is a kind of sickness in itself. It's even a kind of arrogance, the blind insistence on doing it all by yourself, no matter what, because along with it comes the message that no one's help is worth the price in vulnerability it will cost you, that ultimately no one can console you, no one can ease the pain, no one, even God, is that strong if you yourself aren't. Such cussedness betrays a tremendous lack of faith in others, in the leathery stamina of love, and in your own ability to survive embarrassment. The refusal to ask for help is not rugged individualism but ragged individualism, and it is a function of fear.

Not that there's nothing to fear. Asking for help is a formidable art and requires that we lower the drawbridge. We seem naturally to resist help and advice, with its implication of our shortcomings, and this may be especially so for men because vulnerability is generally bred out of them at an early age. Although more women than men seek counseling, take classes, read books, and ask questions, for most of us help is not necessarily pleasant, advice not necessarily easy to take, and guidance often points out the error of our ways, as anyone who's ever entered couples counseling can attest to.

First we have to admit that we *need* help, that something in us or our situation is lacking and can't be remedied without assistance. This takes either some guts or enough desperation so that we don't care anymore what others think. Then we have to admit our need to someone *else* and allow that person to have some say in our affairs, some sway over us, which inevitably triggers the fear of falling into the hands of numbskulls and petty tyrants. Finally, we've got to be willing to make change, to be helped to move beyond the status quo into new territory. The anxiety of asking for help may even be negligible compared to the challenge of putting that help to work on a calling.

Few people understand the dynamics of asking for help better than a man I met many years ago named Percy Ross, who receives two thousand letters *a day* from people asking for his help. The reason he gets so many letters is that he authors a column called "Thanks a Million" that is syndicated in more than seven hundred newspapers. This Minneapolis millionaire is trying to dispose of the fortune it took him nearly sixty years to accumulate by working to redistribute his wealth among people who write to him with their stories of need and sometimes greed. Those that touch him he responds to with a check, a brand of philanthropy he considers "investing in people."

But for every two thousand a day who write him, he conjectures, there are undoubtedly a lot more who think about it but don't, and what holds them back, he figures, is largely pride. "That's what stands in the way of most of them, I'd say. They're embarrassed to be in a position to *need* to ask for help, afraid of getting rejected, maybe even afraid of getting a yes that might force them to put their dreams to the test. Ninety percent of the letters I do get start out with an apology of some kind: 'I never thought I'd ever write this kind of letter,' or 'I don't need money, just advice,' or 'Finally, after three months of starting this letter and tearing it up . . .'

"If you don't ask, though, and keep asking, you don't get. But if you do ask, you just might get. If people say no, you're only as bad off as you would be if you hadn't asked at all, but if they say yes, you've got what you wanted. You've got to ask! Asking is, in my opinion, the world's most powerful—and neglected—secret to success. I certainly wouldn't be where I am today if I hadn't convinced many, many people to help me along the way. The world is full of genies waiting to grant our wishes. There are plenty of people who will gladly give you a hand."

What worries many of us is what the *other* hand is trying to do while its companion is busy granting wishes. This is a question that not surprisingly plagues a lot of us who have had the experience of having help forced on us against our wills, as in "I'm only doing this for your own good." Such help blurs the line between help and manipulation. If others really wanted to help us, they would ask for *our* opinions. "Can I help you? How can I help you? What would be helpful to you?" There are people who, as Robert Furey describes in *Called by Name,* "Blocked our view of God by pretending to be God."

Many of us still have burrs under our saddles when it comes to granting others the opportunity to "guide" us, knowing how easily people can act like amateur preachers and psychotherapists trying to heal, convert, and fix us. They imagine themselves to be the instruments of our deliverance and the answers to our prayers and take as their motto Gore Vidal's comment that "there is no human problem which could not be solved if people would simply do as I advise." The fact is, you need a working set of green lights and red lights when taking on helpers.

A natural antagonism can develop between ourselves and those in positions of authority relative to us, people on whom we're dependent, whether they are parents, teachers, bosses, mentors, doctors, lawyers, or car mechanics. It is human nature to want to retain control over our own lives.

It's also human nature to want to tell others what to do, to finish their sentences for them, especially when we stop seeing their struggle and see only our own reflected in theirs. What kind of help are we likely to offer someone, for instance, whose calling is personally threatening to us in some way—your partner wants to take a job in another city, your kid wants to write a memoir? If we can't set aside our own agendas, even temporarily, we won't be able to see other people except through fogged-up glasses, won't see what they really need. Our support can then end up being tepid instead of the kind of full-throttle enthusiasm Michelangelo offered his apprentice when he said, "Draw Antonio, draw Antonio, draw and do not stop."

Our support for someone can even end up as unconscious sabotage or subtle jabs and underminings disguised as devil's advocacy that can be the emotional and verbal equivalent of flicking lighted cigarette butts at them. In the worst case, our support can be disguised manipulation, even abuse, and I believe special hells are reserved for people who, under the guise of teacher and guardian, use those in their care for their own purposes.

One of the marks of a great intelligence and a courageous soul is the ability to prevent the ego from getting in the way of someone else's growth. Self-restraint is love of the highest order and a discipline that is gymnastic in effort. Even mullahs and mahatmas don't always possess it. Good help is indeed hard to find, but we want to look hard for it, for people who have a good grip on themselves, who wear their jewelry modestly and for whom the gracious bow is still in the book of etiquette. This goes especially for those who stand to have their own lives disrupted in some way by our calling to change and yet are willing to encounter their own resistance to it, even their resentment, be honest enough to talk with us about it, and offer their blessings and support in spite of their misgivings.

If we claim to value growth, if we presume to know anything at all about the value of the search for self, if we want others to honor our borders, then we have to honor theirs; we have to keep our hands in our own pockets and bite our tongues. Each of us has boundaries that are drawn a little differently. A workshop facilitator once demonstrated this: He walked slowly toward each participant and asked that they tell him to stop when he had reached the edge of their comfort zone. These perimeters of "personal space" varied from a foot and a half to six feet.

Nobody can tell you what's right for you to do, any more than they can tell you what your dreams mean. I've seen this happen in groups: Someone will share their dream, and somebody else will inevitably take it upon themselves to be the code breaker, pontificating about what the dream means and what it's instructing the dreamer to do. It comes across as a kind of trespassing, like cutting in line or reaching bodily across somebody else's dinner plate to get the salt shaker. To them it may seem like just friendly advice or feedback, but to the person sharing the dream it may feel more like a hostile takeover. "Quit giving me your damn advice," my brother Ross once blurted at me in a moment of justified frustration. "Just ask me questions and listen."

Help is easier to take if someone leaves it in a bowl on the back porch and lets us come to it on our own terms, rather than attempting to stuff it in our ears. Better still if someone can do it with humor, making us laugh and then, while our mouths are open, feeding us.

Instead of just searching for advice on what to do to respond to your callings, tell others what they can do *for* you. Guide the guides by telling them *exactly* what kind of help you need. If you don't specify, if you just tell people to help you, or that you feel stuck, they're likely to try to diagnose what sort of help you *seem* to need and administer it however they see fit. "You know what your problem is . . . ?" Don't give anyone that much rope. Tell them precisely what you need. "I need fifteen minutes a day of listening and asking questions. I need the name of someone who teaches photography here in town. I want your advice on how to go about teaching abroad. I'm hoping you can loan me five hundred dollars to take a marketing seminar. Tell me I'm not crazy."

While preparing for the rigors of full-time freelance writing, for example, I plied a lot of writers with drinks and victuals, beseeching them for the lowdown. I became the reporter I was. What is it really like? What do you love and hate about it? What skills are essential to cultivate before making the leap? What do you wish someone had told *you?* Among the advice I was given was the strong suggestion to break down all long-term goals into bite-size pieces because by disassembling the call it won't seem so intimidating. The only goals with any power, I was told, are the ones on tomorrow's to-do list because they're the only ones I can get my hands on. The big ones are out of my control. You can't become a famous writer overnight, one fellow said, but you *can* write two pages a day.

Another suggestion is from Richard Bolles: Make a list of what you think it takes to succeed at your calling—the skills, the know-how, the personality traits. Then make another list of those that *you* possess, and subtract it from the first list, to figure out what you'll need in order to prevail. Then either develop these or hook up with people who have them.

People such as Percy Ross insist that anyone coming to them for help present a good case. "Would *you* buy your act?" he asks. Start with the declaration of a clear need and a well-defined purpose. Certainty, he says, inspires confidence. Consider this letter he once received: "Dear Mr. Ross, I'm writing to ask if you would pay for the cost of helicopter flying lessons. I just may want to make a career of piloting after I earn my license. I figure the lessons are approximately $100 an hour, with forty hours needed to obtain a private license. M. M., Knoxville, TN."

To which Mr. Ross responded: "Dear Miss M: I figure you're asking for $4,000 for something you *might* want to do. So now *you* figure out why I'm not mailing you a check."

Percy also says always ask for essentials, not extras. "Ask for what truly delights, empowers, or helps you grow. Ask for muscle, not fat." Don't ask, as one Florida woman did, for $80,000 for a big red car, a white mink coat, green alligator shoes, and a white poodle. Don't write "Dear Mr. Ross, my fingernails look gross because I keep biting them when I get nervous. I'd love new acrylic nails, designed with pretty, real gold art work. They cost about $600. Will you help a cute seventeen-year-old? C. B., Hollywood, CA."

"I don't give to self-centered individuals or causes. Few people do. I want to know how the fulfillment of your request will help others as well as yourself. It's also easier to *ask* for help, I think, if you feel like you're serving a worthy cause, something bigger than just yourself. I also want to know that my help is going to be appreciated and put to good use, so give me some evidence that the help I offer will make a real difference." Something like the following:

"Dear Mr. Ross, I'm imprisoned in Arkansas, and have been writing a book about the effectiveness of punishment and the social reaction to crime. I'm doing everything in my power to better myself while incarcerated. I've alienated my family and have no friends. That's my past, though, not my future. What I would like most is a good dictionary to help me in my writing. Believe it or not, this would be the most wonderful asset in the world right now to me, next to freedom. J. G. W., Tucker, AR."

Percy sent him a dictionary and wrote, "You've been faced with a bad situation and turned it into a positive experience. More power to you! When your book gets published, I'd like to buy a copy. Good luck!"

Genies like Percy Ross are a species of the Muses, who, as P. L. Travers reminds us, don't merely inspire and aid mortals. They also make their own music and dance and art and song, and so they need to be honored in their own right, honored for taking time out from their own callings to be of service to us. No one, not even the Muses, makes a career out of completely unselfish benevolence toward others. People don't need a ticker tape parade, but an offer of thanksgiving goes a long way as a gesture of gratitude. "We all want something in return for our help," says Percy. "We all want recognition. So it helps to be a little strategic, to give some thought to what someone will gain from helping you, whether it's emotional, spiritual, practical, or financial."

I have always been fascinated by the "Acknowledgments" pages at the beginning of books, in which authors thank those who gave them sustenance along the way, and what sort of sustenance was most vital to them. Such acknowledgments are a clear, consistent indication of the kinds of help that are of the greatest value to people while pursuing the most ambitious undertakings of their lives. These include: "Those who believed in me . . . who engaged me in soul talk . . . who listened . . . who helped bring clarity to my thinking . . . who gave me the time to work . . . who took an interest in my progress . . . who restored me with their high spirits . . . who never let go of their end of Ariadne's thread."

THE BEEN-THERE FACTOR

"Friend . . . Good."
— FRANKENSTEIN'S MONSTER

A few years ago, an American woman who lives in the Middle East because her family moved there attended one of my writers' retreats. On the last day, she told the group how alienating and isolating it was for her to live in a culture of chadors and strict observances where no one unveils their feelings, and by contrast what a sheer *relief* it was for her to spend a few days among people who do, people who, in the broadest sense, spoke her language.

This woman was addressing an emotion and urge that are at the heart of helping. Members of support groups call it the been-there factor. Most people join such groups because they're dying to talk to someone who's been there. The been-there factor enables these groups to offer experiential rather than expert advice, which sometimes tells us nothing more than what *can't* be done.

People who have been there empathize and can model the goal for us. They give us permission to be frank, a holding tank for our own experiments, the healing power of being able to help others, and safety in numbers, which, emotionally speaking, is a contradiction in terms for most people. People join such groups for the same reason they join churches and temples: for support, a cheap place to belong, a sense of meaning, and a place to confess.

All this lends itself, at least ideally, to what those in the first women's groups of the feminist movement referred to as "consciousness-raising," which is tremendously useful for those times when our lives feel like record needles stuck in a groove, unable to move on without first being lifted *up*. The kind of "CR" proffered by those who've been there is, among other things, that they can help us *interpret* our call experiences, name them, match words to them the way some people can identify birds by their songs.

One of the most eloquent demonstrations of the power of the been-there factor was dramatized, oddly enough, through a medical study conducted by the VA Medical Center in La Jolla, California. It revealed that preoperative surgery patients who roomed with postop patients healed faster and left the hospital sooner than those paired with other preops. In other words, those who'd been there were living proof that you could make it through. Similarly, those who can most adroitly shepherd us through our attempts to follow a calling are those who have followed their own calls there and back.

When kayaker Ann Linnea, for instance, was nearing the end of her trip around Lake Superior, she met a man in a small marina who had started out from the lake several weeks before on a sailing trip to Florida—which would have taken him through four of the five Great Lakes, up the St. Lawrence River, out into the Atlantic, and then down the entire length of the eastern seaboard—but he lost his nerve in a storm and turned back.

As they sat on the deck of his sailboat, he said to her, "When I seen you come in today in that little boat in that big wind, and heard you've been paddling around the lake all summer, well, I decided then and there I was going to head to Florida after all." Then they made a toast, rum in two cheap glasses, "to people with dreams."

To whatever degree we're searching for people to guide us in saying yes to our dreams, we can do no better than the beneficent influence of those who have said yes to their own because, as Ann Linnea discovered, one person's calling can inspire another's. You never know who's watching you, who's looking to you as a model. People like Ann en-courage us because they teach primarily by example. Their lives are their teachings, and they are committed to that same stubborn questing that, as Marilyn Ferguson wrote in *The Aquarian Conspiracy,* "Brought us from the cave to the moon in a flicker of cosmic time." We place ourselves near them because their enthusiasm is contagious.

We want to be near them because their lives have a certain gracefulness, even when they are beleaguered—maybe especially when beleaguered—and it lifts up our eyes. These people's lives remind us that the life well lived isn't magic but the slow turning of an old stone wheel, an ancient spindle. It has much to do with our ability to capitalize on setbacks, to see through the skin of them to the oracle bones beneath, to transfigure our failures into grist for the mill.

Anyone who is good at taking corners will make a worthy guide, as will anyone in the "helping professions" who specializes in empowering others to make transitions or rites of passage. A guide can be any change agent who is versed in responding to obstacles and helping others manage the discomfort provoked by attempts to reveal the truth to themselves. These can be therapists and counselors, ministers and healers, teachers, psychics, swamis and social workers, or simply anyone whose forte is holding hands and who understands that the biggest part of helping is often just heartfulness. "Once, I thought anyone with enthusiasm about information was a good teacher," says the writer Toni Cade Bambara. "Then anyone who could help me decide how to put my wrath to service. Later, anyone who could lead me back to ancient wisdoms. More recently, anyone who could increase my understanding of all the forces afoot in the universe was a teacher. I now have a more simplistic criterion: anyone with a greater capacity for love than I is a valuable teacher."

One of the most important things about *whoever* ends up counseling us is simply that they're *not* us. They're not in our heads or our shoes or the same thicket of knots into which we've tied ourselves with our endless deliberations about what to do. They possess that elixir called perspective, one of the characteristics of which is *distance.* The closer we are to a thing, the more we're entangled in its intricacies and the less we truly see of it, and this goes as much for our personal dilemmas as for a painting in progress. This also explains why, according to Daniel Goleman in *Vital Lies, Simple Truths,* officials in ancient Italian cities used to seek judges from other places because they would not be ensnarled in local affairs.

We need that distance. We need an outside-looking-in view, a second opinion, a chance to see that we may be too *in it* even to see it anymore. Perspective can be had by asking someone else, "What do you see? What am I overlooking? What is dormant in me that ought to be awakened? What would you do if you were in *my* shoes? What do *you* think my calling is?"

Those who specialize in the skills we need to pursue our individual callings are also people who can help us, and they don't need to be professionals. Although they aren't necessarily the most gainful places to find such people, our own families and partnerships are certainly logical places to look. It's fairly common that within couples, each partner complements the other's life skills, each person having unconsciously chosen the other, in part, for what they themselves lack, which, in a given moment, may be exactly what's needed. Someone who's a loner, for example, and needs to cultivate the courage to make contacts, can learn a lot from the extroversion of the other. One who is loquacious can benefit greatly from one who is laconic. This can help the talkative one keep a low profile while pursuing a call to design or invent or write something that others in their field would gladly sell their souls to have created. One who is by nature fiery and impulsive and is contemplating how to respond to a life-changing call may need to draw on the reserves of an unflappable partner. One who is led by the intellect can be inspired to soften his or her scrutiny of a calling and just follow the heart by the one whose presiding judge is the emotions. Each partner can become a teacher to the other, as long as each is willing to stop living the skill vicariously through the other person and take it on *him- or herself* for a time.

Don't overlook the power contained within even a small circle of friends, which most people sorely underestimate. Some years ago, psychologist Stanley Milgram demonstrated the potential in friendships in what he called the Small World Experiment. He showed that almost any two strangers in America could be connected with one another through no more than five intermediate acquaintances.

We don't even need to look to contemporaries to find the skills that we need. Our mentors can be dead or alive. Consider any three examples of those who have served as guides and exemplars in your own life: living or not, man or woman or animal, mortal or immortal, real or mythic, even a character in a novel. Write down what qualities they each possess that have inspired you and served as shining examples for you. Then write down a single burning question.

Imagine, then, that you're standing in front of each of them in turn. You can see their faces clearly, what they're wearing, what their surroundings are. You pose your question to each, allowing each to answer in his or her own way. Consider how you might act on the advice you receive.

Many people best find the skills they seek in nature, which teaches *entirely* by example, with not a word spoken and no equivocation whatsoever. Wild things are their mentors. They learn about flexibility from trees, about the path of least resistance from water, about the twinship of life and death from volcanoes, about receiving help from birds riding the thermals like surfers. They learn humility from fossils and from the distances that stretch between stars. They learn something about call-and-response from thunder, which answers only to lightning, and from cobbles at the ocean's edge, which won't clatter until rushed at by a wave. From animals, they see the need to do your natural-born thing.

"Everyone needs a spiritual guide," says Gary Kowalski in *The Soul of Animals*. "My own wise friend is my dog. He has deep knowledge to impart. He makes friends easily and doesn't hold a grudge. He enjoys simple pleasures and takes each day as it comes. Like a true Zen master, he eats when he's hungry and sleeps when he's tired. He's not hung up about sex. Best of all, he befriends me with an unconditional love that human beings would do well to imitate."

No matter how much native wisdom we get from wild things, and no matter how much we may enjoy the company of the divine presence, we still need human contact and validation. We need to see our reflections in another person's eyes, someone who will speak out loud to us the messages we need to hear, and someone who isn't busy with a few billion other requests at the same time. Sometimes we just need to be able to crawl up into another person's lap.

THE INNER CAPTAIN

In my sleep, when I dream of being chased, I'm sometimes aware that if only I could get myself to wake up I'd be safe. If I could just get myself to open my eyes, I would break into wakefulness through a barrier that is impenetrable to dream pursuers, leaving them snorting at me from behind the gate.

In the story of Jonah, according to psychologist James Bull, the one who awakens him is the captain, whom Bull equates with "the external counterpart of Jonah's own spirit, the one who resonates to that part of Jonah which is capable of waking up." Or, he adds, the one who never went to sleep to begin with.

The answer to the question of transformative change, he says, and the factor that may separate the successful venturer from the unsuccessful, is largely the ability to activate that part of us: the inner captain, the crier atop the minaret, the shaman with the bull-roarer. It is the single voice within us that, by an act of sheer willpower and remembrance, resurrects the belief in ourselves and reminds us that we are capable and worthy. It is the voice of "yes" in our lives.

This inner captain is also the agent inside who is willing to counter conventional wisdom, make decisions that are *not* based on maintaining the status quo, and rebel against the stranglehold of negative thinking. This captain, says Daniel Goleman, is also the court jester, the designated deviant, the watchdog and whistleblower, the investigative reporter, the boat rocker. We have to build up this agent as surely as we have to keep the vision of our calling *firmly* in mind by making an altar to it somewhere in the house, putting a picture of it up on the refrigerator, making a mantra of it, and not letting it get out of our sight. Even negative reinforcement may do the trick. It may be profitable, for instance, to touch our indignation. The rankling prospect of living below our potential and being less than we know ourselves to be can be a stimulus to action, rather than living with a permanent limp in our stride, continuing to serve the good captain's nemesis, an inner tyrant who keeps us at our lives like galley rowers bowed over the oars.

When that affirmative voice isn't forthcoming from within, we may have to try and trigger it, or bolster it, from without. We may need to find someone or some way to remind ourselves of it. In trying to gather the gumption I needed to take a particularly brassy risk, I once plowed through all the banana boxes in my garage that were filled with files and letters and memorabilia. I pulled out anything positive ever said about me and committed to paper by bosses, colleagues, editors, professors, or book reviewers. I found old letters of recommendation, performance reviews, office memos, newspaper clips, even letters to the editor—a complete written history of my professional strengths, which I read and reread like love letters for a few weeks.

Sometimes we just pray for strength and guidance. This prayerful and beseeching part of us, in its attempts to reconnoiter with the holy and bring us around right, reawakens us to a singular and consoling fact about that object of our prayers: we are somehow heard. Our calls, however clumsy, are responded to by one that, as the poet Kabir once said, "Hears the delicate anklets that ring on the feet of an insect as it walks."

A N   E Y E
F O R   T H E   H I D D E N   T E A C H E R

One of the "laws of manifestation" states that when the student is ready, the teacher will appear. I take this not so much in the literal sense, that a mentor will suddenly materialize and initiate us into the mysteries of our calling or conduct us through it, but that when we're finally open to being taught, we'll see teachings where previously we saw nothing. It's as if we had turned on a black light under which we can suddenly see the messages written in invisible ink on the surface of things. The messages were there all along, but we weren't seeing them in the right light. With the proper illumination, people and events and even our own dreams become scrolls written in a heiroglyph that we now understand.

Rather than waiting and hoping for teachers to appear, we can *create* teachers by asking of whatever comes our way, "What is the teaching here? What can I learn from this?" We can develop an eye for the hidden teacher, the one we don't meet in the classroom but out in the field where nothing is ever wasted. We can find teachers in the raw encounters of life—the things we stumble over that are gifts of wisdom and anguish rolled into one; the unexpected places we find passion; the thick disguises of people who bruise and displease us; words spoken to us at just the right moment, pronouncements that catch our breath.

Seen in the right light, we can feel grateful for things we wouldn't ever think we'd feel grateful for. We can see the star in Asterion, the Minotaur.

I recently had a black light shine on just such an experience, a literal object lesson in the emotional mechanics of violence and the terrible ease with which the sense of having been violated can escalate into a never-ending Ping-Pong of vengeance. Most important, it was a lesson in the power of a solitary act of forgiveness, the need for which I can unflinchingly say has been among the longest-standing calls of my own life.

I had gone to see an exhibit called "Wisdom and Compassion: The Sacred Art of Tibet," at an art museum in San Francisco, during which a group of monks traveling with the Dalai Lama were creating a six-foot-wide circular mandala—a sort of spiritual rendering of the cosmos—made of colored sand ground from gemstones. For nearly a month, they worked silently, bent over the low platform that cradled the growing sacrament. They laid out their intricate geometry of devotion by hand, surrounded constantly by onlookers who stood sometimes for hours, as I did, simply watching; our busy lives were uncharacteristically forgotten.

Although the mandala didn't fit my taste in art, I was nonetheless absorbed by the artistry that went into it, the craft of mindfulness and concentration. I was also astonished that anyone could stoop over for so long without complaint. The greatest measure of the project's drama and poignancy, however, came from knowing that it was temporary. In the Buddhist tradition of nonattachment, the monks intended from the very start to dismantle it after a few months on exhibit and scatter its remains in the sea. All that work wasted, I thought to myself.

But on the day before the final ritual celebrating its completion, just as the monks were putting the finishing touches on the mandala, a madwoman jumped over the velvet ropes, climbed onto the platform, and trampled it with her feet, screaming something about "Buddhist death cults." It was as shocking as it was inconceivable, a desecration not unlike wiping your backside on the Shroud of Turin, and an awful and profane misunderstanding of someone else's intentions. When I read about it, sitting in my kitchen the morning after, my head filled with images of frontier justice. But when I reached the end of the article, my rage turned into disbelief. In stark contrast to my own malevolent response, the monks' was one of exoneration. "We don't feel any negativity," said one of them. "We don't know how to judge her motivations. We are praying for her for love and compassion."

My mother once told me that as a child I would occasionally steal into my older brother Marc's room and vandalize some architectural project he had spent weeks working on in his uncommonly meticulous fashion. I don't know why I did that. In fact, I don't remember doing it. But according to my mother, he would simply say, "It's all right. I was done with it anyway." And she, astonished, would think to herself, "This cannot be my child." Sitting in my kitchen reading the newspaper, I felt as astounded as my mother once had been. Coming from a long line of avengers—people who have demanded eyes for eyes and teeth for teeth—I have always had a difficult time with forgiveness. I have hung on to certain betrayals all my life, refusing to let go of things I long ago lost forever.

But when I heard that the museum officials were considering pressing charges against the marauder, it seemed that to do so would almost be a dishonor to the monks' gesture of absolution, an act that greatly defused the situation, drained much of the bitterness from it, and set a very hard example to follow.

I have since taken a critical look at my own reaction, at the awful instinctiveness of it, and at the alternative provided by the very men who should have been the *most* outraged but weren't. I was incensed by this incident precisely because I had seen the mandala and the monks with my own eyes, so perhaps I could achieve forgiveness in the same manner. Perhaps I would find forgiveness more quickly if I saw this madwoman for myself, bathed myself in her presence just as I did in the mandala's, and wondered how many grains of sand *she* is made of, and who it was who worked on *her.*

The real teaching of the mandala turned out, for me, not to be in its execution, but in its demise, and how its creators responded to the death of their creation. Once again, life imitates art: We know it's going to end, but still it is shocking sometimes how it ends, and how little any of it turns out the way we had intended. The grace is in how we respond to the challenges and affronteries put in our paths.

The monks reminded me that to forgive is indeed divine, but that ordinary people can do it, and a single act of forgiveness has the power to break an escalation of violence before it can become a juggernaut. And although I will admit that revenge can be unmistakably sweet, I also believe that in the long run the succor of revenge is no competition for that of forgiveness. Laws that punish wrongdoers may have little or no effect on setting your own soul to rights after you've been done wrong. That task is hard, human work, although as the monks evidenced, even a single act of amnesty has a kind of divine contagion. I took with me, permanently, a few grains of the wisdom and compassion that were demonstrated at that impermanent exhibit.

MENTORING AND TOR-MENTORING

We turn to God for help when our foundations are shaking, only to learn that it is God who is shaking them.
— CHARLES WEST

The term "mentor" comes from a character in *The Odyssey* by the same name. He was an old man who was entrusted by Ulysses with the care and education of his son, Telemachus, while Ulysses was away at the Trojan War, a job that ran into quite a bit of overtime, as Ulysses finished up with the war but was then blown around the Aegean for the next ten years.

It so happened, too, that Athena, goddess of wisdom and daughter of Zeus, had a fondness for Ulysses. Disguised as Mentor, she would often help guide the young Telemachus. What this suggests is that the gods operate through the medium of our mentors, and one of the prime characteristics of mentors has traditionally been that they're "enthusiastic." That is, god-inspired. Through good mentoring, we can touch that part of ourselves, we can be helped with what psychologist Daniel Levinson calls "the realization of the Dream," with the awakenings in our lives.

A mentor is a kind of soulmate and carrier of souls, a kindred spirit who sees something special in us, not just as we already are but as we could become. It is someone, as actor-director Elia Kazan once said of his own mentor, who sees "the great possibilities." The best mentors are also those who are students at the same time, other people's mentorees.

Such guides are also possessed of a great faith, the kind it takes to realize big Dreams. Their faith is in something they can't see or measure or make rational or pin down for anyone like a specimen. But their faith is an essential tool of the trade, and one for which they make no apologies, despite the fact that it may come across to others as damn foolishness or superstition. They know that even *science* is an adaptive thing, tilting at the mysterious, helping us survive and giving us hope even as it threatens to undo us. And they know that both science and faith can *certainly* move mountains. These people know that the invisible faculties of faith, intuition, and instinct are real forms of knowledge, and that the fourth-dimensional grace of gods and guardian angels, spiritual guides and fairy godmothers, Brother Sun and Sister Moon, are worth invoking if they help us get by. They also know that even left field is still in the ballpark.

❦

The kind of calling Len Edgerly received was destined to take him *deep* into left field, and the kind of faith he needed to go there was greatly enhanced through his relationship to a man he sought out for help, someone who refused the mantle of mentor but was delighted to be, as he put it, Len's "tor-mentor."

At the time he met Alvaro Cardona-Hine, Len was vice president and general manager of the Northern Gas Company in Wyoming, and at "the very beginning of the serious part" of deciding whether to leave to become a writer. In the fall of 1990, a week after having won a literature fellowship through the Wyoming Arts Council, he went to Taos, New Mexico, to participate in a writers' workshop. There he met Alvaro, who came one evening to give a reading as a guest of the workshop leader, Natalie Goldberg.

He was someone Len describes as "like a character from Central Casting in terms of his image as an artist: the beret, the longish hair, the goatee. He's a very striking figure. He also carries himself with a sense of what his art is really about, and he wears his life comfortably, unlike how I was wearing my own at the time, conflicted between my art and my corporate job. I really felt stuck and needed help in moving through the confusion."

Len had long had "mentor on the mind," as he puts it, and he found in Alvaro not only inspiration and a dead ringer for the longed-for life but also someone in whom success in business and art had fused. He was "an artist who understood power and a powerful person who understood art." Alvaro had, in his own forties, left a corporate job for the artist's life as writer, painter, and composer. In Len, Alvaro saw himself as a younger man; and in Alvaro, Len saw himself as an older man.

This perception of oneself in another person is one of the cornerstones of what Carl Jung called generativity, in which elders turn around and begin helping, serving even, the generation coming up behind them. It's part of the work of individuation, of people-making and culture making. It's an essential part of growing up and old, Jung said—a station of the cross. If elders aren't encouraging younger people, a vital link in the chain is missing, a gap opens in the bucket brigade, and the water buckets are dropped onto empty ground. "We have to do it," Alvaro says. "It's my place in life now to be doing this kind of guiding. I have people coming once a week to paint with me, for instance, and I don't charge them anything."

Generativity, the passing of the baton from elder to younger, is *inherent* in mentoring. The original Mentor was a gift, in a sense, from father to son, from sovereign to successor. "We all need someone higher, wiser and older," Ray Bradbury once said, "to tell us we're not crazy after all, that what we're doing is all right. All right, hell, fine!"

❦

After the writing workshop ended, Len drove up to visit Alvaro at his gallery in the little town of Truchas, high in the Sangre de Cristo mountains south of Taos, and asked Alvaro if he could study with him. Shortly afterward, Len asked if Alvaro would consent to being a mentor. At this point, a few complications arose.

Though he felt called to learn from Alvaro, Len also felt ambivalent. "It was hard to relax completely into the idea of an older man guiding me, without the immature echoes of my resistance to being guided by my father, who was a good guide in terms of values and integrity. But unwittingly his guidance was more about where the guide wanted me to go than where I myself wanted to go. I felt on guard against someone taking over the steering wheel." Parents usually don't make very good mentors because there is too much of the caretaker role mixed in. The parent-child relationship has too many fuzzy boundaries, and its primary impulses are toward conformity as opposed to freedom.

Alvaro insists that freedom, however, is critical to a mentoree. "To develop your own voice and vision," he says, "requires a certain independence from others, from the temptation to try to please them. Certainly you can learn from them, and a certain amount of imitation is naturally one of the first stages in learning, but it's best to do the learning from the point of view of having an independent existence."

Perhaps this belief sprung in part from Alvaro having been primarily self-taught in all three of his disciplines. Already inclined toward self-mentoring, perhaps he picked up on Len's ambivalence to being guided, as well as to "some of the projections I was aiming his way," as Len described it. "I projected a lot of my grandiose ambitions to be a writer onto him and generally thought about him in exaggerated terms. He didn't want that."

Len received Alvaro's letter in response to his request for mentoring with some relief. In it, Alvaro wrote, "I feel as if you're trying to put too tight a frame on it, and I myself balk at the title of mentor. There's a paradox here: if I'm to be a mentor, my first task is to awaken you to your own mentorship. Otherwise the thing gets dishonest and I end up doing it for my own aggrandizement. There are a lot of people who love to be in that position, but true teaching has nothing to do with it. Therefore, my task as your nonmentor will always be to keep throwing you back onto yourself, with love and respect. Over and beyond that, I will always be your friend."

Alvaro admits he has sometimes referred to himself as a "tor-mentor," which he prefers to nonmentor, or even antimentor. To be tormented means to be turned around, to have a twist put in your tendencies, and this is much of what Alvaro did for Len in his dual roles as noble captain and savage captain, Captain Kirk and Captain Hook.

A tor-mentor, Alvaro says, is someone who both comforts *and* confronts, a trickster who runs tire tracks across the lawn, who elevates the tweak to an art form, who tolerates reasonableness only up to a point and then escalates from push to shove to get you moving again. It is someone who supplants the fear that you don't matter with the fear that you really *do* matter. It is someone who will gently lure you toward the trials you need for your unfoldment, toward the edge of the diving board. Just such a person once wondered aloud to me whether I was "hiding out a little, not taking the kind of risks that could really mean something to your career," and I spent the next several years turning *that* one over in my mind like a pig on a spit.

A tor-mentor is supportive but won't mechanically slather on reassurance at every turn when what we may need is an honest acknowledgment that the path is slippery when wet, and it's often wet. The outcome is iffy, as it is with all risks, and every dream has its small print. This is much preferable to the usual utopian rah-rah: "Everything's going to turn out just fine. Don't worry. Piece of cake." It can be the difference between support and false reassurance. At the worst it's a forgiveable overprotectiveness, most likely a testament to someone's own anxiety around struggle and suffering. At worst, it can be a dangerous misrepresentation of the facts and a lack of faith that someone is strong enough to handle the truth. "Pie in the sky is no substitute for bread in the here and now," writes Alan Keith-Lucas in *Giving and Taking Help*.

Those who fall on hard times, says psychotherapist Karlfried Graf Durkheim, should not turn to "that friend who offers refuge and comfort and encourages the old self to survive. Rather, they should seek out someone who will faithfully help them to risk themselves, so that they may endure the suffering and pass courageously through it, thus making of it a raft that leads to the far shore."

In helping Len make it to the far shore, Alvaro wasted no time in tor-mentoring him. First he insisted that Len acknowledge his *own* power to guide himself, and that somewhere in the private chambers of his soul is a box with a compass in it. It's geared to true north and wouldn't steer him wrong. As for Len's sense of confusion, Alvaro reminded him always to "look at perplexity as the road up," and look to his own writing for the clarity he needed. "The calling actually began clarifying itself," says Len, "in my asking for help. Suddenly

I'd spoken it, made it real. I'd gone public. It now existed between me and another person."

Alvaro next made it clear that he wasn't afraid to make fun of the king. "At the time I met him," Len says, "the story I was peddling about myself was, 'Oh, I have this terrible decision I have to make. I have this really good job as a business executive, and I have resources from my family that would enable me not to work, and just be an artist, and I don't know what to do.' And he just laughed at me and said to his wife, 'Barbara, I want you to meet a man who has a terrible problem. He can't decide whether to keep this really good job he likes, or to live independently through the generosity of his family.'

"At first it really hurt to have him laughing at what seemed like a really serious problem. But I realized it was a delightful problem to have, and I really appreciated him showing that to me. He didn't buy into my version of myself, which was a man with a problem. It was the beginning of the problem resolving itself."

Alvaro then instigated a sharp turn in Len's trajectory by suggesting that he turn from prose, the form for which he won his literature fellowship, toward poetry. "Amazingly," recalls Len, "that advice struck me as just right. I never predicted that would be a path I would have enjoyed or taken, but there was a rightness to it, a sense of coming home, a yes-of-course." About this advice, Alvaro says, "I made that suggestion based on seeing his work. I was just following instinctively what I thought his process was. It wasn't imposition."

Alvaro's next order of business was impressing upon Len that life is stirred with a slow spoon and that things take time. "Meeting Alvaro didn't speed up my process. It slowed it down. He encouraged me to be more patient than I was being, to push the horizon back and think in terms of the change happening over the course of, say, five years (it ended up taking five and a half). At that time, five years seemed like forever, but it was his way of saying that I had time to experiment with my writing and to let the corporate life unfold in a more complete way and come to a more natural close, instead of me just jumping ship."

Alvaro also helped Len come back to focusing on the ground directly in front of his feet, rather than peering into the fog bank of the future, which "seemed like it would never come." He helped Len hold his vision firmly but also do the hard, mortal work in the here and now. He told Len to begin his mentorship by writing a poem a week for a year, which he did. He also told Len that there would be a sign when the time was right to leap, and that it would be unequivocal. Actually, Len would receive several signs, and they all came together in the early months of 1996.

The first sign appeared during the annual driving trip and father-and-son get-together in Florida that Len and his father had begun five years earlier. "I got to talking rather frankly with him about my situation, and took the risk of telling him that the life I really wanted to be living is one in which I see what I can accomplish as a poet. It was something I'd never dared tell him, and though I really wanted his blessing and his understanding, a green light in the father-son dimension, I thought he'd be disappointed and angry if I left the corporate world, that quitting to be a poet would seem, to him, akin to running off to join the circus. But his reaction was very supportive: 'If that's what you want to do, then that's what I want you to do.' He even expressed some remorse at the thought that he'd perhaps urged me into a life that didn't really fit me, and he felt bad about that. Later, he made an offer of financial support."

Perhaps his father's reaction grew in part out of the fact that he had left corporate life himself a few years before, retiring his position as CEO of State Street Bank in Boston. "I think he came to appreciate the value of an independent life versus a corporate life." Perhaps, too, his response reflected Len's own growing confidence in his ability to manage the leap, something he feels he wouldn't have been able to communicate a few years earlier.

The second sign: Len got a promotion with a 40 percent increase in salary, which turned up the heat on his need to make a decision, because "if I got too used to that lifestyle, it would have made it only harder to leave."

The third sign: A conference center that he and his wife, Darlene, had had on the drawing board for nearly five years, now called The Center at Garden Creek, in Casper, began coming together. Alvaro heartily encouraged them because he saw in it a way Len could help himself make the transition. The center would be a bridge for him to the world, so that the isolation of writing wouldn't overwhelm him.

What Len refers to as "the road of omens" also included a peculiar incident that seemed to speak rather poetically to his unfolding drama: He found blood on his briefcase. His cat had laid a kangaroo rat on the handle, leaving a dark red stain, before picking it up and moving it to another room and then another. In a poem Len composed about the incident, he wrote, "Each time you reach for the redness you feel danger, knowing death is close at hand."

All these signs, Len says, "Came together with tremendous synchronicity, in the same period of a month or two, and the fur on the back of my neck told me the decision was coming. When I started looking at the signs, all the data was there to confirm rationally my gut feeling that yes, this is the right time. By then, too, I'd had more than five years of pretty serious activity as a poet, gotten published in literary magazines, and had the feeling that this was a reasonable path to pursue."

Just before Len made that final decision, though, he asked Alvaro for one last bit of counsel: "If I were to quit my job and become a full-time poet, what kinds of things do you think I'd need to do to become the best poet I could become?" To which Alvaro responded, "Grapple more with the spiritual questions than the craft questions. The writing flows from the quality of the life. Also, always question your writing. Never get comfortable with it. Keep reinventing it."

As a testament to how nerve-racking that decision was, however, Len made one last desperate lurch for the power and prestige he'd left behind. A senate seat from Wyoming had suddenly opened up, which prompted a wide open race. Len began making serious inquiries about running.

"My wife wrote it off to temporary insanity. My father told me he had absolutely no interest in supporting me in that endeavor. I thought maybe this was what the past five years were *really* all about, setting me up to run for the senate. But it turned out to be just a great escape plan. I had a sense of real failure in leaving my job. I was so afraid that without my corporate identity and everything I'd worked for, I'd just evaporate as a person. Here I was having finally decided to live the life of an artist, and I was suddenly considering some frenzied lust for power in the political arena. What it did for me, though, was help get me through a couple of weeks of living with the abyss.

"By the way, I did *not* run this idea of running for the senate by Alvaro."

Len is now a comfortable distance from the abyss, and he describes the terrain on the far side of it by saying that "it feels like I've exhaled after holding my breath for a very long time. It feels like waking up from a long nap in the wrong place. And what I've learned most from my acquaintance with Alvaro is to dare to dream a wonderful life, to go toward the things that are beckoning at the deepest levels, and the rest will take care of itself."

sixteen

HEARTBREAKTHROUGH:
THE CONSEQUENCES
OF SAYING YES

If a cross section had been made in any wall of the old adobe house I moved into when I first moved to New Mexico, it would have looked like an ant colony, except that instead of ants, the colonists would have been mice. When I decided to get rid of them, I didn't realize the extent of their empire.

I also didn't realize that making good on my sympathy for animals—a kind of clemency that operates with the force of a calling in my life—would necessitate that I purchase an arsenal of nonlethal mousetraps that cost considerably more than your basic Last Supper affair—cheddar cheese, spring-loaded. Nor did I count on having to personally escort forty-four mice out to the edge of my property line, half of them during New Mexico's snowiest winter in ten years, and many of them at night.

Often I would hear one or more of the mousetraps click shut just as I was crawling into bed. I would have to get up, put on clothing and boots, and tromp outside with a flashlight, because if I left them until morning, they'd be half-dead in the tiny traps. It was a routine that got old fast, though it slowed down measurably after the thirty-fifth mouse, when, in a sudden sprint in adaptation, they began figuring out how to outmaneuver the traps. They would hold the trap doors open with their tails while grabbing the peanut butter and then back out. Increasingly, I simply had to learn to live with them.

All this was the price I paid for following the call for commiseration which on hundreds of occasions has found me chasing insects and birds and bats around a dozen different homes, trying to trap them in empty yogurt containers and shoe boxes and put them outside, rather than kill them, or beating a path to the checkout counter to pay an arm and a leg for a mousetrap—though on one occasion an old man standing behind me in line consecrated these inconveniences by saying, "Good for you. You'll probably come back as a mouse."

⚜

Just as in monastic life, where there are periods of being a candidate and a novitiate before taking vows, so in life our calls are also tested. We are tempted away and distracted; we hear the siren song of old habits and addictions; we feel pure laziness and amnesia; we discover the cold necessities of life. Joseph Campbell called this part of the heroic journey "the road of trials," which winds between The Epiphany and The Grind, between the heart flushed with heroic song and the heart with its human frailties. On this road, we answer the elemental question of whether our commitments are real or imagined. The ordeals on this endless road, the dragons that have to be slain over and over again, serve to test us, like the Sphinx who confronted Oedipus before he could continue his journey. They teach us humility and a sense of proper perspective, and they help reveal our hidden powers.

The first power for which we may be tested is our ability to prevail over setbacks; in mythic parlance, to transmute their flax into gold. "On every fourth step, you are meant to fall down," says actress Naomi Newman in her monologue *Snake Talk*. "Not occasionally, not once, not twice, but on every fourth step. The ground opens up, the wind blows, a branch hits you in the head, you trip on stones, your heart breaks, you've got to fold the laundry, and they've closed the two left lanes. Here on the fourth step, all the forces gather together to stop you. And some people, when they fall down, they lie there for the rest of their lives. And some people learn how to fall-down-get-up. That is one move. Fall-down-get-up."

Each stumble is a psychological life-or-death moment, a defining moment, and provides the suspense without which a story isn't a story, and the moment might be high drama, like Dorothy's in the castle of the demoness, or low drama, like Jonah's sitting alone in the fish-stinking belly of the whale, incubating.

We may set out on the road in a great caravan, or set out to sea with champagne splattered lustily on our bows, but somewhere out there we come to realize that life is a great devourer, and dreams get swallowed at an alarming rate. Deserted bones litter many a dead beach, reminders of the temptations to which all of us are, always, in danger of succumbing. Furthermore, the soul doesn't care at all what price we have to pay to follow our calls. Our happiness and security and status simply don't matter to it, although our courage, faith, and aliveness do. Unfortunately, as Helen Keller once observed, "There is plenty of courage among us for the abstract, but not for the concrete." Dreams rarely stir up much trouble, but acting on them does.

Isaac Newton's third law of motion pretty well sums it up—every action has its equal and opposite reaction. This dynamic explains why, as Barbara Sher puts it in *Wishcraft,* "When we move, we shake." To say yes to a calling is to move toward it, and to move toward it is to confront the paradoxical universe. We move toward light and are beset by shadows, move toward wholeness and are pried apart, reach for a dream and are rudely awakened. When we set foot on alien turf, some part of us senses danger and leaps to the defense. When we say yes, no crouches in the bushes, or bunches at the scrimmage line, ready to charge. While one foot moves forward with surety, the other catches on a root like a lasso. We rise and fall on mountainous waves. One moment the bow points heavenward, and the next moment its snout is driven into the sea, the watery tonnage rolling over the decks.

When you make the leap necessary to follow a calling, a big fish may or may not be waiting for you off the starboard side. When you go to sign up for a class or a group, it may be closed out. When you finally speak up, whether about something going on in your family or something going into the river upstream, you may be told to butt out. When you begin working to regain someone's trust, they may test you. If nothing gives when you add a new commitment to an in basket already overflowing with fixed commitments, then you may find yourself wearing out your stamina by pushing against an immovable object. When you start going public with your calling, you'll begin hearing people's rash opinions about it. "You shall know the truth," Flannery O'Connor once said, "and it shall make you odd."

You may finally get it together to become an artist just when the art market drops off a cliff. You may start sending your writing out to editors and encounter rejection that would stun a panhandler. You may start your own business at home and quickly realize that you didn't count on the solitude, on feeling so marooned, on how much you'd miss the scene around the water cooler back at the office. Your missionary zeal may take a beating when the people you desire to serve resent you for it.

If your call involves you in service, you may have to open to the scope of suffering in the world. Your call may trigger envy and animosity in your partner, who isn't following his or her calling, and your relationship may become a bullring of conflicting loyalties, a love triangle that devolves into a wreck-tangle. You may pursue your dream of counseling others and find that some of the changes you help propel people into are hellish for them, and you then feel responsible and guilty. You may reach for the apple highest in the tree and end up pulling a muscle in your lower chakras.

Some people who have ignored a calling for a long time and then suddenly begin to act on it sometimes tend to go overboard, like Jonah. They become obsessed with the call, heedless of anything but the fruition of their authenticity. They listen to no one's voice but their own and are propelled by a reactionary singlemindedness that has them strapping themselves to the call for fear that if they let go for even a moment, if they slacken their pace or persistence, if they fall back into any old patterns or relationships, the whole thing will slip through their fingers.

In taking on your calls, watch what you wish for, because you may get it. It's one thing to wish devoutly for a thing, and often quite another to get it. You may thank the lords of manifestation for bringing you a certain job offer and only later realize that it turned you into a workaholic. You may pride yourself on having the courage to stop whatever you were doing and do something new but underestimate the effort and ungainliness involved in being a rookie again. You may follow the call to make good on a talent, and in the process find out that the true dimensions of that talent aren't quite what you thought.

"The gods have two ways of dealing harshly with us," Oscar Wilde once said. "The first is to deny us our dreams, and the second is to grant them."

In following calls, we also need to make some rough peace with the force of chaos and the laws of motion, because following a call often has the effect of placing us at the foaming edge of evolution, moving us from a life that's simpler and less effortful to one that's more demanding, more complex, more of a juggle and a struggle. Sometimes, too, when we move, *everything* starts moving; the ground fibrillates beneath our feet, the rules change, the scenery flies by, the colors are all sucked upward in a twister and swirled together. We step into the slipstream, push off into the surging river, head out with the wagon train; and it's okay to carry a snippet of apron string in your pocket to use as a rosary. You can't just dismiss chaos the way shopkeepers shoo beggars from the cafés and fruit stands, like flies.

I once rode bareback on an elephant at the head of a Barnum and Bailey circus parade (on assignment). It was an experience I cannot wholeheartedly recommend but that has much in common with the effects of climbing aboard a calling. The only way to stay up there was to hang on to the elephant's ears, which flapped disagreeably, making the experience a bit like hanging on to a pile driver for stability. I had to be willing to be flexible and flappable. If I had been unflappable, I would have gotten bucked.

Anyone whose goal is "something higher," author Milan Kundera says, must expect someday to suffer vertigo, which is not just the fear of falling, but also the *desire* to fall; it is the voice of the emptiness below us that tempts and lures us. The poet John Berryman, in singing the praises of ordeal, says that we shouldn't merely expect it but *hope* for it. "Artists are extremely lucky who are presented with the worst possible ordeal which will not actually kill them. Beethoven's deafness, Goya's deafness, Milton's blindness, that kind of thing. Among the greatest pieces of luck for high achievement is ordeal. I hope to be nearly crucified."

For anyone who has tremendous resistance to a calling, the move from no to yes can be a dizzying experience. There are crises of healing just as there are crises of suffering, and the realignment from no to yes is like the resetting of bones, the transplanting of organs. Your yes will be as challenging as any dramatic psychological change and may entail your taking responsibility for something you previously denied. For example, you may finally say yes to marriage; step down from or up to power; withdraw your projections; forgive someone; or confront who, or how, you really are. The change will be as uproarious as that which Copernicus provoked when he claimed that the Earth revolves around the sun and not the other way around. As Robert Johnson says, such a change is a relocation of the center of our own universe from ourselves to something bigger than ourselves, from I to Thou. It is a revolution as disruptive to the individual soul as the Copernican revolution was to religion and science.

THE   TROUBLE   WITH
EXPECTATIONS

One night, either the wind or my aching back woke me up at 3:50 A.M. I remember wondering, as I lay there on the heating pad, how the mourning dove's nest was holding up out there in that wind.

I had discovered it a few weeks before, when I was climbing up the ladder to get onto the roof. I startled a bird out from under the eaves where it had been sitting on a nest that contained two translucent eggs. For a few days before my discovery, I had seen a mourning dove, perhaps the same one, collecting twigs with a very choosy eye from the ground in my backyard and flying off to what I imagined was a nest in the making.

I was very excited by the realization that because of the nest's accessibility, I could look forward to seeing the baby birds later in the spring. I'd often felt so isolated from the web of things, having lived until then within honking distance of cities, that the nest felt like a special dispensation from nature. I felt, in an odd way, honored, as if my house had passed some rigorous inspection.

In the morning the wind was still blowing fiercely, and when I went out to check on the nest, it was gone. I was exceedingly aggrieved and angry. I looked at the wind heaving the trees around and felt sickened by its indifference, and I fixated on the mourning dove's great care in choosing each twig and fitting it in its place. All that work, I thought, and the mindless wind comes up one night, roving around like a thug, and just throws it down on the ground.

I took the loss personally because at that time I, too, was struggling to bring a certain calling to life amid great odds, and I was feeling decidedly helpless within a process that was shaking the nest with *me* in it. I felt out of control and frustrated with my helplessness. I still don't know, so late in the game, how to make peace with being out of control, a condition so intrinsic to life that it seems ludicrous that I'm not wired better to accept it.

For half an hour, I searched that hard ground beneath the eaves, looking for the nest, for the eggs, hanging on to my rescue fantasies that maybe the mother bird somehow carried the eggs to safety, or perhaps they fell into the bunch grass instead of on the rocks, and I could bring off the baby birds myself.

I eventually did find one of the eggs. It had cracked open on the stones at the foot of the ladder. Yolk and dried blood were spattered on it. It looked like a car wreck in which someone had died. I wondered, Does a bird feel something like the pain of a phantom limb on losing its eggs? Does it start all over again, or does the bird have to wait until next year? Does a mourning dove mourn?

I decided to bury the broken egg in my garden, under the budding coreopsis, to try to salvage something from the wreck, to make a little sense of what I knew wasn't a matter of sense or senselessness, just a random act of wildness. It would give me some comfort, a bit of shelter from the wind.

We take our chances out there in the world. We go ahead and build our nests, dreams, callings, in the face of a blowing wind. We hope they're secure, but we don't know, and we need, always, to hold on, but not tightly, willing to let go at a moment's notice. We also need to fashion affirmative responses to the setbacks we endure, the little and big ruinations of our plans and expectations.

I know a man who once opened a gallery that exhibited only one artist's work, and then one day, way ahead of schedule, the artist died, as did, of course, the gallery. We make ourselves cupbearers for the calls we hear, hoping, naturally, for the best. Who could predict that the artist on whom you've staked your future would up and die; that some catastrophe in pork bellies would undo your best-laid plans; that a country upon whose economy or exports your business depends would erupt in civil war; that the lawless wind would knock your nest out of the eaves, spilling out its precious contents?

If life ends up conforming perfectly to our plans, we're lucky, not clever. When we leap, we don't know what the consequences will be, but we are not foolish for leaping anyway. We just never know what we're going to get. We might dance rain out of the sky or we might pull down a tornado. Like the young sorcerer Ged in *A Wizard of Earthsea,* we might be practicing our calling one fine afternoon and end up conjuring a demon who's a little more than we bargained for. We may follow our calling and, after heroic efforts, just when we're ready to rest under a tree with the fruits of our labor, we're called to rally again, and maybe yet again after that. Great struggles aren't inevitably followed by great triumphs and then great vacations. Sometimes great struggles are followed by more great struggles. *Maybe* triumph and reward ensue, and maybe not.

In Annie Dillard's book *An American Childhood,* she tells the story of her father quitting the family firm to follow a long-held dream of sailing the Mississippi River from their home in Pittsburgh to New Orleans, home of the music he loved, Dixieland jazz. On the adventure he'd long imagined, he found the river lonesome. "He wasn't so much free as loose," Dillard writes. "He was living alone on beans in a boat and having witless conversations with lockmasters. He mailed out sad postcards."

It doesn't serve us to press to our oars as if there aren't any rocks in the water, as if we can't be troubled with obstacles, as if they simply don't fit into our grand schemes, and then when they suddenly appear, to resent them their interruptions. It doesn't serve the cause to set out with a "failure is not in my vocabulary" attitude. Life is likely to make a liar out of you.

If we insist that only X is a good outcome, then whenever Y happens, we'll fight against it and be in turmoil. This is actually the natural response because every time something doesn't live up to our expectations, it recapitulates the original betrayals in our young lives, the ones when paradise was lost—someone didn't come when we cried; someone died unexpectedly; our needs weren't met; people were imperfect; we didn't get what we wanted. Some of that outrage is still in there.

It is more fruitful to adopt the old pioneer maxim: Expect nothing, be prepared for anything. As the English novelist G. K. Chesterton advises, "An adventure is only an inconvenience rightly considered. An inconvenience is only an adventure wrongly considered." An ordeal may serve the purpose of shaking us loose from our moorings in order to set us up for important changes we can't see or imagine yet.

Perhaps many of us carry the expectation that if we're following the *right* call, if we're doing the brave thing, no ordeals will drag us down with their despicable gravity. If it's meant to be, doors will swing open and whatever we touch will spontaneously burst into flame or gold. If we bear the cross, we'll automatically get to wear the crown, but if we run into opposition, it means something's wrong. More likely, however, it means something within us is *changing* and that our expectations are having a rude light thrown on them.

Lee Glickstein had this experience when he first began offering the Speaking Circles^{SM}, which didn't get off the ground right away. One class had only four people in it, and on some Wednesday nights only *one* would show up. He asked himself: Do I still offer the class for only four people? Is it worth the time and energy? If I keep teaching, will these four people tell their friends and will the next class double in size? Or is this just not working?

He decided to offer the classes anyway. "The only reason I didn't pull the plug," he says, "was that I knew this was what I was supposed to do, and I followed it even when I forgot why. I gave it all I had. I stuck with it and stuck with it and stuck and stuck and stuck, and it finally took off. I had to keep putting it out in the world, saying 'I do this, I do this, I do this.' When you express to the world, 'This is what I do, this is what I know, this is what I'm here for, I'm available,' then you set up some dynamic. Things come."

Lee also taught the class because he needed the experience; the people who came still needed what he had to offer; and it seemed dangerous to him to get caught up in the numbers game, believing that touching three or four people's lives isn't as important as touching ten or twenty or a hundred, believing that you can't save the world if so few of its members show up at your classes. You never really know the effect your efforts have on people unless they tell you, and if you had the choice to have a profound effect on one person's life or a modest effect on a thousand, which would you choose?

⋄

Expectations are setups, and chances are excellent that they'll come back to haunt us, though the laws of chance do cut both ways; sometimes what we hope for doesn't materialize, and sometimes what we wouldn't dare hope for does materialize. Expectations narrow our focus so that, when circumstances have to pry open our retinas, we tend to resent the circumstances and not the expectations.

Although it's almost impossible not to have expectations, it pays to be aware of them, to have at least a working familiarity with what we *think* is going to happen when we say yes to a calling. Otherwise, we get caught off guard too easily and end up courting cynicism, which theologian Matthew Fox describes as "having had high ideals and empty results." The results may not have been actually empty, of course, but because they didn't match our expectations, we didn't consider them rightly.

As we pursue our callings and as circumstances unfold it also pays to stay open to a great variety of possible outcomes, even those that would never enter our minds. Listen for further instructions buried in the fling of activities. Think of how commonplace it is for people to exclaim that if anyone had told them a year ago that they'd be moving to Alaska or having a baby or entering the seminary or living in Ninevah, they'd have been incredulous.

If anyone had told Miriam Spongberg that at thirty-six years old she would move with a baby back home with her parents and that twenty years later she would still be there, she certainly would have been incredulous.

A year earlier, she wasn't even sure she could *have* a baby. She had endometriosis, an abnormality of the lining of the uterus that often results in infertility. But when she became pregnant, she felt it was "meant to be." Marriage, however, wasn't. She was in a relationship at the time, but there were no signs of impending matrimony. Concerned that she might never get another chance at being a mother, Miriam decided to have the baby on her own, without benefit—and I use the term advisedly—of a husband.

When people think of unwed mothers, they generally think of teenagers, not thirty-five-year-old women. When Miriam herself thought about having a family, she always assumed it would happen the old-fashioned way: Girl grows up, gets married, moves in with husband, has children. Even so, marriage and motherhood were not ultimately inseparable in her mind.

"If it had been the 1950s, it would have been a much bigger deal. But it was the 1970s. It was something I felt I could do, though I had no role models for doing it. But, then, I didn't when I went to graduate school in Illinois, either."

Miriam did practice what she calls "magical thinking," which she describes in this way: "Because it's meant to be, it will somehow work out. I'm generally a very practical person, so it was unusual for me to block out practical considerations the way I did, because if I had thought it all the way through, I probably wouldn't have done it. It wasn't reality based. It was based on a sense of destiny, which is a kind of magical thinking in itself. But sometimes there's a place for magical thinking, like when you feel the presence of the force of destiny. Right and wrong, practical and impractical, these weren't the issues. Following was the issue."

Some of what Miriam expected to happen by following this call did, in fact, happen. Certain people did flip out. She had financial challenges, though no more than those of many single parents. She had to be resourceful in finding male role models for the child, William. A few things also occurred that Miriam *never* expected to happen but did. For instance, in stark contrast to her magical thinking, and possibly as a way to balance it with practicality, she decided to make "the biggest sacrifice," which was to move back in with her parents, thereby living rent free and having grandparents around. In the eyes of her peers, who felt that only scrambled eggs return to the nest, this was an unpardonable sin. Friends suggested that Miriam should have gone on welfare, or moved in communally with others, or done *anything* but move back home with her parents.

"I paid for it, too. Though it was the only way I could have afforded to raise William on my own, and I had immediate tactical support, and my mother loved the arrangement, it also meant moving in with my father." Unfortunately, when William was four, Miriam's mother died, and she was left with her father, whom she describes as "a difficult old man, volatile and self-centered." By then he was also eighty, however, and began to see the value of having her with him, and he promised to give her the house when he died. So Miriam stayed, and she's still staying. William has left home, her father is in his midnineties, and she is still there, caring for him. "It's like I still have a child to care for, and I was really looking forward to the empty nest. I prepared myself for it, I expected it to happen, but it didn't happen. I feel trapped."

Still, she says, it was worth it. "I'm really glad I had the baby, and even glad I moved in with my parents. I just have to keep remembering that I chose it, that this isn't something that happened *to* me. I made a choice."

THE FIRST SIXTY YEARS ARE THE HARDEST

Off the coast of French Guiana, on the Atlantic side of South America, lies a place called Devil's Island. Once the world's most notorious penal colony, it was where the French sent men they wanted to disappear. I visited the island some forty years after the prison was closed down and abandoned, and in that time the jungle had almost completely reclaimed it, tearing the buildings stone from stone, splitting the walls apart with its muscular vines, rotting the iron bars clean through with its humid breath, reducing nearly everything to rubble. The term "vegetative state" is clearly misused. That prison is a textbook case of the power of entropy, the spontaneous and unremitting tendency in the universe toward disorder, and one that acts on the architecture of all things and all plans.

We need to guard our handiwork and our callings against this simple and adamant impulse toward dishevelment. We don't say yes to a call once and only once. In most cases, we must renew our commitment regularly, lest it be overtaken. We have to keep coming back to the task, knowing that the only thing scarier than showing up is not showing up. Our efforts are always haunted by ghosts and the emotions and associations we have wrapped up in the idea of being ourselves, following our own path, and letting our personal power have its say.

An acquaintance of mine who is a writer well into his eighth decade once told me this: If you're determined to be a writer, just remember, the first sixty years are the hardest.

The rub lies in the fact that the jungly fears and distractions that always attend a calling will, like all life, hang on desperately, growing and regrowing no matter how often we mow the lawn. We need vigilance and stamina to keep them from breaking down the walls. A work in progress, Annie Dillard says, can quickly become feral, reverting to a wild state virtually overnight. "It is a lion you cage in your study, a lion growing in strength. You must visit it every day and reassert your mastery over it. If you skip a day, you are, quite rightly, afraid to open the door. You enter its room with bravura, holding a chair at the thing and shouting, 'Simba!' "

Even faith is subject to the insistencies of decay. Faith is tested not just once but repeatedly and needs our watchfulness. Says theologian Frederick Buechner, "Faith is not a seamless garment, but a ragged garment with the seams showing, the tears showing, a garment . . . clutched about us like a man in a storm." Do not, he says, try to evade or resolve the tensions of faith, the forces that would crack it apart, but live them out, be willing to be nearly drawn and quartered by them. Let faith take tea with the demons. Let devotion hear the siren's song. Let piety read the daily paper and serve in the soup kitchens.

To offset the forces of inertia and pessimism and simply abide, we need to know what will propel us *past* the long arm of Murphy's Law. When the hard questions arise, such as "Why bother?" we need answers that will satisfy even the cynic in us. We need to know where we'll go for strength and camaraderie, what we'll do when the backlash hits, how to unmask enemies to reveal the allies beneath, what the payoffs will be. We especially need to know where we'll find a sense of *meaning* in our works in progress.

"Those who have a why to live," Friedrich Nietzsche once said, "can bear with almost any how." From understanding why we pursue a calling and why it's important to us comes the perseverance we need to manage the how-to part, to endure the times when we have to recommit to a call, when we can't make sense of the ticker tape of events, when all the signals are mixed and all the dreams jumbled and the clarity we had on Monday crumbles on Tuesday. These are times when we're no longer who we thought we were, and, in fact, we're not sure of *anything* except that we feel like giving up and letting the jungle take over.

The poet Marge Piercy spoke of this kind of discipline when she wrote, "I love people who harness themselves, an ox to a heavy cart, who pull like water buffalo, with massive patience." Writer Michael Ventura calls it "the talent of the room," a term he coined in an essay on the vagaries of the writing life. "Unless you have the talent of the room, your other talents are worthless. Writing is something you do alone in a room, and before any issues of style, content, or form can be addressed, the fundamental questions are: How long can you stay in that room? How many hours a day? How do you behave in that room? How often can you go back to it? How much fear (and, for that matter, how much elation) can you endure by yourself? How many years—how many *years*—can you remain alone in a room?"

Again and again we are brought around to facing the challenge of simple discipline—not easy, simple. We do it or we don't, and the callings work themselves out accordingly. We either do or we don't comprehend that a call asks us to have the patience of weavers and plowhands. Nonetheless we will sometimes find ourselves prowling back and forth like something caged, but the fate of all faith is that it will eventually be tested. "We don't know enough to despair," says Sam Keen. "Despair is hidden arrogance: I have seen the future and it doesn't work. Hope is rooted in trust in the unknown. Work, wait, and hope. That is enough."

PULLING THE SWORD FROM THE ROCK

Give me a condor's quill!
Give me Vesuvius' crater for an inkstand!
— HERMAN MELVILLE

I sometimes listen to small children babbling and singing to themselves in restaurants and parks and supermarkets where their parents have once again gotten onto the longest line. Children enjoy simply listening to the sound of their own voices, as if they were circuses come to town, or a way to send sound waves out into the world and see how strong they really are. So I listen, and I remember a little of what I'd forgotten from the singing lessons I took many years ago. The voice is a *personal* instrument, and in singing, I heard how I hold myself back, how I tighten my jaw and throat, as if to control what comes out, how I use decibels to try to make up for what I lack in craft, and how I breathe from my chest and not my belly and so deny my voice a full bellows. I heard the sound of the internal critic yelling, "No!" But I also heard the shift, the moment when my voice "took," deepened and solidified, and the note on which it happened suddenly broke and became laughter, as if someone came up behind me and started tickling.

On the road of trials, we encounter many tests, but there are also many blessings that lie on the other side of those tests. Whether we take them on with enthusiasm or resignation, we can pull the sword from the rock and come into power. We encounter in ourselves a true heroism, which, as André and Pierre-Emmanuel Lacocque describe in their book, *Jonah*, lies in "the confrontation with one's destiny, one's raison d'être, one's vocation."

We clean out the gutters and downspouts, get a load off our chests, feel at peace with our own innards. We get to get on with it, to lay our hands on whatever it is we've been hankering to lay our hands on—freedom, adventure, peace of mind, our own talents, our own souls, reconciliation, right livelihood, a sense of movement, a feeling of *fit*. We experience genuine satisfaction, which in old Aramaic means to be surrounded by fruit. We feel gratitude even in the face of hardship and exhilaration at doing our thing, and authenticity comes to have real meaning to us.

We also get to feel like we're not on the lam all the time, running from the houndings of God, tempting the fates that deliver wake-up calls, suffering so many chase dreams. It's absurd to think that Jonah, for instance, could have run *anywhere* and been out of the sight of Yahweh, any more than a fish could hide by swimming from one end of a fishbowl to the other, or a person could avoid the demands of individuation by disappearing into a crowd. By saying yes to our calls, we align ourselves with natural forces instead of pitting ourselves against them. We take our places alongside florescing orchards and stalking animals who are simply expressing their inherent natures. We find ourselves speaking in the vowel sounds of pure relief.

A call has the effect of setting a weight down on one side of a scale; equilibrium cannot be restored until an equal weight, a response, is apportioned on the other side. It's like someone leaving a message on the answering machine, writing a letter, asking a question. It leaves another shoe waiting to be dropped and thus creates a kind of apprehension, an imbalance in the nature of things. By responding to the call, we have a sense of *relief,* an almost physical sensation, a coming back to the center of gravity. "Whence solace comes?" the English novelist Thomas Hardy once asked, and then answered, "In cleaving to the Dream." In doing so, we comfort ourselves, and the dream embraced becomes a compress for our fevers, a lullaby, a basket to catch our falling days, a shawl we can swing across our shoulders on cold nights when we're alone and the stars pierce our skin with their eyes, though if you have never been so alone, then you do not need such a shawl.

In cleaving to the call, we may also find relief in another sense. In the Bible, Moses, who was called to speak to the pharaoh and protested that he was a terrible speaker, was relieved of his speech impediments when he finally consented. When the writer John Haines finally decided to abandon art and devote himself entirely to poetry, the severe migraines he had long suffered vanished completely. When we follow a call, we are relieved of the regrets that would have ensued if we had not done so.

We want our lives to catch fire and burn blue, not smolder. We want to use ourselves up, leave this life the way we entered it—complete—and die with a yes on our lips and not a no, making that last transition, that final threshold, with some grace, with eyes wide open and not squeezed shut as if for a blow. We don't want to enter kingdom come kicking and screaming and begging for more time. Following our calls is one way to love our lives, to flood them with light that can shine back out of them, and to make life easier to explain to ourselves when it's over and we're wondering "What was *that* all about?" By following our calls, we just may be able to face death more squarely. Although we may never *really* be ready for it, we'll never be readier.

The fear of death has always seemed to me to be largely the fear that we're not *living* the way we want to. I once knew a woman whose husband of twenty-five years died after a very long illness, and shortly afterward she told me something that I didn't understand at the time but do now. She said that the more she loved him, the easier it became to consider losing him. In my early twenties then, I thought this would make it *harder* to lose him, not easier. Now, I understand: Loving him more left less for her to regret not having done, not having said.

Every time we honor a calling, we also ameliorate our fear of what lies hidden in us and the unknown hidden in the world. We're not so scared of our own shadows. Having free dived into the sea of our own psyches in pursuit of

dreams and passions, having climbed down the well into our own unconscious, having swapped stories with our ape-men and spent a few witching
hours with our demons and daimons, we're not so scared of the dark anymore,
and the branches that scrape against our windows on windy nights are only
branches scraping against windows.

We begin to realize that our deepest nature, the center of ourselves, or
God within, is the *source* of our callings. This realization leads to what
Stephen Nachmanovitch, in *Free Play,* calls "heartbreakthrough." It also lends
itself to a certain gracefulness. We experience less of a rift between that inner
world and the outer one, between the instinctual and the rational within us.
We're no longer so petrified by the Gorgon's glare of our own resistance. As a
consequence of becoming practiced at following calls in all their myriad
forms, even our most spontaneous reactions take on the quality of well-
considered decisions, from momentary flashes of intuition to the most visionary callings in which we hear our names, like the prophets heard theirs, called
out twice. Rather than being at odds, reason and instinct become nearly
indistinguishable.

Our personal voice and the Larger Voice that wants to speak through us,
call it what you will, also speak as one. Where the personal voice and the
transpersonal voice coincide—like the thermal cracks that line tectonic plates
deep beneath the ocean, pouring forth boiling water and creating life where it
wouldn't otherwise be able to exist—life-giving energy pours through us into
the world.

Then we have some reason to expect miracles, though the major miracle
in the pursuit of callings begins with the miracle of being willing to face ourselves rather than run, even when no one could blame us for running. Whatever miraculous occurrences come to us by following a call, they're really only
echoes of this first one, this triumph of the need to know over the fear of
knowing. "Joy and hope and trust are things one achieves," says philosopher
Ernest Becker, "after one has been through the forlornness."

When we give ourselves as a gift to the life of the spirit, that life recipro-
cates. If sustained, this dynamic makes our lives a seamless broadloom of call-
and-response, an endless exchange of gifts. Dancer Anna Halprin says,
"Interest will follow sincerity. If my passion for my subject is real, audiences
will know it and respond." By the laws of affinity, she says, like attracts like
and people and material will gravitate to our integrity and receptivity. "When
the flower opens," the poet Kabir wrote, "the bees will come."

Of course when the dung appears, the flies will come, and this brings up an important point about the laws of affinity. "It's a bit of a simplification that your passion draws to you what you need," says community builder Stephan Brown. "The right motivation is crucial. It has to be coming from a place of true service, from a balanced and holistic personality. Otherwise, you're not so much inspiring people to follow you as seducing them. Hitler certainly meets the definition of someone with a force field who drew a lot of people to support him, but it wasn't exactly service oriented."

Still, our right actions and devoted enthusiasms seem to set up something akin to a magnetic field that draws to us benedictions and resources that can help us realize the calling. I've seen it work this way far too many times, for far too many people, to be cynical of it at this point. When people begin to follow their calls, the way opens up, even after they have kept the gods drumming their fingers for decades, pacing around in the front hall while they take forever in the boudoir getting ready. Opportunities wash up on shore; people take an interest; out of the corner of your eye, you spy synchronicities; the right book or the right person crosses your path. Sometimes even the money follows. Perhaps it's nothing more mysterious than the universe supporting growth, and life loving itself.

As we follow our calls, it is also important to shout a few hosannas about our progress, to throw our caps in the air in celebration of how far we've come from where we started, and to be unafraid that if we count our blessings out loud, we'll somehow jinx everything. We shouldn't be *reduced* to counting our blessings. ("Oh well, at least I still have . . .") Celebration ought to be part of the path, beginning with acknowledgment that the fulfillment of the call *is* part of the gratitude for the call. Besides, since we may not even reach our goals, or they may change radically before we arrive at them, it's vital to give ourselves plenty of gratification along the way, honoring ourselves for the work we've done, spilling not just tears but champagne. Sometimes half of success is simply noticing it.

చ

There is a tiny church south of Taos, New Mexico, called the Santuario de Chimayo, and one day, while sitting in its adobe silence, I noticed on a window ledge high above the old wooden pews a bust of Jesus with a completely unfamiliar expression on his face. He was beaming with joy.

I was sure, at first, that it must have been some lesser saint, but it was

Jesus. It just wasn't the Jesus I was accustomed to, and indeed, every other rendition of him in that church—and there are probably a hundred—portray him as either stricken or bloodstained, and these portrayals attest to how rare this gorgeous joy is in the world, even among our holiest.

S E T T I N G   T H E   G O D S   T O   D A N C I N G

"I said to the almond tree, 'Sister, speak to me of God,'
and the almond tree blossomed."
— N I K O S   K A Z A N T Z A K I S
A N O N Y M O U S   Q U O T E   I N   <u>R E P O R T   T O   G R E C O</u>

The price of freedom, Thomas Jefferson once said, is the blood of patriots. Matt Thomas is one such patriot, and he has chronicled in agonizing detail the price he has paid for his efforts to help others find freedom. He has been knocked unconscious twenty-two times, sustained eight neck injuries, four back injuries, two broken ribs, and sprained just about everything that can be sprained.

Matt Thomas is the founder of Model Mugging, a hands-on self-defense course in which women learn how to go all out against a heavily padded assailant. The central philosophy is that teaching women how to fight with full force deprograms them from being passive when attacked. It is a course Matt created after one of his black belt karate students was raped by an unarmed attacker. She felt that she had disgraced the martial arts, but Matt felt it was the other way around. Martial arts training takes place in well-lit and comfortably padded dojos, students wear loose-fitting clothes and have time to warm up, 90 percent of the training is from a standing position, and students pull all their punches, to avoid hurting anyone. None of this happens during real assaults.

Teaching women to protect themselves, to fight for life, grew out of Matt's loss of his mother. His father, an American bomber pilot during World War II, abandoned his Japanese mother and pretended to have been killed in action. When he turned up in a private investigator's photographs consorting with Korean bar girls, she was undone by the betrayal and resolved to do the Japanese thing. She walked into the sea, carrying her young son with her. But he screamed at the top of his lungs, so she brought him back to shore and put him in an orphanage. The day after he was adopted by an American couple, she knelt in front of a train.

The women who have taken Matt's classes—over fifty thousand by now—learned how to fight for their lives by learning, first of all, how to yell "No!" at the top of their lungs at those who would deprive them of their lives. This resounding, primal "No!" is really a "Yes!" to life, and with every "Yes!" they articulate and sustain Matt's call "to preserve life."

The return on his investment is incalculable, of course, but he does get glimpses of it from time to time. A mother approached him once and said, "What you taught my daughter saved her life." Another woman told him that she had been contemplating suicide before taking the class, but afterward she changed her mind, telling Matt that he had given her "a new lease on life." She was, by the way, one of only three women in a class Matt almost canceled for lack of enrollment. A pregnant woman told Matt that eight years earlier, her husband had beaten her so severely while she was pregnant that he killed their unborn child. She divorced him, and over the following years she had been unable to get pregnant again. But a month after taking Matt's class, she got pregnant. She told Matt, "My body finally knew that it was safe."

"All I could think to do," Matt says, "was bow to her, because of the lesson in courage and transformation she gave me, and what it taught me about my work in the world."

That which propels us to say yes to our callings can save the world: the green shooting force of soul, a love of life and the good fight, an almost unreasonable sort of faith, a crying need. We can draw this lesson from the story of Jonah: By following a call, we not only can change the nature of things—as soon as Jonah said yes, the storm subsided—but we can also help reform society, as evidenced by the illumination and redemption of Ninevah.

After Jonah delivered his sermon, God himself changed his mind about the Ninevites from vengeance to compassion, which suggests that by delivering ourselves up to our callings we can effect changes of heart at the deepest and highest levels. We can bring good graces down on ourselves, foster healing, restore faith, spare the rod. We can see that there's some give in the Fabric, some play in the ropes that bind the mortal with the immortal.

Such change is a function of our being in dialogue with what is greater than ourselves, a dialogue we enter into when we say yes to our callings and strike up a conversation with the deep self, the same kind of call-and-response dialogue that is so essential to the flowering of community, to world building, to the ox-work of peacemaking. We cease talking only to ourselves and enter into colloquy with Others. We don't just dream, but, as Rollo May put it, we dream in a socially useful way.

In saying yes to our calls, we bring flesh to word and form to faith. We bring substance to dreams, to passions, and to the ancient urgencies. We ground ourselves in life and bring ourselves into being as alchemists and magicians in their finest hours. By following our calls, we come as close as seems possible to embodying the gods and knowing some of what it means to have their power—to make bodies out of clay, rain out of vapors, gold out of lead, fruit out of the idea of fruit. We touch dolls with a wand and make their wooden eyes flutter. We give life. By doing so, we please the gods and the goddesses. It is as if we're their very arms and legs, and when we act with enthusiasm, we set them to dancing.

Having resolved some of the splits within ourselves, we also become more adept at resolving splits between ourselves and others, and in the world. With the ability to be in relationship to what moves beneath the surface in our own lives—like Persephone shuttling between earth and the Underworld, or like shamans who, in the service of their tribes, traverse the membrane between the solid and spirit worlds—we ourselves may become navigators for others, if only by example.

You also serve the world even if your callings direct you into remote business, seemingly far removed from the world's deep hungers. Some people do as much good for the world by sitting quietly on a hillside or in a monastery and contemplating beauty or silence or God, as others do by sitting in an office cranking out another manifesto. Some writers, for instance, whose greatest connection to the world happens precisely in solitude, lament that they feel they're wasting their time with the indulgent writing of stories while Rome burns. The world is cracking apart, they say—the seas are being poisoned, the sky shot through with holes, the tigers hunted down and slaughtered, entire peoples shoved from their ancestral homes—and they're sitting there in their carpeted offices day after indecent day writing *stories*. How could they? They should be out there *doing* something. I would remind them that stories are steam shovels that can move earth, not by lifting heavy objects but simply by naming things.

When I was working at the *Cincinnati Enquirer,* I once received a phone call from a woman who told me that an article I'd written about the will to live had saved a man's life. He was someone she worked with at the local hospice, someone who had given up trying until she pulled up a chair and read him the story. She said it completely changed his mind, brought him "back to life," as she put it. She also completely changed my sense of my own work. I no longer despaired of being a solitary voice in the wilderness, uncertain whether it mattered a whit that I told my stories, followed my calling, in fact did anything at all.

But it does matter, and here's why I think so:

Recently I spent a day hiking deep into Redwood National Forest along the California coast, and at one point I stopped beside a creek to tape-record some thoughts. In the middle of a sentence I was jolted by a loud, sharp crack some fifty feet behind me, like the side of a house splitting. A huge branch broke off and smashed to the forest floor, leaving me hyperventilating.

But I got it on tape, thus proving, at least to my mind, that if a tree falls in the forest and no one is around to hear, it *does* make a sound. And if one lone person hears a calling and follows the heart, and then speaks out with honesty and conviction, in the truest voice they have, then however deep the forest, it, too, will make a sound.

R E S O U R C E S

I am greatly indebted to the people who generously shared their personal stories of calling with me. In hopes of facilitating a *continued* dialogue between
these people and any readers of this book who want to contact them regarding
their organizations, their services, or just their stories, the following pages
include the names and addresses of those interviewees who are interested in
such correspondence.

John Amodio
2755 25th St.
Sacramento, CA 95818
    ❖

Stephan Brown
683 Connie St.
Santa Rosa, CA 95407
(707) 578-5196
    ❖

Mark Dubois
WORLDWISE
401 San Miguel Way
Sacramento, CA 95819
Fax: (916) 739-6951
e-mail:
bankreform@igc.apc.org
    ❖

Len Edgerly
The Center at Garden
Creek
Box 323

Casper, WY 82602
(307) 235-0000
e-mail:
LenEdgerly@aol.com
    ❖

Lee Glickstein
450 Taraval St., #218
San Francisco, CA
94116
(800) 610-0169
    ❖

John Graham
P.O. Box 759
Langley, WA 98260
    ❖

Michael Hall
P.O. Box 6759
Santa Fe, NM 87502
(505) 466-0877

Anna Halprin
15 Ravine Way
Kentfield, CA 94904
(415) 461-5362
    ❖

Gordon Hempton
Sound Tracker
P.O. Box 550
Port Angeles, WA
98362
(360) 452-0797
e-mail:
ghempton@olypen.com
homepage:
www.olypen.com/
ghempton/

Gene K. Hoffman
312 East Sola St.
Santa Barbara,
CA93101-1266
(805) 966-3686

❖

Jan Hoffman
343 West St.
Amherst, MA 01002-
2928
(413) 253-9427
e-mail: krh@scire.
hampshire.edu

❖

Mark Holland
ETSU-UT at Kingsport
University Blvd.
Kingsport, TN 37660
e-mail:
Hollandm@Access.
ETSU-TN.edu

❖

Ron Jones
1201 Stanyan
San Francisco, CA
94117
(415) 566-8470

❖

John Kotre
348 Burr Oak
Ann Arbor, MI 48103

❖

Ann Kreilkamp
P.O. Box 132
Kelly, WY 83011-0132
e-mail:
AKCrone@aol.com

Ann Linnea
PeerSpirit
P.O. Box 550
Langley, WA 98260
(360) 321-8404

❖

Bo Lozoff
Prison Ashram Project/
Human Kindness
Foundation
Rte. 1, Box 201-N
Durham, NC 27705
(919) 304-2220

❖

Sharon Matola
The Belize Zoo
P.O. Box 1787
Belize City, Belize
Central America
Phone and fax: 011-
501-81-3004

❖

Jack Meanwell
244 Forest Ave.
Ludlow, KY 41016

❖

Arnold Mindell
2305 N.W. Kearney,
#320
Portland, OR 97210
Fax: (503) 796-0779

Fran Peavey
3181 Mission St., #30
San Francisco, CA
94110
(510) 428-0240
Fax: (510) 601-5683
e-mail:
fpeavey@igc.apc.org

David Roche
4104 24th St., Suite
311
San Francisco, CA
94114
(800) 820-8971

Rose (aka Robin) Sierra
P.O. Box 1638
Flat Rock, NC 28731
www.rsierra.net

Miriam Spongberg
1117 Mountain Blvd.
Oakland, CA 94611

Matt Thomas
Model Mugging
859 N. Hollywood,
#127
Burbank, CA 91505
(818) 843-1848

BIBLIOGRAPHY

Abrams, Jeremiah, and Connie Zweig. *Meeting the Shadow.* J. P. Tarcher, 1991.

Absher, Tom. *The Calling.* Alicejames Books, 1987.

———. *Men and the Goddess: Feminine Archetypes in Western Literature.* Park Street Press, 1990.

Anderson, Walt. *Therapy and the Arts.* Harper & Row, 1977.

Atkinson, Robert. *The Gift of Stories.* Bergin & Garvey, 1995.

Bach, Marcus. *The World of Serendipity.* DeVorss & Co., 1970.

Bacovcin, Helen. *The Way of a Pilgrim.* Doubleday, 1992.

Baumeister, Roy. *Escaping the Self.* HarperCollins, 1991.

Bayles, David, and Ted Orland. *Art and Fear.* Capra Press, 1993.

Berman, Phillip. *The Courage to Grow Old.* Ballantine Books, 1989.

Beyer, Bryan. *Obadiah, Jonah.* Lamplighter Books, 1982.

Bierlein, J. F. *Parallel Myths.* Ballantine Books, 1994.

Bly, Robert. *A Little Book on the Human Shadow.* HarperSanFrancisco, 1988.

Branden, Nathaniel. *How to Raise Your Self-Esteem.* Bantam Books, 1987.

Bridges, William. *Transitions.* Addison-Wesley, 1980.

Brown, Tom. *The Tracker.* Berkley Books, 1978.

Bryant, Dorothy. *The Kin of Ata.* Random House, 1971.

Buechner, Frederick. *The Hungering Dark.* Harper & Row, 1969.

———. *Now and Then: A Memoir of Vocation.* HarperSanFrancisco, 1983.

———. *The Sacred Journey.* HarperSanFrancisco, 1982.

Burka, Jane, and Lenora Yuen. *Procrastination.* Addison-Wesley, 1983.

Cameron, Julia. *The Artist's Way.* J. P. Tarcher, 1992.

Campbell, Joseph. *The Hero with a Thousand Faces.* Princeton University Press, 1973.

———. *Historical Atlas of World Mythology, Vol. II: The Way of the Seeded Earth, Part I: The Sacrifice.* Harper & Row, 1988.

————. *Inner Reaches of Outer Space: Metaphor as Myth and as Religion.* Harper & Row, 1986.

————. *The Power of Myth.* Anchor Books, 1988.

Carlisle, Thomas John. *You! Jonah!* William Eerdmans, 1968.

Chinen, Allan. *Beyond the Hero: Classic Stories of Men in Search of Soul.* J. P. Tarcher, 1993.

————. *Once upon a Midlife.* J. P. Tarcher, 1992.

Chiron Dictionary of Greek and Roman Mythology. Chiron Publications, 1994.

Clift, Jean Dalby, and Wallace Clift. *The Archetype of Pilgrimage.* Paulist Press, 1996.

Coelho, Paulo. *The Alchemist: A Fable about Following Your Dream.* HarperSanFrancisco, 1993.

Colgrove, Sukie. *By Way of Pain: A Passage into Self.* Park Street Press, 1988.

Combs, Allan, and Mark Holland. *Synchronicity: Science, Myth and the Trickster.* Paragon House, 1990.

Cooper, David A. *Silence, Simplicity and Solitude: A Guide for Spiritual Retreat.* Bell Tower, 1992.

Cooper, J. C. *Symbolism: The Universal Language.* The Aquarian Press, 1981.

Cousineau, Phil. *Soul: An Archaeology.* HarperSanFrancisco, 1994.

Cousins, Norman. *Anatomy of an Illness.* Bantam Books, 1979.

————. *Human Options.* W. W. Norton, 1981.

Crum, Jessie. *The Art of Listening.* Re-Quest Books, 1978.

Dass, Ram, and Paul Gorman. *How Can I Help: Stories and Reflections on Service.* Alfred A. Knopf, 1985.

de Chardin, Teilhard. *The Phenomenon of Man.* Harper & Row, 1959.

Dillard, Annie. *Pilgrim at Tinker Creek.* Bantam Books, 1974.

————. *The Writing Life.* Harper & Row, 1989.

Dossey, Larry. *Meaning and Medicine.* Bantam Books, 1991.

————. *Healing Words.* HarperSanFrancisco, 1993.

Douglas-Klotz, Neil. *Prayers of the Cosmos: Meditations on the Aramaic Words of Jesus.* HarperSanFrancisco, 1990.

Dreifuss, Gustav, and Judith Riemer. *Abraham: The Man and the Symbol.* Chiron Publications, 1995.

Duff, Kat. *The Alchemy of Illness.* Pantheon Books, 1993.

Durkheim, Karlfried Graf. *The Way of Transformation.* Unwin Paperbacks, 1980.

Dyer, Wayne. *Your Erroneous Zones.* Avon Books, 1976.

Edwards, Lloyd. *Discerning Your Spiritual Gifts.* Cowley Publications, 1988.

Eliade, Mircea. *Rites and Symbols of Initiation.* Harper & Row, 1958.

Epel, Naomi. *Writers Dreaming.* Vintage Books, 1993.

Erlich, Gretel. *A Match to the Heart.* Pantheon, 1994.

Estes, Clarissa Pinkola. *The Gift of Story.* Ballantine Books, 1993.

———. *Women Who Run with the Wolves: Myths and Stories of the Wild Woman Archetype.* Ballantine, 1992.

Faraday, Ann. *The Dream Game.* Harper & Row, 1974.

Farnham, Suzanne, and Joseph Gill, R. Taylor McLean, and Susan Ward. *Listening Hearts: Discerning Call in Community.* Morehouse Publishing, 1991.

Feder, Alaine and Bernard. *The Expressive Arts Therapies.* Prentice-Hall, 1981.

Fields, Rick. *Chop Wood, Carry Water.* J.P. Tarcher, 1984.

Foster, Steven. *The Book of the Vision Quest.* Prentice-Hall, 1988.

Fox, Matthew. *The Reinvention of Work.* HarperSanFrancisco, 1994.

Fritz, Robert. *The Path of Least Resistance.* Stillpoint Publishing, 1984.

Fuller, Edmund. *Bulfinch's Mythology.* Dell Publishing, 1959.

Furey, Robert. *Called by Name.* Crossroad Publishing Co., 1994.

Furth, Gregg. *The Secret World of Drawings: Healing through Art.* Sigo Press, 1988.

Gerzon, Mark. *Coming into Our Own: Understanding the Adult Metamorphosis.* Delacorte Press, 1992.

Ghiselin, Brewster. *The Creative Process.* New American Library, 1952.

Glickstein, Lee. *Be Heard Now.* Leeway Press, 1996.

Goldberg, Phillip. *The Intuitive Edge.* J. P. Tarcher, 1983.

Goleman, Daniel. *Vital Lies, Simple Truths: The Psychology of Self-Deception.* Simon & Schuster, 1985.

Goodman, Ellen. *Turning Points.* Fawcett, 1979.

Graves, Robert. *The Greek Myths, Vols. I & II.* Penguin Books, 1955.

Halifax, Joan. *The Fruitful Darkness: Reconnecting with the Body of the Earth.* HarperSanFrancisco, 1994.

Hall, Michael. *Pioneer Journal.* Golden Heart Publications, 1987.

Halpern, Sue. *Migrations to Solitude.* Pantheon, 1992.

Halprin, Anna. *Moving Toward Life: Five Decades of Transformational Dance.* Wesleyan University Press, 1995.

Hannah, Barbara. *Encounters with the Soul.* Sigo Press, 1981.

Hardy, Lee. *The Fabric of This World: Inquiries into Calling, Career Choice, and the Design of Human Work.* William Eerdmans Publishing Co., 1990.

Hawken, Paul. *Growing a Business.* Simon & Schuster, 1987.

Hillman, James. *A Blue Fire: Selected Writings.* Edited by Thomas Moore. HarperCollins, 1989.

———. *Revisioning Psychology.* Harper & Row, 1976.

———. *The Soul's Code.* Random House, 1996.

———. *We've Had a Hundred Years of Psychotherapy and the World's Getting Worse.* HarperSanFrancisco (with Micheal Ventura), 1992.

Homer. *The Odyssey.* Translated by W. H. D. Rouse. New American Library, 1937.

Houston, Jean. *The Possible Human.* J. P. Tarcher, 1982.

Huang, Chungliang Al, and Jerry Lynch. *Mentoring: The Tao of Giving and Receiving Wisdom.* HarperSanFrancisco, 1995.

Huxley, Aldous. *The Doors of Perception.* Harper & Row, 1954.

Hyde, Lewis. *The Gift: Imagination and the Erotic Life of Property.* Vintage Books, 1979.

Johnson, Robert. *Ecstasy: Understanding the Psychology of Joy.* Harper & Row, 1987.

———. *The Fisher King and the Handless Maiden.* HarperSanFrancisco, 1993.

———. *Transformation.* HarperSanFrancisco, 1991.

Jung, Carl Gustave. *Memories, Dreams, Reflections.* Vintage Books, 1963.

———. *The Portable Jung.* Edited by Joseph Campbell. Penguin Books, 1971.

Kast, Verena. *Sisyphus: A Jungian Approach to Midlife.* Daimon Verlag, 1991.

Kazantzakis, Nikos. *Report to Greco.* Simon & Schuster, 1965.

Keen, Sam. *Fire in the Belly.* Bantam Books, 1991.

———. *Hymns to an Unknown God: Awakening the Spirit in Everyday Life.* Bantam Books, 1994.

Keith-Lucas, Alan. *Giving and Taking Help.* University of North Carolina Press, 1972.

Keyes, Margaret Frings. *The Inward Journey: Art As Therapy for You.* Celestial Arts, 1974.

Kidd, Sue Monk. *When the Heart Waits: Spiritual Direction for Life's Sacred Questions.* Harper & Row, 1990.

Koestler, Arthur. *The Roots of Coincidence.* Random House, 1972.

———. *The Act of Creation.* Arkana, 1989.

Kornfield, Jack. *The Path with Heart.* Bantam, 1993.

Kotre, John. *The White Gloves: How We Create Ourselves Through Memory.* The Free Press, 1995.

Kübler-Ross, Elisabeth. *Death: The Final Stage of Growth.* Prentice-Hall, 1975.

Lacocque, André and Pierre-Emmanuel. *Jonah: A Psycho-Religious Approach to the Prophet.* University of South Carolina Press, 1990.

Levine, Stephen. *A Gradual Awakening.* Anchor Books, 1979.

———. *Who Dies: An Investigation of Conscious Living and Conscious Dying.* Anchor Books, 1982.

Levoy, Gregg. *This Business of Writing.* Writer's Digest Books, 1992.

Lewis, Roy. *Choosing Your Career, Finding Your Vocation.* Paulist Press, 1989.

Linnea, Ann. *Deep Water Passage.* Little, Brown & Co., 1995.

Lozoff, Bo. *We're All Doing Time.* Hanuman Foundation, 1985.

Luke, Helen. *Dark Wood to White Rose: Journey and Transformation in Dante's Divine Comedy.* Parabola Books, 1989.

———. *Old Age: Journey into Simplicity.* Parabola Books, 1987.

Maisel, Eric. *Fearless Creating.* J. P. Tarcher/Putnam, 1995.

———. *Staying Sane in the Arts.* J. P. Tarcher/Putnam, 1992.

Maslow, Abraham. *Toward a Psychology of Being.* Van Nostrand Reinhold, 1968.

May, Rollo. *Freedom and Destiny.* W. W. Norton & Co., 1981.

McNiff, Shaun. *Art As Medicine.* Shambhala, 1992.

———. *Fundamentals of Art Therapy.* Charles Thomas Publishing, 1988.

Mead, Jane, and Reid Sherline. *Acts of Faith.* Timken Publishers, 1995.

Merton, Thomas. *A Thomas Merton Reader.* Image Books, 1974.

———. *No Man Is an Island.* Image Books, 1987.

Metzger, Deena. *Writing for Your Life.* HarperSanFrancisco, 1992.

Metzger, Deena, Linda Hogan, and Brenda Peterson, eds. *Between Species: Women and Animals.* Ballantine Books, 1997.

Mindell, Arnold. *Dreambody: The Body's Role in Revealing the Self.* Sigo Press, 1982.

———. *River's Way.* Penguin, 1985.

———. *Working on Yourself Alone.* Penguin, 1990

———. *Working with the Dreambody.* Penguin, 1985.

Moore, Robert, and Douglas Gillette. *The King Within.* William Morrow & Co., 1992.

Moore, Thomas. *Care of the Soul.* HarperCollins, 1992.

Munro, Eleanor. *On Glory Roads: A Pilgrim's Book about Pilgrimage.* Thames & Hudson, 1987.

Myers, William H. *God's Yes Was Louder Than My No: Rethinking the African-American Call to Ministry.* William Eerdmans Publishing, 1994.

Nachmanovitch, Stephen. *Free Play: The Power of Improvisation in Life and the Arts.* J. P. Tarcher, 1990.

National Geographic Society. *Journey into the Unknown: The Story of Exploration,* 1987.

Nemeck, Francis Kelly, and Marie Theresa Coombs. *Called by God.* The Liturgical Press, 1992.

Paine, Wingate. *The Book of Surrender.* Prentice-Hall, 1987.

Pearce, Joseph Chilton. *Evolution's End: Claiming the Potential of Our Intelligence.* HarperSanFrancisco, 1992.

Pearson, Carol. *Awakening the Heroes Within.* HarperSanFrancisco, 1991.

———. *The Hero Within.* Harper & Row, 1986.

Peavey, Fran. *By Life's Grace: Musings on the Essence of Social Change.* New Society Publishers, 1994.

———. *Heart Politics.* New Society Publishers, 1986.

Peavey, Fran, Tova Green, and Peter Woodrow. *Insight and Action.* New Society Publishers, 1994.

Peck, M. Scott. *The Different Drum: Community Making and Peace.* Simon & Schuster, 1987.

———. *The Road Less Traveled.* Simon & Schuster, 1978.

Progoff, Ira. *At a Journal Workshop: Revised.* Dialogue House, 1992.

———. *Jung, Synchronicity and Human Destiny.* The Julian Press, 1973.

———. *The Practice of Process Meditation: The Intensive Journal Way to Spiritual Experience.* Dialogue House, 1980.

Rhyne, Janie. *The Gestalt Art Experience.* Wadsworth, 1973.

Rilke, Rainer Maria. *Letters to a Young Poet.* Vintage Books, 1984.

Ross, Percy. *Ask for the Moon and Get It.* Putnam, 1987.

Sanford, John. *The Man Who Wrestled with God.* Paulist Press, 1981.

Schmookler, Andrew Bard. *Out of Weakness.* Bantam Books, 1988.

Shaw, Robert. *The Call of God: The Theme of Vocation in the Poetry of Donne and Herbert.* Cowley Publications, 1981.

Sheehy, Gail. *Pathfinders.* Bantam Books, 1981.

Shekerjian, Denise. *Uncommon Genius.* Penguin Books, 1990.

Sher, Barbara. *Wishcraft.* Ballantine Books, 1979.

———. *I Could Do Anything If I Only Knew What It Was.* Delacorte, 1994.

Siegel, Bernie. *Peace, Love and Healing.* Harper & Row, 1989.

Simms, George. *Keeping Your Personal Journal.* Paulist Press, 1978.

Simon, Sidney. *Getting Unstuck: Breaking through the Barriers to Change.* Warner Books, 1988.

Sinetar, Marsha. *Do What You Love, The Money Will Follow: Discerning Your Right Livelihood.* Paulist Press, 1987.

————. *Ordinary People as Monks and Mystics.* Paulist Press, 1986.

Singer, June. *Boundaries of the Soul.* Anchor Books, 1994.

Some, Malidoma Patrice. *Ritual: Power, Healing and Community.* Swan/Raven & Co., 1993.

Standen, Rodney. *The Changing Face of the Hero.* The Theosophical Publishing House, 1987.

Steinem, Gloria. *Revolution from Within: A Book of Self-Esteem.* Little, Brown & Co., 1992.

Stephan, Naomi. *Finding Your Life Mission.* Stillpoint Publishing, 1989.

Sullivan, Paula Farrell. *The Mystery of My Story: Autobiographical Writing for Personal and Spiritual Development.* Paulist Press, 1991.

Talbot, Michael. *The Holographic Universe.* HarperCollins, 1991.

Tart, Charles. *Waking Up: Overcoming the Obstacles to Human Potential.* Shambhala, 1987.

Taylor, Ellen Gunderson. *Jonah.* Tyndale House Publishers, 1989.

Tolkien, J. R. R. *The Trilogy.* Ballantine Books, 1965.

Travers, P. L. *What the Bee Knows: Reflections on Myth, Symbol and Story.* Penguin, 1989.

van Gennep, Arnold. *The Rites of Passage.* University of Chicago Press, 1960.

Vardey, Lucinda. *God in All Worlds: An Anthology of Contemporary Spiritual Writing.* Pantheon, 1995.

von Franz, Marie-Louise. *On Divination and Synchronicity: The Psychology of Meaningful Chance.* Inner City Books, 1980.

Wakefield, Dan. *The Story of Your Life.* Beacon Press, 1990.

Walsh, Roger. *The Spirit of Shamanism.* J. P. Tarcher, 1990.

Watts, Alan. *On the Taboo against Knowing Who You Are.* Vintage Books, 1972.

————. *The Wisdom of Insecurity.* Pantheon Books, 1951.

Zinsser, William. *Inventing the Truth: The Art and Craft of Memoir.* Houghton Mifflin, 1987.

A B O U T

T H E   A U T H O R

GREGG LEVOY, author of *This Business of Writing* (Writer's Digest Books) is a fulltime lecturer and seminar leader in the business, educational, and human-potential arenas. He has keynoted and presented *Callings* workshops at the Smithsonian Institution, the National League of Cities, Microsoft, BP Amoco, American Express, the Universities of California/Arizona/Nevada/Wisconsin/Texas and others, the American Counseling Association, the National Career Development Association, The International Association of Career Management Professionals, Esalen Institute, Omega Institute, and others, and has been a frequent guest of the media, including ABC-TV, CNN, NPR, and PBS.

A former adjunct professor of journalism at the University of New Mexico, and former columnist and reporter for the *Cincinnati Enquirer* and *USA Today*, he has written about the subject of callings for the *New York Times Magazine, Washington Post, Omni, Psychology Today, Reader's Digest*, and many others, as well as for corporate, promotional, and television projects. His website is www.gregglevoy.com.